Modern JavaScript Web Development Cookbook

Easy solutions to common and everyday JavaScript development problems

Federico Kereki

BIRMINGHAM - MUMBAI

Modern JavaScript Web Development Cookbook

Commissioning Editor: Kunal Chaudhari
Acquisition Editor: Larissa Pinto
Content Development Editor: Flavian Vaz, Onkar Wani
Technical Editor: Rutuja Vaze
Copy Editor: Safis Editing
Project Coordinator: Kinjal Bari
Proofreader: Safis Editing
Indexer: Rekha Nair
Graphics: Alishon Mendonsa
Production Coordinator: Deepika Naik

First published: December 2018

Production reference: 1211218

Published by Packt Publishing Ltd.
Livery Place
35 Livery Street
Birmingham
B3 2PB, UK.

ISBN 978-1-78899-274-9

www.packtpub.com

This book is more than deservedly dedicated, with my continued love, to Sylvia Tosar.

`mapt.io`

Mapt is an online digital library that gives you full access to over 5,000 books and videos, as well as industry leading tools to help you plan your personal development and advance your career. For more information, please visit our website.

Why subscribe?

- Spend less time learning and more time coding with practical eBooks and Videos from over 4,000 industry professionals

- Improve your learning with Skill Plans built especially for you

- Get a free eBook or video every month

- Mapt is fully searchable

- Copy and paste, print, and bookmark content

PacktPub.com

Did you know that Packt offers eBook versions of every book published, with PDF and ePub files available? You can upgrade to the eBook version at `www.PacktPub.com` and as a print book customer, you are entitled to a discount on the eBook copy. Get in touch with us at `service@packtpub.com` for more details.

At `www.PacktPub.com`, you can also read a collection of free technical articles, sign up for a range of free newsletters, and receive exclusive discounts and offers on Packt books and eBooks.

Contributors

About the author

Federico Kereki is a Uruguayan systems engineer, with a master's degree in education, and over 30 years' experience as a consultant, system developer, university professor, and writer. He is currently a subject matter expert at Globant, and he has taught CS courses at Universidad de la República, Universidad ORT Uruguay, and Universidad de la Empresa.

He has written for the *Linux Journal* and the *LinuxPro Magazine* in the USA, *Linux+* and *Mundo Linux* in Europe, and websites such as Linux.com and IBM DeveloperWorks. He has also written booklets on computer security, and two books—*Essential GWT*, and *Mastering JavaScript Functional Programming*.

This book couldn't have been possible without the continued support from my wife, Sylvia Tosar, who provided everything so I could work on this book—which was started while in a stint working in Pune, India, 10,000 miles away from home; continued for a short while in London, England; and only finished back home in Montevideo, Uruguay, but always with her by my side, in person or thanks to the internet.

About the reviewers

Bruno Joseph Dmello is currently working at Truckx as a web development consultant. He has six years' experience in web application development serving a variety of domains, including entertainment, social media, enterprise, and IT services. He is a JavaScript enthusiast, with four years' experience of working with it. Bruno follows Kaizen and enjoys the freedom of architecting new things on the web. He has also contributed to the community by authoring books such as *Web Development in Node.js and MongoDB* (version2, version 3), *What You Need To Know About Node.js* (free ebook), and *JSON Essentials* (version 2), and by being a reviewer.

Sasan Seydnejad has more than a decade of experience in developing web user interfaces and frontend applications using JavaScript, CSS, and frameworks such as Angular and React.

He specializes in modular SPA design and implementation, responsive mobile-friendly user interfaces, client application architecture, and UX design. He has worked and consulted for various tech companies, including Nokia and Trading Central. He is also the author of the book *Modular Programming with JavaScript*, by Packt Publishing.

Xun (Brian) Wu is the founder and CEO of smartchart.tech. He has 17+ years of extensive, hands-on experience on design and development with blockchain, big data, Cloud, UI, and system infrastructure. He has co-authored a number of books, including *Seven NoSQL Databases in a Week*, *Hyperledger Cookbook*, and *Blockchain Quick Start Guide*. He has been a technical reviewer on more than 40 books for Packt. He serves as a board adviser for several blockchain start-ups and owns several patents on blockchain. Brian also holds an NJIT computer science master's degree. He lives in New Jersey with his two beautiful daughters, Bridget and Charlotte.

I would like to thank my parents, wife, and kids for their patience and support throughout this endeavor.

Packt is searching for authors like you

If you're interested in becoming an author for Packt, please visit `authors.packtpub.com` and apply today. We have worked with thousands of developers and tech professionals, just like you, to help them share their insight with the global tech community. You can make a general application, apply for a specific hot topic that we are recruiting an author for, or submit your own idea.

Table of Contents

Preface

Since its origins more than 20 years ago, JavaScript has evolved from a basic language designed to enhance web pages by adding some interactivity to them, to a full language that has been used to develop quite large, modern websites of very high complexity, with highly interactive behaviors and fast response times, that successfully challenge classic desktop applications. Not only has JavaScript become *the* tool for web development, it has also occupied a place in server development, starting to edge out more conventional languages and frameworks such as PHP, Java, and .NET, since developers can also use their JavaScript knowledge when working with Node. Finally, two other areas, mobile application and desktop program development, both previously reserved for specific languages, have also become part of JavaScript's wide range of tools.

Given this wide scope of JavaScript usage, in this book, we'll start by providing insights on the new features of the latest version of JavaScript, which can be applied everywhere, and also cover several modern tools that will help you with development. Then, we'll move on to using the language for specific areas, starting with the development of a services-based server, going on to create a web page that will use those services, then creating a mobile native version of the same web page, and ending up by producing a desktop executable program—each and every one of our products based on JavaScript and our set of tools.

Who this book is for

This book is for developers who want to explore the latest JavaScript features, frameworks, and tools for building complete web applications, including server- and client-side code. A basic working knowledge of JavaScript is required, and you will be introduced to the latest version, dated June 2018, to keep up with the latest developments and functionality in the language.

What this book covers

In this book, we will cover several subjects and the book is divided into five parts. In part one, in the first two chapters we'll get an overview of JavaScript tools and features:

- Chapter 1, *Working with JavaScript Development Tools*, is where we'll study and install several tools that will help our development, such as Visual Studio Code for development, npm for package management, Git for version control, Prettier for source code formatting, ESLint for code quality checks, and Flow for data type checks, among others.
- Chapter 2, *Using Modern JavaScript Features*, we will see how to use types in your code, and also go into more recent additions to JavaScript, dealing with strings, scopes, functions, async calls, class-oriented programming, modules, and even a touch of **Functional Programming (FP)**.

In part two, the next three chapters, we'll move on to developing server-side code using Node, ending by writing a complete RESTful server:

- Chapter 3, *Developing with Node*, covers the basics of Node, and learn how to use JavaScript for server development. We'll cover themes such as streaming, accessing databases, and executing external processes, among others.
- Chapter 4, *Implementing RESTful Services with Node*, we'll see how to develop a server with Express, serving static files, and dealing with **Cross-Origin Resource Sharing (CORS)** permissions and with authentication rules, tying it all together by building a RESTful set of services.
- Chapter 5, *Testing and Debugging Your Server*, will teach you how to debug your code and write unit tests for it by using more tools, including Winston, Morgan, Jest, Postman, and Swagger.

After having worked on the server, we'll move to browsers, which makes up part three of this book. We devote the next five chapters to developing web applications with React and using the server we just developed as our backend, so we'll be going *full stack* with our development:

- Chapter 6, *Developing with React*, we'll learn about the React framework, set it up to use the development tools, and then we'll create a **Single Page Application (SPA)**, which we'll expand in the following chapters.
- Chapter 7, *Enhancing Your Application*, deals with styling your application with SASS and StyledComponents, making it adaptive and responsive, and covers accessibility and internationalization concerns.

- Chapter 8, *Expanding Your Application*, we'll see how to handle state with Redux, a powerful tool that will be necessary for larger-scale websites, and we'll also include topics such as routing, authorization, and code splitting for performance.
- Chapter 9, *Debugging Your Application*, we'll cover themes such as logging and using browser and standalone tools for enhanced debugging
- Chapter 10, *Testing Your Application*, is where we will write unit tests for our code using Jest, and we'll also see how to use Storybook to simplify both development and testing.

It so happens that a variant of React, React Native, can be used to develop mobile applications, and that will be our next topic for the following two chapters which make up for part four of this book:

- Chapter 11, *Creating Mobile Apps with React Native*, we'll see how to install and use React Native to build a mobile version of our web pages, which will work with different sized devices, in landscape or portrait mode, taking advantage of native features.
- Chapter 12, *Testing and Debugging Your Mobile App*, we'll cover how to debug and test our code, using some tools we have already seen, such as Jest and Storybook, plus a few new ones, specific for mobile development.

Finally in part five, for the last chapter of the book we'll use both our server and client-side knowledge, to develop native desktop applications with Electron:

- Chapter 13, *Creating a Desktop Application with Electron*, is where we'll see that we can use Electron together with the tools we have already seen, React and Node, to produce, debug, and test native desktop applications, which you can distribute to users, who will be able to install them on their own machines just as they'd do with any other desktop program.

To get the most out of this book

The book assumes you already have basic knowledge of JavaScript, and works up from there. Modern features of the language are explained, so we can develop code in the best way. Best practices for the language are also introduced and followed in all the code. Knowledge of HTML and CSS will also be required for the web and mobile applications.

All the code in the book runs on Windows, macOS, and Linux machines, so you shouldn't have any problems with regard to whatever computer you use. Some experience with terminal/command-line tools will come in handy, but most of the work will be done with a graphic interface.

Download the example code files

You can download the example code files for this book from your account at www.packtpub.com. If you purchased this book elsewhere, you can visit www.packtpub.com/support and register to have the files emailed directly to you.

You can download the code files by following these steps:

1. Log in or register at www.packtpub.com.
2. Select the **SUPPORT** tab.
3. Click on **Code Downloads & Errata**.
4. Enter the name of the book in the **Search** box and follow the onscreen instructions.

Once the file is downloaded, please make sure that you unzip or extract the folder using the latest version of:

- WinRAR/7-Zip for Windows
- Zipeg/iZip/UnRarX for Mac
- 7-Zip/PeaZip for Linux

The code bundle for the book is also hosted on GitHub at https://github.com/ PacktPublishing/Modern-JavaScript-Web-Development-Cookbook. In case there's an update to the code, it will be updated on the existing GitHub repository.

We also have other code bundles from our rich catalog of books and videos available at https://github.com/PacktPublishing/. Check them out!

Download the color images

We also provide a PDF file that has color images of the screenshots/diagrams used in this book. You can download it here: https://www.packtpub.com/sites/default/files/ downloads/9781788992749_ColorImages.pdf.

Conventions used

There are a number of text conventions used throughout this book.

`CodeInText`: Indicates code words in text, database table names, folder names, filenames, file extensions, pathnames, dummy URLs, user input, and Twitter handles. Here is an example: "Keep in mind that you won't always be needing `util.promisify()`."

A block of code is set as follows:

```
// Source file: src/roundmath.js

/* @flow */
"use strict";

// continues..
```

When we wish to draw your attention to a particular part of a code block, the relevant lines or items are set in bold:

```
// Source file: src/flowcomments.js

let someFlag /*: boolean */;
let greatTotal /*: number */;
let firstName /*: string */;

function toString(x /*: number */) /*: string */ {
    return String(x);
}

let traffic /*: "red" | "amber" | "green" */;

// continues...
```

Any command-line input or output is written as follows:

```
> npm install moment --save
> npm run addTypes
```

Bold: Indicates a new term, an important word, or words that you see on screen. For example, words in menus or dialog boxes appear in the text like this. Here is an example: "VSC provides full access to commands through its **Command Palette...** as seen in the following screenshot."

Warnings or important notes appear like this.

Tips and tricks appear like this.

Sections

In this book, you will find several headings that appear frequently (*Getting ready, How to do it..., How it works..., There's more...,* and *See also*).

To give clear instructions on how to complete a recipe, use these sections as follows:

Getting ready

This section tells you what to expect in the recipe and describes how to set up any software or any preliminary settings required for the recipe.

How to do it...

This section contains the steps required to follow the recipe.

How it works...

This section usually consists of a detailed explanation of what happened in the previous section.

There's more...

This section consists of additional information about the recipe in order to make you more knowledgeable about the recipe.

There's more...

This section consists of additional information about the recipe in order to make you more knowledgeable about the recipe.

See also

This section provides helpful links to other useful information for the recipe.

Get in touch

Feedback from our readers is always welcome.

General feedback: Email `feedback@packtpub.com` and mention the book title in the subject of your message. If you have questions about any aspect of this book, please email us at `questions@packtpub.com`.

Errata: Although we have taken every care to ensure the accuracy of our content, mistakes do happen. If you have found a mistake in this book, we would be grateful if you would report this to us. Please visit `www.packtpub.com/submit-errata`, selecting your book, clicking on the Errata Submission Form link, and entering the details.

Piracy: If you come across any illegal copies of our works in any form on the internet, we would be grateful if you would provide us with the location address or website name. Please contact us at `copyright@packtpub.com` with a link to the material.

If you are interested in becoming an author: If there is a topic that you have expertise in and you are interested in either writing or contributing to a book, please visit `authors.packtpub.com`.

Reviews

Please leave a review. Once you have read and used this book, why not leave a review on the site that you purchased it from? Potential readers can then see and use your unbiased opinion to make purchase decisions, we at Packt can understand what you think about our products, and our authors can see your feedback on their book. Thank you!

For more information about Packt, please visit `packtpub.com`.

Working with JavaScript Development Tools

1

The recipes we'll be seeing here are as follows:

- Installing Visual Studio Code for development
- Extending Visual Studio Code
- Adding Fira Code font for better editing
- Adding npm for package management
- Doing version control with Git
- Formatting your source code with Prettier
- Documenting your code with JSDoc
- Adding code quality checks with ESLint
- Adding Flow for data types checks

Introduction

JavaScript has gone beyond a simple tool for adding small effects or behaviors to web pages, and has now become one of the world's most-used languages, applied to all sorts of developments. Given the complexity and variety of packages, libraries, and frameworks these days, you wouldn't start working without a full set of tools, and in this chapter we will aim to set up a good development environment, so you can work in a most efficient fashion.

Let's start by setting up some tools that will come in handy for all our JS development. It's been said that a bad craftsman blames his tools, so let's avoid even a hint of that by making some good choices!

Installing Visual Studio Code for development

The first tool we'll need is an **Integrated Development Environment** (**IDE**), or at least a powerful code editor. Some people make do with a simple editor, possibly something like vi or Notepad, but in the long run, all the wasted time in doing everything by hand doesn't pay. There are many options, such as (in alphabetical order) Atom, Eclipse, IntelliJ IDEA, Microsoft Visual Studio, NetBeans, Sublime Text, WebStorm, and Visual Studio Code. Personally, I've opted for the latter, though of course you may work perfectly well with any of the others.

The term IDE isn't really very well-defined. An IDE usually integrates many tools, providing a more seamless experience for the developer. Editors meant for development work provide some similar functionality by means of plugins or extensions. While this can certainly approximate the ease of use of an IDE, there may be some problems, such as a harder installation or configuration, or an interface that might be harder to figure out, but in the end, you may get practically the same feature set.

Visual Studio Code (**VSC**) is basically a source code editor, developed by Microsoft in 2015. Despite the similar name, it's not related to Microsoft's more powerful IDE, Visual Studio. The editor is free and open source, and the latest version is (currently) 1.29.1, dated November 2018, though new releases come out monthly. It can be used for JS development, but also for other languages, so if you wanted to, say, do your server-side coding in PHP, you could perfectly well use VSC for that too. However, from our point of view, the fact that VSC ships with IntelliSense for basically all the frontend languages (JS, TypeScript, JSON, HTML, CSS, LESS, SASS) is a good selling point. See https://code.visualstudio.com/docs/editor/intellisense for more on this.

A nice touch is that VSC is written in JS, based on Node, and packaged for the desktop by using the Electron framework. (We'll get to see these topics in Chapter 13, *Creating a Desktop Application with Electron*.) This automatically lets you use VSC in Linux, macOS, and Windows, which is a good advantage if you work in a team and not everybody shares the same development environment preferences.

A commonly held misconception is that VSC is based on the Atom editor. Though VSC shares the same editor component (Monaco), VSC itself is distinct from Atom. A source of this misunderstanding may be the fact that Electron, when created in 2013, was originally called *Atom Shell*; the name change to Electron happened in 2015.

In the past, I've worked extensively with Eclipse, Microsoft Visual Studio, and NetBeans. However, nowadays I work exclusively with VSC. Why do I prefer it? My reasons (your mileage may vary!) include the following:

- *Availability for multiple operating systems*: I personally use it on Mac and Linux all the time, and sometimes on Windows
- *Actively developed and maintained*: With updates (including bug fixes) provided on a regular basis
- *Very good performance*: VSC feels quite speedy
- *IntelliSense support*: Out of the box for all JS needs
- *Extensions available through plugins*: These become integrated into your work flow, adding new functionality
- *Integrated debugging*: As we'll see in `Chapter 5`, *Testing and Debugging Your Server*
- *Integrated source code management*: Through Git (see the *Doing version control with Git* section, later)
- *Integrated terminal*: You can run commands or launch processes without leaving VSC

On the other hand, there are also some disadvantages; the main two being as follows:

- The interface, configuration, and design of plugins usually varies from one to another, so you'll have to deal with frequent inconsistencies.
- VSC has no knowledge of projects or the links between tools needed to create, for example, a `React` frontend application that communicates with a `Node` backend server. VSC at most recognizes folders, but how you organize them, and where you place your pieces of code, is totally up to you.

How to do it...

How do you install VSC? Instructions are different for each operating system, and may vary over time, so we'll just point you to downloading the appropriate package for your system at `https://code.visualstudio.com/download`, and following the correct platform-specific instructions at `https://code.visualstudio.com/docs/setup/setup-overview`. For Linux distributions, instead of downloading and installing some package by yourself, there may be another way out. For example, with OpenSUSE, there exists a repository that will allow you to install and update VSC through OpenSUSE itself; check out `https://en.opensuse.org/Visual_Studio_Code` for instructions on this, or `https://code.visualstudio.com/docs/setup/linux` for even more distribution-specific instructions.

If you want to live on the edge, and get to see new features as early as possible, there's also an *Insiders build*. You may install both the normal VSC stable build and the Insiders build, and work with whichever you prefer. Be warned, though, that you may find unexpected bugs, but you can help the VSC development team get rid of those by letting them know!

How it works...

After having installed it, open VSC and try out its settings to start configuring things the way you prefer, see the following screenshot. The bottom-left gear menu provides access to several related items, such as keyboard shortcuts, the color scheme, and icon set. If you have worked with VSC in the past, you'll have access to more recent files and folders:

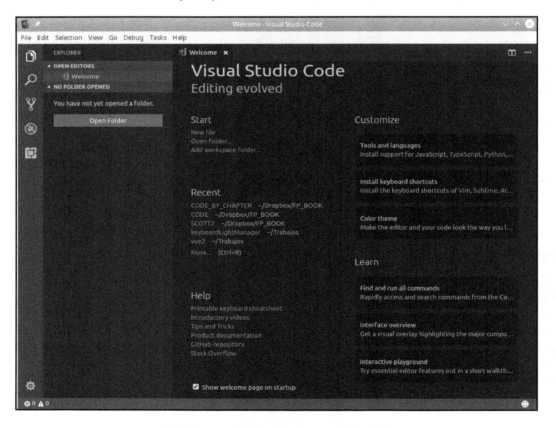

The Welcome screen in VSC, and the settings gear at the bottom left

Configuring VSC is sort of unusual, but maybe to be expected, due to its JS origins. Basically, as seen in the following screenshot, you get a split screen, showing all the available configuration items (more than four hundred!) on the left, in JSON format, and you may change their values by writing new ones on the right side. If you mouse over any setting, you'll get to see the possible values, and you can select a new one just by clicking on it:

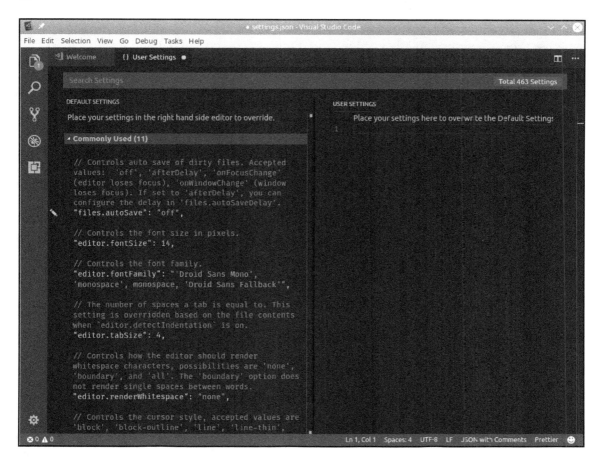

Configuring VSC is done by editing a JSON file with your personal choices

Do you want to pick a different editor for your work, or at least check out what's available out there? You may check out `www.slant.co/topics/1686/~javascript-ides-or-editors` for a long list of candidates, with pros and cons for each. At the current time (October 2018) the page shows 41 options, with Visual Studio Code at the top of the list.

One extra advantage of VSC has to do with updates. It will periodically check to see whether there's a new available version, and it will let you download and install it. (On the other hand, if you use Linux and install VSC through a repository, it may get updated automatically, without you even having to confirm it.) After that, you'll get an information screen with the changes for the last month; as seen in the following screenshot:

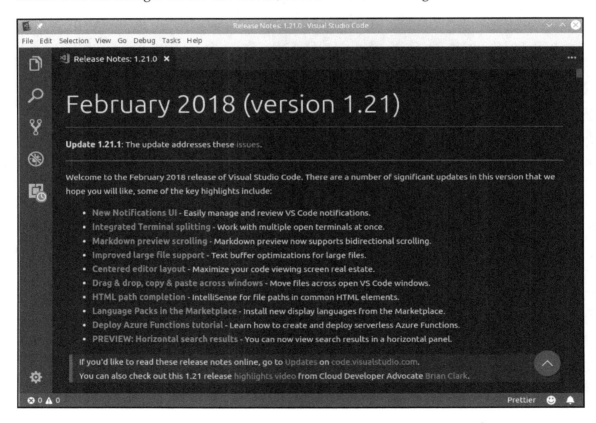

After each monthly update, you'll be informed of VSC's new features

Configuration of VSC goes beyond what we have just mentioned; see the following sections to find out more ways of extending its power and making it better for you to use.

Extending Visual Studio Code

VSC includes many out-of-the-box features, with which you can actually get started and working with no problems. By means of extensions, you can add support for languages, debugging, code quality, and many more functions. Configuring visual aspects is also provided, and you can change VSC's theme, shortcuts, and general preferences. However, you will want to add even more functionality to VSC, and that's where extensions (plugins) come in.

> You can even develop your own extensions for VSC, though we won't be getting into that subject in this book. If you are interested, check out https://code.visualstudio.com/docs/extensions/overview. Extensions can be written in either JS or TypeScript (see the *Adding Flow for data types checks* section), and of course you can develop them by using VSC itself!

How to do it...

Extensions are optional installable additions to VSC, which provide specific new functions. Installing new extensions is a breeze. You can bring up the menu of all the available extensions by going to **View** | **Extensions** in the main menu (where you can also find a keyboard shortcut for it) or by clicking the Extensions icon at the bottom of the Activities bar at the left of VSC.

You will first get the list of currently installed extensions, as demonstrated in the following screenshot:

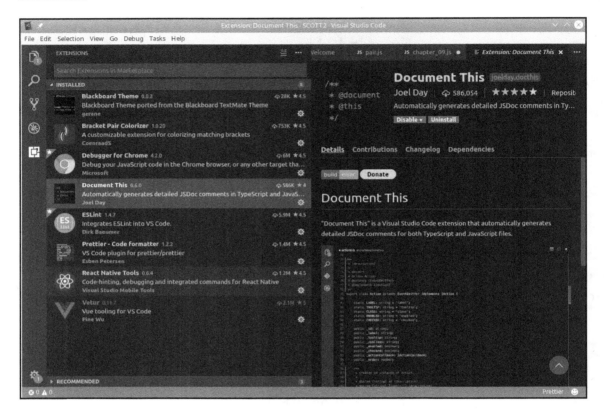

The list of already-installed extensions

If you want, you can disable any specific extension: click on it at the left side of the screen, and then click on **Disable** at the right. You can also fully uninstall any extension, and it's a sure bet that you'll do this quite a lot; the only way to find out if an extension works for you is by experimenting! Take a look at the following screenshot:

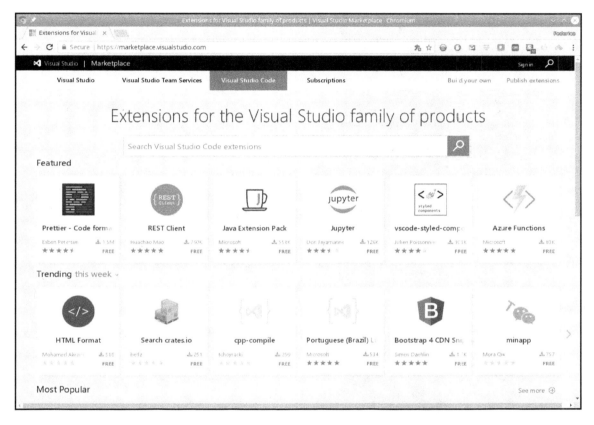

The VSC Marketplace is a good place to search for new extensions

Finding new extensions is also a breeze. You can either go to the VSC Marketplace at `https://marketplace.visualstudio.com/` as seen in the preceding screenshot or directly search from within VSC, by typing in the search box, as seen in the following screenshot. I'd recommend paying attention to the total number of installs (the higher the better) and the rating from 1 to 5 stars (also, the higher the better). We'll be using several extensions; see, for example, in this chapter the *Formatting your source code with Prettier* and *Documenting your code with JSDoc* sections; there will be more in later chapters:

You can also search for new extensions from within VSC by just typing some keywords

Extensions are updated automatically, and you won't have to do much. Periodically, I'd recommend having a look at your list of extensions, and possibly searching again for new ones; there have been cases of new versions deprecating old ones, but with a new name, so an update wouldn't have worked. And, finally, be ready to experiment and find for yourself which extensions make you tick!

Adding Fira Code font for better editing

If you want to try a topic that can quickly lead to a (warm? heated?) discussion, say out loud that the best font for programming is such and such, and just wait! I don't want to start any arguments, but I can certainly recommend a font that can make your JS code look much better, and become more readable.

 An article in Slant, at `https://www.slant.co/topics/67/~best-programming-fonts`, lists over 100 programming fonts; did you even think so many were available?

The key to a better font hinges on the concept of ligatures. In typography, a ligature occurs when two or more letters are joined, becoming a single character. OK, the proper technical word would be glyph, but let's not make it more complicated than needed!

 Some ligatures you may not be aware of are these: the ampersand character *(&)* was originally a ligature of the letters *E* and *i*, spelling out *et* in Latin, meaning *and*. Similarly, the German *ß* character was a ligature of two *s* letters, next to each other, and the Spanish *Ñ* originally was a pair of *N* characters, one written on top of the other.

In JS, there are many symbols that are written as two or more characters, just because no other way is available. For example, the greater than or equal to symbol is typed as >=, which doesn't look as good as the mathematical symbol ≥, does it? Other combinations are <= (less than or equal to), => (for arrow functions, which we'll meet in `Chapter 2`, *Using Modern JavaScript Features*), the binary shift operators << and >>, the equality operators == and === (plus the corresponding != and !==), and more.

 Do not confuse *ligatures* with *kerning*. Both have to do with showing adjacent characters, but the former refers to joining characters and replacing them with a new one, while the latter deals with reducing the distance between characters. If you place an *f* next to an *i*, kerning would make them closer without overlapping (in the same way that you can reduce spacing between *A* and *V* because of the letters' shapes), while a ligature would replace both characters with *fi*, actually joining both letters.

How to do it...

While there are many monospaced fonts (meaning all characters have the same width, which helps with onscreen alignment and indentation), there are not so many that also provide ligatures. In my case, after experimenting with many, I can recommend using Fira Code, available online at `https://github.com/tonsky/FiraCode`. This font provides lots of ligatures, not only for JS but for other programming languages as well. Take a look at following illustration for all the possibilities:

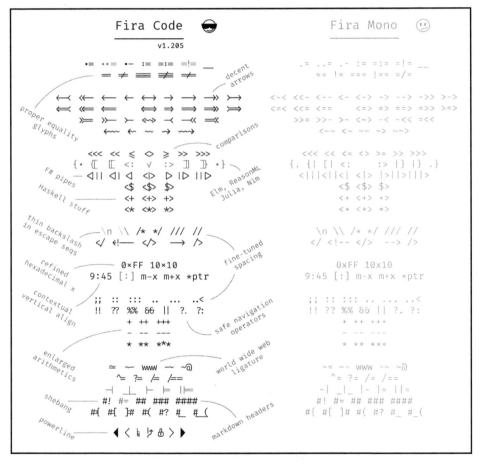

All the available ligatures, as seen in the figure taken from
https://raw.githubusercontent.com/tonsky/FiraCode/master/showcases/all_ligatures.png

Download the latest version (1.206, as of December 2018) and install it, according to the standard procedures for your operating system. Afterwards, you'll have to change a pair of VSC settings, as seen earlier in this chapter; just add the following lines, and save your configuration:

```
"editor.fontFamily": "'Fira Code', 'Droid Sans Mono', 'Courier New'",
"editor.fontLigatures": true,
    .
    .
    .
```

The first line defines what font you want to use (and in CSS style, I also provided alternatives, just in case I took my settings to a different machine where `Fira Code` wasn't available) and the second line tells VSC to enable onscreen ligatures.

How it works...

After doing the changes in the previous section, when you open VSC, you'll be able to see code as in the following screenshot:

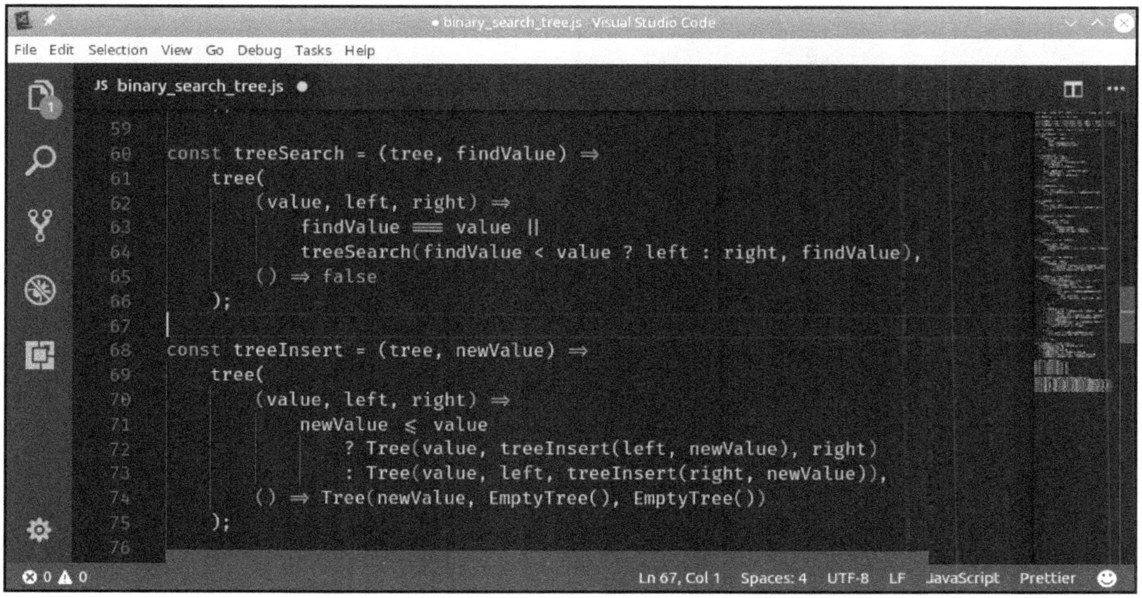

A sample listing, showing several ligatures; see lines 60 (=>), 63 (=== and ||), or 71 (<=)

Note that you don't have to do anything at all when you type in your code. If you want an arrow ligature, you will have to type the two characters = and > as usual; the way they will look on screen is just a result of font rendering. Similarly, if you want to search for an arrow, seek =>, as that's what will be saved to disk.

Now we have got VSC configured to our liking, let's start more packages to help with source code management and other features.

Adding npm for package management

When working either on the frontend or the backend, you will surely want to use already available libraries and frameworks, and that begets an interesting problem: how to deal with those packages' own needs, more packages, which themselves need even more packages, and so on. In Chapter 3, *Developing with Node*, we'll work with Node, but we need to get ahead of ourselves, and install npm (the package manager of Node) now to be able to set up several other tools.

npm also is the name of a gigantic repository of software, at https://www.npmjs.com/, which counts has around 600,000 packages you can observe that in the following screenshot and it grows at a daily rate of more than 500 packages, according to counts such as at http://www.modulecounts.com/, a place that tracks several well-known code repositories:

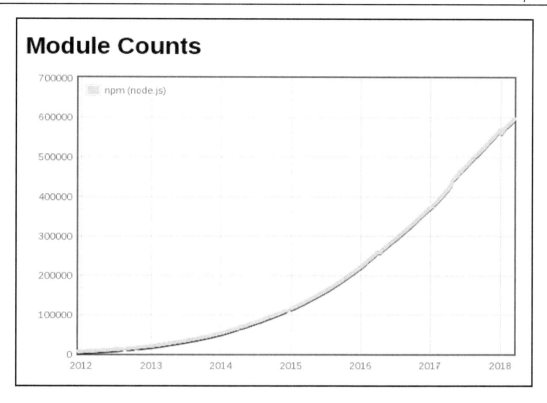

The growth of the npm repository seems exponential, according to data from www.modulecounts.com.

It can be safely said that it's probably impossible that a modern JS application doesn't require at least one, and more likely several, packages from npm, so adding a package manager will be mandatory; let's see a couple of them.

How to do it...

To get npm, you must first install Node, and that will come in handy for Chapter 3, *Developing with Node*, and the following ones. We won't copy the details here from the web (see https://docs.npmjs.com/getting-started/installing-node) but we can resume as follows:

1. Install Node, either by downloading it and then doing a manual installation (the most common way for Windows) or by adding an appropriate repository and then using your Linux package manager to install Node (that's the way I do this in my OpenSuse machines). Be careful, and pick the **Long Term Support** (**LTS**) version, recognizable by its even major number (such as 8.x.x, for example), unless you feel adventurous enough to use the latest development version, and you don't mind risks such as things stopping working!

2. Verify that Node is correctly installed. At the command line, type node -v and get the current version; in my machine, it's v9.7.1, but this will surely change by the time you try this out, and yes, I'm feeling adventurous and not using the LTS version!

3. Check if npm is up to its latest version with the npm -v command. If it's not (refer to the following code snippet), you'll have to update it:

```
> npm -v
5.5.1

    |                                    |
    |   Update available 5.5.1 → 5.7.1   |
    |      Run npm i -g npm to update     |
    |                                    |
```

If you are working without a package manager (meaning you can get updates for your software automatically, without having to go and look for each on a one-by-one basis) you could also be interested in installing nvm, though it's optional; for more on this, see https://github.com/creationix/nvm.

How it works...

We'll be back to using npm in several places in this text. You'll have to use it in order to install several packages (some of which appear in this very chapter, such as JSDoc or Prettier) and later on we'll see how to configure an application, so all its required packages will be available and up to date.

You can find complete documentation for all `npm` features at `https://docs.npmjs.com/`.

Creating a project with npm

If you pick any empty directory and just install a package, you'll get some warnings related to a missing file, and you'll also find some new elements:

```
~ > md sample
~ > cd sample
~/sample > npm install lodash
npm WARN saveError ENOENT: no such file or directory, open
'/home/fkereki/sample/package.json'
npm notice created a lockfile as package-lock.json. You should commit this
file.
npm WARN enoent ENOENT: no such file or directory, open
'/home/fkereki/sample/package.json'
npm WARN sample No description
npm WARN sample No repository field.
npm WARN sample No README data
npm WARN sample No license field.

+ lodash@4.17.11
added 1 package from 2 contributors and audited 1 package in 1.945s
found 0 vulnerabilities

~/sample> dir
total 4
drwxr-xr-x 3 fkereki users  20 Mar 15 11:39 node_modules
-rw-r--r-- 1 fkereki users 313 Mar 15 11:39 package-lock.json
```

What's happening here? Let's explain the results step by step, and then add whatever's missing. When you install modules, they (plus all their dependencies, and their dependencies' dependencies, and so on) are placed by default in a `node_modules` directory. This is a good measure, because all the code that will go in that directory is code that you haven't actually written, and that will eventually get updated by `npm` without your direct control. We can verify that quickly by going to the newly created directory and checking out its contents:

```
~/sample> cd node_modules
~/sample/node_modules> dir
total 36
drwxr-xr-x 3 fkereki users 20480 Mar 15 11:39 lodash
```

But, how would you control what packages (and their versions) are to be installed? That's the point of the missing `package.json` file, which, among other things that we'll meet later in the book, lets you specify what packages you want. (We'll also use it to specify parameters for other tools, such as Babel or ESLint, as we'll see later in this chapter.) You can create this file by hand, but it's easier to use `npm init` and just answer a few questions. This will create the required file, which will eventually describe all the dependencies of your project, plus other features (such as build or deploy procedures) that we'll see later:

```
~/sample> npm init
This utility will walk you through creating a package.json file.
It only covers the most common items, and tries to guess sensible defaults.
See `npm help json` for definitive documentation on these fields
and exactly what they do.
Use `npm install <pkg>` afterwards to install a package and
save it as a dependency in the package.json file.

Press ^C at any time to quit.
package name: (sample) simpleproject
version: (1.0.0)
description: A simple project to show package.json creation
entry point: (index.js)
test command:
git repository:
keywords:
author: Federico Kereki
license: (ISC)
About to write to /home/fkereki/sample/package.json:

{
  "name": "simpleproject",
  "version": "1.0.0",
  "description": "A simple project to show package.json creation",
  "main": "index.js",
  "scripts": {
    "test": "echo \"Error: no test specified\" && exit 1"
  },
  "author": "Federico Kereki",
  "license": "ISC"
}
Is this ok? (yes)
```

Let's quickly go over each field, but remember these are only the basic ones; you can find more complete, official descriptions at `https://docs.npmjs.com/files/package.json`. As we skipped some answers, not all fields are present in the produced project file, but you can add everything later:

- `name`: Whatever name you want to assign to the project; by default, the directory's name.
- `version`: The semantic version number for your project. You would update this number whenever you create a newer version. See `https://semver.org/` for more information on semantic versioning.
- `description`: A simple description of your project, used by the npm search command.
- `main`: The name of the primary entry point to your program. It's common to use `index.js` for this.
- `test command`: A command (script) that you would run in order to execute unit tests for your code. We'll also be seeing this later in the book.
- `git repository`: If you are going to use source control, here you would give the details for it. We'll get to this in the *Doing version control with Git* section later in this chapter.
- `scripts`: This is an object that contains script commands you can run with npm run; for example, you could write scripts to build a project, deploy it, check it for code quality rules, and so on.
- `author`: Who created the project.
- `license`: Whatever license you want to assign to your project; this is meant for other people to know how they may use your package (permissions, restrictions) should you allow it. You can find a (quite long!) list of possible licenses at `https://spdx.org/licenses/`, and be careful when selecting one; there are legal aspects involved!

But, where are the packages? Let's see about that in the next section.

Installing packages for different purposes

There are two ways of installing npm packages: globally or locally:

- If you plan to use the package from the command line, install it globally; for example, npm install prettier -g would install the prettier command so you can use it anywhere. (We'll see more of prettier in the *Formatting your source code with Prettier* section.) You may need to run the command as an administrator, or with sudo.
- Otherwise, if you just need the package for your project, install it locally.

Installing packages locally can also be done in more than one way:

- If you need the package for your own project, then you install it as a production package with npm install lodash --save
- Instead, if you need the package in order to build your project, but not as a part of the final, produced code, install it as a development package with npm install eslint --save-dev

 There are many shorthand versions for commands and options, such as just i for install, or -D for --save-dev, but I am more comfortable spelling everything out. If you want to learn more about this, just try npm --help.

After running these two latter commands, if you inspect package.json, you'll notice that some lines were added:

```
~/sample> cat package.json
{
  "name": "simpleproject",
  "version": "1.0.0",
  "description": "A simple project to show package.json creation",
  "main": "index.js",
  "scripts": {
    "test": "echo \"Error: no test specified\" && exit 1"
  },
  "author": "Federico Kereki",
  "license": "ISC",
  "dependencies": {
    "lodash": "^4.17.5"
  },
  "devDependencies": {
    "prettier": "^1.11.1"
  }
}
```

The `dependencies` and `devDependencies` entries refer to the production and development packages you require. If you are writing your software, and you decide you need a new package, there are two ways of doing this:

- Add an entry to `package.json`, in the proper place, and then do `npm install` to get it
- Alternatively, use `npm install` with either `--save` or `--save-dev`, and `package.json` will be updated by `npm`

> To remove a dependency, use `npm uninstall` instead. You must include `--save` or `--save-dev` in order to also remove the reference from `package.json`.

If you need specific versions, you will have to learn about semantic versioning. Version rules may become complex, and we'll just see the main ones; check `https://docs.npmjs.com/files/package.json#dependencies` and `https://github.com/npm/node-semver#versions` for a complete description:

4.5.6	Version 4.5.6, and none other
^4.0.0	Latest compatible version 4.x.x
^4.2.0	Latest compatible version 4.2.x
>5.6.7	A version greater than 5.6.7
~8.7.6	A version approximately equivalent to 8.7.6; should be 8.7.x

There's more...

Maintaining your packages and updating them is an important task, and if you are part of a development team, with people possibly even in different regions or countries, it becomes mandatory that everybody should be working with the same configuration at all times. If the project is very dynamic (meaning that packages will be added, removed, or updated frequently), `npm` can become a bit slow and also produce consistency or security problems; to address this situation, in 2016 Facebook released a new package manager, `yarn`. (See `https://yarnpkg.com/en/`.)

> If you want to see the rationale for the changes, see the original blog post about yarn at `https://code.facebook.com/posts/1840075619545360`.

A key feature is that you can seamlessly replace npm with yarn, and just start using the latter, because it shares the same feature set (apart from some minor differences) while working in a faster, more reliable, and more secure way. For instance, yarn can manage downloads in parallel, and even work with cached packages, so it would even be possible to do some updates without a connection to the internet!

Installation is quite simple, and a bit ironic. Use npm with npm install -g yarn, and from that moment on, you will be able to use yarn directly and forget npm. See https://yarnpkg.com/en/docs/install for more complete documentation on the installation process.

For more details on comparing npm and yarn commands, check out https://yarnpkg.com/lang/en/docs/migrating-from-npm/ or https://shift.infinite.red/npm-vs-yarn-cheat-sheet-8755b092e5cc.

Doing version control with Git

In modern software development, it goes without saying that you will need some SCM (Software Configuration Management) software to keep track of all changes in your code. Today, the most-used tool is Git, which we'll also be using. Git was created in 2005 by Linus Torvalds (who also created Linux!) for the development of the Linux kernel; not a small task considering that its source is over 25 million lines of code!

Linux is not the only major operating system controlled with Git; in February 2017, Microsoft itself decide to migrate the development of Microsoft Windows to Git, and developed customizations to enhance remote work.

We won't be delving into how Git works, what commands to use, and so on, because that would be material enough for a book! We will focus on how to use Git with VSC. This is rather simple because not only was VSC written with Git access in mind, but there are also some extensions that can make work even easier, so you don't have to memorize lots of commands and options; take look at following illustration:

Git has lot of commands, but you can cope very well with a few selected ones.
This XKCD comic is available online at https://xkcd.com/1597/.

How to do it...

Personally, I have a GitHub account, and I decided to use it for the code for this book. This is not only a way of being able to quickly share all the code with readers, but also (and quite important!) a way to ensure I wouldn't be able to accidentally lose my work, which I am quite capable of doing! See `https://github.com/fkereki/modernjs` for all code. I will assume that you have an appropriate `Git` server, and that you are able to initialize a project, connect it to the server, and so on. Also, VSC needs `Git` to be pre-installed in your machine; if you haven't installed it, checkout `https://git-scm.com/book/en/v2/Getting-Started-Installing-Git` to get started.

VSC provides full access to commands through its **Command Palette....** as seen in the following screenshot. You can search for a command there, and after clicking on it, VSC will ask for all possible parameters one at the time, so you don't have to do them by memory:

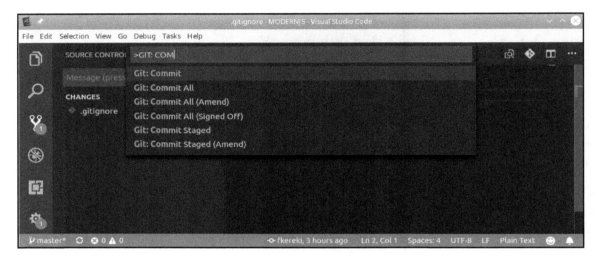

You can enter Git commands through VSC's command palette, and you'll get asked for the required parameters, if any

Committing code is quite frequent, so you can directly do it by clicking on the source control icon (third from the top, at the left) and entering the commit message that you want. In that screen, you can also revert local changes and more; mouse over to get all possible features.

There's more...

There is a single Git extension that I would recommend for VSC: look for GitLens (also called **Git Supercharged**) and install it. This extension provides access to practically all Git information.

Take a look at the following screenshot:

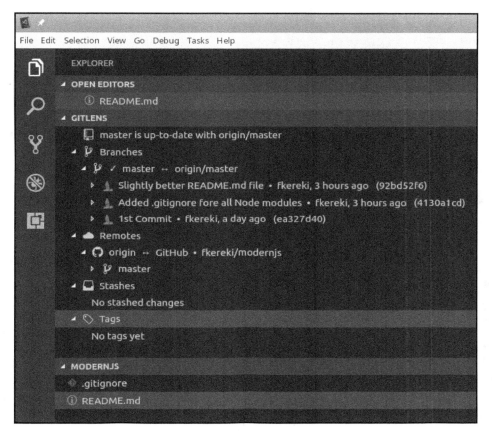

GitLens in use

Among other features, `GitLens` provides the following:

- A lens, to show recent commit and author information
- An explorer, to browse repositories and file histories
- A blame annotation, to show who made the last change to a line, as with git blame
- The ability to search for commits in different ways, and much more

For more detailed information, see `http://gitlens.amod.io/`. Pay particular attention to customization at `https://github.com/eamodio/vscode-gitlens/#configuration`, because most features can be twiddled to better suit your work style. You can access them through the standard **Settings** page (look for all configuration items whose names start with *GitLens*), or by opening the Command Palette and looking for **GitLens: Open Settings**, which will open a special setup screen as seen in the following screenshot:

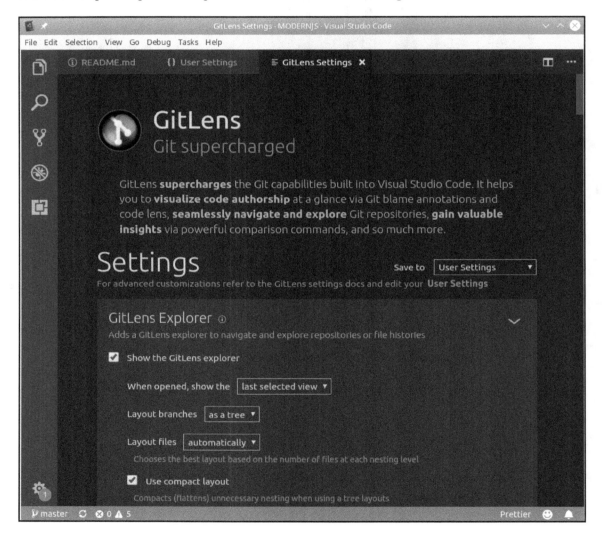

Gitlens also provides a special onscreen settings feature, which allows you to configure practically every aspect of the tool

Now that we have a development environment set up, and we have chosen and installed a minimum set of tools, let's go further and add some optional, but highly recommended, additional packages that will help produce better code.

Formatting your source code with Prettier

If you work in a project with several other developers, sooner or later arguments as to how code should be formatted are certain to pop up, and they can keep going for a long time! Deciding upon a single standard for your source code is really needed, but if formatting depends on each person, it's certain that you will end with even more "standards" than team members! Take a look at the following illustration. Something you don't want to have in a team is extra friction or aggravation, and style arguments can take forever:

You cannot afford to have more than one standard.
This XKCD comic is available online at https://xkcd.com/927/.

The problem is worsened by the fact that modern JS projects will not only include JS source code, but also possibly TypeScript or Flow (see the *Adding Flow for data types checks* section later), JSX (see Chapter 6, *Developing with React*), JSON, HTML, CSS or SCSS, and even more.

After having tried out many source code formatters, I finally decided to use Prettier for all purposes. Prettier is an *opinionated* code formatter, which supports all the languages that I listed previously, reformatting source code according to a set of rules, thus ensuring that all code conforms to an expected style.

If you want to read the original description for `Prettier`, see the blog post at `https://jlongster.com/A-Prettier-Formatter`, where the author describes the rationale for the project and gives some details on implementation and options.

What does it mean, that it is *opinionated*? Many (or most) code formatters provide a very big set of configuration options that you can twiddle in order to get the code to look as you wish. On the other hand, `Prettier` has its own set of rules, with little leeway for configuration, and thus cuts short all arguments. Moreover, you can get it to work seamlessly with VSC, meaning that whenever you save the code, it will get reformatted.

Let's see some examples of this *opinionating*. Working with arrow functions (which we shall see in more detail in the *Defining functions* section of Chapter 2, *Using Modern JavaScript Features*), if the function has a single parameter, enclosing it in parentheses is optional:

```
const plus1= (x)=> 1+x
```

However, `Prettier` decides that in this case the parentheses should not be included. Also, note that it added several spaces for clarity, as well as the (optional) missing semicolon:

```
const plus1 = x => 1 + x;
```

Similarly, if you use promises (we'll see them in the *Doing async calls compactly* section of Chapter 2, *Using JavaScript Modern Features*) you may write something such as the following:

```
fetch('http://some.url').then((response) => {
    return response.json();
}).then((myJson) => {
    console.log(myJson);
}).catch(e => { /* something wrong */ });
```

However, it will get reformatted to the more usual following code:

```
fetch("http://some.url")
    .then(response => {
        return response.json();
    })
    .then(myJson => {
        console.log(myJson);
    })
    .catch(e => {
        /* something wrong */
    });
```

Note how each `.then(...)` was pushed to a separate line, according to the most common style for JS. The formatting rules that `Prettier` applies are derived from usual practice, and it wouldn't be possible to list them all here. But, what really matters is that by using this tool, you may be certain that your whole team will be working in the same fashion.

 If your team grumbles about some rule or other, remind them of the saying *there's a right way, a wrong way, and the Army way!* After adopting `Prettier`, there will be no place for style discussions any more, and peace will eventually reign.

How to do it...

Installing `Prettier` is very simple: you should just add the VSC extension, which you can find by searching for `Prettier Code Formatter`; as a check, the latest version (as of December, 2018) is 1.16.0, and the author is Esben Petersen. The plugin itself can be found in the VSC marketplace, at `https://marketplace.visualstudio.com/items?itemName=esbenp.prettier-vscode`. You can also install it globally (as we saw in the *Installing packages for different purposes* section earlier in this chapter) to be able to use it in scripts or from the command line with `npm` or `yarn`. See `https://prettier.io/docs/en/install.html`, and I'd recommend doing that.

There is one change you will want to make in the VSC preferences. Go to **File | Preferences | Settings**, and add the following line to your user configuration, so every file will be formatted automatically whenever you save it:

```
"editor.formatOnSave": true,
.
.
.
```

If you'd rather only apply `Prettier` to JS, then you should use this instead:

```
"[javascript]": {
    "editor.formatOnSave": true
},
.
.
.
```

As we said, `Prettier` is pretty opinionated as to how code should look, and there are only a few options that you can change. The available options can be set in `package.json` (which makes it easier for all the team to share them) in a `"prettier"` key. Some of the possibilities (meaning the ones you might want to modify) are as follows:

Option	Default value	Meaning
arrowParens	false	For arrow functions with a single parameter, whether to enclose it in parentheses.
bracketSpacing	true	Include a space after the opening brace of an object, and before the closing brace.
jsxBracketSameLine	false	If `true`, the ending > for a multiline JSX element will be added at the end of the last line; if `false`, it will be on a separate line.
printWidth	80	Maximum line size.
semi	true	Add semicolons at the end of every line, even if not needed.
singleQuote	false	Use single quotes for strings.
tabWidth	2	Indentation size.
trailingComma	none	Specify whether to add trailing commas or not, wherever possible. Options are `none` (never add such commas), `es5` (add them where ES5 allows, as in arrays or objects), or `all` (add them even to function arguments).
useTabs	false	Use tabs for indentation.

Personally, the only ones I use are `tabWidth:4` and `printWidth:75`, but the latter is for the sake of the book only, not for other work. My `package.json` thus includes the following; I have it just before the `dependencies` key, but you can place it elsewhere:

```
"prettier": {
    "tabWidth": 4,
    "printWidth": 75
},
.
.
.
```

You can also use `Prettier` independently of VSC, and in that case the configuration options should go in a `.prettierrc` file. See `https://prettier.io/docs/en/cli.html` and `https://prettier.ic/docs/en/configuration.html` for more on this.

Finally, if you want to avoid `Prettier` code formatting for some reason or another, you can do the following:

- Avoid all formatting for a given file by adding its path and name to a `.prettierignore` text file at the project root
- Avoid reformatting a single sentence by preceding it with a `// prettier-ignore comment`

For the latter option, remember to use the appropriate comment style depending on the source code language. For example, in an HTML file's you would use `<!-- prettier-ignore -->`, while in CSS, it should be `/* prettier-ignore */`, and for JSX, `{/* prettier-ignore */}`.

How it works...

There are two ways of using `Prettier`. The first is to configure VSC to automatically format the code whenever you save it; following the instructions we saw earlier when we installed VSC, change the editor **Format on save** option to **true**, and you'll be set. Of course, you can also format the code whenever you want by right clicking and selecting the **Format Document** option.

You can also use `Prettier` online. Go to `https://prettier.io/playground/`, paste your code into the left panel, and you'll instantly get a formatted version in the right panel. Take a look at the following screenshot for an example of code reformatting:

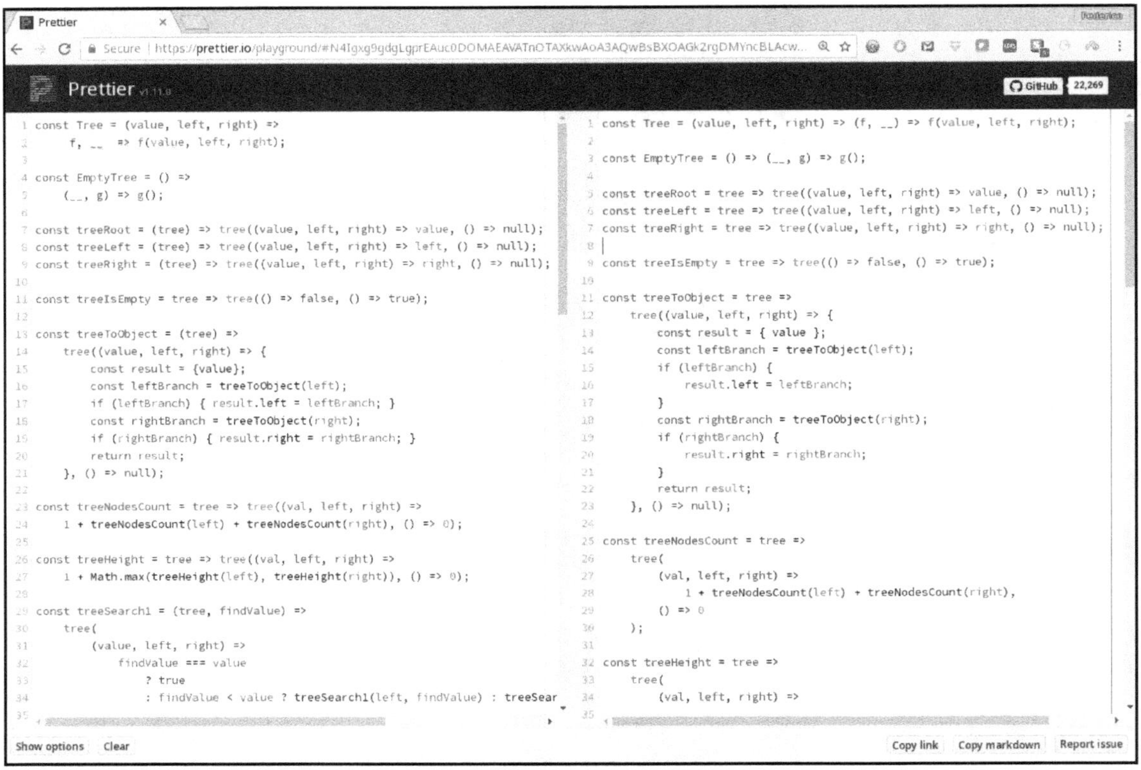

Prettier online can be used to experiment with configuration parameters, or for a quick code reformatting session

If you want to experiment with the few available options, click **Show Options** at the bottom-left corner, and you'll be able to configure Prettier, according to what we saw in the previous section, see the following screenshot:

If you want to dynamically experiment with (the few available) Prettier settings, you can do so in the online playground

When preparing the code for this book, I set the right margin at 75, because that's what will fit in a printed page. I also set indentation to 4 characters, because I find it clearer. Other than that, I left everything as the default; fewer style arguments to deal with this way!

Documenting your code with JSDoc

A good rule for maintainability is that code should be documented. JSDoc (or JSDoc3; the name reflects the current version, 3.6.0) is an API documentation generator, which can produce an HTML website with full documentation for your code. You only have to add comments (in a specific format) to your source code, and JSDoc will scan the code to pick them up and generate the documentation. Let's first see how those comments should be written, and then turn to a tool to make the work easier with VSC.

The official web page for JSDoc is at http://usejsdoc.org/, and the source code can be found at https://github.com/jsdoc3/jsdoc.

How to do it...

The main idea for JSDoc is to document your APIs, including functions, classes, methods, and whatnot. JSDoc comments are expected to precede the code that is being documented. Comments start with /** and end with */; the double star distinguishes them from normal comments.

Don't go overboard with stars, because if you write three or more, then the comment will also be ignored; JSDoc expects two stars, no more, no less.

The following code block shows the simplest possible example, how you might document a function by providing a description of its goals and arguments:

```
/**
 * Solves the Hanoi Towers puzzle, for any number of disks.
 *
 * @param {number} disks - How many disks to move
 * @param {string} from - The starting pole's name
 * @param {string} to - The destination pole's name
 * @param {string} extra - The other pole's name
 */
const hanoi = (disks, from, to, extra) => {
    if (disks === 1) {
        console.log(`Move disk 1 from post ${from} to post ${to}`);
    } else {
        hanoi(disks - 1, from, extra, to);
        console.log(`Move disk ${disks} from post ${from} to post ${to}`);
        hanoi(disks - 1, extra, to, from);
    }
};
```

The `@param` notation is a block tag, which introduces a code item, in this case, a parameter of the function. A (partial) list of common tags is as follows:

`@author`	The developer's name.
`@class`	Defines a class.
`@constructor`	Marks a function a constructor.
`@copyright, @license`	Legal details.
`@deprecated`	Marks a function or method as deprecated.
`@exports`	An exported module member.
`@function, @callback`	Defines a function, and more specifically, one used as a callback.
`@param`	What parameters are expected. The data type may be added within braces.
`@property or @prop`	A property of an object.
`@return or @returns`	What the function or method returns.
`@throws or @exception`	An exception thrown by a method.
`@version`	A library's version.

There are more tags, such as `@private`, to identify a member as private, but since JS doesn't really provide that feature, I skipped it. Other tags are more specific, and you may not use them, such as `@generator` or `@mixin`. If you want to see the complete list of possible block (and also a couple of inline) tags, checkout `http://usejsdoc.org/index.html`.

A confession: we won't be using `JsDoc` very much in this book, but only because all the needed explanations will be given in the text itself. For normal work, I'd always use it, but in this book it would mainly be redundant.

How it works...

Writing this sort of comment can quickly become tedious, but you can use the *Document This* VSC extension to automatically generate the needed template, which you will then complete. You can find the extension at `https://marketplace.visualstudio.com/items?itemName=joelday.docthis`, but it's simpler to install it through VSC itself: search for `Document This` and it will quickly appear.

After including this extension, if you right-click on the code, a new command will appear that will automatically generate (mostly empty) comments for you to complete.

As for generating the automatic documentation, checkout `http://usejsdoc.org/about-commandline.html`; we won't go into this because it's fairly straightforward. You can configure `JSDoc`, and also change the template it uses for the generated page; see `http://usejsdoc.org/about-configuring-jsdoc.html` and `http://usejsdoc.org/about-configuring-default-template.html` for these topics. See the following screenshot:

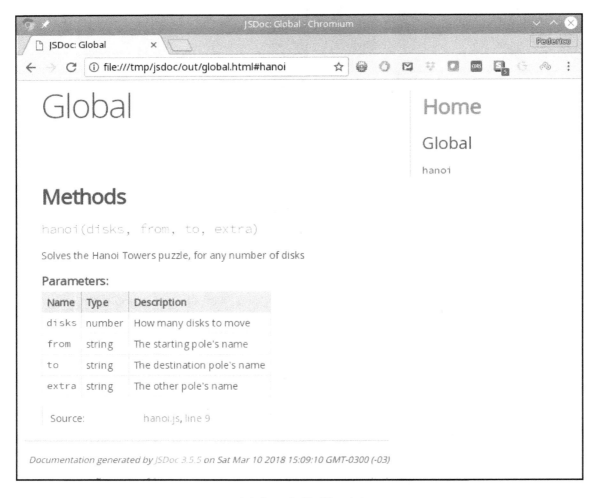

A simple example of the JSDoc output

Of course, documenting a single function won't be your use case! But for our purposes, it's enough; for normal use, you'd get an index with links to every class, function, and so on, fully documenting your code.

You have set up your working environment, and you are able to write documented, well-indented code in the latest version of JS, but that's still not proof against some error that may be committed, so let's now look into ways of enhancing your code more deeply.

Adding code quality checks with ESLint

JS is a very potent language, but there's also great potential for misuse. For example, most people would agree that if a==b is true, and b==c is also true, then a==c should be true too, but because of the data type conversion rules that JS applies for the == cperator, you have the following:

```
""==0   // true
0=="0"  // true
""=="0" // false!?
```

Another example follows; what does this very simple function return?

```
function mystery() {
    return
    {
        something: true
    }
}
```

If you answered *an object*, you would have been bitten by a missing semicolon. This code is actually interpreted by JS as follows:

```
function mystery() {
    return ;
    {
        something: true;
    }
}
```

Note the semicolon after return. This function returns undefined, and something is interpreted as a label for an expression that happens to be true; bad! These kinds of situations are common enough, and even if you know what you are doing, getting at least a warning about possible problems with your code could help root out a bug, and that's the kind of warning that ESLint produces.

The *gotcha* shown previously is only one of many that JS has for unaware developers. Google for *JavaScript gotchas* and you'll get several lists of possible errors.

How to do it...

Linters are a class of programming tools that analyze your source code, and raise warnings and errors about poor-quality uses or constructs that could even imply bugs. We are going to use ESLint, created by Nicholas Zakas in 2013; the tool's current version is 5.10.0, as of December, 2018.

 The first `lint` program was written in 1978 by Stephen Johnson, at Bell Labs, where he also worked on Unix, **yet another compiler compiler (yacc)**, and the portable C compiler, which made it easier to output code for different computer architectures.

`ESLint` is based upon pluggable rules, which may be enabled or disabled at will, or configured according to your specific preferences. (You could even develop your own rules, but that's beyond the scope of this book.) There are also bundles of rules that let you avoid having to individually configure dozens of distinct rules.

Installing ESLint is quite simple, and just requires doing the following:

```
npm install eslint eslint-config-recommended --save-dev
```

Then, you will have to add ESLint options to the `package.json` configuration file; let's get into this. First, we'll add a script to apply ESLint to our complete source directory (which has only a single file at this time!) with `npm run eslint`:

```
"scripts": {
    "build": "babel src -d out",
    "eslint": "eslint src",
    "test": "echo \"Error: no test specified\" && exit 1"
}
```

We must also specify some configuration for ESLint itself. We'll add a completely new section for this:

```
"eslintConfig": {
    "parserOptions": {
        "ecmaVersion": 2017,
        "sourceType": "module"
    },
    "env": {
        "browser": true,
        "node": true
    },
    "extends": "eslint:recommended",
    "rules": {}
}
```

Let's go item by item:

- `parserOptions` lets you specify what JS version you want to process (I'm going with 2017, for ES8), and whether you are going to use modules (I'm indicating this, in advance of what we'll see in the *Organizing code in modules* section of `Chapter 2`, *Using Modern JavaScript Features*).

- `env` lets you specify the environment(s) you are going to work with, and that really means that some global variables will be assumed to exist. In this case, I'm saying I will be working both with code for browsers and for `Node`, but there are plenty more possible environments; checkout the *Specifying Environments* section at `https://eslint.org/docs/user-guide/configuring`. Later on, we will be adding some more environments, for example, for unit testing.

- `extends` lets you select a predefined set of rules, which you will later be able to modify to suit your tastes. I'm going with the recommended set; you can read more about it at `https://github.com/kunalgolani/eslint-config`. The available sets of rules change only whenever the `ESlint` major version changes, so they are reasonably stable. Furthermore, the `recommended` set represents a usually agreed upon list of rules, so before you start tinkering with specific changes, give it a try as is. The complete set of rules is available at `https://eslint.org/docs/rules/`, and the recommended rules can be found at `https://github.com/eslint/eslint/blob/master/conf/eslint-recommended.js`.

- `rules` lets you change some of the rules to better suit your style. We'll see good reasons for this soon.

 If (and only if) you are planning to use some `Babel` feature that is not yet supported by `ESLint`, you should install and use the `babel-eslint` package from `https://www.npmjs.com/package/babel-eslint`. This will also require adding a line to the `.eslintrc.json` file to change the parser that `ESLint` uses. However, keep in mind that it's highly unlikely you will require this change!

How it works...

If we use `npm run eslint` as is, we will get the following result:

```
> npm run eslint
> simpleproject@1.0.0 eslint /home/fkereki/sample
> eslint src


/home/fkereki/sample/src/eight_queens.js
  32:1 error Unexpected console statement no-console
> X 1 problem (1 error, 0 warnings)
```

The standard rules do not allow using `console.log(...)`, since you don't probably want to include them in your shipped application; this is the `no-console` rule at `https://eslint.org/docs/rules/no-console`. We can enable or disable rules on a global or local basis. If we approve of this `console.log(...)`, we must then disable the `no-console` rule locally. We'll do this by adding a comment to the source code, just before the problem line:

```
// eslint-disable-next-line no-console
console.log(`Solutions found: ${solutions}`);
```

If you had used `// eslint-disable no-console`, you would have disabled the `no-console` rule for the whole source file; `// eslint-disable` with no further specification would have disabled *all* rules for the file. After this, if you use `npm run eslint`, you'll get no errors.

Now, let's set a global rule. Some people don't like the `solutions++` line because not everybody feels comfortable with the `++` operator; there's a `no-plusplus` rule for this, at `https://eslint.org/docs/rules/no-plusplus`, but by default it's not enabled in the recommended set, so we will enable it globally by adding to the `rules` section in `package.json`:

```
"rules": {
    "no-plusplus": "error"
}
```

After this, if you run `ESLint`, you'll get a new error, and the developer that supposedly did it should fix the code:

```
/home/fkereki/sample/src/eight_queens.js
  13:9  error  Unary operator '++' used  no-plusplus
```

The possible configurations for a rule are `"off"` (if you want to disable it), `"warn"` (if you want to get a warning, but accept it), and `"error"` (rejecting the file). Some rules accept extra configurations, but those are specific; you'll have to read the rule documentation in order to learn about the possible changes. See `https://eslint.org/docs/rules/no-empty` for a specific example with the `no-empty` rule, which disallows empty blocks of code but has an extra option to allow them in `catch` statements.

Deciding what rules to enable or disable is something that usually happens at the beginning of a project, and it can be expected that some new rule changes will happen over time. In any case, no matter what you pick, ideally you should work only with `"off"` and `"error"`; if developers get used to warnings, they finally end up not paying attention to them, and that can be bad! Get used to the whole list of rules at `https://eslint.org/docs/rules/`.

Finally, all projects will be using an `out/` directory for the output file, which you would then distribute. If you care to look at some files within it, you don't need `ESLint` protesting about possible errors in generated code. To avoid this, you can add a small section to the `package.json` file:

```
"eslintIgnore": ["**/out/*.js"],
```

There's more...

Of course, all these checks are very good, but if you had to stop working, save everything, and run a separate tool each time you wanted to check for problems in your code, it would soon become unbearable. However, with VSC you can add a plugin to interact with ESLint in real time. Go to the extensions view and search for ESLint; you should find and install an extension, currently at version 1.7.2 (March 2018), written by Dirk Baeumer.

Once you install this extension, errors will be shown on screen with a wavy red underline, and if you mouse over them, you'll get an explanation about the failed rule. Take a look at the for an example:

```
 9
10    const finder = (column = 0) ⇒ {
11        if (column === SIZE) {
12            [eslint] Unary operator '++' used. (no-plusplus)
13            solutions++; // count it
14        } else {
15            const testRowsInColumn = j ⇒ {
16                if (j < SIZE) {
17                    if (checkPlace(column, j)) {
18                        places[column] = j;
19                        finder(column + 1);
20                    }
21                    testRowsInColumn(j + 1);
22                }
23            };
24            testRowsInColumn(0);
25        }
26    };
```

The ESLint plugin in action, showing problems with the code in real time

There are very few configuration items for `ESLint`; the only one I use is `"eslint.alwaysShowStatus": true`, so the status bar will show whether `ESLint` is enabled or not.

An interesting package that you could consider is the web `DeepScan` tool at `https://deepscan.io/home/`. `DeepScan` is advertised as *beyond Lint*, insofar as it can also detect runtime problems having to do with implicit type conversions, null checks, unreachable code, and more. For the time being, `DeepScan` is considered to be in beta stage and there are no paid plans yet. You can use it free for open source projects; for example, you can use it automatically with a GitHub project.

Adding Flow for data types checks

Let's finish this chapter by considering a tool that turns JS into a (sort of) new language, a *typed* one. One of the characteristics of JS is being untyped; for example, a variable can hold, or a function may return, any kind of value, there's no way to declare what type(s) should be stored in a variable or returned from a function. In this section, we will add Flow, a tool developed by Facebook, which allows for data type controls.

 Angular developers do not go for Flow, and opt for TypeScript instead. (OK, not Angular developers only; you can use TypeScript practically everywhere!) This version of JS was developed by Microsoft, and also includes data typing in a style very similar to Flow. TypeScript has its own transpiler, and you won't need Babel or Flow, so configuration will be a tad simpler. Instead of ESLint, you'll use TSLint, but you need not forego ESLint's rules: install tslint-eslint-rules; (see https://github.com/buzinas/tslint-eslint-rules) and you'll get the best of both worlds.

We will be getting into how to fully use Flow in the *Adding types* section of Chapter 2, *Using JavaScript Modern Features*, but let me give you a preview of what we expect; then, we'll get to install all the needed packages, and afterwards we'll go into more details. Imagine you wrote a highly complex function to add two numbers:

```
function addTwoNumbers(x, y) {
    return x + y;
}

console.log(addTwoNumbers(22, 9)); // 31, fine
```

However, since JS won't check types and has some conversion rules, the following two lines would also work:

```
console.log(addTwoNumbers("F", "K")); // FK - oops...
console.log(addTwoNumbers([], {}));   // [object Object]! more oops...
```

You could, on principle, add a lot of data type checking code to your function to verify typeof(x)==="number", but that can become a chore. (Although, of course, for some cases it's the only solution.) However, many errors can be detected before even running the code, as would happen here.

If you modify the function to include data type declarations, `Flow` will be able to detect the two wrong uses, and you will be able to solve the situation before even running the code:

```
function addTwoNumbers(x: number, y: number) {
    return x + y;
}
```

Basically, that's all there is! Of course, there are many details about what data types are available, defining new ones, using interfaces, and much more, but we'll get to that in the next chapter. For the time being, let's just install it with the promise that we will learn more about its use very shortly.

How to do it...

Installing `Flow` depends on whether you are working with `Babel` (as would be the case for client-side browser code) or not (as you would do for server-side code). We will see how to deal with `Node` starting in `Chapter 3`, *Developing with Node*; here, we'll just consider Babel.

To start, execute the following command to get the needed Flow packages, including the Babel and ESLint ones:

```
npm install flow-bin babel-preset-flow eslint-plugin-flowtype --save-dev
```

Then, add the `"flow"` preset for Babel in `package.json`:

```
"babel": {
    "presets": ["env", "flow"]
},
```

Add some lines to the `ESLint` configuration, also in `package.json`:

```
"eslintConfig": {
    "parserOptions": {
        "ecmaVersion": 2017,
        "sourceType": "module"
    },
    "env": {
        "browser": true,
        "node": true
    },
    "parser": "babel-eslint",
    "extends": ["eslint:recommended", "plugin:flowtype/recommended"],
    "plugins": ["flowtype"],
    "rules": {
        .
```

```
        .
        .
        .
    }
},
```

Add a `"flow"` script in `package.json`:

```
"scripts": {
    "build": "babel src -d out",
    "flow": "flow",
    .
    .
    .
},
```

Finally, perform `npm run flow init` to initialize `Flow`, only once, to create a
`.flowconfig` file with information that will be used by the `Flow` process. (See `https://flow.org/en/docs/config/` for more information on this file.)

 The `.flowconfig` file doesn't really match the style of other configuration files, and should really be a JSON file instead, possibly part of `package.json`. However, this is a still pending item; you can check `https://github.com/facebook/flow/issues/153` to monitor advances, but for the time being, you'll have to deal with `.flowconfig` as is.

How it works...

With the configuration you just wrote, you are set! Just do `npm run flow` whenever you start to work, to run a background process that will check your code incrementally and let you know about possible data type problems. However, you may even skip this step if you work with VSC; see the next section.

Configuring Flow's linting

Even though `ESLint` has us well covered for avoiding JS bad coding practices, it doesn't do much with regard to data types, but `Flow` can help us in this area.

There is a set of rules you can apply, and you will configure them through the
`.flowconfig` file we mentioned in the previous section:

```
[lints]
all=warn
unsafe-getters-setters=off
```

The first line, `all=warn`, is a *catch-all*, which defines the standard setting for all rules;
possible values are `off`, `warn`, and `error`. After that, you can specify settings for individual
rules; for example, in the preceding code I decided to ignore warnings about unsafe getters
or setters. Some rules are as follows:

- `sketchy-null`, which applies whenever you test the value of a variable that
  could be false (for example, zero) but also null or undefined, in the context of
  something like `if (x) { ... }`. This warning is meant to remind you that the
  variable might have a value you weren't considering.
- `sketchy-null-bool`, `sketchy-null-number`, `sketchy-null-string`, and
  `sketchy-null-mixed` are more granular versions of `sketchy-null`, and apply
  only to the specified data types.
- `unclear-type` warns about using `any`, `Object`, or `Function` as data type
  annotations.
- `untyped-import` and `untyped-type-import` warn you against importing
  from untyped files.
- `unsafe-getters-setters` advises against using getters or setters, because of
  their side effects.

 Read the complete current set of `Flow` linting rules at `https://flow.org/
en/docs/linting/rule-reference/`, where you will also find examples of
each rule.

You should also set `include_warnings` to `true`, in order to be able to get warnings in
VSC:

```
[options]
include_warnings=true
```

Whatever settings you include in .fontconfig will apply globally to your entire project, but you can also change them on a file-by-file basis, or even for a single line of code, along the same lines as with ESLint. You can disable warnings for a line by using a flowlint-next-line comment and listing the rules you want to change:

```
// flowlint-next-line sketchy-null-bool:off
if (x) {
    // ...
}
```

There is another comment, flowlint, that applies to the complete file. Checkout https://flow.org/en/docs/linting/flowlint-comments/ for more possibilities.

Using Flow within VSC

As we have been doing previously, we'll want to see Flow problems right in VSC. There's a simple solution: just go to **Extensions**, search for Flow Language Support, and install the package; that's it!

You'll also have to change two settings for VSC:

- Add "flow.useNPMPackagedFlow": true and this will remove the need to do npm run flow at the beginning; the extension will do that on its own
- Add "javascript.validate.enable": false to avoid clashes between Flow's syntax and JS

After that, you will be able to see `Flow` errors onscreen; see following screenshot for an example:

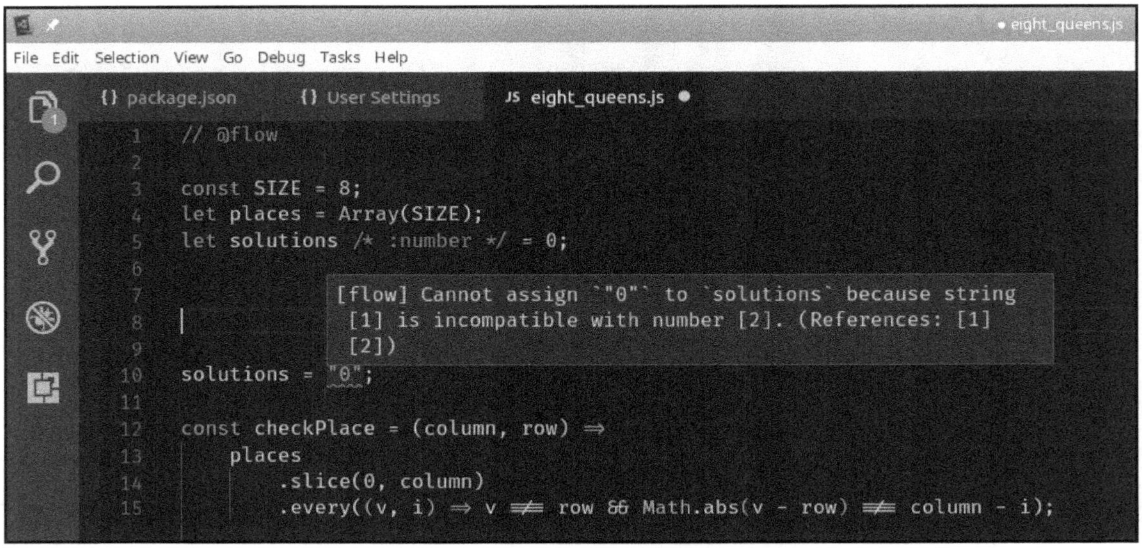

```
                                                                        ● eight_queens.js
File  Edit  Selection  View  Go  Debug  Tasks  Help

   {} package.json        {} User Settings        JS eight_queens.js ●
    1    // @flow
    2
    3    const SIZE = 8;
    4    let places = Array(SIZE);
    5    let solutions /* :number */ = 0;
    6
    7              [flow] Cannot assign `"0"` to `solutions` because string
    8    |         [1] is incompatible with number [2]. (References: [1]
    9              [2])
   10    solutions = "0";
   11
   12    const checkPlace = (column, row) ⇒
   13        places
   14            .slice(0, column)
   15            .every((v, i) ⇒ v ≢ row && Math.abs(v - row) ≢ column - i);
```

The VSC Flow extension lets you catch data type errors in real time; however, error messages are not always very clear

Using Modern JavaScript Features

2

The recipes we will be covering in this chapter are as follows:

- Adding types
- Working with strings
- Enhancing your code
- Defining functions
- Programming functionally
- Doing async calls compactly
- Working with objects and classes
- Organizing code in modules
- Determining a feature's availability

Introduction

In the previous chapter, we set up our working environment with many tools that we will be using throughout this book. In this chapter, we will get ourselves prepared for the rest of this book, and we will be considering some interesting and powerful modern features of JavaScript that can you help be more effective and write better code.

We will be considering several new language features that will come handy—but definitely not everything! JS has really grown into a big language, and there are some features that you're not likely to ever need. From the very start, we will also work more seriously with `Flow`, aiming to forego the usage of *untyped JS*, for a safer way of developing code.

It may be important to highlight that JS has evolved through the years, and that there isn't a single standard version. The most recent one is (formally) called ECMAScript 2018, which is usually shortened to ES2018. The current list of versions of the language is as follows:

- ECMAScript 1, June 1997
- ECMAScript 2, June 1998, essentially equal to the previous version
- ECMAScript 3, December 1999, adding several new functionalities
- ECMAScript 5, December 2009 (there never was an ECMAScript 4; that version was abandoned) also known as JS5
- ECMAScript 5.1, June 2011
- ECMAScript 6 (ES2015 or ES6), June 2015
- ECMAScript 7 (ES2016), June 2016
- ECMAScript 8 (ES2017), June 2017
- ECMAScript 9 (ES2018), June 2018

ECMA was originally an acronym meaning **European Computer Manufacturers Association**, but nowadays the name is simply considered a name by itself. You can go to its site at https://www.ecma-international.org/ and view the standard language specification at https://www.ecma-international.org/publications/standards/Ecma-262.htm.

Whenever we refer to JS in this text without further specification, the latest version (that is, ES2018) is what we mean. No browsers fully implement this version, and further on in this book, we'll solve this problem by using Babel, a tool that will convert the modern features into equivalent, but older and compatible code, so even if you program in the latest fashion, users with older browsers will still be able to run your code. The tools we'll be using will install Babel on their own, so we won't have to do that, but if you're curious, you can read more at https://babeljs.io/.

A very good source for all JS-related things is the **Mozilla Developer Network** (**MDN**), which has been going strong with all sorts of web documentation for over ten years. Take a look to their site at https://developer.mozilla.org/bm/docs/Web/JavaScript; we'll be frequently making reference to it. You can also read http://es6-features.org/ for a wealth of examples of ES6 features.

Adding types

In the previous chapter, we installed `Flow` so that we could add data types check to JS, but we didn't really get into its syntax or rules. Let's get into that now, before getting into JS-specific features.

Getting started

`Flow` will not check every file unless you expressly require it to. For a file to be checked, you must add a simple comment to the very top, as shown in the following code snippet. `Flow` will ignore any files that lack this comment, so even if you were adding the tool to an already existing project, you could do it gradually, adding files one at a time:

```
/* @flow */
```

Starting with Flow's controls, you just have to specify what data type you expect any variable to be, and `Flow` will check that it's always used correctly. Fortunately, `Flow` is also capable of determining data types by value; for example, if you assign a string to a variable, it will assume that this variable is meant to contain strings. Adapting an example from `https://flow.org/en/docs/usage/`, you could write the following:

```
/* @flow */

function foo(x: ?number): string {
    if (x) {
        return x;
    } else {
        return "some string";
    }
}

console.log(foo("x"));
```

The `:?number` and `:string` annotations specify that x is an optional numeric parameter, and that `foo` should return a string. Can you see two problems with the rest of the code? If you use `npm run flow`, you'll get a report showing what the problem is. First, you cannot `return x`, because of the data types mismatch between the variable and the expected return value:

```
Error -----------------------------------------------------------
---------------- src/types_examples.js:5:16

Cannot return x because number [1] is incompatible with string [2].
```

```
  2 |
[1] [2] 3 | function foo(x /* :?number */) /* :string */ {
  4 |       if (x) {
  5 |           return x;
  6 |       } else {
  7 |           return 'some string';
  8 |       }
```

Second, you are trying to call a function but passing a parameter of the wrong type:

```
Error-------------------------------------------------------------
--------------- src/types_examples.js:12:17

Cannot call foo with 'x' bound to x because string [1] is incompatible with
number [2].

  [2] 3 | function foo(x /* :?number */) /* :string */ {
  :
  9 | }
  10 |
  11 | // eslint-disable-next-line no-console
[1] 12 | console.log(foo('x'));
  13 |
```

All of the preceding code is (except for the type declarations) valid JS, so it would have been accepted; Flow tells you about the problems so that you can fix them. Now, let's get into greater detail, and see all of the possibilities that this tool gives us.

 If you want to ignore Flow's warnings for any line, precede it with a comment like // @FlowFixMe and follow with the reason why you want to skip that situation. See https://flow.org/en/docs/config/options/#toc-suppress-comment-regex for more on this.

How to do it...

There are many ways to define types so that you can deal with simple and complex cases with no problems. Let's start with the simpler, basic types, and then move on to more specific cases.

Basic types in Flow

The possible data types definitions can be found at `https://flow.org/en/docs/types/`
—we won't copy them all here, but rather show you the main ones through a few examples.
Please look at the full documentation because there's a great variety of possibilities that you
should be aware of:

`:boolean`	Boolean values.
`:number`	Numeric values.
`:string`	Strings.
`:null`	Null values. You wouldn't just be declaring that a certain variable should always be null; rather, you'll be using these with advanced types such as *unions*, which we'll get to see in the next section.
`:void`	Void (undefined) value.
`:mixed`	Any type, but will still get checked for consistency. For instance, if at one point `Flow` knows that the variable is a Boolean, then using it as a string would be flagged as wrong.
`:any`	Any type, and `Flow` won't do any checks for it. This amounts to disabling type checks on whatever is of *any* type.
`function foo(x: ?boolean)`	A function with an optional `boolean` parameter. This is the same as declaring that the argument can either be a `boolean`, `null`, or also `undefined`.
`function bar() :string`	A function that returns a string result.
`{ property ?: number }`	An optional object property; if present, it could be numeric or undefined, but not `null`.
`: Array&lt;number>` `: number[]`	An array of numbers, in two different styles. If you want to deal with fixed length arrays, *tuples* may apply; go to `https://flow.org/en/docs/types/tuples/` to find out more.

We will find out how to assign or define types for these definitions in
the *Defining types for arrow functions* recipe, later in this chapter.

We can see some examples of the definitions in the following code. I disabled ESLint's rule about unused variables to avoid obvious problems:

```
// Source file: src/types_basic.js

/* @flow */
/* eslint-disable no-unused-vars */

let someFlag: boolean;
let greatTotal: number;
let firstName: string;

function toString(x: number): string {
    return String(x);
}

function addTwo(x: number | string, y: number | string) {
    return x + y;
}

function showValue(z: mixed): void {
    // not returning anything
    console.log("Showing... ", z);
}

let numbersList: Array&lt;number>;
numbersList = [22, 9, 60]; // OK
numbersList[1] = "SEP"; // error; cannot assign a string to a number

let anotherList: number[] = [12, 4, 56];

// continues...
```

The addTwo() definition has a hidden problem: are you sure that x and y will always be of the same type? Actually, x could be a number and y could be a string, and Flow wouldn't complain. We have no easy way of testing this, and a runtime check for typeof x === typeof y would be needed.

When you define an object, you should provide data types for all of its properties and methods. Object definitions are considered to be *sealed*, meaning that you cannot change the object types. If you cannot or won't do this, start with an empty object, and then Flow will let you add properties at will:

```
// ...continued

let sealedObject: { name: string, age?: number } = { name: "" };

sealedObject.name = "Ivan Horvat"; // OK

sealedObject.id = 229; // error: key isn't defined in the data type

sealedObject = { age: 57 }; // error: mandatory "name" field is missing

let unsealedObject = {};
unsealedObject.id = 229; // OK
```

If a function expects an object with some properties, and it receives an object with those properties plus some extra ones, Flow won't complain. If you don't want this, use *exact objects*; see https://flow.org/en/docs/types/objects/#toc-exact-object-types. However, this also causes problems, such as disabling the spread operator; see https://github.com/facebook/flow/issues/2405 for a (two year long!) discussion.

Now, let's turn to more complex definitions, which you will probably end up using, since they better match usual business requirements and program specifications.

Union types

The basic definitions of the previous section may be enough for plenty of code, but as you start working with more complex problems, you'll need some more advanced Flow features, and you may want to define types separately so that you can reuse them elsewhere. Due to this, in this and the following sections, we'll look at more advanced types.

In JS, it's common that a variable may have, at different times, different data types. For that situation, you can use *union types*:

```
// Source file: src/types_advanced.js

let flag: number | boolean;
flag = true; // OK
flag = 1; // also OK
```

```
flag = "1"; // error: wrong type

let traffic: "red" | "amber" | "green"; // traffic is implicitly string
traffic = "yellow"; // error: not allowed

type numberOrString = number | string;
function addTwo(x: numberOrString, y: numberOrString) {
    return x + y;
}

// continues...
```

For some occasions in which you have objects that have different properties depending on some internal value, you can also use *disjoint* unions; see `https://flow.org/en/docs/types/unions/`.

Class types

`Flow` supports classes and mostly in an automatic way. Every time you define a class, it becomes a type by itself, so you don't have to do anything else; you can just use it elsewhere. (We'll be seeing more about classes in a short while, in the *Working with Objects and Classes* section.) You can assign types to properties and methods in the same way as for objects and functions. Using our `Person` class again as an example, the following code shows how to define it with `Flow`:

```
// Source file: src/types_advanced.js

class Person {
    // class fields need Flow annotations
    first: string;
    last: string;

    constructor(first: string, last: string) {
        this.first = first;
        this.last = last;
    }

    initials(): string {
        return `${this.first[0]}${this.last[0]}`;
    }

    fullName(): string {
        return `${this.first} ${this.last}`;
    }
```

```
    get lastFirst(): string {
        return `${this.last}, ${this.first}`;
    }

    set lastFirst(lf: string) {
        // very unsafe; no checks!
        const parts = lf.split(",");
        this.last = parts[0];
        this.first = parts[1];
    }
}

let pp = new Person("Jan", "Jansen"); // OK
let qq = new Person(1, 2); // error: wrong types for the constructor
let rr: Person; // OK, "Person" type is understood and can be used
```

However, there is a problem you may encounter. If you have distinct classes, even with exactly the same shape, they won't be considered equivalent by `Flow`. For instance, even if `Animal` and `Pet` are equivalent, the assignment of `Pet` to `Animal` (or vice versa) won't be allowed:

```
// Source file: src/types_advanced.js

class Animal {
 name: string;
 species: string;
 age: number;
}

class Pet {
 name: string;
 species: string;
 age: number;
}

let tom: Animal;
tom = new Pet(); // error: Pet and Animal are distinct types
```

In this particular case, if you were to say that `Pet` extends `Animal`, then you could assign `Pet` to `Animal`, but not the other way round. A more general solution would involve creating an `interface` and using it in several places:

```
// Source file: src/types_advanced.js

interface AnimalInt {
 name: string;
 species: string;
```

```
   age: number;
}

class Animal2 implements AnimalInt {
 name: string;
 species: string;
 age: number;
}

class Pet2 implements AnimalInt {
 name: string;
 species: string;
 age: number;
}

let tom2: AnimalInt; // not Animal2 nor Pet2
tom2 = new Pet2(); // OK now
```

Note that the `interface` definition, which includes three fields, doesn't exempt you from declaring those fields when you define `Animal2` or `Pet2`; in fact, if you were to forget some of these fields, `Flow` would point out the error, because neither of the three is marked as optional.

Type aliases

When your types become more complex or when you want to reuse the same definition in several places, you can create a type alias:

```
// Source file: src/types_advanced.js

type simpleFlag = number | boolean;

type complexObject = {
 id: string,
 name: string,
 indicator: simpleFlag,
 listOfValues: Array&lt;number>
};
```

After defining types in this fashion, you can just use them anywhere, even in the definition of new types, as we did in `complexObject`, where we defined a field to be of the previously defined `simpleFlag` type:

```
// Source file: src/types_advanced.js

let myFlag: simpleFlag;
```

```
let something: complexObject = {
  id: "B2209",
  name: "Anna Malli",
  indicator: 1,
  listOfValues: [12, 4, 56]
};
```

Type aliases can even be generic, as we'll see in the next section. You can also export types from a module, and import them for usage anywhere; we'll get to that in the *Working with libraries* section.

Generic types

In functional programming, it's quite usual to work with the identity function, which is defined as follows:

```
// Source file: src/types_advanced.js

const identity = x => x;
```

> In combinatory logic, which we won't be going into, this corresponds with the I *combinator*.

How would you write a type definition for this function? If the argument is a number, it will return a number; if it's a string, it'll return a string and so on. Writing all possible situations would be a chore and not very **Don't Repeat Yourself (DRY)**. Flow provides a solution, with *generic types*:

```
// Source file: src/types_advanced.js

const identity = <T>(x: T): T => x;
```

In this case, T stands for the generic type. Both the argument of the function and the result of the function itself are defined to be of T type, so Flow will know that whatever type the argument is, the result type will be the same. A similar syntax would be used for the more usual way of defining functions:

```
// Source file: src/types_advanced.js

function identity2<T>(x: T): T {
    return x;
}
```

`Flow` also checks that you don't accidentally restrict a generic type. In the following case, you would always be returning a number, while `T` might actually be any other different type:

```
// Source file: src/types_advanced.js

function identity3<T>(x: T): T {
    return 229; // wrong; this is always a number, not generic
}
```

You need not restrict yourself to a single generic type; the following nonsense example shows a case with two types:

```
// Source file: src/types_advanced.js

function makeObject<T1, T2>(x: T1, y: T2) {
    return { first: x, second: y };
}
```

It's also possible to define a parametric type with a generic type that can later be specified. In the following example, the type definition for `pair` allows you to further create new types, each of which will always produce pairs of values of the same type:

```
// Source file: src/types_advanced.js

type pair<T> = [T, T];

type pairOfNumbers = pair<number>;
type pairOfStrings = pair<string>;

let pn: pairOfNumbers = [22, 9];

let ps: pairOfStrings = ["F", "K"];
```

There are more ways you can use generic types; check `https://flow.org/en/docs/types/generics/` for a complete description of available possibilities.

Opaque types for safer coding

In `Flow` (and TypeScript as well), types that are structurally the same are considered to be compatible and one can be used instead of the other. Let's consider an example. In Uruguay, there is a national identification card with a DNI code: this is a string that's formed by seven digits, a dash, and a check digit. You could have an application that lets you update people's data:

```
// Source file: src/opaque_types.js

type dniType = string;
type nameType = string;

function updateClient(id: number, dni: dniType, name: nameType) {
    /*
        Talk to some server
        Update the DNI and name for the client with given id
    */
}
```

What could happen? If you don't define better types, there's nothing preventing you from doing a call such as `updateClient(229, "Kari Nordmann", "1234567-8")`; can you spot the switched values? Since both `dniType` and `nameType` are just bottom strings, even though they imply totally different concepts, `Flow` won't complain. `Flow` ensures that types are used correctly, but since it doesn't handle semantics, your code can still be obviously wrong.

Opaque types are different, since they obscure their internal implementation details from the outside, and have much stricter compatibility rules. You could have a file called `opaque_types.js` with the following definitions:

```
// Source file: src/opaque_types.js

opaque type dniType = string;
type nameType = string; // not opaque!
```

Then, in a different source file, we could attempt the following:

```
// Source file: src/opaque_usage.js

import type { dniType, nameType } from "./opaque_types";
import { stringToDni } from "./opaque_types";

let newDni = "1234567-8"; // supposedly a DNI
```

```
let newName = "Kari Nordmann";

updateClient(229, newName, newDni); // doesn't work; 2nd argument should be
a DNI
updateClient(229, newDni, newName); // doesn't work either; same reason
```

How can we fix this? Not even changing the definition of `newDni` would help:

```
let newDni: dniType = "1234567-8"; // a string cannot be assigned to DNI
```

Even after this change, `Flow` would still complain that a string isn't a DNI. When we work with opaque types, if we want to do type conversions, we must provide them on our own. In our case, we should add such a function to our file with type definitions:

```
// Source file: src/opaque_types.js

const stringToDni = (st: string): dniType => {
    /*
        do validations on st
        if OK, return a dniType
        if wrong, throw an error
    */
    return (st: dniType);
};

export { stringToDni };
```

Now, we can work! Let's see the code:

```
// Source file: src/opaque_usage.js

updateClient(229, stringToDni(newDni), newName); // OK!
```

This is still not optimal. We know that all DNI values are strings, so we should be able to use them as such, right? This isn't the case:

```
// Source file: src/opaque_usage.js

function showText(st: string) {
    console.log(`Important message: ${st}`);
}

let anotherDni: dniType = stringToDni("9876543-2");
showText(anotherDni); // error!
```

The `anotherDni` variable is of `dniType`, but as opaque types carry no information as to the real types, trying to use it as a `string` fails. You could, of course, write a `dniToString()` function, but that seems to be overkill—and would quickly get out of control in a system with potentially dozens of data types! We have a fallback: we can add a subtyping constraint, which will allow the opaque type to be used as a different type:

```
// Source file: src/opaque_types.js

opaque type dniType : string = string;
```

This means that `dniType` may be used as `string`, but not vice versa. Using opaque types will add safety to your code, since more errors will be caught, but you can also get a certain measure of flexibility through these constraints, which will make your life easier.

Working with libraries

Today, it's highly likely that any project you create will depend on third-party libraries, and it's very likely that those weren't written with `Flow`. By default, `Flow` will ignore these libraries and won't do any type checking. This means that any data type errors you might commit when using the library will be unrecognized, and you'll have to deal with them in the old-fashioned way, through testing and debugging—a throwback to worse times!

To solve this problem, `Flow` lets you work with **library definitions (libdefs)** (see `https://flow.org/en/docs/libdefs/`) that describe the data types, interfaces, or classes for a library, separately from the library itself, like header files in C++ and other languages. Libdefs are `.js` files, but they are placed in a `flow-typed` directory at the root of your project.

 You can change this directory by editing the `.flowconfig` configuration file, but we won't meddle with it. If you are interested in effecting such a change, see the `[libs]` documentation at `https://flow.org/en/docs/config/`.

There exists a repository of library definitions, `flow-typed`, in which you can find already made files for many popular libraries; see `https://github.com/flowtype/flow-typed` for more information. However, you don't need to directly deal with that, because there is a tool that does the work for you, though at some times it will pass the buck back to you!

The main objection against Flow these days, and a point for TypeScript, is that the list of supported libraries in terms of data type descriptions is far greater for the latter. There are some projects that attempt to make Flow work with TypeScript's descriptions, but so far this is still pending, though some good results have been shown.

First, install the new tool:

```
npm install flow-typed --save-dev
```

Then, add a script in package.json to simplify the work:

```
scripts: {
    .
    .
    .
    addTypes: "flow-typed install",
    .
    .
    .
```

Using npm run addTypes will scan your project and attempt to add all possible libdefs. If it cannot find an appropriate definition for a library (this isn't unusual, I'm sorry to say), it will create a basic definition using any everywhere. For instance, I added the moment library to the project:

```
> npm install moment --save
> npm run addTypes
```

After this, the flow-typed directory was added to the project root. In it, there a lot of files appeared, including moment_v2.3.x.js with the type definitions for the moment library. For libraries without a libdef, files were also created, but you may ignore them.

If you need a libdef, and it doesn't exist, you may be able to create it by yourself. (And, please, contribute your work to the flow-typed project!) I added npm install fetch --save, but when I tried to get the libdef, it wasn't found. So, I can either keep working without the definitions (the standard situation!) or I can try to create the appropriate file; none is really an optimal situation.

I would suggest adding the flow-typed directory to .gitignore so that those files won't get uploaded to Git. Since it's standard practice to do npm install every time you pull from the repository, now you also have to use npm run addTypes—or, better yet, create a script that will do both commands!

Working with strings

Strings have been a feature of JS since the very first version, but nowadays there are some more features available.

How to do it...

In the following sections, we'll see many functions that we'll be using through the rest of this book, such as interpolation (to build up strings out of several parts) or tagged strings (which we'll use to style components in the *Creating StyledComponents for inline styling* section of Chapter 7, *Enhancing Your Application*), to show just two examples.

Interpolating in template strings

Everybody has, at one time or another, used common operators to build up a string, as in the following code fragment:

```
let name = lastName + "," + firstName;
let clientUrl = basicUrl + "/clients/" + clientId + "/";
```

JS has now added *template literals*, providing an easy way to include variable text and produce multiple line strings. String interpolation is quite simple, and the preceding code could be rewritten as follows:

```
let name = `${lastName}, ${firstName}`;
let clientUrl = `${basicUrl}/clients/${clientId}/`;
```

 Template literals were earlier known as *template strings*, but current JS specifications don't use that expression any more. For more information, go to https://developer.mozilla.org/en-US/docs/Web/JavaScript/Reference/Template_literals.

Template literals are delimited by back-tick characters (` ... `). You use ${ ... } wherever you want some value or expression to be substituted:

```
let confirm = `Special handling: ${flagHandle ? "YES" : "NO"}`;
```

Of course, it's easy to go overboard and start pushing too much logic when interpolating. I would recommend avoiding code such as the following for just that reason:

```
let list = ["London", "Paris", "Amsterdam", "Berlin", "Prague"];
let sched = `Visiting ${list.length > 0 ? list.join(", ") : "no cities"}`;
// Visiting London, Paris, Amsterdam, Berlin, Prague
```

If `list` had been empty, `"Visiting no cities"` would have been produced instead. It's far clearer if you push logic out of templates; even if the resulting code is somewhat larger, it will gain in clarity:

```
let list = ["London", "Paris", "Amsterdam", "Berlin", "Prague"];
let destinations = list.length > 0 ? list.join(", ") : "no cities";
let sched = `Visiting ${destinations}`;
```

 We'll fight the temptation to include logic in templates later, when we work in React (from Chapter 6, *Developing with React*, to Chapter 10, *Testing your Application*) and see how we can render components.

Tagged templates

A tagged template is a more advanced form of the templates we've been looking at. Basically, it's another way to call a function, but with a syntax similar to a template string. Let's look at an example and then explain it:

```
// Source file: src/tagged_templates.js

function showAge(strings, name, year) {
    const currYear = new Date().getFullYear();
    const yearsAgo = currYear - year;
    return (
        strings[0] + name + strings[1] + year + `, ${yearsAgo} years ago`
    );
}

const who = "Prince Valiant";
const when = 1937;
const output1 = showAge`The ${who} character was created in ${when}.`;
console.log(output1);
// The Prince Valiant character was created in 1937, 81 years ago

const model = "Suzuki";
const yearBought = 2009;
const output2 = showAge`My ${model} car was bought in ${yearBought}`;
console.log(output2);
// My Suzuki car was bought in 2009, 9 years ago
```

The `showAge()` function is called with the following:

- An array of strings, corresponding to each constant part of the template, so `strings[0]` is `The` and `strings[2]` is `.` in the first case, for example
- A parameter for each expression included; in our case, there's two of them

The function may do any calculations and return any type of value—possibly not a string! In our example, the function produces an *enhanced* version of the original string, adding how many years ago something happened—when a comic strip character was created or an automobile was bought, for example.

 We'll be using tagged templates in the *Creating StyledComponents for inline styling* section of `Chapter 7`, *Enhancing Your Application*; the styled-component library we'll use depends totally on this feature to allow for more readable code.

Writing multiline strings

Another feature of the new template literals is that they can span several lines. With earlier versions of JS, if you wanted to produce multiple lines of text, you had to insert newline characters (`"\n"`) in the output string, like so:

```
let threeLines = "These are\nthree lines\nof text";
console.log(threeLines);
// These are
// three lines
// of text
```

With template strings, you can just write the line as desired:

```
let threeLines = `These are
three lines
of text`;
```

However, I would recommend against this practice. Even if the code may seem more legible, when it gets indented, the result looks ugly, since continuation lines *must* start at the first column—do you see why? Check out the following code—the continuation lines are pushed to the left, breaking the visual continuity of the indented code:

```
if (someCondition) {
    .
    .
    .
    if (anotherCondition) {
```

```
        .
        .
        .
        var threeLines = `These are
three lines
of text`;
    }
}
```

You can use a backslash to escape characters that are not meant to be part of templating:

```
let notEscaped1 = `this is \$\{not\} interpolation\\nright? `;
// "this is ${not} interpolation\nright? "
```

 You might want to look into String.raw (see https://developer.mozilla.org/en-US/docs/Web/JavaScript/Reference/Global_Objects/String/raw) for an alternative to this way of avoiding templating. You can just avoid templating altogether, since an informal poll has shown that practically no developers know of it and it isn't such a great advantage after all.

Repeating strings

Let's finish with several new string-related functions. Most are pretty simple to understand, so the explanations will mostly be brief. For a complete list of all available string functions, both old and new, see https://developer.mozilla.org/en-US/docs/Web/JavaScript/Reference/Global_Objects/String.

You can iterate any string using the .repeat(...) method:

```
"Hello!".repeat(3); // Hello!Hello!Hello!
```

Padding strings

You can pad a string to a given length by adding repeated strings either at the left or at the right of the original text by using .padStart(...) and .padEnd(...):

```
"Hello".padStart(12);        // "       Hello"
"Hello".padStart(12,"XYZ");  // "XYZXYZXHello"
"Hello".padStart(3);         // "Hello"; no effect here

"Hello".padEnd(12);          // "Hello       "
"Hello".padEnd(12,"XYZ");    // "HelloXYZXYZX"
"Hello".padEnd(4);           // "Hello"; no effect here either
```

Among possible uses, you may pad a number with zeroes to the left. We have to transform the number into a string because the padding methods are only available for strings:

```
let padded = String(229.6).padStart(12, "0"); // "0000000229.6"
```

 The reason for using padStart and padEnd instead of padLeft and padRight has to do with left-to-right and right-to-left languages. It was felt that start and end were not ambiguous, while left and right would be. For example, in Hebrew, the start of a string is printed at the right and its end is to the left.

Searching in strings

There are new functions to determine whether a strings starts with, ends with, or includes a given string. This can give you much relief from using indexOf(...) and length-related calculations:

```
"Hello, there!".startsWith("He"); // true
"Hello, there!".endsWith("!");    // true
"Hello, there!".includes("her");  // true
```

 Each of these methods has a position as an optional second parameter, which specifies where to do the search; see https://developer.mozilla.org/en-US/docs/Web/JavaScript/Reference/Global_Objects/String/startsWith, https://developer.mozilla.org/en-US/docs/Web/JavaScript/Reference/Global_Objects/String/endsWith, and https://developer.mozilla.org/en-US/docs/Web/JavaScript/Reference/Global_Objects/String/includes for more information.

Trimming strings

You may trim a string at both ends, or only at one, by using .trim(...), .trimStart(...), and .trimEnd(...):

```
"   Hello, there!   ".trim();      //    "Hello, there!"
"   Hello, there!   ".trimStart(); //    "Hello, there!   "
"   Hello, there!   ".trimEnd();   // "   Hello, there!"
```

 Originally, .trimStart() was .trimLeft(), and .trimEnd() was .trimRight(), but the names were changed for the same reason as .padStart() and .padEnd() were.

Iterating over strings

Strings are now iterable objects (such as arrays are), meaning that you can use `for...of` to iterate over them, character by character:

```
for (let ch of "PACKT") {
    console.log(ch);
}
```

The spread operator (read about it in depth, in the *Spreading and joining values* section of this chapter) will also work, hence transforming a string into an array of single characters:

```
let letters = [..."PACKT"];
// ["P", "A", "C", "K", "T"]
```

Enhancing your code

Now, let's go over several useful new functions of JS, which have to do with basic needs and features. This won't be exhaustive, since JS is quite big, after all! However, we will touch on the most interesting features that you will be likely to use.

How to do it...

The features in this section aren't linked by a common thread, apart from the fact that they will help you to write shorter, more concise code and help you to avoid possible common errors.

Working in strict mode

Let's start with a change that you probably won't need! JS was somewhat cavalier as to some errors and, instead of warning or crashing, it would just silently ignore them. In 2015, a new *strict* mode was included, which changed the JS engine's behavior to start reporting these errors. To enable the new mode, you had to include a single line before anything else, with a simple string:

```
"use strict";
```

Including this string would enforce strict mode for your code. What errors were caught? A brief list includes the following:

- You cannot create a global variable by accident. If you misspelled a variable's name in a function, JS would have created a new global variable and just moved on; in strict mode, an error is produced.
- You cannot use `eval()` to create variables.
- You cannot have function parameters with duplicate names, as in `function doIt(a, b, a, c)`.
- You cannot delete non-writable object properties; for example, you cannot delete `someObject.prototype`.
- You cannot write to some variables; for instance, you cannot do `undefined=22` or `NaN=9`.
- The `with` statement is forbidden.
- Some words (such as `interface` or `private`, for example) were reserved for keywords in future versions of JS.

 The previous list isn't complete and there're a few more changes and restrictions. For full details, read `https://developer.mozilla.org/en-US/docs/Web/JavaScript/Reference/Strict_mode`.

Should you use this? For your main script, `"use strict"` is optional, but for modules and classes, it's implied. So, most code will always run in strict mode, so you'd really get used to including that string. That said, if you are using `Babel`, the required string is already provided for you by the transpiler. On the other hand, Node's modules will require it, as we'll see in the next chapter.

Scoping variables

The concept of *scope* is associated with the idea of *visibility*: scope is the context in which defined elements (such as variables or functions) can be referenced or used. Clasically, JS provided only two types of scope: *global* scope (accessible everywhere) and *function* scope (accessible only within the function itself). Since scopes have been around since the beginning of JS, let's just remember a couple of rules, with not much elaboration:

- Scopes are hierarchically arranged, and *child* scopes can access everything in the *parent* scope, but not the other way round.

- Access to the *parent* scope will be disabled if you redefine something at an inner scope. References will always be to the child definition, and you cannot access the equally named element in the outer, encompassing scope.

JS5 introduced a new type of scope, called *block* scope, that lets you work in a more careful way. This allows you to create variables for a single block, without existence outside of it, even in the rest of the function or method where they were defined. With this concept, two new ways of defining variables, other than using `var`, were added: `let` and `const`.

The new declarations are not subject to *hoisting*, so if you are not used to declaring all variables at the top of your code before they are used, you may have problems. Since the usual practice is starting functions with all declarations, this isn't likely to affect you. See `https://developer.mozilla.org/en-US/docs/Glossary/Hoisting` for more details.

The first option, `let`, allows you to declare a variable that will be limited to the block or statement where it is used. The second option, `const`, adds the proviso that the variable isn't supposed to change value, but rather be constant; if you try to assign a new value to a constant, an error will be produced. The following simple examples show the new behaviors:

Using `const` for a constant value needs little explanation, but what about `let`? The reason harkens back to the origin of the `BASIC` programming language. In that language, you assigned values to variables with code like `37 LET X1 = (B1*A4 - B2*A2) / D;` this particular line was taken from Darmouth College's `BASIC` manual facsimile, dated October 1964. See `http://www.bitsavers.org/pdf/dartmouth/BASIC_Oct64.pdf` for more information.

```
// Source file: src/let_const.js

{
    let w = 0;
}
console.log(w); // error: w is not defined!

let x = 1;
{
    let x = 99;
}
console.log(x); // still 1;

let y = 2;
for (let y = 999; 1 > 2; y++) {
```

```
    /* nothing! */
}
console.log(y); // still 2;

const z = 3;
z = 9999; // error!
```

Using `let` also solves a classic problem. What would the following code do? Here it is:

```
// Source file: src/let_const.js

// Countdown to zero?
var delay = 0;
for (var i = 10; i >= 0; i--) {
    delay += 1000;
    setTimeout(() => {
        console.log(i + (i > 0 ? "..." : "!"));
    }, delay);
}
```

If you were expecting a countdown to zero (10... 9... 8... down to 2... 1... 0!) with suitable one second delays, you'll be surprised, because this code emits −1! eleven times! The problem has to do with closures; by the time the loop ends, the `i` variable is −1, so when the waiting (timeout) functions run, `i` has *that* value. This can be solved in several ways, but using `let` instead of `var` is the simplest solution; each closure will capture a different copy of the loop variable, and the countdown will be correct:

```
// Source file: src/let_const.js

var delay = 0;
for (let i = 10; i >= 0; i--) { // minimal fix!
    delay += 1000;
    setTimeout(() => {
        console.log(i + (i > 0 ? "..." : "!"));
    }, delay);
}
```

For more on blocks and `let`/`const`, check out https://developer.mozilla.org/en-US/docs/Web/JavaScript/Reference/Statements/block, https://developer.mozilla.org/en-US/docs/Web/JavaScript/Reference/Statements/const and https://developer.mozilla.org/en-US/docs/Web/JavaScript/Reference/Statements/let at MDN.

Spreading and joining values

A new operator, . . ., lets you expand an array, string, or object, into independent values. This is harder to explain than to show, so let's see some basic examples:

```
// Source file: src/spread_and_rest.js

let values = [22, 9, 60, 12, 4, 56];

const maxOfValues = Math.max(...values); // 60
const minOfValues = Math.min(...values); // 4
```

You can also use it to copy arrays or concatenate them:

```
// Source file: src/spread_and_rest.js

let arr1 = [1, 1, 2, 3];
let arr2 = [13, 21, 34];

let copyOfArr1 = [...arr1]; // a copy of arr1 is created

let fibArray = [0, ...arr1, 5, 8, ...arr2]; // first 10 Fibonacci numbers
```

 If you apply the spread operator to a string, the effect is to separate it into individual characters, much as if you had used .split(); for instance, console.log(..."JS") shows ["J", "S"], so this case isn't particularly interesting.

You can also use it to clone or modify objects; in fact, this is a usage we're going to meet again later, in Chapter 8, *Expanding Your Application*, mostly when we use Redux:

```
// Source file: src/spread_and_rest.js

let person = { name: "Juan", age: 24 };

let copyOfPerson = { ...person }; // same data as in the person object

let expandedPerson = { ...person, sister: "María" };
// {name: "Juan", age: 24, sister: "María"}
```

This is also useful for writing functions with an undefined number of arguments, avoiding the old style usage of the `arguments` pseudo-array. Here, instead of splitting an element into many, it joins several distinct elements into a single array. Note, however, that this usage only applies to the last arguments of a function; something such as `function many(a, ...several, b, c)` wouldn't be allowed:

```
// Source file: src/spread_and_rest.js

function average(...nums: Array&lt;number>): number {
    let sum = 0;
    for (let i = 0; i &lt; nums.length; i++) {
        sum += nums[i];
    }
    return sum / nums.length;
};

console.log(average(22, 9, 60, 12, 4, 56)); // 27.166667
```

 If you are wondering why I called `arguments` a pseudo-array, the reason is because it *looks* somewhat like an array, but only provides the `.length` property; see more at `https://developer.mozilla.org/en-US/docs/Web/JavaScript/Reference/Functions/arguments`. In any case, you won't be dealing with it, thanks to the spread operator.

Destructuring arrays and objects

Another powerful construct provided by JS nowadays is the destructuring assignment. This is also harder to explain than to show, so once again let's directly get to some examples! The simplest case lets you split an array into variables:

```
let [a, b, c] = [22, 9, 60]; // a=22, b=9, c=60
```

More interesting still is that you can swap or twiddle variables around! Following on from the preceding example, we'd have the following:

```
[a, b] = [b, a];        // a and b are swapped! a=9, b=22
[c, b, a] = [b, a, c]; // and now a=60, b=9, c=22
```

You can also assign default values to missing variables, ignore values you don't care for, and even apply the `rest` operator:

```
// default values
let [d, e = 1, f = 2, g] = [12, 4]; // d=12, e=4, f=2, g=undefined

// ignoring values
```

```
let [h, , i] = [13, 21, 34];        // h=13, i=34

// using with rest
let [j, k, ...l] = [2, 3, 5, 8];    // j=2, k=3, l=[5,8]
```

This can also be applied to objects, letting you pick attributes and even renaming them, as with the flag and name in the following code. Assigning values by default is also possible:

```
let obj = { p: 1, q: true, r: "FK" };

let { p, r } = obj;            // p=1, r="FK"
let { q: flag, r: name } = obj; // Renaming: flag=true, name="FK"
let { q, t = "India" } = obj;   // q=true; t="India"
```

One interesting usage of this is allowing a function to return many values at once. If you want to return, say, two values, you can either return an array or an object and use destructuring to separate the returned values in a single sentence:

```
function minAndMax1(...nums) {
    return [Math.min(...nums), Math.max(...nums)];
}

let [small1, big1] = minAndMax1(22, 9, 60, 12, 4, 56);
```

Alternatively, you can use an object and an arrow function just for variety; note the extra parentheses we used, since we are returning an object. We are also renaming attributes, by the way:

```
const minAndMax2 = (...nums) => ({
    min: Math.min(...nums),
    max: Math.max(...nums)
});

let { min: small2, max: big2 } = minAndMax2(22, 9, 60, 12, 4, 56);
```

You can find many examples of spreading and destructuring in MDN if you visit the following links:

https://developer.mozilla.org/en-US/docs/Web/JavaScript/Referenc e/Operators/Spread_syntax

https://developer.mozilla.org/en-US/docs/Web/JavaScript/Referenc e/Functions/rest_parameters

https://developer.mozilla.org/en-US/docs/Web/JavaScript/ Reference/Operators/Destructuring_assignment

Doing powers

Finally, let's introduce a newly added operator, `**`, which stands for power calculations:

```
let a = 2 ** 3; // 8
```

This is just a shortcut for the existing `Math.pow()` function:

```
let b = Math.pow(2, 3); // also 8
```

An exponential assignment operator also exists, which is similar to `+=`, `-=`, and the rest:

```
let c = 4;
c **= 3; // 4 cubed: 64
```

This is an operator that you won't probably using very often, unless you deal with interest calculations and financial formulas. A final reminder: just as in math, the exponentiation operator groups from right to left, so `2 ** 3 ** 4` is calculated as `2 ** (3 ** 4)`; be careful!

Defining functions

JS isn't a functional programming language by definition, but it includes practically everything that a full-fledged functional language would provide. In our case, we won't be delving too deeply into this programming paradigm, but let's see some important features that will simplify your work.

How to do it...

JS has always included functions, which can be defined in many ways, but now there is yet one more function definition style that will provide several advantages; read on.

Writing arrow functions

After reading the preceding paragraph, did you try to count how many ways there are to define a function in JS? There are actually far more than you probably think, including at least the following:

- *A named function declaration*: `function one(...) {...}`
- *An anonymous function expression*: `var two = function(...) {...}`

- *A named function expression*: `var three = function someName(...) {...}`
- *An immediately-invoked expression*: `var four = (function() { ...; return function(...) {...}; })()`
- *A function constructor*: `var five = new Function(...)`
- *The new style, an arrow function*: `var six = (...) => {...}`

You are probably quite used to the first trio, while the two that follow may be not so common. However, what we now care about is the last style, called an *arrow function*. Arrow functions work pretty much in the same fashion as functions defined in the other ways, but there are three key differences:

- Arrow functions do not have an `arguments` object
- Arrow functions may implicitly return a value, even if no `return` statement is provided
- Arrow functions do not bind the value of `this`

In fact, there are some more differences, including the fact that you cannot use arrow functions as constructors, they don't have a prototype property, and they cannot be used as generators. For more on this, see `https://developer.mozilla.org/en-US/docs/Web/JavaScript/Reference/Functions/Arrow_functions`.

The first difference is handled simply by using the spread operator, as we saw earlier in this chapter. So, let's focus on the last two items, which are more interesting, instead.

Returning values

An arrow function may have a block of code with some return statements in it or it may just be an expression. The former case is most similar to the standard way of defining a function; for example, we could write a function to add three numbers as follows, using both styles. We should add data types to the definitions, but we'll get to that soon:

```
function addThree1 (x, y, z) {
    const s = x + y + z;
    return s;
}

const addThree2 = (x, y, z) => {
    const s = x + y + z;
    return s;
};
```

If you can do this just by returning an expression, you can then write an equivalent version; just write whatever you want to return immediately after the arrow:

```
const addThree3 = (x, y, z) => x + y + z;
```

There's a special case: if you are returning an object, then you must place it within parentheses because otherwise JS will confuse it with a block of code. For Redux (which we'll be seeing in the *Managing State with Redux* section of Chapter 8, *Expanding Your Application*), you might want to write an *action creator* that returns an *action*, namely an object with a `type` attribute and possibly some more:

```
const simpleAction = (t, d) => {
    type: t;
    data: d;
};

console.log(simpleAction("ADD_KEY", 229)); // undefined
```

What's happening here? JS is interpreting the braces as a block, and then `type` and `data` are considered to be *labels* (see https://developer.mozilla.org/en-US/docs/Web/JavaScript/Reference/Statements/label if you don't remember these!), so the whole *object* is really a block that just doesn't return anything, and JS returns an `undefined` result. Just placing the object in parentheses will work as expected:

```
const simpleAction = (t, d) => ({
    type: t;
    data: d;
});

// this works as expected
```

Handling this in arrow functions

A well-known JS problem is how to handle `this`, because its value isn't always what you expect! Modern JS solves this with arrow functions that, unlike common functions, inherit the proper `this` value. A well-known example is as follows: you would expect the following code to display JAVASCRIPT after a few seconds, but rather `undefined` will be shown (don't mind the fact that you could have coded `show()` in a simpler way; I wanted to highlight a general problem and not a particular solution):

```
// Source file: src/arrow_functions.js

function Show(value: mixed): void {
    this.saved = value;
```

```
        setTimeout(function() {
            console.log(this.saved);
        }, 1000);
    }

    let w = new Show("Doesn't work..."); // instead, "undefined" is shown
```

There are three ways of solving this:

- Using `.bind()` to properly bind the timeout function to the correct value of `this`
- Using a closure and defining a local variable (usually called `that`) to store and save the original value of `this`
- Using arrow functions, which will work without any extra work

We can see these three solutions in the following code:

```
// Source file: src/arrow_functions.js

function Show1(value: mixed): void {
    this.saved = value;
    setTimeout(
        function() {
            console.log(this.saved);
        }.bind(this),
        1000
    );
}

function Show2(value: mixed): void {
    this.saved = value;
    const that = this;
    setTimeout(function() {
        console.log(that.saved);
    }, 2000);
}

function Show3(value: mixed): void {
    this.saved = value;
    setTimeout(() => {
        console.log(this.saved);
    }, 3000);
}

let x = new Show1("This");
let y = new Show2("always");
let z = new Show3("works");
```

> We will get to see the `.bind()` idea in React in the *Defining Components* section of `Chapter 6`, *Developing with React,* where we will deal with `this` related problems.

Defining types for arrow functions

Finally, let's see how types would be defined for arrow functions. We can have a couple more implementations of the `toString()` function we saw earlier in the *Basic types in Flow* section:

```
// Source file: src/types_basic.js

const toString2 = (x: number): string => {
    return x + "";
};

type numberToString = number => string;
const toString3: numberToString = (x: number) => String(x);
```

Defining default argument values

An interesting new feature for functions is the possibility of defining default values for missing arguments. We could write a function to calculate n^{th} roots that, by default, would calculate square roots:

```
// Source file: src/default_arguments.js

function root(a: number, n: number = 2): number {
 return a ** (1 / n);
}

// Or, equivalently:
// const root = (a: number, n: number = 2): number => a ** (1 / n);

console.log(root(125, 3));      // 5
console.log(root(4));           // 2
console.log(root(9, undefined)); // 3
```

As seen in the third example, passing `undefined` is equivalent to omitting the value. This means that you can provide default values for any parameter: a call such as `someFunction(undefined, 22, undefined)` would use default values for the first and third arguments, and 22 as the second one.

Default values can also be used for methods and constructors. In the following `Counter` class, the `inc()` method, if not provided with a number, will increment the counter by 1. Also, when constructing the counter, if you don't provide an initial value, zero will be used:

```
// Source file: src/default_arguments.js

class Counter {
    count: number; // required by Flow

    constructor(i: number = 0) {
        this.count = 0;
    }

    inc(n: number = 1) {
        this.count += n;
    }
}

const cnt = new Counter();
cnt.inc(3);
cnt.inc();
cnt.inc();

console.log(cnt.count); // 5
```

As a last detail, you can use values from previous arguments to calculate the default values of later ones. A simple nonsense example shows this; I'll skip type declarations since they are not relevant here:

```
// Source file: src/default_arguments.js

function nonsense(a = 2, b = a + 1, c = a * b, d = 9) {
    console.log(a, b, c, d);
}

nonsense(1, 2, 3, 4);                   // 1 2 3 4
nonsense();                             // 2 3 6 9
nonsense(undefined, 4, undefined, 6);  // 2 4 8 6
```

Using default values is a very practical way to simplify the usage of functions, particularly in the case of complex APIs with many parameters, but allowing sensible values for whatever the user omits.

Programming functionally

Functional programming is often more declarative than imperative, with higher level functions that can do complete processing in a simpler, straightforward way. Here, let's look at several functional programming techniques that you should really adopt for your own code.

How to do it...

Functional programming has always been present in JS, but recent versions of the language have added well-known features of other languages that you can use to shorten your code, also making it simpler to understand.

Reducing arrays to values

A simple question: how many times have you looped through an array to, say, add its numbers? The odds are, many times! This kind of operation —going through an array element by element performing some calculation to arrive at a final result—is the first one we will be implementing in a functional way, with .reduce().

 The name .reduce() pretty much tells us what it does: it *reduces* a complete array to a single value. In other languages, this operation is called *fold*.

The most usual example, which most texts and articles show, is summing all of the elements of an array, and, since I'm traditionally minded, let's do just that! You must provide an initial value for your calculation (in this case, since we want a sum, it would be a zero) and a function that will update the calculated value when accessing each array element:

```
// Source file: src/map_filter_reduce.js

const someArray: Array&lt;number> = [22, 9, 60, 12, 4, 56];

const totalSum = someArray.reduce(
    (acc: number, val: number) => acc + val,
    0
); // 163
```

How does it work? Internally, `.reduce()` starts by taking your initial value (zero, in this case) and then it calls the reducing function, giving it the accumulated total (`acc`) and the first element of the array (`val`). The function must update the accumulated total: in this case, it would calculate *0 + 22*, so the next total would be *22*. After, `.reduce()` would call the function again, passing it 22 (the updated total) and 9 (the second array element), and 31 would become the new accumulated total. This will proceed systematically through the complete array, until the final value (163) is computed. Note that all aspects of loop control are automatic, so there is no way you can err somewhere, and the code is quite declarative: you could almost read it as "reduce `someArray` to a value by summing all elements, starting with zero".

 There are some more possibilities for `.reduce()`: check out `https://developer.mozilla.org/en-US/docs/Web/JavaScript/Reference/Global_Objects/Array/reduce` for more information. You can also use `.reduceRight()`, which essentially works in the same fashion, but starting at the end of the array and proceeding backwards; see `https://developer.mozilla.org/en-US/docs/Web/JavaScript/Reference/Global_Objects/Array/ReduceRight` for more information.

Of course, you are not limited to processing arrays of numbers; you can deal with any data type, and the final result can also be any type. For example, you could use `.reduce()` to turn an array of names into an HTML bulleted list, as follows:

```
// Source file: src/map_filter_reduce.js

const names = ["Juan", "María", "Sylvia", "Federico"];

const bulletedList =
    "&lt;ul>" +
    names.reduce((acc, val) => `${acc}&lt;li>${val}&lt;/li>`, "") +
    "&lt;/ul>";

//
&lt;ul>&lt;li>Juan&lt;/li>&lt;li>María&lt;/li>&lt;li>Sylvia&lt;/li>&lt;li>Fe
derico&lt;/li>&lt;/ul>
```

With a little practice, it's safe to say that you'll probably be able to transform any kind of calculation over an array into a `.reduce()` call with shorter, clearer code.

Mapping arrays

A second type of very common operation is to go through an array and produce a new array by doing some kind of process to each element. Fortunately, we also have a way to do that functionally by using `.map()`. The way this function works is simple: given an array and a function, it applies the function to each element of the array and produces a new array with the results of each call.

Suppose we called a web service and got back an array with people data. We just wanted their ages so that we are able to do some other process; say, calculate the average age of the people who used the service. We can manage this simply:

```
// Source file: src/map_filter_reduce.js

type person = { name: string, sex: string, age: number };

const family: Array&lt;person> = [
    { name: "Huey", sex: "M", age: 7 },
    { name: "Dewey", sex: "M", age: 8 },
    { name: "Louie", sex: "M", age: 9 },
    { name: "Daisy", sex: "F", age: 25 },
    { name: "Donald", sex: "M", age: 30 },
    { name: "Della", sex: "F", age: 30 }
];

const ages = family.map(x => x.age);
// [7, 8, 9, 25, 30, 30]
```

Using `.map()` is, like `.reduce()`, a much shorter and safer way to process an array. In fact, most times, the two operations are used one after the other, with some possible `.filter()` operations mixed in to select what should or should not be processed; let's get into that now.

> The `.map()` operation also has some extra features; see `https://developer.mozilla.org/en-US/docs/Web/JavaScript/Reference/Global_Objects/Array/map` for a complete description. Also, if you really want to affect the original array, rather than producing a new one, take a look at the `.forEach()` method at `https://developer.mozilla.org/en-US/docs/Web/JavaScript/Reference/Global_Objects/Array/forEach`.

Filtering arrays

The third operation we are considering is `.filter()`, which will scan a complete array and generate a new one, but only with the elements that satisfy some condition, as given by you via a function. Following our example, we could pick only the males in the service result by writing the following:

```
// Source file: src/map_filter_reduce.js

const males = family.filter(x => x.sex === "M");
// an array with Huey, Dewey, Louie, and Donald records
```

Having these three operations makes it simple to do sequences of calls and generate results with little code. For example, could we find out the age of the eldest of the males in the family? Yes, quickly—with just a few lines of code:

```
// Source file: src/map_filter_reduce.js

const eldestMaleAge = family
    .filter(x => x.sex === "M")
    .map(x => x.age)
    .reduce((acc, val) => Math.max(acc, val), 0); // 30
```

This style of chained operations is quite common: in this case, we first select the males, then we pick their ages, and then we reduce the array to a single value, the maximum: neat!

Producing functions from functions

Let's finish this section on functional aspects by looking at a quintessential functional programming tool: **Higher Order Functions (HOFs)**: functions that produce functions as results! In later chapters, we'll actually meet more usages of HOFs; here, let's work out a simple example.

 The following example is taken from my previous book for Packt, *Mastering JavaScript Functional Programming*. Chapter 2, *Thinking Functionally - A First Example*, and Chapter 6, *Producing Functions - Higher-Order Functions* will be of particular interest with regard to HOFs. See more
at `www.packtpub.com/web-development/mastering-javascript-function al-programming`.

Suppose you have developed an e-commerce site. The user selects products, adds them to his/her shopping cart, and at the end clicks on a **BILL ME** button so that his/her credit card will be charged. However, if the user were to click twice or more, he/she would be billed several times rather than once. Your application might have something along these lines in its HTML:

```
&lt;button id="billBtn" onclick="billUser(sales, data)">Bill me&lt;/button>
```

Somewhere among your scripts, there would be some code like the following. I'm not including data type declarations because they are not relevant to our code; we don't really know or care what the arguments to billUser() would be:

```
function billUser(sales, data) {
    window.alert("Billing the user...");
    // actually bill the user
}
```

Now, what could you do in order to avoid repeated clicks on the button? There are several not-quite-so-good solutions, such as the following:

- Do nothing, just warn the user, and hope they pay attention!
- Use a global flag to signal the fact that the user clicked once.
- Remove the onclick handler from the button after the user clicks.
- Change the onclick handler to something else that won't bill the user.

However, all of these solutions are somewhat lacking, depend on global objects, need you to mess with the billing function, are tightly linked with the user view, and so on. Since requiring that some functions are executed only once isn't such an outlandish requirement, let's specify the following:

- The original function should be unchanged and do its thing—nothing more
- We want a new function that will call the original one, but only once
- We want a general solution so that we can apply it in different situations

We will write a function, once(), that will take a function as its argument and produce a new function, but that will *do its thing* only once. The logic is not long, but study it carefully:

```
// Source file: src/functional_code.js

const once = fn => {
    let done = false;
    return (...args) => {
        if (!done) {
            done = true;
```

```
            fn(...args);
        }
    };
};
```

Some analysis of our new function is as follows:

- The definition shows that `once()` takes a generic function (`fn()`) as an argument
- The `return` statement shows that `once()` returns another function
- We are using the spread operator to deal with functions with any number of arguments
- We are using a closure for the `done` variable, which remembers whether `fn()` was invoked or not

 I left out type definitions for clarity, but in the source code provided with this book, full definitions are provided. Can you work them out on your own? A tip: the output of the `once()` function should be the same type as the input to it.

With this new function, you could have coded the button as follows. When the user clicks on the button, the function that will get called with `(sales, data)` as arguments isn't `billUser()`, but rather the result of having applied `once()` to `billUser()` —and that would have resulted in a new function that would have called `billUser()` only once:

```
&lt;button id="billButton" onclick="once(billUser)(sales, data)">
Bill me
&lt;/button>;
```

This is the concept of a higher order function: a function that receives functions as arguments and produces a new function as a result. Usually, there are three kinds of possible transformations that we could desire:

- *Wrapping functions*: We do this so that they keep their original functionality, but add some new feature; for example, we could add logging or timing so that the original function still does its thing, but log its parameters or produce timing information
- *Altering functions*: We do this so that they will differ in some key point with the original version; this is what we did with `once()`, which produces a new version of a function that runs only a single time
- *Other changes*: These changes include turning a function into a promise (we'll see this when we get to `Node`, in the *Using Promises instead of error first callbacks* section of `Chapter 3`, *Developing with Node*) and more

Doing async calls compactly

When Ajax started appearing, it was commonly used with callbacks, which themselves could have callbacks of their own, with more callbacks within, which eventually led to coining the term *callback hell*. As a way out of that impractical programming style, two other styles of working with services and asynchronous calls appeared: promises and `async`/`await`—though in truth, the latter also use promises!

Getting started

Let's see both styles by using a simple example. This book was written in three different cities: Pune, India; London, England; and Montevideo, Uruguay, so let's do some work related to those cities. We will write code that will get weather information for those cities:

- For Montevideo alone
- For London and then for Pune, in series, so that the second call won't start until the first is done
- For the three cities in parallel, so that all three requests will be processed at the same time, gaining time by the overlap

We will not get into details such as using this or that API, getting a private key, and so on, and we'll just fake it by accessing the free *The Weather Channel* page. We will use the following definitions for all our coding, which we'll do in `Node`, using the `axios` module; don't worry about the details now:

```
// Source file: src/get_service_with_promises.js

const axios = require("axios");

const BASE_URL = "https://weather.com/en-IN/weather/today/l/";

// latitude and longitude data for our three cities
const MONTEVIDEO_UY = "-34.90,-56.16";
const LONDON_EN = "51.51,-0.13";
const PUNE_IN = "18.52,73.86";

const getWeather = coords => axios.get(`${BASE_URL}${coords}`);
```

The `BASE_URL` constant provides the basic web address, to which you must attach the coordinates (latitude, longitude) of the desired city. On its own, we would get a page like the one shown in the following screenshot:

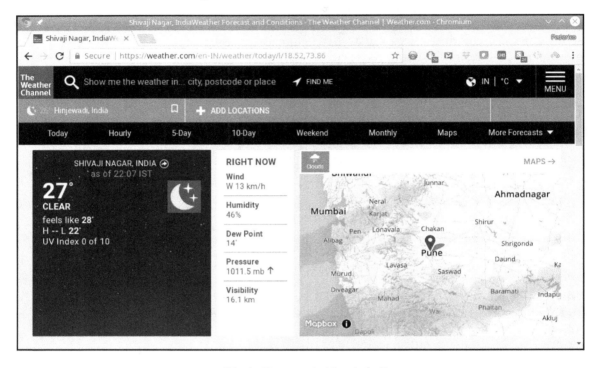

we will be using Ajax to get weather information for cities

In real life, we would not be getting a web page but rather an API, and then process the returned results. In our case, since we don't actually care for the data, but for the methods we'll use to do the calls, we'll be content with just showing some banal information, such as how many bytes were sent back. Totally useless, I agree, but this is enough for our example!

We'll be using `axios` in several places in this book, so you may want to read its documentation, which can be found at `https://github.com/axios/axios`.

How to do it...

Using functions as callbacks is the most classic way of dealing with async calls, but this has several disadvantages, such as code that is harder to read and series difficulties in dealing with some not-too-uncommon cases. Here, we'll look at two alternative ways of working.

Doing Ajax calls with promises

The first way we can do web service calls is by using promises, and they were (up to the appearance of the more modern `async`/`await` statements, which we'll be seeing in the next section) the favorite method. Promises were available some time back (first around 2011 through jQuery's deferred objects, and afterwards by means of libraries such as `BlueBird` or `Q`), but in recent JS versions, they became native. Since promises cannot really be considered something new, let's just see some examples so that we can move on to more modern ways of working—no, we won't be even considering going further back than promises, and directly work with callbacks!

Do native promises imply that libraries won't be needed again? That's a tricky question! JS promises are quite basic, and most libraries add several methods that can simplify your coding. (See `http://bluebirdjs.com/docs/api-reference.html` or `https://github.com/kriskowal/q/wiki/API-Reference` for such features from `Bluebird` or `Q`.) Hence, while you may do perfectly well with native promises, in some circumstances, you may want to keep using a library.

Getting the weather data for Montevideo is simple if we use the `getWeather()` function that we defined previously:

```
// Source file: src/get_service_with_promises.js

function getMontevideo() {
    getWeather(MONTEVIDEO_UY)
        .then(result => {
            console.log("Montevideo, with promises");
            console.log(`Montevideo: ${result.data.length} bytes`);
        })
        .catch(error => console.log(error.message));
}
```

The `getWeather()` function actually returns a promise; its `.then()` method corresponds to the success case and `.catch()` corresponds to any error situations.

Getting data for two cities in a row is also simple. We don't want to start the second request until the first one has been successful, and that leads to the following scheme:

```javascript
// Source file: src/get_service_with_promises.js

function getLondonAndPuneInSeries() {
    getWeather(LONDON_EN)
        .then(londonData => {
            getWeather(PUNE_IN)
                .then(puneData => {
                    console.log("London and Pune, in series");
                    console.log(`London: ${londonData.data.length} b`);
                    console.log(`Pune: ${puneData.data.length} b`);
                })
                .catch(error => {
                    console.log("Error getting Pune...", error.message);
                });
        })
        .catch(error => {
            console.log("Error getting London...", error.message);
        });
}
```

 This is not the only way to program such a series of calls, but since we won't actually be directly working with promises, let's just skip the alternatives.

Finally, in order to do calls in parallel and optimize time, the `Promise.all()` method will be used to build up a new promise out of the three individual ones for each city. If all calls succeed, the bigger promise will also do; should any of the three calls fail, then failure will also be the global result:

 For more information on `Promise.all()`, check out `https://developer.mozilla.org/en-US/docs/Web/JavaScript/Reference/Global_Objects/Promise/all`. If you'd rather build a promise that succeeds when *any* (instead of *all*) of the involved promises succeeds, you should use `Promise.race()`; see `https://developer.mozilla.org/en-US/docs/Web/JavaScript/Reference/Global_Objects/Promise/race`.

```
// Source file: src/get_service_with_promises.js

function getCitiesInParallel() {
    const montevideoGet = getWeather(MONTEVIDEO_UY);
    const londonGet = getWeather(LONDON_EN);
    const puneGet = getWeather(PUNE_IN);

    Promise.all([montevideoGet, londonGet, puneGet])
        .then(([montevideoData, londonData, puneData]) => {
            console.log("All three cities in parallel, with promises");
            console.log(`Montevideo: ${montevideoData.data.length} b`);
            console.log(`London: ${londonData.data.length} b`);
            console.log(`Pune: ${puneData.data.length} b`);
        })
        .catch(error => {
            console.log(error.message);
        });
}
```

Note how we use a destructuring assignment to get the data for each city. The result of calling these functions may be as follows; I added some spacing for clarity:

```
Montevideo, with promises
Montevideo: 353277 bytes

London and Pune, in series
London: 356537 b
Pune: 351679 b

All three cities in parallel, with promises
Montevideo: 351294 b
London: 356516 b
Pune: 351679 b
```

Organizing web calls with promises is a straightforward method, but the usage of possibly nested .then() methods can become hard to understand, so we really should give a look to an alternative. We'll do just that in the next section.

Doing Ajax calls with async/await

The second way, `async/await`, is more modern but, deep inside, actually also works with promises, but simplifyies the job. There are some important definitions that we should take into account:

- An `async` function will contain some `await` expressions, depending on promises
- `await` expressions pause the execution of the `async` function until the promise's resolution
- After the promise's resolution, processing is resumed, with the returned value
- If an error is produced, it can be caught with `try ... catch`
- `await` can only be used in async functions

How does this affect our coding? Let's review our three examples. Getting information for a single city is simple:

```
// Source file: src/get_service_with_async_await.js

async function getMontevideo() {
    try {
        const montevideoData = await getWeather(MONTEVIDEO_UY);
        console.log("Montevideo, with async/await");
        console.log(`Montevideo: ${montevideoData.data.length} bytes`);
    } catch (error) {
        console.log(error.message);
    }
}
```

We are still using a promise (the one returned by `axios` via the `getWeather()` call), but now the code looks more familiar: you wait for results to come, and then you process them—it almost looks as if the call were a synchronous one!

Getting data for London and then Pune in sequence is also quite direct: you wait for the first city's data, then you wait for the second's, and then you do your final process; what could be simpler? Let's see the code:

```
// Source file: src/get_service_with_async_await.js

async function getLondonAndPuneInSeries() {
    try {
        const londonData = await getWeather(LONDON_EN);
        const puneData = await getWeather(PUNE_IN);
        console.log("London and Pune, in series");
        console.log(`London: ${londonData.data.length} b`);
        console.log(`Pune: ${puneData.data.length} b`);
```

```
        } catch (error) {
            console.log(error.message);
        }
    }
```

Finally, getting all data in parallel also depends on the `Promise.all()` method we saw in the previous section:

```
// Source file: src/get_service_with_async_await.js

async function getCitiesInParallel() {
    try {
        const montevideoGet = getWeather(MONTEVIDEO_UY);
        const londonGet = getWeather(LONDON_EN);
        const puneGet = getWeather(PUNE_IN);

        const [montevideoData, londonData, puneData] = await Promise.all([
            montevideoGet,
            londonGet,
            puneGet
        ]);

        console.log("All three cities in parallel, with async/await");
        console.log(`Montevideo: ${montevideoData.data.length} b`);
        console.log(`London: ${londonData.data.length} b`);
        console.log(`Pune: ${puneData.data.length} b`);
    } catch (error) {
        console.log(error.message);
    }
}
```

The parallel call code is really quite similar to the pure promises' version: the only difference here is that you `await` results, instead of using `.then()`.

We have seen two ways of dealing with asynchronous service calls. Both are very much in use, but in this text, we'll tend to favor `async/await`, given that the resulting code seems clearer, with less extra baggage.

Working with objects and classes

If you want to start a lively discussion, ask a group of web developers: is *JavaScript an object oriented language, or merely an object based one?*, and retreat quickly! This discussion, while possibly arcane, has gone on year after year, and will probably continue for a while. A usual argument for the *object-based* opinion has to do with the fact that JS didn't include classes and inheritance and was prototype oriented. This argument has been voided now because the latest versions of JS provide two new keywords, `class` and `extends`, which behave in pretty much the same way as their counterparts in other *official* OO languages. However, keep in mind that the new classes are just *syntactical sugar* over the existing prototype-based inheritance; no new paradigm or model was truly introduced.

 JS could do inheritance, but it was harder. To see how this was achieved in the old fashioned way, look at `https://developer.mozilla.org/en-US/docs/Learn/JavaScript/Objects/Inheritance`, and you'll have to agree that using `class` and `extends` is much better than assigning prototypes and constructors by hand!

How to do it...

If you have worked with other common programming languages, such as Java, C++, and Python, the concepts of classes and objects should already be clear to you; we'll assume that's the case and look at how these concepts apply in modern JS.

Defining classes

Let's start with the basics and look at how classes are defined in modern JS. Afterwards, we'll move to other features that are interesting, but that you might not use that often. To define a class, we simply write something like the following:

```
// Source file: src/class_persons.js

class Person {
    constructor(first, last) {
        this.first = first;
        this.last = last;
    }

    initials() {
        return `${this.first[0]}${this.last[0]}`;
    }
```

```
    fullName() {
        return `${this.first} ${this.last}`;
    }
}

let pp = new Person("Erika", "Mustermann");
console.log(pp); // Person {first: "Erika", last: "Mustermann"}
console.log(pp.initials()); // "EM"
console.log(pp.fullName()); // "Erika Mustermann"
```

The new syntax is much clearer than using functions for constructors, as in older versions of JS. We wrote a .constructor() method, which will initialize new objects, and we defined two methods, .initials() and .fullName(), which will be available for all instances of the Person class.

 We are following the usual convention of using an initial uppercase letter for class names and initial lowercase letters for variables, functions, methods, and so on.

Extending classes

We can also extend a previously existing class. To refer to the original constructor, use super(), and to refer to the parent's method, use super.method(); see the redefinition of .fullName() here:

```
// Source file: src/class_persons.js

class Developer extends Person {
    constructor(first, last, language) {
        super(first, last);
        this.language = language;
    }

    fullName() {
        // redefines the original method
        return `${super.fullName()}, ${this.language} dev`;
    }
}

let dd = new Developer("John", "Doe", "JS");
console.log(dd); // Developer {first: "John", last: "Doe", language: "JS"}
console.log(dd.initials()); // "JD"
console.log(dd.fullName()); // "John Doe, JS dev"
```

You are not limited to extending your own classes; you can also extend the JS ones, too:

```
// Source file: src/class_persons.js

class ExtDate extends Date {
    fullDate() {
        const months = [
            "JAN",
            "FEB",
            "MAR",
            "APR",
            "MAY",
            "JUN",
            "JUL",
            "AUG",
            "SEP",
            "OCT",
            "NOV",
            "DEC"
        ];

        return (
            months[this.getMonth()] +
            " " +
            String(this.getDate()).padStart(2, "0") +
            " " +
            this.getFullYear()
        );
    }
}

console.log(new ExtDate().fullDate()); // "MAY 01 2018"
```

If you don't need a special constructor, you can omit it; the parent's constructor will be called by default.

Implementing interfaces

JS doesn't allow multiple inheritance, and it doesn't provide for implementing interfaces either. However, you can build your own ersatz interfaces by using *mixins*, using a higher order function (as we saw earlier, in the *Producing functions from functions* section), but with a class as a parameter, and adding methods (but not properties) to it. Even if you don't get to actually use it, let's look at a short example, because it gives another example of working in a functional way.

Read https://developer.mozilla.org/en-US/docs/Glossary/Mixin for a definition. As an alternative, you can use TypeScript; see https://www. typescriptlang.org/docs/handbook/interfaces.html for the latter.

Let's take our `Person` class from earlier, once again. Let's imagine a couple of interfaces: one could provide an object with a method that produced the JSON version of itself, and another could tell you how many properties an object has. (OK, none of these examples are too useful, but bear with me; the method we'll use is what matters.) We will define two functions that receive a class as an argument and return an extended version of it as a result:

```js
// Source file: src/class_persons.js

const toJsonMixin = base =>
    class extends base {
        toJson() {
            return JSON.stringify(this);
        }
    };

const countKeysMixin = base =>
    class extends base {
        countKeys() {
            return Object.keys(this).length;
        }
    };
```

Now, we can create a new `PersonWithMixins` class (not a very good name, is it?) by using these two mixins, and we can even provide a different implementation, as with the `.toJson()` method. A very important detail is that the class to extend is actually the result of a function call; check it out:

```js
// Source file: src/class_persons.js

class PersonWithTwoMixins extends toJsonMixin(countKeysMixin(Person)) {
    toJson() {
        // redefine the method, just for the sake of it
        return "NEW TOJSON " + super.toJson();
    }
}

let p2m = new PersonWithTwoMixins("Jane", "Roe");
console.log(p2m);
console.log(p2m.toJson());    // NEW TOJSON {"first":"Jane","last":"Roe"}
console.log(p2m.countKeys()); // 2
```

Being able to add methods to an object in this way can be a workaround for the problem of being able to implement interfaces. This is important to show how JS can let you work in an advanced style, seemingly beyond what the language itself provides, so that you won't be feeling that the language hinders you when trying to solve a problem.

> Using `Flow`, we will get to use the usual Java-style implements and interface declarations, but they will only be used for type checking; see the *Implementing interfaces* section for more details.

Static methods

Often, you have some utility functions that are related to a class, but not to specific object instances. In this case, you can define such functions as static methods, and they will be available in an easy way. For instance, we could create a `.getMonthName()` method, which will return the name of a given month:

```
// Source file: src/class_persons.js

class ExtDate extends Date {
    static getMonthName(m) {
        const months = [
            "JAN",
            "FEB",
            .
            .
            .
            "DEC"
        ];
        return months[m];
    }
    fullDate2() {
        return (
            ExtDate.getMonthName(this.getMonth()) +
            " " +
            String(this.getDate()).padStart(2, "0") +
            " " +
            this.getFullYear()
        );
    }
}

console.log(new ExtDate().fullDate2()); // "MAY 01 2018"
console.log(ExtDate.getMonthName(8));   // "SEP"
```

Static methods must be accessed by giving the class name; since they do not correspond to objects, they cannot be used with this or an object itself.

Using getters and setters

JS now lets you define *dynamic* properties that, instead of being a stored value in the object, are calculated on the spot. For example, with the previous `Person` class, we could have a *getter* for `lastFirst`, as follows:

```
// Source file: src/class_persons.js

class Person {
    constructor(first, last) {
        this.first = first;
        this.last = last;
    }

    // initials() method snipped out...

    fullName() {
        return `${this.first} ${this.last}`;
    }

    get lastFirst() {
        return `${this.last}, ${this.first}`;
    }

    // see below...
}
```

With this definition, you could access a `.lastFirst` property as if it actually were an attribute of the object; no parentheses are needed:

```
pp = new Person("Jean", "Dupont");
console.log(pp.fullName()); // "Jean Dupont"
console.log(pp.lastFirst); // "Dupont, Jean"
```

You can complement a getter with a *setter*, and it will perform any operations you want it to. For example, we may want let the user assign a value to `.lastFirst` and then change `.first` and `.last` appropriately.

Working somewhat cavalierly (no checks on arguments!), we could add the following definition to our `Person` class:

```
// Source file: src/class_persons.js

class Person {
    // ...continued from above

    set lastFirst(lf) {
        // very unsafe; no checks!
        const parts = lf.split(",");
        this.last = parts[0];
        this.first = parts[1];
    }
}

pp.lastFirst = "Svensson, Sven";
console.log(pp); // Person {first: " Sven", last: "Svensson"}
```

Of course, having a property and having a getter or a setter for the same property is not allowed. Also, getter functions cannot have parameters, and setter functions must have exactly one.

 You can find more information on getters and setters at `https://developer.mozilla.org/en-US/docs/Web/JavaScript/Reference/Functions/get` and `https://developer.mozilla.org/en-US/docs/Web/JavaScript/Reference/Functions/set`, respectively.

The previous sections do not exhaust all of the possibilities of JS as to classes and objects (not by a long shot!), but I opted to go over the most likely ones for clarity.

Organizing code in modules

As today's JS applications become more and more complex, working with namespaces and dependencies becomes ever more difficult to handle. A key solution to this problem was the concept of *modules*, which allows you to partition your solution in independent parts, taking advantage of encapsulation to avoid conflict between different modules. In this section, we'll look at how to work in this fashion. However, we'll start with a previous JS pattern, which may become useful in its own way.

Node, which we'll be working with starting with the next chapter, also does modules but in a different fashion, so we'll postpone the discussion of its modules for now.

How to do it...

Organizing code is such a basic need when dealing with hundreds or thousands of or even larger code bases, and so many ways of dealing with the problem were designed before JS finally defined a standard. First, we'll look at the more classic *iffy* way (we'll see what this means soon) and then move on to more modern solutions, but be aware that you may encounter all of these styles when reading other people's code!

Doing modules the IIFE way

Before modules became widely available, there was a fairly common pattern in use, which basically provided the same features that today's modules do. First, let's introduce a sample fragment of code, and then examine its properties:

```
// Source file: src/iife_counter.js

/* @flow */

/*
    In the following code, the only thing that needs
    an explicit type declaration for Flow, is "name".
    Flow can work out on its own the rest of the types.
*/

const myCounter = ((name: string) => {
    let count = 0;

    const inc = () => ++count;

    const get = () => count; // private

    const toString = () => `${name}: ${get()}`;

    return {
        inc,
        toString
    };
```

```
}) ("Clicks");

console.log(myCounter); // an object, with methods inc and toString

myCounter.inc(); // 1
myCounter.inc(); // 2
myCounter.inc(); // 3

myCounter.toString(); // "Clicks: 3"
```

Defining a function and immediately calling it is called an IIFE, pronounced *iffy*, and stands for *Immediately Invoked Function Expression*.

 IIFEs are also known as *Self-Executing Anonymous Functions*, which doesn't sound as good as *iffy*!

We defined a function (the one starting with `name => ...`), but we immediately called it (with `("Clicks")` afterwards). Therefore, what gets assigned to `myCounter` is not a function, but its returned value, that is, an object. Let's analyze this object's contents. Because of the scoping rules for functions, whatever you define inside isn't visible from the outside. In our particular case, this means that `count`, `get()`, `inc()`, and `toString()` won't be accessible. However, since our IIFE returns an object including the two latter functions, those two (and only those two) are usable from the outside: this is called the *revealing module pattern*.

 A question: where is the `"Clicks"` value stored, and why isn't the value of `count` lost from call to call? The answer to both questions has to do with a well-known JS feature, *closures*, which has been in the language since its beginning. See `https://developer.mozilla.org/en-US/docs/Web/JavaScript/Closures` for more information on this.

If you have followed on so far, the following should be clear to you:

- Whatever variables or functions are defined in the module aren't visible or accessible from the outside, unless you voluntarily reveal them
- Whatever names you decide to use in your module won't conflict with outside names because of normal lexical scoping rules
- The captured variables (in our case, `name`) persist so that the module can store information and use it later

All in all, we must agree that IIFEs are a *poor man's module* and their usage is quite common. Browse the web for a bit; you are certain to find examples of it. However, ES6 introduced a more general (and clearer and easier to understand) way of defining modules, which is what we'll be using: let's talk about this next.

Redoing our IIFE module in the modern way

The key concept in modules is that you'll have separate files, each of which will represent a module. There are two complementary concepts: importing and exporting. Modules will import the features they require from other modules, which must have exported them so that they are available.

First, let's look at the equivalent of our counter module from the previous section, and then comment on the extra features we can use:

```
// Source file: src/module_counter.1.js

/* @flow */

let name: string = "";
let count: number = 0;

let get = () => count;
let inc = () => ++count;
let toString = () => `${name}: ${get()}`;

/*
    Since we cannot initialize anything otherwise,
    a common pattern is to provide a "init()" function
    to do all necessary initializations.
*/
const init = (n: string) => {
    name = n;
};

export default { inc, toString, init }; // everything else is private
```

How would we use this module? Let's hold on the explanations about some internal aspects and answer that first.

To use this module in some other file from our application, we would write something as follows, with a new source file that imports the functions that our module exported:

```
// Source file: src/module_counter_usage.js

import myCounter from "module_counter";

/*
    Initialize the counter appropriately
*/
myCounter.init("Clicks");

/*
    The rest would work as before
*/
myCounter.inc(); // 1
myCounter.inc(); // 2
myCounter.inc(); // 3
myCounter.toString(); // "Clicks: 3"
```

OK, so using this module to provide a counter isn't so different after all. The main difference with the IIFE version is that here, we cannot do an initialization. A common pattern to provide this is to export a `init()` function that will do whatever is needed. Whoever uses the module must, first of all, call `init()` to set things up properly.

 There's no need to immediately call the `init()` function, as would happen with the IIFE version, and you could delay it until necessary. Also, the `init()` function could be called more times in order to reset the module. These possibilities provide extra functionality.

Adding initialization checks

If you wish, you can make the `.init()` function more powerful by having the module crash if used without initialization:

```
// Source file: module_counter.2.js

/* @flow */

let name = "";
let count = 0;

let get = () => count;

let throwNotInit = () => {
```

```
    throw new Error("Not initialized");
};
let inc = throwNotInit;
let toString = throwNotInit;

/*
    Since we cannot initialize anything otherwise,
    a common pattern is to provide a "init()" function
    to do all necessary initializations. In this case,
    "inc()" and "toString()" will just throw an error
    if the module wasn't initialized.
*/
const init = (n: string) => {
    name = n;
    inc = () => ++count;
    toString = () => `${name}: ${get()}`;
};

    export default { inc, toString, init }; // everything else is private
```

In this fashion, we can ensure proper usage of our module. Note that the idea of assigning a new function to replace an old one is very typical of the Functional Programming style; functions are first class objects that can be passed around, returned, or stored.

Using more import/export possibilities

In the previous section, we exported a single item from our module by using what is called a default export: one per module. There is also another kind of export, *named* exports, of which you can have several per module. You can even mix them in the same module, but it's usually clearer to not mix them up. For example, say you needed a module to do some distance and weight conversions. Your module could be as follows:

```
// Source file: src/module_conversions.js

/* @flow */

type conversion = number => number;

const SPEED_OF_LIGHT_IN_VACUUM_IN_MPS = 186282;
const KILOMETERS_PER_MILE = 1.60934;
const GRAMS_PER_POUND = 453.592;
const GRAMS_PER_OUNCE = 28.3495;

const milesToKm: conversion = m => m * KILOMETERS_PER_MILE;
const kmToMiles: conversion = k => k / KILOMETERS_PER_MILE;
```

```
const poundsToKg: conversion = p => p * (GRAMS_PER_POUND / 1000);
const kgToPounds: conversion = k => k / (GRAMS_PER_POUND / 1000);

const ouncesToGrams: conversion = o => o * GRAMS_PER_OUNCE;
const gramsToOunces: conversion = g => g / GRAMS_PER_OUNCE;

/*
 It's usually preferred to include all "export"
 statements together, at the end of the file.
 You need not have a SINGLE export, however.
*/
export { milesToKm, kmToMiles };
export { poundsToKg, kgToPounds, gramsToOunces, ouncesToGrams };
export { SPEED_OF_LIGHT_IN_VACUUM_IN_MPS };
```

You can have as many definitions as you want, and you can export any of them; in our case, we are exporting six functions and one constant. You do not need to pack everything into a single export; you can have several, as we have already shown you. Exports are usually grouped together at the end of a module to help a reader quickly find everything that the module exports, but sometimes you may find them all throughout the code; we won't be doing that. You can also export something in the same line where you define it, as in export const LENGTH_OF_YEAR_IN_DAYS = 365.2422, but we won't use that style either, for consistency.

When importing a module with named exports, you just have to say which of the exports you want. You can import from different modules; you'll just require several import statements. It's a standard practice to group all of them at the start of your source file. You can also rename an import, as in the case of poundsToKg in the following code, which we'll use as p_to_kg. In reality, you would do this if you had identically named imports from two different modules; in our particular example, it doesn't really make sense:

```
// Source file: src/module_conversion_usage.js

/* @flow */

import {
    milesToKm,
    ouncesToGrams,
    poundsToKg as p_to_kg
} from "./module_conversions.js";
console.log(`A miss is as good as ${milesToKm(1)} kilometers.`);

console.log(
    `${ouncesToGrams(1)} grams of protection `,
    `are worth ${p_to_kg(1) * 1000} grams of cure.`
);
```

So far, we have seen how to export JS elements—functions and constants in our example—but you could also export classes, objects, arrays, and so on. In the next section, we'll get back to Flow, and see how types can also be exported and imported.

Using Flow types with modules

Exporting data types (including generics, interfaces, and so on) is quite similar to normal exports, except that you must include the word `type`. If you wanted to use the conversion type elsewhere, in the original module, you would add the following:

```
export type { conversion };
```

Correspondingly, wherever you wanted to import that type, you would add something like this:

```
import type { conversion } from "./module_conversions.js";
```

Note, however, an important detail: you cannot export or import data types in the same sentence in which you deal with standard JS elements: `export` and `export type` are distinct, separate statements, and so are `import` and `import type`.

Determining a feature's availability

To round off this chapter, let me introduce two web tools that can help you be aware about what features you can safely use and which will make a transpiler (such as `Babel`, which we mentioned at the start of this chapter) necessary.

How to do it...

Your first resource will be `https://kangax.github.io/compat-table/`, which provides very thorough and complete tables showing, feature by feature, what is supported on JS engines everywhere. Depending on your specific needs, you might be able to totally dispense with transpiling, but it's certain you should be careful before taking such a measure!

The following screenshot shows Kangax at work:

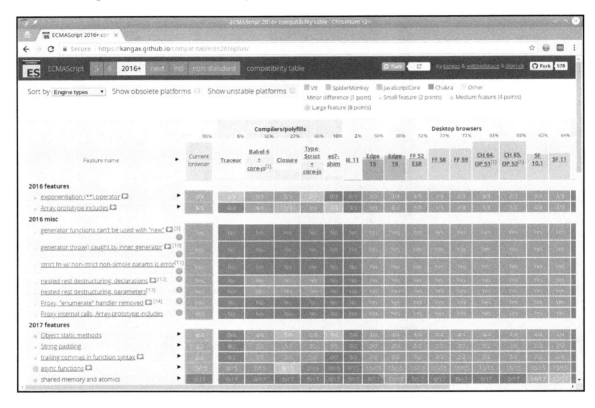

The Kangax website lets you determine what features are (or are not) provided by browsers, versions of Node, and so on

A second web tool that you should be aware of is *Can I use...* at https://caniuse.com/. In this site, you can search for any feature (be it JS, HTML, or CSS), and you'll get to see what browser versions support it or not. A comment is relevant: this site only provides information for desktop and mobile browsers; you cannot see if a feature is supported in Node, for example. The following screenshot shows *Can I use...* at work:

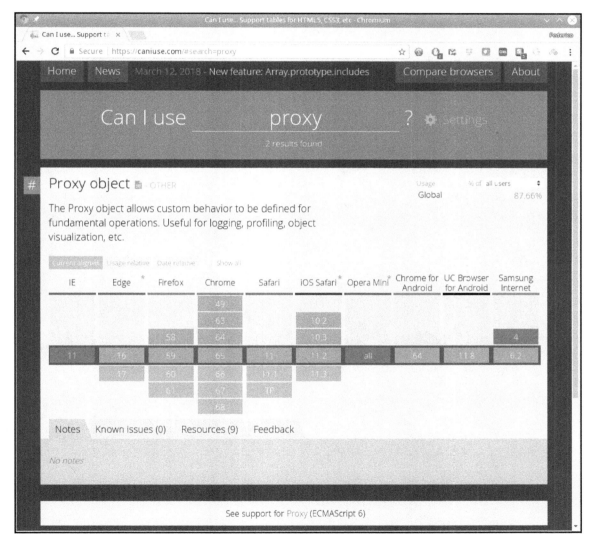

The *Can I Use...* site lets you find out what browsers support (or don't) a given feature

Developing with Node

3

The recipes we will be seeing in this chapter are as follows:

- Checking Node's setup
- Working with modules
- Using Flow with Node, directly
- Using Flow with Node through preprocessing
- Running your Node code with Nodemon
- Using promises instead of error first callbacks
- Working with streams to process requests
- Compressing files with streams
- Working with a database
- Executing external processes with exec()
- Using spawn() to run a command, and communicating with it
- Using fork() to run Node commands

Introduction

We installed Node in the *Installing Node and npm* section of Chapter 1, *Working with JavaScript Development Tools*, but that was only for setting npm up. Node can be used not only as a web server, which is the most common usage, but also to write shell line commands or even desktop applications, as we'll see in Chapter 13, *Creating a Desktop Application with Electron*. However, some configuration and development practices are common for all those environments, and that will be the objective of this chapter. In this chapter, we will get started on Node development.

Checking Node's setup

For starters, let's verify Node is working, by creating a very basic server; we'll get into more details in the next Chapter 4, *Implementing RESTful Services with Node*, but now we just want to make sure everything is fine. In other chapters, we will use Node more seriously, but the objective here is to verify that it works OK.

How to do it...

Getting ahead a bit, let's set up a very basic server, which will answer all the requests by sending back a 'Server alive!' string. For this, we will need to follow three steps:

1. Use require() to import the http module of Node—we'll see more on modules in the next section; for the time being, just assume that require() is equivalent to import.
2. Then, use the createServer() method to set up our server.
3. After that, provide a function that will answer all requests by sending back a text/plain fixed answer.

The following code represents the most basic possible server, and will let us know whether everything has worked correctly. I have named the file miniserver.js. The line in bold does all the work, which we'll go over in the next section:

```
// Source file: src/miniserver.js

/* @flow */
"use strict";

const http = require("http");

http
    .createServer((req, res) => {
        res.writeHead(200, { "Content-Type": "text/plain" });
        res.end("Server alive!");
    })
    .listen(8080, "localhost");

console.log("Mini server ready at http://localhost:8080/");
```

How it works...

We wrote a server; now, let's see it run. With this very simple project, we can just directly run the server code. In later sections in this chapter, we'll see that using Flow types will require some extra preprocessing; we can skip that part for now, however. We can start our server with the following command line:

```
> node src/miniserver.js
Mini server ready at http://localhost:8080/
```

To verify if everything is working fine, just open a browser and go to `http://localhost:8080`. The following screenshot shows the (admittedly not very impressive) result:

Our minimalistic server is running, showing that we have Node working properly

Now that we know that everything is OK, let's get started with some basic techniques that we will be using in several other places of the book.

Why are we running the server at port 8080 instead of 80? To access ports below 1024, you need administrative (root) rights. However, that would make your server highly unsafe; a hacker that somehow managed to get into it would have maximum rights at your machine! Thus, the standard practice is to run Node with normal rights, at ports over 1024 (such as 8080, for example) and set up a reverse proxy to send traffic on ports 80 (HTTP) or 443 (HTTPS).

Working with modules

In the *Organizing code in modules* section of `Chapter 2`, *Using JavaScript Modern Features*, we saw how modern JS works with modules. However, with `Node`, we have a little setback: it doesn't do modules the modern JS way—unless you are willing to work with experimental features!

Why doesn't `Node` work with the modern JS modules? The reason harkens back to several years before the new modules with `import` and `export` statements existed, and `Node` implemented the CommonJS module format. (We'll be seeing more about those modules in the next section.) Obviously, libraries meant to be used with `Node` were also developed using that format, and nowadays there are an uncountable number of modules that follow those guidelines.

However, since the new standard for modules appeared, a pressure began to apply to use the new syntax—but that posed some problems beyond just adjusting the language; can you have *two* radically different module styles coexisting? (Because, no one can magically transform all the existing code that uses CommonJS into the new format, right?) There are some other differences. ES modules are meant to be used in asynchronous fashion, while CommonJS modules are synchronous; for most cases, this doesn't cause a difference, but there are cases that must be considered.

The solution that was arrived at isn't considered definitive yet. For the time being (since version 8.5) you can enable the ES modules by using the `--experimental-modules` command line flag. If you invoke node with it, it will recognize the ES modules, if their extension is `.mjs` instead of plain `.js`. Hopefully, by version 10, it won't be needed, but that cannot be ensured, and there's also a certain risk that some details might change by then!

This solution, using the new `.mjs` file extension to identify new-style modules, is whimsically known as the **Michael Jackson Solution** because of the initials of the three words.

So, if I were writing this book in one or two years' time, I'd probably be telling you to just go ahead, start using the `.mjs` file extension, and use the new style modules.

See `https://nodejs.org/api/esm.html` for current information about this feature.

However, at this time, it should not be considered a totally safe step—the feature is clearly marked as *experimental* at this point of time—so let's keep going with the current (old) standard, and learn how to work with the old-fashioned modules. Let's create a math module you might want to use for financial coding, so we get to see a Node style module built from scratch.

How to do it...

With Node modules, there are two important changes in how we export and import elements. Any file can be a module, as with ES modules. In a nutshell, in order to import something from a module, you'll have to use a require() function, and the module itself will use an exports object to specify what it will export.

JS math operators (addition, subtraction, and so on) don't do rounding, so let's write a roundmath.js module that will perform arithmetic, but rounding to cents, for an imagined business-related application. First, we get started with the common two lines that enable Flow, and set strict mode:

```
// Source file: src/roundmath.js

/* @flow */
"use strict";

// continues...
```

 Don't forget to add the "use strict" line in all your modules, before the rest of your code, as we mentioned in the *Working in strict mode* section in the previous chapter. JS modules are strict by definition, but that doesn't apply to Node modules, which are *not* strict.

Then, let's define our functions. Just for variety, we'll have a couple of internal (not exported) functions, and several ones that will be exported:

```
// ...continued

// These won't be exported:

const roundToCents = (x: number): number => Math.round(x * 100) / 100;
const changeSign = (x: number): number => -x;

// The following will be exported:

const addR = (x: number, y: number): number => roundToCents(x + y);
```

```
const subR = (x: number, y: number): number => addR(x, changeSign(y));

const multR = (x: number, y: number): number => roundToCents(x * y);

const divR = (x: number, y: number): number => {
    if (y === 0) {
        throw new Error("Divisor must be nonzero");
    } else {
        return roundToCents(x / y);
    }
};

// continues...
```

Finally, as per usual conventions, all exports will be together, at the bottom, so it will be easy to see everything that a module exports. Instead of the modern `export` statement, you assign whatever you want to export, to an `exports` object. If you want to keep variables or functions private, all you need do is skip assigning them; in our case, we are only exporting four of the six functions we coded:

```
// ...continued

exports.addR = addR;
exports.subR = subR;
exports.multR = multR;
exports.divR = divR;
```

How it works...

How would we use this module, and how does it work? If we wanted to import some of its functions from other modules, we'd write something as follows; see how we use some of the operations we designed:

```
// Source file: src/doroundmath.js

/* @flow */
"use strict";

const RM = require("./roundmath.js");

console.log(RM.addR(12.348, 4.221)); // 16.57
console.log(RM.changeSign(0.07)); // error; RM.changeSign is not a function
```

The first two lines are the usual. Then, we require() whatever modules we need; in this case, a single one. Also, per convention, all such requirements are grouped together, at the start, to make it simpler to understand the needs of a module, without having to go all through the code. In our case, RM gets assigned the exports object, so you can refer to RM.addR(), RM.subR(), and so on, and this makes clear to the reader that you are using something from the RM module.

If you want to write a bit less, you can take advantage of the *destructuring statement* (which we met in the *Destructuring arrays and objects* section in the previous chapter) and directly assign the desired methods to individual variables:

```
/* @flow */
"use strict";

const { multR, divR } = require("./roundmath.js");

console.log(multR(22.9, 12.4)); // 283.96
console.log(divR(22, 7)); // 3.14
```

It is better if you get used to only importing modules that you'll need. In other cases (which we'll see in later chapters) we can use tools to just remove whatever modules you don't actually use, and if you require() everything, that wouldn't be possible.

Using Flow with Node, directly

Since we are using Flow, and Node doesn't actually know about the data types, there will obviously be problems if we just try to execute our data-typed code. There are two solutions for this: one not so elegant, but that speeds up development, and another more powerful one, but that will require extra work. Let's here consider the first, simpler solution, and leave the second one for the next section.

How to do it...

It so happens that Flow provides two ways of specifying types: the way that we have been using so far, with extra type notations, and another more verbose one, through the comments. Of course, JS doesn't *know* about type definitions, so the first style won't work unless we do extra work (as we'll see) but using comments is totally safe.

To define types with comments, all `Flow` specific definitions must be enclosed in comments starting with `/*:` (note the extra colon) and finishing with the usual `*/`, for simple basic types, or `/*::` and `*/` for everything else. We can revisit some examples we saw earlier in `Chapter 2`, *Using JavaScript Modern Features*. Simple cases are as follows:

```
// Source file: src/flowcomments.js

let someFlag /*: boolean */;
let greatTotal /*: number */;
let firstName /*: string */;

function toString(x /*: number */) /*: string */ {
    return String(x);
}

let traffic /*: "red" | "amber" | "green" */;

// continues...
```

More complex definitions, including optional parameters, types and opaque types, class attributes, and so on, require the longer comments:

```
// ...continued

/*::
type pair<T> = [T, T];
type pairOfNumbers = pair<number>;
type pairOfStrings = pair<string>;

type simpleFlag = number | boolean;

type complexObject = {
    id: string,
    name: string,
    indicator: simpleFlag,
    listOfValues: Array<number>
};
*/

class Person {
    /*::
    first: string;
    last: string;
    */

    constructor(first /*: string */, last /*: string */) {
        this.first = first;
```

```
        this.last = last;
    }

    // ...several methods, snipped out
}

// continues...
```

You can also export and import data types:

```
// ...continued

/*::
import type { dniType, nameType } from "./opaque_types";
*/

/*::
export type { pairOfNumbers, pairOfStrings };
*/
```

How it works...

Why and how does this work? Flow is able to recognize both the /*::   ...   */ and
/*:   ...   */ comments, and thus can do its job perfectly well. Since the Flow code is all
hidden away in comments, from the point of view of the JS engine, the Flow parts do not
even exist, so an obvious advantage of this way of working is that you can directly execute
your code.

Why would you *not* like this? The evident criticism is that the code looks, to put it mildly,
ugly. If you were used to, say, TypeScript, having to wrap all type-related things in
comments can become a chore, and the code will also be harder to read. Also, there is a risk
that you'll mistype a comment (forgetting one of those many colons is a possibility) and
then Flow will just ignore your definitions, posing a possible risk of letting a bug go
through.

Is there an alternative? Yes, there is, but it will require some extra processing, while giving
us the benefit of using standard Flow notation; let's turn to that now.

Using Flow with Node through preprocessing

Working with comments is a bit overly verbose. If you'd rather work with straightforward type annotations and extra statements, you will have to turn to some preprocessing, to get rid of the Flow paraphernalia before attempting to run your Node code. The good thing with this is that the required processing can be quite efficient, and practically unnoticeable when you develop; let's get into it, and see how we can get to keep Flow definitions, while not breaking our Node code.

How to do it...

We want to use the shorter, more concise style of Flow, but Node cannot execute code with such additives.The solution to our conundrum is easy: just remove everything related to Flow before attempting to run! There is a package, flow-remove-types, that does just that. To start, as usual, you'll have to install the needed package:

```
npm install flow-remove-types --save-dev
```

To continue, you will have to enable it by adding a new script. We were writing our code in the src/ directory, so let's send the Flow-cleaned output to the out/ directory. In that directory, we will get the version of the code that we will use in our server:

```
"scripts": {
    "build": "flow-remove-types src/ -d out/",
    "addTypes": "flow-typed install",
    "update": "npm install && flow-typed install",
    "flow": "flow",
        .
        .
        .
},
```

To finish, we should also tell Git to ignore the out/ directory. We were already ignoring the node_modules and flow-typed directories, so let's add one more:

```
**/node_modules
**/flow-typed
**/out
```

We are specifying `**/out` instead of just `out/`, because we are sharing a single `Git` repository between many projects, for the sake of the book. If, as is more common, you had a separate repository for each project, then you would simply specify `out`.

How it works...

What will change from the moment you start using `flow-remove-types`? First, obviously, you cannot just run your project with a simple `node src/somefilename.js`; first you'll have to strip Flow by `npm run build`. The effect of this command will be to create a copy in `out/`, of everything in `src/`, but without type declarations. Then, you will be able to run the project by doing `node out/somefilename.js`—filenames won't be changed.

When `flow-remove-types` package cleans up your files, it replaces all type declarations with whitespaces, so the transformed output files have exactly the same number of lines, and every function starts at exactly the same line as before, removing the need for sourcemaps and keeping the output legible. The following code shows how part of our module from the *Working with modules* section would look after the process:

```
/* @flow */
"use strict";

// These won't be exported:

const roundToCents = (x: number): number => Math.round(x * 100) / 100;

const changeSign = (x: number): number => -x;

// The following will be exported:

const addR = (x: number, y: number): number => roundToCents(x + y);

const subR = (x: number, y: number): number => addR(x, changeSign(y));

const multR = (x: number, y: number): number => roundToCents(x * y);

const divR = (x: number, y: number): number => {
    if (y === 0) {
        throw new Error("Divisor must be nonzero");
    } else {
        return roundToCents(x / y);
    }
};
```

If you would rather have a smaller-sized output (after all, reading code with all those blank spaces can be a bit tiresome) you can produce a source map and remove all spaces, by adding a couple of parameters to your build script, or by adding a different script, as shown in the following code snippet:

```
"scripts": {
    "build": "flow-remove-types src/ -d out/",
    "buildWithMaps": "flow-remove-types src/ -d out/ --pretty --
sourcemaps",
    .
    .
    .
},
```

 The Node debugger included in VSC fully supports source maps, so producing briefer code won't be a problem. We'll get to see more about this in Chapter 5, *Testing and Debugging Your Server*.

Now we have a way to keep working with Node and Flow together, but running our code has become just a tad more complex; let's see if we can fix that!

Running your Node code with Nodemon

With the work we have done so far, after each and every change, running our updated Node code would require that we perform the following:

1. Stop the current version of the code, if it's still running.
2. Rerun the build process to update the out directory.
3. Run the new version of the code.

Doing all of this, for every single small change, can quickly become boring and tiresome. But, there is a solution: we can install a watcher, that will monitor our files for changes and do everything mentioned here by itself, freeing us from the repetitive chore. Let's then see how we can set a tool to watch out for changes, and do all the steps shown on its own.

How to do it...

We will want to install and configure `nodemon`, which will take care of everything for us, running updated code as necessary. First, obviously, we must install the mentioned package. You could do it globally with `npm install nodemon -g`, but I'd rather do it locally:

```
npm install nodemon --save-dev
```

Then, we'll need to add a couple of scripts:

- `npm start` will build the application and run our main file
- `npm run nodemon` will start the monitoring

```
"scripts": {
    "build": "flow-remove-types src/ -d out/",
    "buildWithMaps": "flow-remove-types src/ -d out/ --pretty --
        sourcemaps",
    "start": "npm run build && node out/doroundmath.js",
    "nodemon": "nodemon --watch src --delay 1 --exec npm start",
    .
    .
    .
},
```

Now, we are ready to monitor our application for changes, and restart it as needed!

How it works...

The command most interesting for us is the second one. When you run it, `nodemon` will start monitoring, meaning it will watch whatever directory you selected (out, in this case) and whenever it detects some file change, it will wait one second (to make sure, for example, that all files are saved) and then it will rerun the application. How did I do this?

Initially, I started `nodemon`. When you do `npm run nodemon`, the project is built and then run, and `nodemon` keeps waiting for any changes; see the following screenshot:

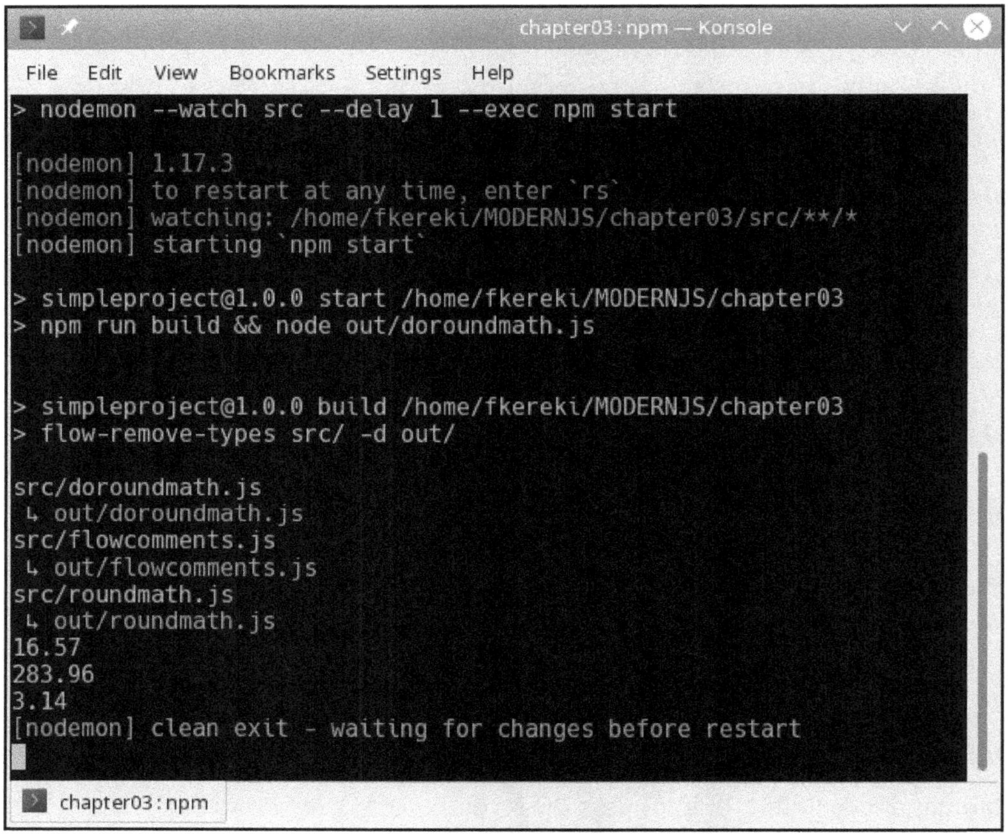

When you start nodemon, it builds the project, runs it, and keeps watching out for any changes that need a restart

Afterwards, I just added a simple `console.log()` line, so a file would be changed; the following screenshot was the result, showing the rebuilt and restarted code, plus the extra output line:

```
283.96
3.14
[nodemon] clean exit - waiting for changes before restart
[nodemon] restarting due to changes...
[nodemon] starting `npm start`

> simpleproject@1.0.0 start /home/fkereki/MODERNJS/chapter03
> npm run build && node out/doroundmath.js


> simpleproject@1.0.0 build /home/fkereki/MODERNJS/chapter03
> flow-remove-types src/ -d out/

src/doroundmath.js
 ↳ out/doroundmath.js
src/flowcomments.js
 ↳ out/flowcomments.js
src/roundmath.js
 ↳ out/roundmath.js
16.57
283.96
3.14
ADDED TEXT JUST FOR THE CHANGE
[nodemon] clean exit - waiting for changes before restart
```

chapter03:npm

After any change in a watched file, nodemon will restart the project. In this case, I had just added a line logging ADDED TEXT JUST FOR THE CHANGE.

That's all there is to it. The application will be rebuilt and restarted automatically, without us having to manually rerun `npm start` each and every time; a big help!

> Read more about `nodemon` at `http://nodemon.io/` and `https://github.com/remy/nodemon`.

Using promises instead of error first callbacks

Now, let's start considering several techniques that will come in handy when writing services.

Node runs as a single thread, so if every time it had to call a service, or read a file, or access a database, or do any other I/O-related operation, it would have to wait for it to finish, then attending requests would take a long time, blocking other requests from being attended, and the server would show a very bad performance. Instead, all operations such as those are always done asynchronically, and you must provide a callback that will be called whenever the operation is finished; meanwhile, Node will be available to process other clients' requests.

 There are synchronous versions of many functions, but they can only be applied for desktop work, and never for web servers.

Node established a standard that all callbacks should receive two parameters: an error and a result. If the operation failed somehow, the error argument would describe the reason. Otherwise, if the operation had succeeded, the error would be null or undefined (but, in any case, a *falsy* value) and the result would have the resultant value.

This means that the usual Node code is full of callbacks, and if a callback itself needs another operation, that means yet more callbacks, which themselves may have even more callbacks, resulting in what is called *callback hell*. Instead of working in this fashion, we want to be able to opt for modern promises, and, fortunately, there is a simple way to do so. Let's see how we can simplify our code by avoiding callbacks.

How to do it...

Let's start by seeing how a common error first callback works. The fs (file system) module provides a readFile() method that can read a file, and either produce its text or an error. My showFileLength1() function attempts to read a file, and list its length. As usual with callbacks, we have to provide a function, which will receive two values: a possible error, and a possible result.

This function must check whether the first argument is null or not. If it isn't null, it means there was a problem, and the operation wasn't successful. On the other hand, if the first argument is null, then the second argument has the file read operation result. The following code highlights the usual programming pattern used with Node callbacks; the lines in bold are the key ones:

```
// Source file: src/promisify.js

/* @flow */
"use strict";

const fs = require("fs");

const FILE_TO_READ = "/home/fkereki/MODERNJS/chapter03/src/promisify.js";
// its own source!

function showFileLength1(fileName: string): void {
    fs.readFile(fileName, "utf8", (err, text) => {
        if (err) {
            throw err;
        } else {
            console.log(`1. Reading, old style: ${text.length} bytes`);
        }
    });
}
showFileLength1(FILE_TO_READ);

// continues...
```

This style of coding is well-known, but doesn't really fit modern development, based on promises and, even better, async/await. So, since version 8 of Node, there has been a way to automatically transform an error-first callback function into a promise: util.promisify(). If you apply that method to any old-style function, it will turn into a promise, which you can then work in simpler ways.

How it works...

The util module is standard with Node, and all you have to do to use it is the following:

```
const util = require("util");
```

The `util.promisify()` method is actually another example of a Higher Order Function, as we saw in the *Producing functions from functions* section of `Chapter 2`, *Using JavaScript Modern Features*.

Using `util.promisify()`, we can make `fs.readFile()` return a promise, which we'll process with the `.then()` and `.catch()` methods:

```
// ...continued

function showFileLength2(fileName: string): void {
    fs.readFile = util.promisify(fs.readFile);

    fs
        .readFile(fileName, "utf8")
        .then((text: string) => {
            console.log(`2. Reading with promises: ${text.length} bytes`);
        })
        .catch((err: mixed) => {
            throw err;
        });
}
showFileLength2(FILE_TO_READ);

// continues...
```

You could have also written `const { promisify } = require("util")`, and then it would have been `fs.readFile = promisify(fs.readFile)`.

This also allows us the usage of `async` and `await`; I'll be using an arrow `async` function, just for variety:

```
// ...continued

const showFileLength3 = async (fileName: string) => {
    fs.readFile = util.promisify(fs.readFile);

    try {
        const text: string = await fs.readFile(fileName, "utf8");
        console.log(`3. Reading with async/await: ${text.length} bytes`);
    } catch (err) {
        throw err;
    }
};
showFileLength3(FILE_TO_READ);
```

There's more...

Keep in mind that you won't always be needing `util.promisify()`. There are two reasons for this:

- Some libraries (such as `axios`, which we already used) already return promises, so you don't have to do anything
- Some other methods (such as the `http.request()` method of `Node`; see `https://nodejs.org/dist/latest-v9.x/docs/api/http.html#http_http_request_options_callback`) have a different signature altogether, without even an error argument

In any case, aiming for a standard usage will help, so we'll adopt the promise-based style for the rest of the book.

Working with streams to process requests

If you have to work with a large enough set of data, it's fairly obvious that it will cause problems. Your server may not be able to provide all the required memory, or even if that doesn't prove to be a problem, the needed processing time would surpass the standard waiting time, causing timeouts—plus the fact that your server would close out other requests, because it would be devoted to handling your long-time processing one.

`Node` provides a way to work with collections of data as streams, being able to process the data as it flows, and piping it to compose functionality out of smaller steps, much in the fashion of Linux's and Unix's pipelines. Let's see a basic example, which you might use if you were interested in doing low-level `Node` request processing. (As is, we will be using higher-level libraries to do this work, as we'll see in the next chapter.) When a request comes in, its body can be accessed as a stream, thus allowing your server to deal with any size of requests.

 The response that will be sent to the client is also a stream; we'll see an example of this in the next section, *Compressing files with streams*.

Streams can be of four kinds:

- *Readable*: Which can (obviously!) be read. You would use this to process a file, or, as in our following example, to get a web request's data.
- *Writable*: To which data can be written.
- *Duplex*: Both readable and writable, such as a web socket.
- *Transform*: Duplex streams that can transform the data as it is read and written; we'll see an example of this for zipping files.

How to do it...

Let's write some simple code to process a request, and just show what was asked. Our main code for the request process will be the following:

```
// Source file: src/process_request.js

const http = require("http");

http
    .createServer((req, res) => {
        // For PUT/POST methods, wait until the
        // complete request body has been read.

        if (req.method === "POST" || req.method === "PUT") {
            let body = "";

            req.on("data", data => {
                body += data;
            });

            req.on("end", () => processRequest(req, res, body));

        } else {
            return processRequest(req, res, "");
        }
    })
    .listen(8080, "localhost");

// continues...
```

The `processRequest()` function will be quite simple, limited to showing its parameters. This kind of code can become helpful if you need to better understand how to process requests, as we'll see in the next chapter. We will get parameters both from the URL and the request body:

```
// ...continued

const url = require("url");
const querystring = require("querystring");

function processRequest(req, res, body) {
  /*
  Get parameters, both from the URL and the request body
  */
  const urlObj = url.parse(req.url, true);
  const urlParams = urlObj.query;
  const bodyParams = querystring.parse(body);

  console.log("URL OBJECT", urlObj);
  console.log("URL PARAMETERS", urlParams);
  console.log("BODY PARAMETERS", bodyParams);

  /*
   Here you would analyze the URL to decide what is required
   Then you would do whatever is needed to fulfill the request
   Finally, when everything was ready, results would be sent
   In our case, we just send a FINISHED message
  */

  res.writeHead(200, "OK");
  res.end(`FINISHED WITH THE ${req.method} REQUEST`);
}
```

The output of this code, which we'll see next, will be the the request `url` object (`req.url`), its parameters, and the parameters in the body.

How it works...

Let's run the simple server we just wrote, to see how it works. We can build and run it with the following two lines:

```
> npm run build
> node out/process_request.js
```

After the server is running, we can test it by using `curl`—we'll get back to this in the *Testing simple services from the command line* section of Chapter 5, *Testing and Debugging Your Server*, and we'll see our FINISHED... message:

```
> curl "http://127.0.0.1:8080/some/path/in/the/server?alpha=22&beta=9"
FINISHED WITH THE GET REQUEST
```

The quote characters around the URL are needed, because the & character has a special meaning by itself for shell line commands.

The server console will show the following output, but what we care about right now are the URL parameters, that match with what was provided in the `curl` call:

```
URL OBJECT Url {
  protocol: null,
  slashes: null,
  auth: null,
  host: null,
  port: null,
  hostname: null,
  hash: null,
  search: '?alpha=22&beta=9',
  query: { alpha: '22', beta: '9' },
  pathname: '/some/path/in/the/server',
  path: '/some/path/in/the/server?alpha=22&beta=9',
  href: '/some/path/in/the/server?alpha=22&beta=9' }
URL PARAMETERS { alpha: '22', beta: '9' }
BODY PARAMETERS {}
```

This was easy, but if the service request had been a POST, we would have listened to events to build up the `body` of the request. Refer to the following:

- `'data'` is fired whenever there is more data to be processed. In our case, on each event we add to the `body` string, so as to build up the request body
- `'end'` is fired when there is no more data. Here, we use it to recognize when we have got the complete body of the request, and are then ready to move on and process it.
- `'close'` (when a stream is closed) and `'error'` events do not apply here, but are also available for stream processing.

If we were to do `curl -X "POST" --data "gamma=60" --data "delta=FK"` `"http://127.0.0.1:8080/other/path/"` to perform a `POST`, passing a couple of body parameters, the console output would change:

```
URL OBJECT Url {
 protocol: null,
 slashes: null,
 auth: null,
 host: null,
 port: null,
 hostname: null,
 hash: null,
 search: null,
 query: {},
 pathname: '/other/path/',
 path: '/other/path/',
 href: '/other/path/' }
URL PARAMETERS {}
BODY PARAMETERS { gamma: '60', delta: 'FK' }
```

Read more about streams (a lot of information!) at `https://nodejs.org/api/stream.html`.

Compressing files with streams

We can see more examples of using streams, of several types, such as in cases where we wanted to zip a file. In this recipe, we will be using a readable stream to read from a source, and a writable stream to put the zipped result.

How to do it...

The code is quite straightforward, and short, too. We just have to `require` the needed modules, create an input stream for the file that we'll read, an output stream for the file that we'll create, and pipe the first stream to the second one; nothing could be simpler:

```
// Source file: src/zip_files.js

const zlib = require("zlib");

const fs = require("fs");
```

```
const inputStream = fs.createReadStream(
    "/home/fkereki/Documents/CHURCHES - Digital Taxonomy.pdf"
);

const gzipStream = zlib.createGzip();

const outputStream = fs.createWriteStream(
    "/home/fkereki/Documents/CHURCHES.gz"
);

inputStream.pipe(gzipStream).pipe(outputStream);
```

How it works...

We use the `fs` module to produce two streams: a readable one, with which we will be reading a given file (here, a fixed one, but it would be trivial to read any other one) and a writable one, where the gzipped output will go. We will pipe the input stream through the `gzip` module, which will compress the input before passing it on to the output.

We could as easily have produced a server that would have sent the zipped file to the client, to download. The following is the required code; the key difference is that the zipped stream now goes to the `response` stream. We must also provide some headers, so the client will know that a zipped file is being sent:

```
// Source file: src/zip_send.js

const zlib = require("zlib");
const fs = require("fs");

const http = require("http");

http
    .createServer(function(request, response) {
        // Tell the client, this is a zip file.
        response.writeHead(200, {
            "Content-Type": "application/zip",
            "Content-disposition": "attachment; filename=churches.gz"
        });

        const inputStream = fs.createReadStream(
            "/home/fkereki/Documents/CHURCHES - Digital Taxonomy.pdf"
        );
```

```
        const gzipStream = zlib.createGzip();

        inputStream.pipe(gzipStream).pipe(response);
    })
    .listen(8080, "localhost");
```

If you `npm run build` and then `node out/zip_send.js`, opening `127.0.0.1:8080` will get what is shown in the following screenshot; you get the zipped file to download:

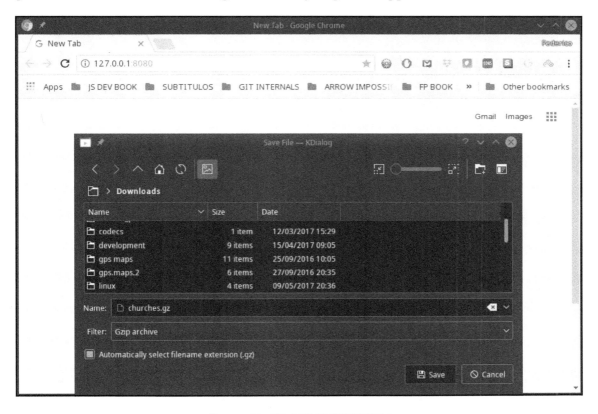

Streams are also used to zip and send a file to the browser

 Read more about `fs` at `https://nodejs.org/api/fs.html`, and about `zlib` at `https://nodejs.org/api/zlib.html`.

Working with a database

Let's now see how you would access a database, such as `MySQL`, `PostgreSQL`, `MSSQL`, `Oracle`, or more. (We will be needing this in `Chapter 4`, *Implementing RESTful Services with Node*, when we get to build a set of services.) Accessing a database is frequently done, so that's what we will be doing. I chose some geographical data (with countries, their regions, and the cities in those), to which we'll later add something else, to work with more complex examples.

Getting ready

Getting a list of countries was easy: I used the data from `https://github.com/datasets/country-codes`, which I pruned down to just the country two-character code (as in the ISO 3166-1 norm) and name. For regions and cities, I used GeoNames' data from `http://download.geonames.org/export/dump/`; in particular, I used `admin1CodesASCII.txt`, which I reworked into `regions.csv`, and `cities15000.zip`, which I edited into `cities.csv`.

 If you want to be able to view CSV files in a clearer format, check out the EXCEL VIEWER extension for VSC.

What you need to know about these three tables is as follows:

- *Countries* are identified by a two-letter code (such as *UY* for Uruguay, or *IN* for India), and have a name
- *Regions* belong to a country, and are identified by the country code, plus a string; in addition, they have a name
- *Cities* are identified by a numeric code, have a name, latitude and longitude, population, and are in a region of a country

This is enough to get started; later, we will be adding some more tables, to experiment a bit more. I used `MariaDB` (the open fork of `MySQL`; see `https://mariadb.com/`) and `MySQL WorkBench` (see `https://www.mysql.com/products/workbench/`) to create the tables and import the data, just because it's even simpler than doing it by hand! I also created a `fkereki` user, with `modernJS!!` as the password, to access the tables.

If you want to use a different database, such as PostgreSQL or Oracle, the following code will be quite similar, so don't worry much about dealing with a specific DB. If you use an ORM, you'll then see some DB-independent ways of accessing data, which could help should you really have to deal with different DB products.

How to do it...

In order to access a MariaDB database, we will install the `mariasql` package from `https://github.com/mscdex/node-mariasql` and then promisify its `.query()` method, to work in an easier fashion. Installation is accomplished with `npm install mariasql --save` and, after a short while (you will see some object code being built), the package will be installed. Follow the steps mentioned next.

Another possibility would be to use `mariasql-promise` from `https://github.com/steelbrain/mariasql-promise`, all of whose methods already return promises. However, getting the connection object and storing it for later use is harder with this library, and that's why I opted for the original one; after all, we only need to modify `.query()` to return a promise.

Getting a connection

First, let's have some constants that we will be using later; apart from the `Flow` and strict usage lines, we just require the `MariaDB` library, the `promisify()` function, and we define four constants to access the database:

```
// Source file: src/dbaccess.js

/* @flow */
"use strict";

const mariaSQL = require("mariasql");
const { promisify } = require("util");

const DB_HOST = "127.0.0.1";
const DB_USER = "fkereki";
const DB_PASS = "modernJS!!";
const DB_SCHEMA = "world";

// continues...
```

Now, let's get a database connection. We just create a new object, and `promisify` its
`.query()` method. The `dbConn` variable will be passed as a parameter to every function
that will need to access the database:

```
// ...continued

function getDbConnection(host, user, password, db) {
    const dbConn = new mariaSQL({ host, user, password, db });
    dbConn.query = promisify(dbConn.query);
    return dbConn;
}

const dbConn = getDbConnection(DB_HOST, DB_USER, DB_PASS, DB_SCHEMA);

// continues...
```

Executing some queries

A simple way of testing if the connection works is by executing a trivial query that returns a
constant value; what really matters here is that the function should work without throwing
any exceptions. We use `await` to get the result of the `.query()` method, that is an array
with all the found rows; in this case, the array will obviously have a single row:

```
// ...continued

async function tryDbAccess(dbConn) {
    try {
        const rows = await dbConn.query("SELECT 1960 AS someYear");
        console.log(`Year was ${rows[0].someYear}`);
    } catch (e) {
        console.log("Unexpected error", e);
    }
}

// continues...
```

Let's try something else: what about finding the ten countries that have more cities? We can
use `.forEach()` to list the results in a frankly not-very-attractive format:

```
// ...continued

async function get10CountriesWithMoreCities(dbConn) {
    try {
        const myQuery = `SELECT
            CI.countryCode,
            CO.countryName,
```

```
            COUNT(*) as countCities
        FROM cities CI JOIN countries CO
        CN CI.countryCode=CO.countryCode
        GROUP BY 1
        CRDER BY 3 DESC
        LIMIT 10`;

        const rows = await dbConn.query(myQuery);
        rows.forEach(r =>
            console.log(r.countryCode, r.countryName, r.countCities)
        );
    } catch (e) {
        console.log("Unexpected error", e);
    }
}

// continues...
```

Updating the database

Finally, let's do some updates. We will first add a new (invented!) country; we will then check whether it exists; we will update it and check the changes, then we will proceed to delete it, and finally we'll verify that it's gone:

```
// ...continued

async function addSeekAndDeleteCountry(dbConn) {
    try {
        const code = "42";
        const name = "DOUGLASADAMSLAND";

        /*
            1. Add the new country via a prepared insert statement
        */
        const prepInsert = dbConn.prepare(
            "INSERT INTO countries (countryCode, countryName) VALUES
(:code, :name)"
        );
        const preppedInsert = prepInsert({ code, name });
        await dbConn.query(preppedInsert);

        /*
            2. Seek the recently added country, return an array of objects
        */
        const getAdams = `SELECT * FROM countries WHERE
countryCode="${code}"`;
        const adams = await dbConn.query(getAdams);
```

```
console.log(
    adams.length,
    adams[0].countryCode,
    adams[0].countryName
);

/*
    3. Update the country, but using placeholders
*/
await dbConn.query(
    `UPDATE countries SET countryName=? WHERE countryCode=?`,
    ["NEW NAME", code]
);

/*
    4. Check the new data, but returning an array of arrays instead
*/
const adams2 = await dbConn.query(
    `SELECT * FROM countries WHERE countryCode=?`,
    [code],
    { useArray: true }
);
console.log(adams2.length, adams2[0][0], adams2[0][1]);

/*
    5. Drop the new country
*/
await dbConn.query(`DELETE FROM countries WHERE countryCode="42"`);

/*
    6. Verify that the country is no more
*/
const adams3 = await dbConn.query(getAdams);
console.log(adams3.length);
} catch (e) {
    console.log("Unexpected error", e);
}
}

// continues...
```

Getting everything together

All we have to do now, to get a complete working example, is just call the three functions:

```
// ...continued

tryDbAccess(dbConn);
get10CountriesWithMoreCities(dbConn);
addSeekAndDeleteCountry(dbConn);
```

Finally, I added a script to automate running all tests, by doing `npm run start-db`:

```
"scripts": {
    "build": "flow-remove-types src/ -d out/",
    "buildWithMaps": "flow-remove-types src/ -d out/ --pretty --
sourcemaps",
    "start": "npm run build && node out/doroundmath.js",
    "start-db": "npm run build && node out/dbaccess.js",
    .
    .
    .
},
```

Let's analyze how the code works, and remark on some interesting points.

How it works...

Running `tryDbAccess()` isn't hard to figure out: the constant query goes to the server, and an array with a single row comes back. The output of our code would have been as follows:

```
Year was 1960
```

The second query gets more interesting. Apart from the details of actually writing the SQL query (which is beyond the objectives of this book) the interesting point is the returned array, each with an object with the selected fields:

```
IN India 1301
BR Brazil 1203
RU Russian Federation 1090
DE Germany 1061
CN China 810
FR France 633
ES Spain 616
JP Japan 605
IT Italy 575
MX Mexico 556
```

Now, let's get to the last example. We are seeing several ways of creating the statement that will be executed.

The `INSERT` uses a prepared statement. A good way to prepare safe queries (meaning, they cannot be involved in SQL injection hacks) is by using prepared strings. The `.prepare()` method is interesting: given a string, it returns a function, that when called with the actual parameters to use, will itself return the string to use in the query. Of course, you can also build the function by hand, as I did in the other examples—but then it's up to you to make sure that the resulting query is safe!

> The `.escape()` method can help building a safe query string, if you don't want to use `.prepare()`. See more at `https://github.com/mscdex/node-mariasql`.

The subsequent `SELECT` uses a string created by hand (nothing too original here) but the `UPDATE` shows another style: using `?` symbols as *placeholders*. In that case, you must also provide an array of values that will replace the placeholders; it's fundamental that the order of the values in the array matches the expected arguments.

Next, the second `SELECT` also uses placeholders, but adds a tweak: passing an object with the `useArray:true` option, the function performs a tad faster, because it doesn't create objects for each row, and simply returns arrays. This has a problem, however, because now you have to remember what each position of the array means.

The results of the code are as expected: first a single line, showing that a country was actually created, with the values we passed; then, the same record but with a changed name, and finally a zero showing that the country doesn't exist any more:

```
1 '42' 'DOUGLASADAMSLAND'
1 '42' 'NEW NAME'
0
```

There's more...

In this section, we have gone through several examples of accessing a database to perform varied operations on it, by means of a direct connection, working with tables and cursors. You could also consider using an **Object-Relational Mapping (ORM)** library, to work with objects instead: the best known possibility is probably `Sequelize` (at `http://docs.sequelizejs.com/`) but there are some more packages (such as `TinyORM`, `Objection.js`, or `CaminteJS`, just to mention some which are still in development, not abandoned).

Executing external processes with exec()

If you are implementing some service with Node, there may be occasions in which you require to do some heavy processing, and that, as we have mentioned before, is a *no-no* because you will block all users. If you need to do this kind of work, Node lets you offload the work to an external process, freeing itself and becoming available for continuing work. The external process will work on its own, in an asynchronous fashion, and when it is done, you will be able to process its results. There are several ways of doing this; let's go into them.

The first option to run a separate command is the child_process.exec() method. This will spawn a shell, and execute a given command in it. Whatever output is generated will be buffered, and when the command finishes execution, a callback function will be called with either the produced output, or an error.

Let's see an example of calling an external process, by accessing the filesystem.

How to do it...

An example, to get a directory listing of all JS files at a given path, could be as follows. (Yes, of course you could and should do this using fs.readDir(), but we want to show how to do it with a child process.)

As shown in the *Using Promises instead of error first callbacks* section earlier in this chapter, we will promisify() the call, to simplify coding:

```
// Source file: src/process_exec.js

const child_process = require("child_process");
const { promisify } = require("util");
child_process.exec = promisify(child_process.exec);

async function getDirectoryJs(path: ?string) {
    try {
        const cmd = "ls -ld -1 *.js";
        const stdout = await child_process.exec(cmd, { cwd: path });
        console.log("OUT", path || "");
        console.log(stdout);
    } catch (e) {
        console.log("ERR", e.stderr);
    }
}
```

How it works...

When we call the `.exec()` method, a separate shell is created, and the command runs in it. If the call is successful, the output will be returned; otherwise, an object with a `.stderr` property will be thrown as an exception. A possible couple of runs are as follows:

```
getDirectoryJs("/home/fkereki/MODERNJS/chapter03/flow-typed/npm");
OUT /home/fkereki/MODERNJS/chapter03/flow-typed/npm
-rw-r--r-- 1 fkereki users 4791 Apr 9 12:52 axios_v0.18.x.js
-rw-r--r-- 1 fkereki users 3006 Mar 28 14:51 babel-cli_vx.x.x.js
-rw-r--r-- 1 fkereki users 3904 Apr 9 12:52 babel-eslint_vx.x.x.js
-rw-r--r-- 1 fkereki users 2760 Apr 9 12:52 babel-preset-env_vx.x.x.js
-rw-r--r-- 1 fkereki users 888 Apr 9 12:52 babel-preset-flow_vx.x.x.js
-rw-r--r-- 1 fkereki users 518 Apr 9 12:52 eslint-config-
recommended_vx.x.x.js
-rw-r--r-- 1 fkereki users 14995 Apr 9 12:52 eslint-plugin-
flowtype_vx.x.x.js
-rw-r--r-- 1 fkereki users 73344 Apr 9 12:52 eslint_vx.x.x.js
-rw-r--r-- 1 fkereki users 1889 Mar 28 14:51 fetch_vx.x.x.js
-rw-r--r-- 1 fkereki users 188 Apr 9 12:52 flow-bin_v0.x.x.js
-rw-r--r-- 1 fkereki users 13290 Apr 9 12:52 flow-coverage-report_vx.x.x.js
-rw-r--r-- 1 fkereki users 1091 Apr 9 12:52 flow-remove-types_vx.x.x.js
-rw-r--r-- 1 fkereki users 5763 Apr 9 12:52 flow-typed_vx.x.x.js
-rw-r--r-- 1 fkereki users 1009 Apr 9 12:52 mariasql_vx.x.x.js
-rw-r--r-- 1 fkereki users 0 Mar 28 14:51 moment_v2.3.x.js
-rw-r--r-- 1 fkereki users 5880 Apr 9 12:52 nodemon_vx.x.x.js
-rw-r--r-- 1 fkereki users 4786 Apr 9 12:52 prettier_v1.x.x.js

getDirectoryJs("/boot");
ERR ls: cannot access '*.js': No such file or directory
```

The second parameter for `.exec()` provides an object with possible options. In our case, we are specifying the current working directory (`cwd`) for the command. Another interesting option can let you work with commands that produce lots of output. By default, the maximum buffered output will be 200K; if you need more, you'll have to add an object with the `maxBuffer` option set to a larger value; check `https://nodejs.org/api/child_process.html#child_process_child_process_exec_command_options_callback` for more on these and other options.

There's no limit to the complexity of the command that you can execute, but there's also a risk. Keep in mind the possibility of being hacked: if you are building up your command based on some input provided by an user, you could be on the end of a command injection attack. Imagine you wanted to build something such as `` `ls ${path}` `` and the user had provided `"/; rm -rf *"` as the `path`; what would happen?

There's more...

Using `.exec()` is very good for short commands, with little output. If you don't actually need the shell, you can do even better with `.execFile()`, which runs the desired command directly, without first creating a shell and then running the command in it. See `https://nodejs.org/api/child_process.html#child_process_child_process_execfile_file_args_options_callback` for more information on this.

Using spawn() to run a command, and communicating with it

Using `.exec()` is simple, but you are limited to small-sized outputs, and you cannot also get a partial answer: let's see more about this. Imagine you are preparing a large file to be sent to a client. If you were to read that file with `.exec()`, you wouldn't be able to start sending the file contents to a client until you had read all the file. However, if the file were too large, that would not only imply a delay, but also the possibility of a crash. Using `.spawn()` gives you an interesting addition: the possibility of using streams to communicate, in a bidirectional way, with the spawned process.

How to do it...

Using `.spawn()` is similar to `.exec()` in general terms. Let's now use a separate process to read a directory and send its results back. We will be passing the path we want to process using a stream, and we'll get the list of found files also through streaming.

To start, let's have the main code, which will spawn a process:

```
// Source file: src/process_spawn.js

const path = require("path");
const { spawn } = require("child_process");

const child = spawn("node", [path.resolve("out/process_spawn_dir.js")]);

child.stdin.write("/home/fkereki");

child.stdout.on("data", data => {
    console.log(String(data));
});
```

```
child.stdout.on("end", () => {
    child.kill();
});
```

To finish, we need the child process, which would be as follows:

```
// Source file: src/process_spawn.js

const fs = require("fs");

process.stdin.resume();

process.stdin.on("data", path => {
    // Received a path to process
    fs
        .readdirSync(path)
        .sort((a, b) => a.localeCompare(b, [], { sensitivity: "base" }))
        .filter(file => !file.startsWith("."))
        .forEach(file => process.stdout.write(file + "\n"));

    process.stdout.end();
});
```

How it works...

Spawned processes show yet another case of events. The process stays there, waiting, and the "data" event is fired whenever the process receives any data via the stdin input, as done through the child.stdin.write("/home/fkereki") line. Then, the process reads the directory, with fs.readdirSync(), a synchronous call you shouldn't use in normal Node code, but that is safe in a subprocess, because it won't block anything. The results of the call are sorted, filtered to avoid hidden files, and then lines are written to stdout.

In a similar fashion to the child process, the parent process listens to events coming from the child's stdout. Whenever data arrives ("data" events are fired) it is simply logged with console.log(). When the child signals that no more data will be coming, by performing process.stdout.end(), the "end" event is fired, and the parent recognizes it, and can do whatever it wants.

This way of spawning processes thus allows for bidirectional communication between the parent and child processes, which could be used in many different forms.

Using fork() to run Node commands

The Child_process.fork() method is a special case of .spawn(), which specifically only spawns new Node processes. The spawned child process has a communication channel built in that makes it even simpler to pass messages between the parent process and itself: you just use the .send() method to send a message, and listen to the "message" event on the other side. Let's see how to fork off a second process, and communicate with the first one.

How to do it...

Since the code of the previous section used .spawn() to launch a new Node instance and run some code, it's fairly obvious that we can quickly and simply adjust it to use .fork() instead. Also, we won't have to use stdin and stdout to communicate, opting for messaging instead.

First, let's start with the parent code. It would become the following; the key differences are the usage of .fork() instead of .spawn(), and the way that the file path is sent to the child process:

```
// Source file: src/process_fork.js

const path = require("path");
const { fork } = require("child_process");

const child = fork(path.resolve("out/process_fork_dir.js"));

child.send({ path: "/home/fkereki" });

child.on("message", data => {
    console.log(String(data));
});
```

Then, the child code would also show small variations, in the way messages are received, and data is sent to the parent:

```
// Source file: src/process_fork_dir.js

const fs = require("fs");

process.on("message", obj => {
    // Received a path to process
    fs
        .readdirSync(obj.path)
        .sort((a, b) => a.localeCompare(b, [], { sensitivity: "base" }))
        .filter(file => !file.startsWith("."))
        .forEach(file => process.send && process.send(file));
});
```

How it works...

Using `.fork()` implies that the child process is a `Node` process, so instead of expressly mentioning it, as we did in the previous section, we just have to pass the name of the JS file to be executed.

The second difference, as we mentioned, is that instead of using `stdin` and `stdout` for communication, we can `.send()` a message (in any direction, from parent to child or vice versa) and we listen to the `"message"` event instead of the `"data"` one.

If you analyze the highlighted differences in code, you'll realize that the differences are really minor, and for the special (but not uncommon) case of needing to run a separate `Node` process, `.fork()` is more appropriate, and possibly a tad simpler to use.

4
Implementing RESTful Services with Node

We will cover the following recipes:

- Developing a server with Express
- Adding middleware
- Getting request parameters
- Serving static files
- Adding routes
- Implementing secure connections
- Adding security safeguards with Helmet
- Implementing CORS
- Adding authentication with JWT
- Tying it all together – building a REST server

Introduction

In the last chapter, we looked at a set of important basic Node techniques. In this chapter, we will use them to set up a basic server with Express and build on that until we get to produce a RESTful server that's appropriate for a **Services Oriented Architecture** (**SOA**) setup.

Developing a server with Express

While you can work with plain vanilla `Node` and do everything, today `Express` is surely the most used `Node` framework, allowing you to easily develop servers by providing a whole bunch of basic functionality. First, let's install it and check it's working, and then move on to constructing services and more.

In this recipe, we'll start by doing the basic installation of `Express` so that we can use it in later sections for more advanced work.

 You can learn more about `Express` at `https://expressjs.com/`.

How to do it...

Let's install `Express` and make sure that it works. Installation is basically trivial because it's just another `npm` package, so you just need a simple command:

```
npm install express --save
```

 You can add a `--verbose` optional parameter to the `npm` command to get a more verbose output and be able to see that things are happening.

Next, let's redo our basic test server from the previous chapter, but using `Express`. And, yes, this is way overkill for such a simple feature, but we just want to check that we set everything up in the right fashion! Refer to the following code:

```
// Source file: src/hello_world.js

/* @flow */
"use strict";

const express = require("express");

const app = express();

app.get("/", (req, res) => res.send("Server alive, with Express!"));
```

```
app.listen(8080, () =>
    conscle.log(
        "Mini server (with Express) ready at http://localhost:8080/!"
    )
);
```

How it works...

Running this server is practically the same as with our very basic `Node` one:

```
> npm run build
> node out/hello_world.js
Mini server (with Express) ready at http://localhost:8080/!
```

We can do the same tests as earlier, and note the following:

- Accessing the / address gets back a `Server alive` message
- Other paths produce a 404 (Not Found) error:

```
> curl 127.0.0.1:8080
Server alive, with Express!
```

Trying to access other paths (or /, but not with `GET`) will return a `404` error and a HTML error screen:

The basic Express configuration shows an error screen for 404 (Not Found) errors

The key line is the `app.get("/", (req, res) => ...)` call. Basically, after having created the application object (`app`) you can specify a route (in this case, /), a HTTP method (such as `.get()`, `.post()`, `.put()`, and `.delete()`), and a whole lot more.

Go to `https://expressjs.com/en/4x/api.html#app.METHOD` for more on the available methods.

You can also use `.all()` as a catch-all for every possible method, and a function that will get called when the user hits that particular path. In our case, no matter what the request (`req`) is, the response (`res`) is constant, but obviously you'd want to do more for an actual service!

It goes without saying that you will surely have more than one route, and possibly process not only `GET` methods. You can certainly add many more routes and methods, and we'll get to more advanced routing in upcoming sections.

The other interesting line is `app.listen()`, which specifies what port to listen to, and a function that will be executed when the server starts up; in our case, it's just a log message.

Now that we have managed to get our server running, let's implement some other usual server functionality.

Adding middleware

`Express` bases all of its functionality on a key concept: *middleware*. If you work with plain vanilla Node, you have to write a single large *request handler* that will have to take care of all of the requests your server may receive. By using middleware, `Express` lets you break down this process into smaller pieces, in a more functional, pipeline-ish sort of way. If you need to check security, log requests, handle routing, and so on, all will be done by appropriately placed middleware functions.

First, let's understand how `Express` differs from `Node`, see how we can add some basic middleware of our own, and only then move on to apply the usual functions for common needs. Refer to the following diagram for more information:

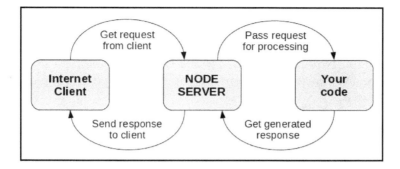

Standard processing, in absence of the Express middleware handling – your code must do all of the processing

In standard processing (see the preceding diagram), `Node` gets requests from internet clients, passes them to your code for processing, gets the generated response, and passes it along to the original client. Your code must handle everything in what amounts, basically, to a very large function, dealing with security, encryption, routing, errors, and so on. If you add `Express` to the mix, the process changes a bit:

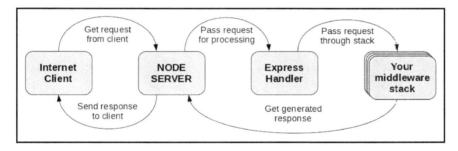

When Express is added, it handles requests by passing them to a middleware stack to produce the response

In this case, you set up a series of functions that will be called in order by `Express`, and each function will deal with a specific aspect of the overall process, simplifying the overall logic. Moreover, you won't have to directly deal with common problems (say, CORS or zipping, to mention just a few) because there are plenty of `Express` packages that already provide such functions; all you have to do is add them to the stack, at the appropriate place.

To get a better idea of how this works, in this recipe let's develop a very basic request logger (we'll learn about it in depth in the *Adding HTTP logging with Morgan* section of `Chapter 5`, *Testing and Debugging Your Server*) and an error reporter.

Getting ready

If you want to add some middleware, you have to place it in the correct order among all of the functions that you define. For example, if you want to log something, you'd probably want to do it before any processing is done, so you'd add that definition at the top of your stack, or very near to it.

Middleware functions receive three parameters: the incoming HTTP request (let's call it req, as we've been doing so far), the outgoing HTTP response (res), and a function that you must call when you want processing to continue with the next piece of middleware in the stack (next()). When your middleware gets called, it must either send a response (by using res.send(), res.sendFile(), or res.end()) or call next() so that the following functions in the stack will get the chance to produce the answer.

Error functions are a bit different, and they add an error (err) parameter to the three we just listed; having four parameters is what marks the function as an error processor in the eyes of Express. If everything works fine, Express skips the error middleware, but if an error occurs, Express will skip every function until it gets to the first available error function.

Let's jump to the end and view our complete middleware example, which will be as follows; we'll explain how it works in the next section:

```
// Source file: src/middleware.js

/* @flow */
"use strict";
const express = require("express");
const app = express();

app.use((req, res, next) => {
    console.log("Logger... ", new Date(), req.method, req.path);
    next();
});

app.use((req, res, next) => {
    if (req.method !== "DELETE") {
        res.send("Server alive, with Express!");
    } else {
        next(new Error("DELETEs are not accepted!"));
    }
});

// eslint-disable-next-line no-unused-vars
app.use((err, req, res, next) => {
```

```
        console.error("Error....", err.message);
        res.status(500).send("INTERNAL SERVER ERROR");
});

app.listen(8080, () =>
    console.log(
        "Mini server (with Express) ready at http://localhost:8080/!"
    )
);
```

How to do it...

Let's start with our logger. We want it to apply to every path so that we can just omit the path. An alternative would be writing `app.use("*", ...)`, which means exactly the same; we'll also use it as an example. Your logic could do anything, and since we want to log requests, we can just list the current timestamp, the `request` method, and the requested path. Afterwards—and this is the most important thing—since we haven't finished dealing with the request, calling `next()` is mandatory, or the request will end up in a processing limbo, never sending anything to the client:

```
app.use((req, res, next) => {
    console.log("Logger... ", new Date(), req.method, req.path);
    next();
});
```

Since we want to have some errors, let's define that the DELETE methods aren't to be accepted, so `next()` will be called, but passing an error object; other requests will just get a simple text answer. Our main request processing code could then be as follows:

```
app.use((req, res, next) => {
    if (req.method === "DELETE") {
        next(new Error("DELETEs are not accepted!"));
    } else {
        res.send("Server alive, with Express!");
    }
});
```

Finally, our error processing code will log the error, and send back a 500 status:

```
// eslint-disable-next-line no-unused-vars
app.use((err, req, res, next) => {
    console.error("Error....", err.message);
    res.status(500).send("INTERNAL SERVER ERROR");
});
```

You'll note the need for disabling the `no-unused-vars` ESLint rule. Recognizing errors just by the function signature is not a very good practice, and if you are setting your error handler at the end of the stack so that there's no other function to call, the next parameter will be unused and cause an error. There is some talk of solving this situation in upcoming versions of `Express`, but for now the point is moot.

> The error code we just showed, basic as it is, could be used in practically every Node server you write. We will be using it as is in our examples.

How it works...

We've set everything up; now, let's see our code working:

```
> npm run build
> node out/middleware.js
```

We can use some curl requests to test this; let's use GET, POST, and DELETE:

```
> curl "http://127.0.0.1:8080/some/path/to/get?value=9"
Server alive, with Express!
> curl -X POST "http://127.0.0.1:8080/a/post/to/a/path"
Server alive, with Express!
> curl -X DELETE "http://127.0.0.1:8080/try/to/delete?key=22"
INTERNAL SERVER ERROR
```

The logged output will be as follows:

```
Logger...  2018-05-08T00:22:20.192Z GET /some/path/to/get
Logger...  2018-05-08T00:22:44.282Z POST /a/post/to/a/path
Logger...  2018-05-08T00:23:01.888Z DELETE /try/to/delete
Error....  DELETEs are not accepted!
```

Now, we now know how to write our own middleware, but it so happens that `Express` provides lots of ready-made functions. Let's give them a whirl and look at how we can use them for several common needs.

Getting request parameters

Let's get to a basic problem: how do you get the request parameters? In our earlier example, in the *Working with streams to process requests* section of the previous chapter, we did it by hand, working with the request stream to get the body, and using parsing functions to extract the parameters. However, `Express` already provides some middleware you can use before any other function in your stack that needs parameters, either from the body or the URL itself. So in this recipe, let's see how we can access the request parameters, which is a very basic need.

How to do it...

Let's see what it takes to access the parameters. First, you have to require the `body-parser` module and ask for the options you want; we'll get into that next:

```
// Source file: src/get_parameters.js

const bodyParser = require("body-parser");
app.use(bodyParser.urlencoded({ extended: false }));
```

Since you want the parameters to be parsed before any processing, the `app.use()` line will be at the top of your stack.

Now, getting into more detail, the `body-parser` module provides four parsers:

- *A URL-encoded body parser*, just like we're using here, to read about the differences in using `extended` true or false. Checkout `https://github.com/expressjs/body-parser` for more information.
- *A JSON body parser*, as in `bodyParser.json()`, to process requests with `Content-Type` is done through `application/json`.
- *A raw body parser*, as with `bodyParser.raw()`, to process `application/octet-stream` contents by default, though this can be changed by providing a `type` option.
- *A text body parser*, like `bodyParser.text()`, to process `text/plain` content.

The three latter parsers may provide extra options; check the documentation for more on that. Note, however, that if you have to deal with multipart bodies, then you cannot rely on a body-parser; see `https://github.com/expressjs/body-parser` for some alternatives, and see what suits you.

How it works...

We only had to add a couple of lines, and everything was set up. We can see our code working by either changing our logger from the previous section, or by writing code like this:

```
// Source file: src/get_parameters.js

app.use("*", (req, res) => {
    console.log(req.query, req.body);
    res.send("Server alive, with Express!");
});
```

URL parameters are automatically separated by Express into req.query, and req.body will be parsed by bodyParser. We can try a couple of service calls, a GET and a POST, to cover all cases:

```
> curl "http://127.0.0.1:8080/birthdays?day=22&month=9&year=1960"
> curl -X POST --data "name=FK" "http://127.0.0.1:8080/persons"
```

The output will be as follows:

```
> node out/get_parameters.js
Mini server (with Express) ready at http://localhost:8080/!
{ day: '22', month: '9', year: '1960' } {}
{} { name: 'FK' }
```

In the first case (GET), we can see that req.query is an object with the three query parameters, while in the second case (POST) there are no query parameters, but the req.body provides the single parameter (name) we provided.

This should convince you of the merits of Express' design, based on a middleware stack, but let's go through some more examples, such as working with static files, routing, security, and more.

Serving static files

We are planning to create a set of REST services, but it's very possible that your server will also have to serve some static files, such as images, PDFs, and so on. On principle, you could do this by hand by setting specific routes for each static asset, and then writing a function that would read the required file and stream its contents to the client; we did something like that in the *Working with streams to process requests* section in the previous chapter.

However, this is such a common and reiterative task that `Express` provides a simpler solution; let's look at how we can simply serve static files.

An even better solution would be to have another server, such as nginx, in your stack and have it handle static files. Standard servers are much better at handling this type of simple request, and will leave your Node code free to handle more complex, demanding tasks.

How to do it...

Let's suppose we want to have some flag icons served for an application. I did the following:

1. I created, at the same level as the /out directory into which the output files go, a /flags directory with some subdirectories: /flags/america/north, /flags/america/south, and /flags/europe.

2. I placed some free flag icons by *GoSquared*, taken from https://www.gosquared.com/resources/flag-icons/ in those directories. For variety, the flags are accessible at the /static path, which doesn't actually exist.

3. I wrote the following code; this is the basic server from earlier, with just some added code (in bold font) to deal with static files:

```
// Source file: src/serve_statics.js

/* @flow */
"use strict";

const express = require("express");
const path = require("path");
const app = express();

app.get("/", (req, res) => res.send("Server alive, with
Express!"));

app.use(
    "/static",
    express.static(path.join(__dirname, "../flags"), {
        immutable: true,
        maxAge: "30 days"
    })
);
```

```
app.use((err, req, res, next) => {
    console.error("Error....", err.message);
    res.status(500).send("INTERNAL SERVER ERROR");
});

app.listen(8080, () =>
    console.log(
        "Mini Express static server ready at
http://localhost:8080/!"
    )
);
```

 If you want to read more about serving static files, check out Node's documentation at `https://expressjs.com/en/starter/static-files.html`.

`app.use()`, in this case, gets a special function, `express.static()`, which takes care of sending files in the given path, with some headers for caching; let's get into the details:

- The first parameter to `app.use()` is the base of the path that the user will select; note that it doesn't need to exist in the actual directory, as in other examples we have seen. We could write `app.use()` if we want to accept all HTTP methods, by the way.
- The first parameter to `express.static()` specifies the path where the files are found. I'm using the `path.join()` function to find out the actual path: `/flags` at the same level as `/out`.
- The second parameter to `express.static()` lets you add options; in our case, I'm sending some caching headers so that browsers will know that the file can be safely cached for 30 days.

 The format for the `maxAge` parameter can be in a format understood by the `ms` package (`https://github.com/zeit/ms`), which is able to convert date and time strings into the equivalent milliseconds, which is standard for JS.

How it works...

Whenever the user specifies a path starting with /static, it is converted into the equivalent starting from /flags, and if the file is found, it will be sent back, with the caching headers included. Check out the following screenshot for an example of this:

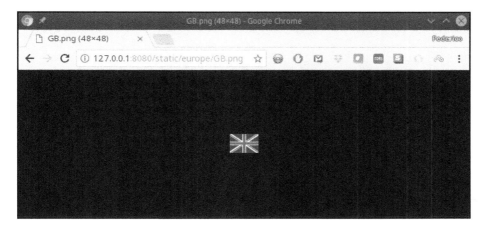

A static flag icon, served from a non-existing path, /static, mapped to an actual path

There's more...

If you want to send static files for some specific reason, without using the method shown in the preceding section, you can use routing and the res.sendFile() method, as shown in the following code:

```
// Source file: src/serve_statics_alt.js

/* @flow */
"use strict";

const express = require("express");
const app = express();
const path = require("path");

const flagsPath = path.join(__dirname, "../flags");

app.get("/uruguay", (req, res) =>
    res.sendFile(`${flagsPath}/america/south/UY.png`)
);
```

```
app.get("/england", (req, res) =>
    res.sendFile(`${flagsPath}/europe/GB.png`)
);

app.get("/license", (req, res) =>
    res.sendFile(`${flagsPath}/license.txt`)
);

app.use((err, req, res, next) => {
    console.error("Error....", err.message);
    res.status(500).send("INTERNAL SERVER ERROR");
});

app.listen(8080, () =>
    console.log(
        "Mini Express static server ready at http://localhost:8080/!"
    )
);
```

If you access `http://127.0.0.1:8080/uruguay`, you'll get my home country's flag, and `http://127.0.0.1:8080/license` will retrieve the MIT license for the icon set I chose; see the latter in the following screenshot:

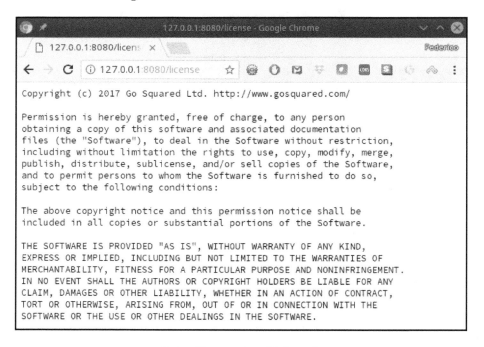

Testing a different route that sends back a text file

Of course, you wouldn't use this method if you had lots of static files to provide, but if you have only a few, then this alternative solution works very well.

You may have noticed that I didn't add headers for caching, but it can certainly be done. Read more on `res.sendFile()` at https://expressjs.com/en/api.html#res.sendFile, in particular the `immutable` and `headers` options.

Adding routes

No matter what kind of server you are building (a RESTful one, as we plan to do, or any other kind), you'll have to deal with routing, and `Node` and `Express` together provide easy ways of doing this.

Going back to our database from the *Working with a database* section in the previous chapter, in a RESTful fashion, we should provide the following routes, allowing for the given methods:

- `/countries` (`GET` to obtain the list of all countries, and `POST` to create a new country)
- `/countries/someCountryId` (`GET` to access a country, `PUT` to update one, and `DELETE` to delete one)
- `/regions` (`GET` to get all regions of all countries, `POST` to create a new region)
- `/regions/someCountryId` (`GET` to get all regions of a given country)
- `/regions/someCountryId/someRegionId` (`GET` to access a region, `PUT` to update one, `DELETE` to delete one)
- `/cities` (`GET` to get all cities – but we won't really want to allow this because of the resulting set size!—plus `POST` to create a new one)
- `/cities/someCityId` (`GET` to access a city, `PUT` to update one, and `DELETE` to delete a city)

You could also allow for extra parameters, for example, to allow paging a result set, or to enable some filtering, but what we care about now is setting up the routes. You could set up all of the necessary routes in the main file, as we have been doing in our short examples so far, but as you start adding more and more routes, some organization is needed to avoid ending up with a thousands-of-lines-long main file.

How to do it...

Thanks to Express, we won't need too much code, with only two new lines to enable our routing; check out the following code:

```
// Source file: src/routing.js

/* @flow */
"use strict";

const express = require("express");
const app = express();

const myRouter = require("./router_home.js");
app.use("/", myRouter);

// eslint-disable-next-line no-unused-vars
app.use((err, req, res, next) => {
    console.error("Error....", err.message);
    res.status(500).send("INTERNAL SERVER ERROR");
});

app.listen(8080, () =>
    console.log("Routing ready at http://localhost:8080")
);
```

The router_home.js module could have the first level of route branching, as shown in the following code:

```
// Source file: src/router_home.js

/* @flow */
"use strict";

const express = require("express");
const routerHome = express.Router();

const routerCountries = require("./router_countries.js");
const routerRegions = require("./router_regions.js");
const routerCities = require("./router_cities.js");

routerHome.use("/countries", routerCountries);
routerHome.use("/regions", routerRegions);
routerHome.use("/cities", routerCities);

module.exports = routerHome;
```

And, going down one more level, we'd have three more files specifying the next levels. For example, routing for countries would be as follows. You'll note a weird extra route, /URUGUAY, which I added just to show you that we can have more routes than a RESTful server would require!

```
// Source file: src/router_countries.js

/* @flow */
"use strict";

const express = require("express");
const routerCountries = express.Router();

routerCountries.get("/", (req, res) => {
    res.send(`All countries... path=${req.originalUrl}`);
});

routerCountries.get("/URUGUAY", (req, res) => {
    res.send(`GET UY (Uruguay)... path=${req.originalUrl}`);
});

routerCountries.get("/:country", (req, res) => {
    res.send(`GET Single country... ${req.params.country}`);
});

module.exports = routerCountries;
```

The regions routing file will be as shown in the following code, and we'll skip the cities routing since it's quite similar to countries routing:

```
// Source file: src/router_regions.src

/* @flow */
"use strict";

const express = require("express");
const routerRegions = express.Router();

routerRegions.get("/", (req, res) => {
    res.send(`Region GET ALL... `);
});

routerRegions.get("/:country", (req, res) => {
    res.send(`Region GET ALL FOR Country=${req.params.country}`);
});

routerRegions.get("/:country/:id", (req, res) => {
```

```
        res.send(`Region GET ${req.params.country}/${req.params.id}`);
});

routerRegions.delete("/:country/:id", (req, res) => {
        res.send(`Region DELETE... ${req.params.country}/${req.params.id}`);
});

routerRegions.post("/", (req, res) => {
        res.send(`Region POST... `);
});

routerRegions.put("/:country/:id", (req, res) => {
        res.send(`Region PUT... ${req.params.country}/${req.params.id}`);
});

module.exports = routerRegions;
```

 You can read more about Express routing at https://expressjs.com/
en/starter/basic-routing.html and https://expressjs.com/en/
guide/routing.html.

How it works...

Of course, our so-called *RESTful server* is, at least for now, a total joke, since it just returns
constant answers, doing nothing at all, but the key parts are practically all here. First, let's
analyze its structure. When you write app.use(somePath, aRouter), it means that all of
the routes starting with the given path will be taken up by the provided router, which will
take care of the routes from the given path onward. First, we write a basic router starting at
/, and then break down the routes by path (/countries, /regions, and /cities),
writing a router for each one. These latter routers will go deeper in the paths, until all of
your routes are mapped out.

To make it clear: when the server receives a request for, say, /regions/uy, the request is
first handled by our main router (at routing.js), which passes it to the home router
(router_home.js), which passes it to the final router (router_regions.js), where the
request is eventually handled.

Now, let's move on to the routes by themselves. There are two kind of routes here: *constant* routes such as `/countries` and *variable* routes such as `/regions/uy/4`, which include some varying items, such as `uy` and `4`, in this case. When you write a route such as `/regions/:country/:id`, Express will pick out the varying parts (here, `:country` and `:id`) and make them available as properties of the `req.params` object (`req.params.country` and `req.params.id`) so that you can use them in your logic.

> You can also use regular expressions to define a path, but remember the joke: a programmer has a problem; a programmer decides to solve it using regular expressions; a programmer now has *two* problems.

So, if we implement some requests on the preceding path, we'll see the functioning router; all we will be lacking is the actual RESTful code to produce some useful results, but we'll get to that later in this chapter:

```
> curl "http://127.0.0.1:8080/regions"
Region GET ALL..

> curl "http://127.0.0.1:8080/regions/uy"
Region GET ALL FOR Country=uy

> curl -X POST "http://127.0.0.1:8080/regions"
Region POST...

> curl -X PUT "http://127.0.0.1:8080/regions/uy/4"
Region PUT... uy/4
```

Of course, trying some methods that aren't allowed will produce an error; try doing a `DELETE` request for `/regions` and you'll see what I mean. We now know how to do any kind of routing, but we still must be able to receive JSON objects, allow for CORS if needed, and some other considerations, so let's keep working and start by enabling secure connections with HTTPS.

Implementing secure connections

Sending data over HTTPS instead of HTTP is a good security practice, and actually mandatory if your server ever has to send sensitive, secure data over the web. There are many kinds of attacks that are avoided by setting up an encrypted connection with the client browser, so let's see how we can implement secure connections with `Node` and `Express`.

In this recipe, we will cover how to enable HTTPS so that our server becomes more secure.

How to do it...

We want to enable HTTPS connections, so we'll have to do a bit of work to install everything we need.

The first step in this installation will be getting yourself a certificate that properly validates the site that you own. Buying it goes beyond this book, so let's do a workaround by generating our own self-signed certificates—which, of course, aren't really secure, but will let us do all of the required configuration!

Let's assume that we want to set up our www.modernjsbook.com site. Working in Linux, you can create the necessary certificate files by executing the following commands and answering some questions:

```
openssl req -newkey rsa:4096 -nodes -keyout modernjsbook.key -out
modernjsbook.csr
openssl x509 -signkey modernjsbook.key -in modernjsbook.csr -req -days 366
-out modernjsbook.crt
```

After doing this, you will end up with three files: a **Certificate Signing Request (CSR)**, a KEY (Private Key), and a self-signed certificate (CRT) file, as follows; in real life, a **Certificate Authority (CA)** would be the actual signer:

```
> dir
-rw-r--r-- 1 fkereki users 1801 May 14 22:32 modernjsbook.crt
-rw-r--r-- 1 fkereki users 1651 May 14 22:31 modernjsbook.csr
-rw------- 1 fkereki users 3272 May 14 22:31 modernjsbook.key
```

Now, when you set up your server, you must read in those files (which should reside in a safe, read-only directory for added security) and pass their contents as options. We will use the `fs` module to do this, as in previous examples, and since reading the files is done only when the server is loaded, `fs.readFileSync()` can be used. Take look at the following code:

```
// Source file: src/https_server.js

/* @flow */
"use strict";

const express = require("express");
const app = express();
const https = require("https");
```

```
const fs = require("fs");
const path = require("path");

const keysPath = path.join(__dirname, "../../certificates");

const ca = fs.readFileSync(`${keysPath}/modernjsbook.csr`);
const cert = fs.readFileSync(`${keysPath}/modernjsbook.crt`);
const key = fs.readFileSync(`${keysPath}/modernjsbook.key`);

https.createServer({ ca, cert, key }, app).listen(8443);
```

 Why port 8443? The reason has to do with security, and we saw why in the *Checking Node's setup* section of the previous chapter; it's the same motive that we had behind using port 8080 instead of port 80.

How it works...

Running the preceding code is enough to get encrypted connections to your server. (Of course, if you use self-signed certificates, the end user will get warnings about the lack of actual security, but you would get valid certificates, wouldn't you?) We can see the result of this in the following screenshot—and keep in mind that with real certificates, the user would get no alerts about your unsafe site!

Installing certificates and using HTTPS instead of HTTP generates a secure server.
Of course, since we made up the certificate by ourselves, Google Chrome doesn't really like the site!

We can also force HTTP users to work with HTTPS by running a *second* server, this time with HTTP, and redirecting all traffic to our first server, which is secure:

```
// Source file: src/http_server.js

/* @flow */
"use strict";

const express = require("express");
const app = express();
const http = require("http");

http.createServer(app).listen(8080);

app.use((req, res, next) => {
    if (req.secure) {
        next();
    } else {
        res.redirect(
            `https://${req.headers.host.replace(/8080/, "8443")}${req.url}`
        );
    }
});
```

A `Node` server can only listen to a single port, so you'd run this server as a separate instance. Now, if you try to use HTTP to access your server, you'll be redirected automatically, a good practice!

Adding secure connections is simple; let's keep on working on more security aspects.

Adding security safeguards with Helmet

Out of the box, `Express` is a very good tool for building your RESTful server, or to provide any other kind of service. However, unless you take some extra precautions, Express doesn't apply all security best practices, which may doom your server. Not everything is lost, in any case, because there are some packages that can help you with those practices, and `Helmet` (at `https://helmetjs.github.io/`) is one of the best for this.

Don't think of `Helmet`—or any other similar package, by the way—as a magic silver bullet that will somehow solve all of your possible present and future security headaches! Use it as a step in the right direction, but you must keep on top of possible menaces and security holes, and not trust any single package to manage everything.

How to do it...

Given that it works with `Express`, `Helmet` is also a piece of middleware. Its installation and setup are rather easy, fortunately. Using `npm` takes care of the first part:

```
npm install helmet --save
```

Putting `Helmet` to work is just a matter of adding it at the top of the middleware stack:

```
const helmet = require("helmet");
app.use(helmet());
```

You're all set! By default, `Helmet` enables the following list of security measures, all of which imply adding, changing, or removing specific headers from your response to a request. For more documentation on specific headers or options, check out `https://helmetjs.github.io/docs/`:

Module	Effect
dnsPrefetchControl	Sets the `X-DNS-Prefetch-Control` header to the disable browsers prefetching (requests done before the user has even clicked on a link) to prevent privacy implications for users, who may seem to be visiting pages they actually aren't visiting (`https://helmetjs.github.io/docs/dns-prefetch-control`).
frameguard	Sets the `X-Frame-Options` header to prevent your page from being shown in an iframe, and thus avoids some *clickjacking* attacks that may cause you to unwittingly click on hidden links (`https://helmetjs.github.io/docs/frameguard/`).
hidePoweredBy	Removes the `X-Powered-By` header, if present, so that would-be attackers won't know what technology powers the server, making targeting and taking advantage of vulnerabilities a bit harder (`https://helmetjs.github.io/docs/hide-powered-by`)
hsts	Sets the `Strict-Transport-Security` header so that browsers will keep using HTTPS instead of switching to the insecure HTTP. (`https://helmetjs.github.io/docs/hsts/`)
ieNoOpen	Sets the `X-Download-Options` header to prevent old versions of Internet Explorer from downloading untrusted HTML in your pages (`https://helmetjs.github.io/docs/ienoopen`).
noSniff	Sets the `X-Content-Type-Options` header to prevent browsers from trying to *sniff* (guess) the MIME type of a downloaded file, to disable some attacks (`https://helmetjs.github.io/docs/dont-sniff-mimetype`).
xssFilter	Sets the `X-XSS-Protection` header to disable some forms of **Cross-side scripting** (**XSS**) attacks, in which you could unwittingly run JS code on your page by clicking a link (`https://helmetjs.github.io/docs/xss-filter`).

You can also opt to enable some extra options, if they apply to your requirements. For notes on how to do this, check out Helmet's documentation at `https://helmetjs.github.io/docs/`: the package, now at version 3.12.0, is often updated, and a plain `npm install` may not be enough to enable the newer features. Take a look at the following table:

Module	Effect
`contentSecurityPolicy`	Lets you configure the `Content-Security-Policy` header to specify what things are allowed to be on your page, and where they may be downloaded from (`https://helmetjs.github.io/docs/xss-filter`).
`expectCt`	Allows you to set the `Expect-CT` header to require **Certificate Transparency** (**CT**), to detect possibly invalid certificates or authorities (`https://helmetjs.github.io/docs/expect-ct/`).
`hpkp`	Lets you configure the `Public-Key-Pins` header to prevent some possible *person-in-the-middle attacks*, by detecting possibly compromised certificates (`https://helmetjs.github.io/docs/hpkp/`).
`noCache`	Sets several headers to prevent users from using old cached versions of files, which might have vulnerabilities or errors, despite newer versions being available (`https://helmetjs.github.io/docs/nocache/`).
`referrerPolicy`	Lets you set the `Referrer-Policy` header to make browsers hide information as to the origin of a request, avoiding some possible privacy problems (`https://helmetjs.github.io/docs/referrer-policy`).

How it works...

There is not much more to be said about using `Helmet`. After you add it to the middleware stack, and configure what to enable or disable, possibly giving some options as detailed in the documentation, `Helmet` will simply verify that the headers included in any response follow the security considerations that we listed in the preceding section.

Let's do a quick check. If you run our `hello_world.js` server, the response for `http://localhost:8080/` will include these headers:

```
Connection: keep-alive
Content-Length: 27
Content-Type: text/html; charset=utf-8
Date: Wed, 16 May 2018 01:57:10 GMT
ETag: W/"1b-bpQ4Q2jOe/d4pXTjItXGP42U4V0"
X-Powered-By: Express
```

The same results, but running `helmet_world.js`, which is essentially the same code but adding `Helmet`, shows more headers, as shown in the following code snippet in bold text:

```
Connection: keep-alive
Content-Length: 27
Content-Type: text/html; charset=utf-8
Date: Wed, 16 May 2018 01:58:50 GMT
ETag: W/"1b-bpQ4Q2jOe/d4pXTjItXGP42U4V0"
Strict-Transport-Security: max-age=15552000; includeSubDomains
X-Content-Type-Options: nosniff
X-DNS-Prefetch-Control: off
X-Download-Options: noopen
X-Frame-Options: SAMEORIGIN
X-XSS-Protection: 1; mode=block
```

You would get even more headers if you were to individually enable some of the optional features, but the difference is clear: we managed to add some security controls with essentially almost zero coding!

 As with all security measures, it's necessary to follow Helmet's functionality so that you can possibly add or remove some new middleware options, and protect your server against new menaces.

Implementing CORS

Whenever the browser requests some resource from a server, there are some validation rules that apply. For many of these interactions, which only ask for information and do not attempt to produce any kind of change in the server, there is no limitation, and the requests are always allowed, as in the following cases:

- *CSS styles* are required via a `<link rel="stylesheet">` tag
- *Images* are required via an `<img>` tag
- *JS code* is required via a `<script>` tag
- *Media* requests via the `<audio>` or `<media>` tags

For other types of requests, the **Same Origin Policy** or **Single Origin Policy** (**SOP**) limits requests to those that are sent to the same origin (meaning the protocol, as in `http://`, host name, as in `modernjsbook.com`, and port, as in `:8080`), refusing any other request that doesn't match one or more of the origin URL elements. This impacts, for example, all Ajax requests, which will be duly rejected.

However, if you are willing to accept requests from some or all servers, you can apply **Cross Origin Resource Sharing** (**CORS**) to enable such requests. Basically, CORS defines an interaction style that lets the server decide whether to allow a cross origin request; instead of blocking every request (as SOP would imply) or allowing all of them (a huge security breach!), rules can be applied to decide one way or the other.

 If you want to read the current specification for CORS, see the Fetch Living Standard document at `https://fetch.spec.whatwg.org/`, specifically Section 3.2. A good article about CORS can be found at `https://developer.mozilla.org/en-US/docs/Web/HTTP/CORS`.

How to do it...

Let's start enabling CORS. Basically, it is just a matter of dealing with some requests by examining some data in their headers and sending back some other headers to the browser so that it will know what to expect. This type of process is very easily solved by applying middleware, and a package for this already exists (`cors`), which can be installed easily with the help of the following code:

```
npm install cors --save
```

You can enable CORS for all routes or only a few. The first way only requires two lines of code (in bold, in the following code), telling `Express` to apply the middleware right at the top, for all requests:

```
// Source file: src/cors_server.js

/* @flow */
"use strict";

const express = require("express");
const app = express();

const cors = require("cors");
app.use(cors());

app.get("/", (req, res) => res.send("Server alive, with CORS!"));
```

```
app.listen(8080, () =>
    console.log("CORS server ready at http://localhost:8080/!")
);
```

You could also enable it specifically for any given route. Picking one example from earlier in this chapter, you could have specified CORS for attempts to get a city; the change would have been minimal:

```
routerCities.get("/:id", cors(), (req, res) => {
    res.send(`GET City... ${req.params.id}`);
});
```

Finally, some requests require a *pre-flight* check, which means that the browser, before sending the actual request, will send an OPTIONS request to verify whether the original request can be accepted. To enable this, you should enable CORS for whatever route, as in the following example, or generically, with a single app.options('*', cors()) line at the beginning of your middleware stack:

```
routerCities.options("/:id", cors());

routerCities.delete("/:id", (req, res) => {
    res.send(`DELETE City... ${req.params.id}`);
});
```

How it works...

The simplest way to verify that CORS is enabled is by simulating calls from different sources using curl or a similar tool. (We'll be seeing more of this in the following chapter, when we get to do some testing.) We can make it even simpler by writing up a small web page that will do a cross-domain GET, adding a dummy header to force CORS, and checking the network traffic. Our page is simplicity itself—totally *no frills*!

```
// Source file: src/cors_request.html

<html>
<head></head>
<body>
    <script type="text/javascript">
        const req = new XMLHttpRequest();
        req.open('GET', 'http://www.corsserver.com:8080/', true);
        req.onreadystatechange = () => {
            if (req.readyState === 4) {
                if (req.status >= 200 && req.status < 400) {
                    console.log(req.responseText)
                } else {
```

```
                          console.warn("Problems!")
                      }
                  }
              };
              req.setRequestHeader("dummy", "value");
              req.send();
          </script>
      </body>
      </html>
```

We will be running our CORS server at `www.corsserver.com:8080` (I'm actually hacking the `/etc/hosts` file on my own machine so that the server is actually in my machine itself), and we'll use the Web Server for Chrome to load and run our page. Check out the following screenshot for the results of doing this:

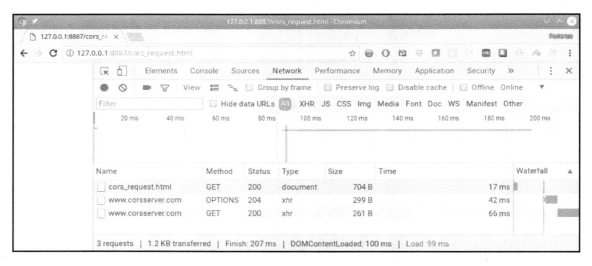

Performing a simple cross domain GET shows that our server got an OPTIONS request, followed by the GET request afterwards

Using CORS is safer than other alternatives, including the old stalwart JSONP (*JSON with Padding,* a way to enable getting information across domains), so adding it to your server should be mandatory. However, as we've seen, it's simplicity itself with just a tad of Express middleware.

Adding authentication with JWT

For any server-based application, one challenge that must be solved is authentication, and our RESTful server therefore will need a solution for that. In traditional web pages, sessions and cookies may be used, but if you are using an API, there's no guarantee that requests will come from a browser; in fact, they may very well come from another server. Adding this to the fact that HTTP is stateless, and that RESTful services are also supposed to be so, we need another mechanism, and **JSON Web Tokens** (**JWT**) is an often used solution.

 JWT is sometimes read aloud as *JOT*; see Section 1 of the RFC at `https://www.rfc-editor.org/info/rfc7519`.

The idea with JWT is that the client will first exchange valid credentials (such as username and password) with a server and get back a token, which will afterwards give them access to the server's resources. Tokens are created using cryptological methods, and are far longer and more obscure than usual passwords. However, tokens are small enough to be sent as body parameters or a HTTP header.

 Sending the token in the URL as a query parameter is a bad security practice! And, given that the token isn't actually a part of a request, putting it in the body also doesn't fit very well, so opt for a header; the recommended one is `Authorization: Bearer`.

After getting the token, it must be supplied with every API call, and the server will check it before proceeding. The token may include all information about the user so that the server won't have to query a database again to re-validate the request. In that sense, a token works like the security passes you are given at the front desk of a restricted building; you have to prove your identity once to the security officer, but afterwards you can move through the building by only showing the pass (which will be recognized and accepted) instead of having to go through the whole identification procedure again and again.

 Check out `https://jwt.io/` for online tools that allow you to work with JWT, and also lots of information about tokens.

We won't be getting into the details of a JWT's creation, format, and so on; read the documentation if you are interested, because we will be working with libraries that will handle all such details for us. (We may just keep in mind that the token includes a *payload* with some *claims* related to the client or the token itself, like an expiration or issue date, and may include more information if we need to—but don't include secret data, because the token can be read.)

In this recipe, let's create a basic server that will be able to first issue a JWT to a valid user, and second check the presence of the JWT for specific routes.

How to do it...

Let's look at how we can add authentication. To work with JWT, we'll be using jsonwebtoken from https://github.com/auth0/node-jsonwebtoken. Install it with the help of the following command:

```
npm install jsonwebtoken --save
```

Our code example for JWT will be larger than in previous examples, and it should be separated into many files. However, I avoided doing this in order to make it clearer. First, we'll need to make some declarations, and the key lines are in bold:

```
// Source file: src/jwt_server.js

/* @flow */
"use strict";

const express = require("express");
const app = express();
const jwt = require("jsonwebtoken");
const bodyParser = require("body-parser");

const validateUser = require("./validate_user.js");

const SECRET_JWT_KEY = "modernJSbook";

app.use(bodyParser.urlencoded({ extended: false }));
```

Almost everything is standard, except for the validateUser() function and the SECRET_JWT_KEY string. The latter will be used to sign the tokens, and most definitely shouldn't be in the code itself! (If somebody could hack their way into the source code, your secret would be out; rather, set the key in an environment variable, and get the value from there.)

As for the function, checking if a user exists and if their password is correct is simple to do, and can be achieved in many ways, such as by accessing a database, active directory, service, and so on. Here, we'll just make do with a hardcoded version, which accepts only a single user. The `validate_user.js` source code is, then, quite simple:

```
// Source file: src/validate_user.js

/* @flow */
"use strict";

/*
    In real life, validateUser could check a database,
    look into an Active Directory, call another service,
    etc. -- but for this demo, let's keep it quite
    simple and only accept a single, hardcoded user.
*/

const validateUser = (
    userName: string,
    password: string,
    callback: (?string, ?string) => void) => {
    if (!userName || !password) {
        callback("Missing user/password", null);
    } else if (userName === "fkereki" && password === "modernjsbook") {
        callback(null, "fkereki"); // OK, send userName back
    } else {
        callback("Not valid user", null);
    }
};

module.exports = validateUser;
```

Let's get back to our server. After the initial definitions, we can place the routes that need no tokens. Let's have a /public route, and also a /gettoken route to get a JWT for later. In the latter, we'll see whether the POST included user and password values in its body, and if they are a valid user by means of the validateUser() function we showed in the preceding code. Any problems will mean a 401 status will be sent, while if the user is correct, a token will be created, expiring in one hour's time:

```
// Source file: src/jwt_server.js

app.get("/public", (req, res) => {
    res.send("the /public endpoint needs no token!");
});

app.post("/gettoken", (req, res) => {
    validateUser(req.body.user, req.body.password, (idErr, userid) => {
```

```
        if (idErr !== null) {
            res.status(401).send(idErr);
        } else {
            jwt.sign(
                { userid },
                SECRET_JWT_KEY,
                { algorithm: "HS256", expiresIn: "1h" },
                (err, token) => res.status(200).send(token)
            );
        }
    });
});
```

Now that the unprotected routes are out of the way, let's add some middleware to verify that a token is present. We expect, according to the JWT RFC, to have an Authorization: Bearer somejwttoken header included, and it must be accepted. If no such header is present, or if it's not in the right format, a 401 status will be sent. If the token is present, but it's expired or has any other problem, a 403 status will be sent. Finally, if there's nothing wrong, the userid field will be extracted from the payload, and attached to the request object so that future code will be able to use it:

```javascript
// Source file: src/jwt_server.js

app.use((req, res, next) => {
    // First check for the Authorization header
    const authHeader = req.headers.authorization;
    if (!authHeader || !authHeader.startsWith("Bearer ")) {
        return res.status(401).send("No token specified");
    }

    // Now validate the token itself
    const token = authHeader.split(" ")[1];
    jwt.verify(token, SECRET_JWT_KEY, (err, decoded) => {
        if (err) {
            // Token bad formed, or expired, or other problem
            return res.status(403).send("Token expired or not valid");
        } else {
            // Token OK; get the user id from it
            req.userid = decoded.userid;
            // Keep processing the request
            next();
        }
    });
});
```

Now, let's have some protected routes (in fact, a single one, /private, just for this example), followed by error checking and setting up the whole server:

```
// Source file: src/jwt_server.js

app.get("/private", (req, res) => {
    res.send("the /private endpoint needs JWT, but it was provided: OK!");
});

// eslint-disable-next-line no-unused-vars
app.use((err, req, res, next) => {
    console.error("Error....", err.message);
    res.status(500).send("INTERNAL SERVER ERROR");
});

app.listen(8080, () =>
    console.log("Mini JWT server ready, at http://localhost:8080/!")
);
```

We're done! Let's see how this all comes together.

How it works...

We can start by testing the /public and /private routes, without any token. The former won't cause any problems, but the latter will be caught by our token testing code and rejected:

```
> curl "http://localhost:8080/public"
the /public endpoint needs no token!

> curl "http://localhost:8080/private"
No token specified
```

Now, let's try to get a token. Check out the following code:

```
> curl http://localhost:8080/gettoken -X POST -d
"user=fkereki&password=modernjsbook"
eyJhbGciOiJIUzI1NiIsInR5cCI6IkpXVCJ9.eyJ1c2VyaWQiOiJma2VyZWtpIiwiaWF0IjoxNT
I2ODM5MDEwLCJleHAiOjE1MjY4NDI2MTB9.cTwpL-
x7kszn7C9OUXhH1kTGhb8Aa7oOGwNf_nhALCs
```

 Another way of testing this would be going to https://jwt.io/ and creating a JWT, including userid:"fkereki" in the payload, and using modernJSbook as the secret key. You would have to calculate the expiration date (exp) by yourself, though.

Checking the token at `https://jwt.io` shows the following payload:

```
{
  "userid": "fkereki",
  "iat": 1526839010,
  "exp": 1526842610
}
```

The `iat` attribute shows that the JWT was issued on 5/20/2018, close to 2:00 P.M. and the `exp` attributes show that the token is set to expire one hour (3,600 seconds) later. If we now repeat the curl request to `/private`, but adding the appropriate header, it will be accepted. However, if you wait (at least an hour!), the result will be different; the JWT checking middleware will detect the expired token, and a 403 error will be produced:

```
> curl "http://localhost:8080/private" -H "Authorization: Bearer
eyJhbGciOiJIUzI1NiIsInR5cCI6IkpXVCJ9.eyJ1c2VyaWQiOiJma2VyZWtpIiwiaWF0IjoxNT
I2ODM5MDEwLCJleHAiOjE1MjY4NDI2MTB9.cTwpL-
x7kszn7C9OUXhHlkTGhb8Aa7oOGwNf_nhALCs"
the /private endpoint needs JWT, but it was provided: OK!
```

With this code, we now have a way to add authentication to our RESTful server. If you want, you could go further and add specific authorization rules so that some users would get access to some features, while others would be restricted. Now, let's try to bring everything together, and build ourselves a small REST set of services.

Tying it all together – building a REST server

In this recipe, let's write at least a part of a complete RESTful server for our world database that we started using in the *Working with a database* section of the previous chapter, according to the routing scheme that we saw in the *Adding Routes* section earlier in this chapter. We'll focus on just working with Regions, but only for the sake of brevity; Countries and Cities are very similar in terms of coding, and the full code is provided with this book.

Our REST services will send JSON answers and require tokens for authorization. We will enable CORS so that we can access them from different web pages. The routes we will process will be as follows:

- `GET /regions` will provide all regions of all countries
- `GET /regions/:country` will return all regions of the given country
- `GET /regions/:country/:region` will return a single region

- DELETE /regions/:country/:region will let us delete a given region
- POST /regions/:country will allow us to create a new region
- PUT /regions/:country/:region will let us create or update a given region

Dealing with countries and cities is quite similar, with only a couple of exceptions:

- Because of the size of the result set, we won't accept GET /cities requests to provide all cities in the world; only GET /cities/:city will be permitted. An alternative would be accepting the request, but sending back a 405 status code, Method not allowed.
- Since country codes cannot be assigned at will, we won't allow POST /countries. Instead, PUT /countries/:country will be required to add a new country, as well as for updating an existing one.

Each type of request will produce the appropriate HTTP status codes; we'll see that in the following sections. Also, GET requests will be sent JSON results, and POST requests will be sent the location of the newly created entity; more on this later.

How to do it...

Let's look at how we can write our server. We'll start with some basic code, skipping parts that we already saw earlier, such as CORS and JWT handling:

```
// Source file: src/restful_server.js

/* @flow */
"use strict";
const express = require("express");
const app = express();
const bodyParser = require("body-parser");
const dbConn = require("./restful_db.js");
app.get("/", (req, res) => res.send("Secure server!"));

/*
    Add here the logic for CORS
*/

/*
    Add here the logic for providing a JWT at /gettoken
    and the logic for validating a JWT, as shown earlier
*/
```

Handling routing is quite standard. Since routes are simple and few, we may put them in the same source file; otherwise, we'd set up separate files for different sets of routes. The handlers for the routes will certainly go in another file (`"restful_regions.js"`) so as not to obscure the main server code. Note that country and region codes are, if present, part of the URL; whenever the name for a region is needed, it goes in the body parameters:

```
// Source file: src/restful_server.js

const {
    getRegion,
    deleteRegion,
    postRegion,
    putRegion
} = require("./restful_regions.js");

app.get("/regions", (req, res) => getRegion(res, dbConn));

app.get("/regions/:country", (req, res) =>
    getRegion(res, dbConn, req.params.country)
);

app.get("/regions/:country/:region", (req, res) =>
    getRegion(res, dbConn, req.params.country, req.params.region)
);

app.delete("/regions/:country/:region", (req, res) =>
    deleteRegion(res, dbConn, req.params.country, req.params.region)
);

app.post("/regions/:country", (req, res) =>
    postRegion(res, dbConn, req.params.country, req.body.name)
);

app.put("/regions/:country/:region", (req, res) =>
    putRegion(
        res,
        dbConn,
        req.params.country,
        req.params.region,
        req.body.name
    )
);
```

Finally, let's look at some more code that we've already seen to finish up the server, error handling and setting up the server itself:

```
// Source file: src/restful_server.js

// eslint-disable-next-line no-unused-vars
app.use((err, req, res, next) => {
    console.error("Error....", err.message);
    res.status(500).send("INTERNAL SERVER ERROR");
});

/*
   Add here the logic for HTTPS, finishing with:

   https.createServer({ ca, cert, key }, app);
*/

app.listen(8080, () =>
    console.log("Routing ready at http://localhost:8080")
);
```

Let's move on and see how it works. We'll show the code for handling routes in the following section.

How it works...

Since we have four kinds of requests, let's split our study of the server code appropriately.

Handling GETs

As we saw previously, there are three possible routes to handle:

- /regions to get all regions of all countries
- /regions/UY to get all regions of a given country—in this case, Uruguay (UY)
- /regions/UY/11 to get a specific region of a country—here, region 11 of Uruguay

We can handle all three cases in a similar way by just changing the SQL SELECT we'll be doing. Handling the results, however, will require a special case, as we'll note in the following code:

```
// Source file: src/restful_regions.js

const getRegion = async (
    res: any,
    dbConn: any,
    country: ?string,
    region: ?string
) => {
    try {
        res.set("Connection", "close");

        let sqlQuery = "";
        let regions;
        if (country == null) {
            sqlQuery = `
                SELECT rr.*
                FROM regions rr
                JOIN countries cc
                ON cc.countryCode=rr.countryCode
                ORDER BY cc.countryCode, rr.regionCode
            `;
            regions = await dbConn.query(sqlQuery);
        } else if (region == null) {
            sqlQuery = `
                SELECT 1
                FROM countries
                WHERE countryCode=?
            `;

            const countries = await dbConn.query(sqlQuery, [country]);
            if (countries.length === 0) {
                res.status(404).send("Country not found");
                return;
            }

            sqlQuery = `
                SELECT rr.*
                FROM regions rr
                JOIN countries cc
                ON cc.countryCode=rr.countryCode
                WHERE rr.countryCode=?
                ORDER BY rr.regionCode
            `;
            regions = await dbConn.query(sqlQuery, [country]);
```

```
    } else {
        sqlQuery = `
            SELECT rr.*
            FROM regions rr
            JOIN countries cc
            ON cc.countryCode=rr.countryCode
            WHERE rr.countryCode=?
            AND rr.regionCode=?
        `;
        regions = await dbConn.query(sqlQuery, [country, region]);
    }

    if (regions.length > 0 || region === null) {
        res.status(200)
            .set("Content-Type", "application/json")
            .send(JSON.stringify(regions));
    } else {
        res.status(404).send("Not found");
    }
} catch (e) {
    res.status(500).send("Server error");
}
};
```

The special case we mentioned in the preceding code is asking for something like
/regions/XYZZY, and providing a wrong country code. In this case, instead of sending an empty set (which could imply that the country does exist, as it doesn't seem to have any regions) we can send a 404, so the second if statement (country provided, region absent) does a special check before proceeding.

We can see this code working with several examples. Getting /regions with no further parameter provides a largish output (22 MB), so adding parameters to allow for filtering or paging could be in order:

> I removed the HTTPS, CORS, and mainly the JWT code from the server to make the examples simpler to follow. Doing this meant that I haven't received extra headers, and have avoided having to provide a JWT in each call. Yes, I cheated a bit, but the source code provided with the book includes everything, so don't worry about it!

```
> curl localhost:8080/regions/
[{"countryCode":"AD", "regionCode":"2", "regionName":"Canillo"},
{"countryCode":"AD", "regionCode":"3", "regionName":"Encamp"},
{"countryCode":"AD", "regionCode":"4", "regionName":"La Massana"},
 .
 .
 .
{"countryCode":"ZW", "regionCode":"7", "regionName":"Matabeleland South"},
{"countryCode":"ZW", "regionCode":"8", "regionName":"Masvingo"},
{"countryCode":"ZW", "regionCode":"9", "regionName":"Bulawayo"}]
```

A request for a specific country (such as /regions/UY) produces an answer very much like the one that we received previously, but including only the regions in the country UY (Uruguay) and a request for a single region gets a single object:

```
> curl localhost:8080/regions/uy/10
[{"countryCode":"UY","regionCode":"10","regionName":"Montevideo"}]
```

Finally, we can try for an error; check out the following screenshot and note the 404 status:

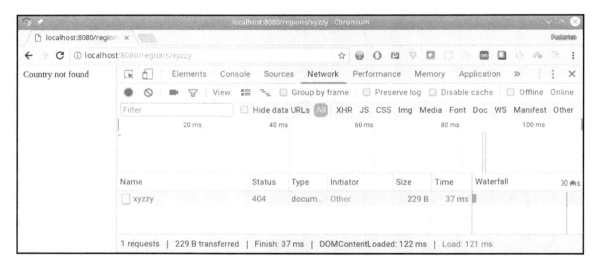

Asking our RESTful server for regions in a non-existent country produces a 404 error

Handling DELETEs

Deleting a region is simple, except that you must check beforehand whether the region has any cities or not. We could solve this by implementing a cascading deletion so that when you delete a region, all of its cities get deleted as well, or we may forbid the deletion outright. In our case, I opted for the latter, but it could be argued that the former is also valid, and would require not very complex logic:

> Why are we checking for cities by ourselves, instead of letting the DB server do it by using foreign keys? The reason is simple: I wanted to show some code that went a bit beyond a single SQL statement. The very same argument could be done for cascade deletions, which you could implement with a hand-crafted SQL sentence, or by setting up special rules in your database. And, let me state that for an actual application, letting the DB do the work would actually be preferable!

```
// Source file: src/restful_regions.js

const deleteRegion = async (
    res: any,
    dbConn: any,
    country: string,
    region: string
) => {
    try {
        res.set("Connection", "close");

        const sqlCities = `
            SELECT 1 FROM cities
            WHERE countryCode=?
            AND regionCode=?
            LIMIT 1
        `;
        const cities = await dbConn.query(sqlCities, [country, region]);
        if (cities.length > 0) {
            res.status(405).send("Cannot delete a region with cities");
            return;
        }

        const deleteRegion = `
                DELETE FROM regions
                WHERE countryCode=?
                AND regionCode=?
            `;

        const result = await dbConn.query(deleteRegion, [country, region]);
```

```
            if (result.info.affectedRows > 0) {
                res.status(204).send();
            } else {
                res.status(404).send("Region not found");
            }
        } catch (e) {
            res.status(500).send("Server error");
        }
    }
};
```

We can test this in a similar way. Deleting a region without cities works, while attempting to do it for a region with cities or for a non-existing region fails:

```
> curl localhost:8080/regions/uy/23 -X DELETE --verbose
*   Trying 127.0.0.1...
* TCP_NODELAY set
* Connected to localhost (127.0.0.1) port 8080 (#0)
> DELETE /regions/uy/23 HTTP/1.1
.
.
.
< HTTP/1.1 204 No Content


> curl localhost:8080/regions/uy/10 -X DELETE --verbose
* Trying 127.0.0.1...
* TCP_NODELAY set
* Connected to localhost (127.0.0.1) port 8080 (#0)
> DELETE /regions/uy/10 HTTP/1.1
> Host: localhost:8080
> User-Agent: curl/7.59.0
> Accept: */*
>
< HTTP/1.1 405 Method Not Allowed
.
.
.
Cannot delete a region with cities


> curl localhost:8080/regions/uy/99 --verbose
* Trying 127.0.0.1...
* TCP_NODELAY set
* Connected to localhost (127.0.0.1) port 8080 (#0)
> GET /regions/uy/99 HTTP/1.1
> Host: localhost:8080
> User-Agent: curl/7.59.0
> Accept: */*
```

```
>
< HTTP/1.1 404 Not Found
  .
  .
  .
Not found
```

See the different status codes that may be returned:

- 204, if a region was deleted with no problems—and in that case, no text response is sent
- 404, if the requested region doesn't exist
- 405, if the request couldn't be accepted (because the regions had cities)

Of course, you might change the workings of the service and, for example, provide for a cascading delete operation if a certain parameter was provided, as in `http://some.server/regions/uy/23?cascade=true`. Also, for some services, this operation may happen without even asking for it; a user might have a set of preferences, and whenever a user is to be deleted, you should also delete their preferences. This would depend on the desired semantics of the service.

Handling PUTs

A `PUT` request means that an existing resource is to be updated. In our case, a pre-condition is that the specified region must exist; otherwise, a `404` error would be appropriate. If the region exists, then we can update it and send a `204` status. If `MySQL` detects that no changes have been made to the region, it lets you know that the `UPDATE` didn't change anything; you could either send a `204` (as I chose to) or a `409` error, but in any case, you are certain that the region has the data you want. We'll also have to do some parameter checking; in this case, just to make sure that a name is given, but the data validation logic could be much more complex:

```
// Source file: src/restful_regions.js

const putRegion = async (
    res: any,
    dbConn: any,
    country: string,
    region: string,
    name: string
) => {
    res.set("Connection", "close");
```

```
        if (!name) {
            res.status(400).send("Missing name");
            return;
        }

        try {
            const sqlUpdateRegion = `
                UPDATE regions
                SET regionName=?
                WHERE countryCode=?
                AND regionCode=?
            `;

            const result = await dbConn.query(sqlUpdateRegion, [
                name,
                country,
                region
            ]);

            if (result.info.affectedRows > 0) {
                res.status(204).send();
            } else {
                res.status(409).send("Region not updated");
            }
        } catch (e) {
            res.status(500).send("Server error");
        }
    };
```

This is easy to test, since there are only two situations (either the region exists or it doesn't), plus a sanity check in case the name is missing. Let's add the missing tilde to a region first; just like before, no content will be received because of the 204 status code:

```
> curl localhost:8080/regions/uy/16 -X PUT -d "name=San Jose" --verbose
*   Trying 127.0.0.1...
* TCP_NODELAY set
* Connected to localhost (127.0.0.1) port 8080 (#0)
> PUT /regions/uy/16 HTTP/1.1
.
.
.
< HTTP/1.1 204 No Content
```

The two error cases (non-existent region, missing name) are quickly taken care of. The former case is detected by MySQL, while the latter is caught by the initial `if` statement:

```
> curl localhost:8080/regions/uy/xyzzy -X PUT -d "name=Colossal Cave" --
verbose
*    Trying 127.0.0.1...
* TCP_NODELAY set
* Connected to localhost (127.0.0.1) port 8080 (#0)
> PUT /regions/uy/xyzzy HTTP/1.1
.
.
.
< HTTP/1.1 409 Conflict
.
.
.
Region not updated

> curl localhost:8080/regions/uy/10 -X PUT --verbose
*    Trying 127.0.0.1...
* TCP_NODELAY set
* Connected to localhost (127.0.0.1) port 8080 (#0)
> PUT /regions/uy/10 HTTP/1.1
.
.
.
< HTTP/1.1 400 Bad Request
.
.
.
Missing name
```

Handling PUT is just about the simplest case; let's finish our study of the server by taking a close look at the most complex request, a POST.

Handling POSTs

Finally, handling POST requests is a bit more complex, since you are supposed to say to which collection (in this case, a country's) you want to add the new resource, and the logic is supposed to do everything, including assigning an ID. This means that our code will be a bit longer, since we'll be adding the need to find an unused region code. There will be another difference: when the resource is created, the URI for the new resource should be returned in the Location header, so that will be another extra requirement.

Finally, once again, we'll have some data validation, as with PUT requests:

```
// Source file: src/restful_regions.js

const postRegion = async (
    res: any,
    dbConn: any,
    country: string,
    name: string
) => {
    res.set("Connection", "close");

    if (!name) {
        res.status(400).send("Missing name");
        return;
    }

    try {
        const sqlCountry = `
            SELECT 1
            FROM countries
            WHERE countryCode=?
        `;
        const countries = await dbConn.query(sqlCountry, [country]);
        if (countries.length === 0) {
            res.status(403).send("Country must exist");
            return;
        }

        const sqlGetId = `
            SELECT MAX(CAST(regionCode AS INTEGER)) AS maxr
            FROM regions
            WHERE countryCode=?
        `;
        const regions = await dbConn.query(sqlGetId, [country]);
        const newId =
            regions.length === 0 ? 1 : 1 + Number(regions[0].maxr);

        const sqlAddRegion = `
            INSERT INTO regions SET
            countryCode=?,
            regionCode=?,
            regionName=?
        `;

        const result = await dbConn.query(sqlAddRegion, [
            country,
            newId,
```

```
            name
        ]);
        if (result.info.affectedRows > 0) {
            res.status(201)
                .header("Location", `/regions/${country}/${newId}`)
                .send("Region created");
        } else {
            res.status(409).send("Region not created");
        }
    } catch (e) {
        res.status(500).send("Server error");
    }
};
```

This is the logic that requires the most queries. We must (1) check that the country exists, (2) determine the maximum region ID for that country, and only then (3) insert the new region and return a 201 status to the user. We can test this in a similar way to what we did for PUT, so let's look at a simple case:

```
> curl localhost:8080/regions/ar -X POST -d "name=NEW REGION" --verbose
*   Trying 127.0.0.1...
* TCP_NODELAY set
* Connected to localhost (127.0.0.1) port 8080 (#0)
> POST /regions/ar HTTP/1.1
.
.
.
< HTTP/1.1 201 Created
< X-Powered-By: Express
< Location: /regions/ar/25
.
.
.
Region created

> curl localhost:8080/regions/ar/25
[{"countryCode":"ar","regionCode":"25","regionName":"NEW REGION'}]
```

Argentina has 24 provinces, numbered from 1 to 24 in the regions table, so if we add a new one, it should be #25, and the Location header in the answer proves that this is so. (We are only returning the route, without the server and port, but we could easily add those pieces of data.) Doing a GET confirms that the POST succeeded.

There's more...

We have set up a barebones RESTful server with `Express`, but there is much more—enough for a book of its own! Let's finish this chapter by taking a very quick glance at several ideas and tools that you might want to consider for your own projects.

Accepting JSON data

We have used `POST` parameters in our examples, but it's also possible to receive, parse, and process JSON input. (This can make it easier to call a REST service, because at the frontend it's very likely you'll be able to readily produce an object with the desired parameters for the request.) Use `express.json()` as middleware, and the request body will include the data from the JSON parameter.

> Go to `http://expressjs.com/en/4x/api.html#express.json` for more information on this.

Adding the PATCH method for partial updates

The PUT method makes you update a complete entity, but sometimes you want to affect only a few fields, and in this case you can allow the `PATCH` method. `PATCH` is similar to `PUT`, but lets you update only some attributes. Adding support for this method is not complex, and is very similar to the `PUT` logic, so you may provide a more powerful server with relatively little extra coding.

> You can read more about PATCH at `https://developer.mozilla.org/en-US/docs/Web/HTTP/Methods/PATCH` and if you care about its specification, at `https://datatracker.ietf.org/doc/rfc5789/`.

Using Restify instead of Express

While `Express` is a very popular and widely used package that can be used to build any kind of server, if you specifically want just a REST server and no other feature, you may consider using other packages, such as `Restify`. The advantages of such a change have to do with the orientation of the package, which provides similar features to `Express`, but requires a bit less code in order to accomplish a RESTful deployment. Some well-known users of `Restify` are `npm` and Netflix, but the list is much longer.

You can read more about `Restify` at `http://restify.com/`.

Allowing filtering, sorting, and pagination

Since REST is basically a style and not a specification for services, there are aspects that aren't specified, and you have some leeway as to their implementation. Three common requirements are *filtering* (so you don't get all entities, but just those that satisfy some condition), *sorting* (so that entities are included in some order), and *pagination* (because showing hundreds or thousands of entities at once isn't practical). Of course, these three requirements interact with each other; if you sort and filter, then paging should apply to the sorted filtered data.

All of these requirements can be handled by adding some query parameters (or possibly headers), but you'll have to study a bit to understand what's the best way for you:

- *Filtering* may be specified with a format such as `filter=price[lt]220`, which would specify that a given attribute (`price`) must be less than (`lt`) a value (`200`). Building up more complex expressions involving logical operators such as `and`, `or`, and `not`, plus optional parentheses, can also be done, at the cost of more complex parsing and interpreting at the server.
- *Sorting* may be specified by parameters such as `sortby=price,name` to order first by `price` and then by `name`. You can add other options to allow for ascending or descending sorting.
- *Paging* can be done by using the `limit` and `offset` parameters, with the same interpretation that's used in SQL `SELECT` statements (see `https://dev.mysql.com/doc/refman/8.0/en/select.html` for more on that) or by specifying a page size and the page number.

Adding the handling of these options to your REST server will make it more powerful, and enable the client to send more specific, optimized requests. There is one more extension that you may want; being able to select extra, related entities, so read on.

Using GraphQL instead of REST

REST services are standard and easy to use, but may imply some overhead, mostly when you don't need just a single entity, but also some related ones; for example, how would you get a country and all of its regions? With our current design, you'd have to do separate calls and join the results by yourself, or otherwise extend your routes yourself. For example, you would do this for `/regions/uy?include=cities` so that the server would add—to each region in `UY`—an array with its cities. While this solution may be apt for a small example like the one we're using, for bigger, more complex databases, with tables related among themselves in many ways, it could easily get out of hand.

There is, however, another option. `GraphQL` is a data query language that was developed by Facebook, and it lets you define, at the client, the structure of the data you require; the server will do whatever is needed to produce exactly that. `GraphQL` lets you get many related resources with a single request by following references to build a complex structure, and sending it along with the minimum delay. You also get tools to help you define your data schema and perform online queries.

Let's look at a very short example, taken from the documentation of GraphQL's own site, at `http://graphql.org/learn/queries/`. Given a database of *Star Wars* movies, you could write the following query that wants to get the hero from a couple of movies, and for each one, the name, the list of movies they appear in, and all of their friends' names:

```
{
    leftComparison: hero(episode: EMPIRE) {
        ...comparisonFields
    }
    rightComparison: hero(episode: JEDI) {
        ...comparisonFields
    }
}

fragment comparisonFields on Character {
    name
    appearsIn
    friends {
        name
    }
}
```

The result of this query is as follows. Note how the object structure follows your specification in the query, and that repeated fields, or foreign key access, were all solved by the GraphQL server, and in a single request:

```
{
    data: {
        leftComparison: {
            name: "Luke Skywalker",
            appearsIn: ["NEWHOPE", "EMPIRE", "JEDI"],
            friends: [
                {
                    name: "Han Solo"
                },
                {
                    name: "Leia Organa"
                },
                {
                    name: "C-3PO"
                },
                {
                    name: "R2-D2"
                }
            ]
        },
        rightComparison: {
            name: "R2-D2",
            appearsIn: ["NEWHOPE", "EMPIRE", "JEDI"],
            friends: [
                {
                    name: "Luke Skywalker"
                },
                {
                    name: "Han Solo"
                },
                {
                    name: "Leia Organa"
                }
            ]
        }
    }
}
```

While totally outside the scope of this chapter (we wanted a RESTful server, after all), GraphQL is a very valid alternative for applications that need to work with complex, linked structures, which would require too much processing and communication time otherwise.

To learn more about GraphQL, check out the official site at https:// graphql.org/.

Implementing a microservice-based architecture

Now that you're able to develop a server by following the structure in this chapter, working in an SOA might evolve into a microservices organization, in which the server, instead of being a monolithic piece of code that can provide multiple services, is organized as a set of distinct mini-servers, loosely coupled, connected by a lightweight protocol, and each having a single responsibility. Services may be created by different groups, even using different languages or libraries, that are only dependent on following a given interface so that other services may freely interact with them as needed.

This structure, based on independent smaller pieces, greatly helps with scalability, modularity, and even development and testing. If changes are needed, their impact will be smaller, and strategies such as continuous delivery and deployment become feasible. Developing the microservices themselves is readily done, and the necessary techniques for doing this are mainly the ones that we saw in this chapter. Only adding the requests from one microserver to another to gather all of the required information is necessary.

A couple of good starting points on the benefits of a microservice-based architecture are the articles by Martin Fowler at https://martinfowler. com/microservices/ and by Chris Richardson at http://microservices. io/patterns/microservices.html.

Testing and Debugging Your Server

5

In this chapter, we will look at the following recipes:

- Adding logging with Winston
- Adding HTTP logging with Morgan
- Configuring your server for different environments
- Unit testing your code
- Measuring your test coverage
- Debugging your code
- Testing simple services from the command line
- Testing more complex sequences of calls with Postman
- Documenting and testing your REST API with Swagger

Introduction

In the previous chapters, we installed Node and created a RESTful server. Is everything ready? Usually, things don't work out that well—bugs will creep in, and you'll have to find out how to fix your code. In this chapter, we'll be getting into practical details, such as testing and debugging your server.

So, after this chapter, you'll have your Node RESTful server ready for deployment and for official production work. Let's get into the necessary tasks.

Adding logging with Winston

Let's start with a simple, basic need: *logging*. Having solid, correct logging set up can help you find problems quickly, while incomplete or otherwise lacking logging can make you look for hours for what could be a simple, trivial problem. A basic rule for any application is to ensure that proper login is set up so that you can be confident that any situation that comes up will at least be recognized and recorded for future analysis.

The first idea you could have is to just use the console family of functions, such as `console.log()`, `console.warn()`, `console.info()`, and more. (For a complete reference, check out `https://developer.mozilla.org/en-US/docs/Web/API/console`.) While these are good for quick debugging, they just don't do it for application-level logging. You should be able to select what kind of logs you want (everything? Errors only?) to decide what logs you see depending on your environment (for example, you'd want to see some kinds of logs in development but not in production), or even to enable or disable logging. And, finally, we want to have some control over the provided information:

- *Timestamping*, to learn at what time each log was written
- *Text formatting*, so logging can be understandable by humans, but also parseable by applications
- *Level setting*, usually on a scale ranging from *error* (the most serious) through *warning*, *informative*, *verbose*, and ending with *debugging* and *silly* (yes, truly!)
- *Destination picking*, like `stdout` or `stderr`, the filesystem, and so on

If you look around in the `npm` listings, you'll find many modules that can do logging: some are generic tools, and other are more specific ones. In our case, we'll use `Winston` for generic, application-level logging, and we'll turn to a different tool, `Morgan`, which is specifically tailored for HTTP traffic logging, as we'll see in the next section.

 You can learn more about `Winston` at `https://github.com/winstonjs/winston`.

How to do it...

We want to install Winston, so the first step will be to apply the time-honored method:

```
npm install winston --save
```

 Currently, version 3.0 is in beta, but by the time you get this book, it will almost certainly be out of beta and ready for production. (By the way, I installed the beta version by using a slightly changed command: npm install winston@next --save; otherwise, I'd have gotten a 2.x.x version.)

For (thorough!) documentation on Winston, check its own GitHub page at https://github.com/winstonjs/winston. Be careful with articles on the web, though, because there are some important changes in version 3, so most code won't work without some updating.

We want to look at a simple example about the usage of Winston. This package has many configuration parameters, so let's try to get a basic, sane configuration going, which you'll be able to extend on your own:

```javascript
// Source file: winston_server.js

/* @flow */
"use strict";

const express = require("express");
const winston = require("winston");

const app = express();

const logger = winston.createLogger({
    transports: [
        new winston.transports.Console({
            level: "info",
            format: winston.format.combine(
                winston.format.colorize({ all: true }),
                winston.format.label({ label: "serv" }),
                winston.format.timestamp(),
                winston.format.printf(
                    msg =>
                        `${msg.timestamp} [${msg.label}] ${msg.level} ${
                            msg.message
                        }`
                )
            )
        )
```

```
        }),
        new winston.transports.File({
            filename: "serv_error.txt.log",
            level: "warn",
            format: winston.format.combine(
                winston.format.timestamp(),
                winston.format.printf(
                    msg =>
                        `${msg.timestamp} [serv] ${msg.level} ${
                            msg.message
                        }`
                )
            )
        }),
        new winston.transports.File({
            filename: "serv_error.json.log",
            level: "warn"
        })
    ]
});

// continues...
```

Winston can handle several transports at the same time, and by *transport*, it means a storage device for whatever you log. A single logger may have multiple transports, but configured differently: for example, you may want to show all logs at the console, but only write a file with warnings and errors, and yet more possibilities include writing a database or sending data to some URL. Formats may also vary (text lines for the console, possibly JSON for a file?), so you have lots of flexibility regarding configuring where your messages will go.

In our case, we are creating three transports:

- *A console output*, for all messages marked as `"info"` and above, using colorized output (we'll see it in a short while), emitting output with a timestamp, a label (`"serv"`, to help distinguish the server's messages from others that might show up in the console, coming from other applications), the error level, and a message
- *A file output*, for all messages marked as `"warn"` and above, in text format
- *Another file output*, for the same messages, but in JSON format

We'll look at how to adapt logging (and other features) later in this chapter, in the *Configuring your server for different environments* section, so you'll be able to be even more flexible in logging and other features.

After having created the logger and defined the transports, all we have to do is use it, wherever we want. I'll start with a very basic server so that we can focus on getting logging to work: we'll just handle two routes—/, which will send back a message, and /xyzzy, which will simulate some program failure, instead of sending back a "Nothing happens" message.

At the beginning, we could log every request by hand—though we'll get a better output with Morgan, as we'll see afterwards. The following code does just that:

```
// ...continued

app.use((req, res, next) => {
    logger.info(`${req.method} request for ${req.originalUrl}`);
    next();
});

// continues...
```

Then, for each route, we can add some info or debug messages, as we may need:

```
// ...continued

app.get("/", (req, res) => {
    logger.info("Doing some processing...");
    logger.debug("Some fake step 1; starting");
    logger.debug("Some fake step 2; working");
    logger.debug("Some fake step 3; finished!");
    res.send("Winston server!");
});

app.get("/xyzzy", (req, res) => {
    logger.info("Adventurer says 'XYZZY'");
    res.say_xyzzy(); // this will fail
    res.send("Nothing happens.");
});

// continues...
```

Handling wrong routes might produce a `warn` message, and in other unplanned situations, a direct `error`. For the former, I'm only listing the required route, and for the latter, both the error message and the traceback stack, to help in future debugging:

```
// ...continued

app.use((req, res) => {
    logger.warn(`UNKNOWN ROUTE ${req.originalUrl}`);
    res.status(404).send("NOT FOUND");
});

// eslint-disable-next-line no-unused-vars
app.use((err, req, res, next) => {
    logger.error(`GENERAL ERROR ${err.message}\n${err.stack}`);
    res.status(500).send("INTERNAL SERVER ERROR");
});

app.listen(8080, () => {
    logger.info("Ready at http://localhost:8080");
});
```

We're set! Let's try it out.

How it works...

After building the project, I ran the `Winston` logging code to catch all the produced logs. I tried it out with a sequence of calls, simulated with `curl`; we'll be looking at how to do this in more complex tasks in later sections in this chapter:

```
> curl localhost:8080/
Winston server!
> curl localhost:8080/
Winston server!
> curl localhost:8080/invented
NOT FOUND
> curl localhost:8080/
Winston server!
> curl localhost:8080/xyzzy
INTERNAL SERVER ERROR
> curl localhost:8080/
Winston server!
> curl localhost:8080/
Winston server!
```

The output on the console can be seen in the following screenshot. The normal lines are in green (yes, hard to see in a black and white book—sorry about that!), the warnings are yellow, and the errors are in red. The request for the non-existing /invented path ended in a warning, and the one for /xyzzy produced an error, since we tried to call a non-existent function:

```
2018-05-28T00:28:54.869Z [serv] info Ready at http://localhost:8080
2018-05-28T00:29:00.816Z [serv] info GET request for /
2018-05-28T00:29:00.817Z [serv] info Doing some processing...
2018-05-28T00:29:04.844Z [serv] info GET request for /
2018-05-28T00:29:04.844Z [serv] info Doing some processing...
2018-05-28T00:29:06.650Z [serv] info GET request for /invented
2018-05-28T00:29:06.651Z [serv] warn UNKNOWN ROUTE /invented
2018-05-28T00:29:08.130Z [serv] info GET request for /
2018-05-28T00:29:08.130Z [serv] info Doing some processing...
2018-05-28T00:29:11.214Z [serv] info GET request for /xyzzy
2018-05-28T00:29:11.214Z [serv] info Adventurer says 'XYZZY'
2018-05-28T00:29:11.214Z [serv] error GENERAL ERROR res.say_xyzzy is not a function
TypeError: res.say_xyzzy is not a function
    at app.get (/home/fkereki/MODERNJS/chapter05/out/winston_server.js:60:9)
    at Layer.handle [as handle_request] (/home/fkereki/MODERNJS/chapter05/node_modules/express/lib/router/layer.js:95:5)
    at next (/home/fkereki/MODERNJS/chapter05/node_modules/express/lib/router/route.js:137:13)
    at Route.dispatch (/home/fkereki/MODERNJS/chapter05/node_modules/express/lib/router/route.js:112:3)
    at Layer.handle [as handle_request] (/home/fkereki/MODERNJS/chapter05/node_modules/express/lib/router/layer.js:95:5)
    at /home/fkereki/MODERNJS/chapter05/node_modules/express/lib/router/index.js:281:22
    at Function.process_params (/home/fkereki/MODERNJS/chapter05/node_modules/express/lib/router/index.js:335:12)
    at next (/home/fkereki/MODERNJS/chapter05/node_modules/express/lib/router/index.js:275:10)
    at app.use (/home/fkereki/MODERNJS/chapter05/out/winston_server.js:47:5)
    at Layer.handle [as handle_request] (/home/fkereki/MODERNJS/chapter05/node_modules/express/lib/router/layer.js:95:5)
2018-05-28T00:29:13.061Z [serv] info GET request for /
2018-05-28T00:29:13.061Z [serv] info Doing some processing...
2018-05-28T00:29:14.158Z [serv] info GET request for /
2018-05-28T00:29:14.158Z [serv] info Doing some processing...
```

Winston's console output for a few dummy requests

What got logged to the different log files? According to our specification, only the warning and the error messages were stored. The text file is basically the same as the console output, and that makes sense because the format specification we selected for those two transports is exactly the same:

```
2018-05-28T00:29:06.651Z [serv] warn UNKNOWN ROUTE /invented
2018-05-28T00:29:11.214Z [serv] error GENERAL ERROR res.say_xyzzy is not a function
TypeError: res.say_xyzzy is not a function
    at app.get
(/home/fkereki/MODERNJS/chapter05/out/winston_server.js:60:9)
    at Layer.handle [as handle_request]
(/home/fkereki/MODERNJS/chapter05/node_modules/express/lib/router/layer.js:95:5)
    at next
(/home/fkereki/MODERNJS/chapter05/node_modules/express/lib/router/route.js:137:13)
    at Route.dispatch
```

```
(/home/fkereki/MODERNJS/chapter05/node_modules/express/lib/router/route.js:
112:3)
    at Layer.handle [as handle_request]
(/home/fkereki/MODERNJS/chapter05/node_modules/express/lib/router/layer.js:
95:5)
    at
/home/fkereki/MODERNJS/chapter05/node_modules/express/lib/router/index.js:2
81:22
    at Function.process_params
(/home/fkereki/MODERNJS/chapter05/node_modules/express/lib/router/index.js:
335:12)
    at next
(/home/fkereki/MODERNJS/chapter05/node_modules/express/lib/router/index.js:
275:10)
    at app.use
(/home/fkereki/MODERNJS/chapter05/out/winston_server.js:47:5)
    at Layer.handle [as handle_request]
(/home/fkereki/MODERNJS/chapter05/node_modules/express/lib/router/layer.js:
95:5)
```

The JSON file, on the other hand, is a bit reduced: each line includes an object with the message and level attributes, because we didn't specify that anything in particular should be added. However, you can change that: read Winston's documentation at `https:/ /github.com/winstonjs/winston/blob/master/README.md`, and you'll have plenty of available possibilities:

```
{"message":"UNKNOWN ROUTE /invented","level":"warn"}
{"message":"GENERAL ERROR res.say_xyzzy is not a function\nTypeError:
res.say_xyzzy is not a function\n at app.get
(/home/fkereki/MODERNJS/chapter05/out/winston_server.js:60:9)\n at
Layer.handle [as handle_request] ...part of the text snipped out...
(/home/fkereki/MODERNJS/chapter05/out/winston_server.js:47:5)\n at
Layer.handle [as handle_request]
(/home/fkereki/MODERNJS/chapter05/node_modules/express/lib/router/layer.js:
95:5)","level":"error"}
```

So, we have a flexible way to log just about whatever we want to, but our HTTP logging was, in particular, a bit too skimpy, and that's a good reason to include Morgan, as we'll see.

There's more...

You may also be interested in looking at other packages, such as Bunyan (`https://github.com/trentm/node-bunyan`) or Pino (`https://github.com/pinojs/pino`); the latter is said to be the logging package with the best performance, but don't take my word for it—try it out! Finally, should you work on developing npm packages, then debug (`https://github.com/visionmedia/debug`), which is basically a wrapper around console methods, could be your package of choice—and being quite simple, it also works for web applications and Node.

Adding HTTP logging with Morgan

In the previous section, we managed to provide a very basic HTTP logging feature when we included some middleware that did Winston logging:

```
app.use((req, res, next) => {
    logger.info(`${req.method} request for ${req.originalUrl}`);
    next();
});
```

While this worked, there is much more information that we could desire, such as the HTTP status code for the response, the processing time it required, and more, so let's add Morgan into the mix, since that package is specific for requests logging.

 You can learn more about Morgan at `https://github.com/expressjs/morgan`.

In this recipe, we'll add Morgan to our software stack so that we can get better logs for all the processed requests.

How to do it...

Let's start by installing `Morgan` with the usual method:

```
npm install morgan --save
```

Now we must include it in our server, and we'll also require the `fs` package in order to write `Morgan`'s logs to a file. Note that I'm adding to our previous server, so the `Winston` parts will be in place, unchanged from what we saw in the previous section:

```
// Source file: src/morgan_server.js

/* @flow */
"use strict";

const express = require("express");
const winston = require("winston");
const morgan = require("morgan");
const fs = require("fs");

const app = express();

// continues...
```

We want to do some general logging to a file, and also all errors (HTTP status code 400 and higher) to the console, so we'll have to add `morgan` twice to our middleware stack. The first parameter to `morgan` defines how the log messages will be formed: you have to provide either a function to generate the message that will be logged, or a string with tokens that `morgan` will replace at runtime. In the following code snippet, I used both styles, just for variety: a function for the file output, and a string for the console:

```
// ...continued

const morganStream = fs.createWriteStream("serv_http_errors.log", {
    flags: "a"
});

app.use(
    morgan(
        (tokens, req, res) =>
            `${new Date().toISOString()} [http] ` +
            `${tokens.method(req, res)} ${tokens.url(req, res)}`,
        {
            immediate: true,
            stream: morganStream
        }
    )
```

```
);

app.use(
    morgan(
        `:date[iso] [http] ` +
            `:method :url (:status) :res[content-length] - :response-time
ms`,
        {
            skip: (req, res) => res.statusCode < 400
        }
    )
);

// continues...
```

The second option to morgan lets you add some options, such as the following:

- immediate, meaning that requests will be logged as soon as they come in (immediate:true) or after they've been processed (immediate:false). The advantage of the former is that you are sure that all requests will be logged, even in the case of a serious crash, but the latter provides more information.
- skip(), a function that lets you decide whether to log a given request or not. In our case, we'll use it to just log requests that get a 400 or higher status.
- stream, to which the output should be written.

When specifying the output format, you have access to several pieces of data, called *tokens* in Morgan's parlance, such as the following, but check the documentation for the full list:

:date[format]	Current date and time in UTC, in several formats
:http-version	HTTP version of the request
:method	HTTP method of the request
:remote-addr	Remote address of the request
:req[header]	The given header of the request, or "-" if the header isn't present
:res[header]	The given header of the response, or "-" if the header isn't present
:response-time	Processing time, in milliseconds
:status	HTTP status of the response
:url	URL of the request

You can see that I used several of these tokens when setting up Morgan's output. Now, let's see this works.

How it works...

Let's give this a whirl, using the same examples that we used for `winston`. Since we set the console output to show only warnings and errors, we'll just see an added pair of lines. Displaying `[http]` instead of `[serv]` helps finding them, among the rest of the console output:

```
.
.
.
2018-05-28T19:27:19.232Z [http] GET /invented (404) 9 - 0.886 ms
.
.
.
2018-05-28T19:27:23.771Z [http] GET /xyzzy (500) 21 - 0.925 ms
.
.
.
```

The (complete) HTTP log went into a file, and is just a list of all of the requests:

```
2018-05-28T19:27:16.871Z [http] GET /
2018-05-28T19:27:17.827Z [http] GET /
2018-05-28T19:27:19.231Z [http] GET /invented
2018-05-28T19:27:20.677Z [http] GET /
2018-05-28T19:27:23.770Z [http] GET /xyzzy
2018-05-28T19:27:25.296Z [http] GET /
```

Note that we opted to do an immediate logging, which means that all requests—even those that might cause everything to crash—get logged, but the outcome itself of the request is then not available. If you wish to also get that information—but, say, only for requests that caused some error—you might add a third `morgan` destination, sharing the same file stream, but only for errors, as shown in the following code snippet:

```
app.use(
    morgan(
        `:date[iso] [http] ` +
            `:method :url (:status) :res[content-length] - :response-time
ms`,
        {
            skip: (req, res) => res.statusCode < 400,
            stream: morganStream
        }
    )
);
```

Using this, the log would then include more data, but only for the requests you picked:

```
2018-05-28T19:36:54.968Z [http] GET /
2018-05-28T19:36:55.453Z [http] GET /
2018-05-28T19:36:56.011Z [http] GET /
2018-05-28T19:36:58.149Z [http] GET /invented
2018-05-28T19:36:58.151Z [http] GET /invented (404) 9 - 1.230 ms
2018-05-28T19:36:59.528Z [http] GET /
2018-05-28T19:37:00.033Z [http] GET /
2018-05-28T19:37:01.886Z [http] GET /xyzzy
2018-05-28T19:37:01.888Z [http] GET /xyzzy (500) 21 - 1.115 ms
2018-05-28T19:37:03.060Z [http] GET /
2018-05-28T19:37:03.445Z [http] GET /
2018-05-28T19:37:03.903Z [http] GET /
```

There's more...

If you wish, you can make `Morgan`'s output to go into `Winston`'s to get a single common logging stream, like so:

```
// Source file: src/morgan_in_winston_server.js

app.use(
    morgan(
        `:method :url (:status) :res[content-length] - :response-time ms`,
        {
            stream: {
                write: message => logger.info(message.trim())
            }
        }
    )
);
```

Some output could be as follows; I highlighted the `morgan` lines:

```
2018-05-28T20:03:59.931Z [serv] info Ready at http://localhost:3080
2018-05-28T20:04:02.140Z [serv] info Doing some processing...
2018-05-28T20:04:02.146Z [serv] info GET / (200) 15 - 3.642 ms
2018-05-28T20:04:02.727Z [serv] info Doing some processing...
2018-05-28T20:04:02.728Z [serv] info GET / (200) 15 - 0.581 ms
2018-05-28T20:04:04.479Z [serv] warn UNKNOWN ROUTE /invented
2018-05-28T20:04:04.480Z [serv] info GET /invented (404) 9 - 1.170 ms
2018-05-28T20:04:05.842Z [serv] info Doing some processing...
2018-05-28T20:04:05.843Z [serv] info GET / (200) 15 - 0.490 ms
2018-05-28T20:04:07.640Z [serv] info Adventurer says 'XYZZY'
```

A few details about the changes I made are as follows:

- Adding `.trim()` gets rid of a possible extra new line character
- Since all messages are sent through `winston`, you don't get your `[http]` distinguishing text in the output
- If you want to send warnings for status like 400 or above, you'll have to write a more complex function that will scan the message text and decide whether to use `logger.info()` or some other method

Configuring your server for different environments

No matter what you develop, it's certain that you'll work at least with a couple of environments, *development* and *production*, and settings for your code won't be the same. For example, you won't use the same configuration for security, to access a database, to log errors, or to connect to analytics services, and so on: when running in your development environment, you'll need a certain setup, and for production there may be many changes.

You could set everything up in your code, but having users, passwords, IPs, and other sensitive data in plain text and saved in a source code repository that might get hacked isn't a good recipe for security. You should deal exclusively with your development configuration and leave the actual deployment to production to a different team, which will safely deal with that configuration.

Node lets you access environment variables and use them for configuration so that you can move that setup outside of your code. In this chapter, let's look at some ways to deal with all this, which will also indirectly help with our testing, later in this chapter.

How to do it...

When you are developing software, you'll obviously work in a different environment than for production; in fact, you could have several environments such as *development, testing, preproduction, production,* and so on. We'll also do this; let's start by going over some of the configurations we have already seen in this book.

In the *Getting a connection* section of `Chapter 3`, *Developing with Node*, when we created our services, we defined four constants to access the database, as follows:

```
const DB_HOST = "127.0.0.1";
const DB_USER = "fkereki";
const DB_PASS = "modernJS!!";
const DB_SCHEMA = "world";
```

In the previous chapter, in the *Adding Authentication with JWT* section, we had a secret that we used for signing:

```
const SECRET_JWT_KEY = "modernJSbook";
```

And, finally, in this very chapter, we decided what levels of logging should be done. However, we hardcoded those levels, without the possibility of making things different in production:

```
const logger = winston.createLogger({
    transports: [
        new winston.transports.Console({
            level: "info",
            format: winston.format.combine(
                winston.format.colorize({ all: true }),
                .
                .
                .
```

We also wrote the following, with some hardcoding:

```
const morganStream = fs.createWriteStream("serv_http_errors.log", {
    flags: "a"
});

app.use(
    morgan(
        `:date[iso] [http] ` +
            `:method :url (:status) :res[content-length] - :response-time
ms`,
        {
            skip: (req, res) => res.statusCode < 400
```

It's worth pointing out that changes between development and production need not be limited to listing or not listing; you could also change the logging format, the files where logs should be written, and so on.

The key to changing configurations *on the fly* is the usage of environment variables, which are provided via the `process.env` object. Every configuration variable in your environment will appear as a property of that object. If we write and run a program that just consists of a single `console.log(process.env)` line (or if we do `node -e "console.log(process.env)"` at the command line) you'll get an output similar to the following:

```
> node show_env.js
{ GS_LIB: '/home/fkereki/.fonts',
 KDE_FULL_SESSION: 'true',
 PILOTPORT: 'usb:',
 HOSTTYPE: 'x86_64',
 VSCODE_NLS_CONFIG: '{"locale":"en-us","availableLanguages":{}}',
 XAUTHLOCALHOSTNAME: 'linux',
 XKEYSYMDB: '/usr/X11R6/lib/X11/XKeysymDB',
 LANG: 'en_US.UTF-8',
 WINDOWMANAGER: '/usr/bin/startkde',
 LESS: '-M -I -R',
 DISPLAY: ':0',
 JAVA_ROOT: '/usr/lib64/jvm/jre',
 HOSTNAME: 'linux',
 .
 .
 .
 . many, many lines snipped out
 .
 .
 .
 PATH: '/home/fkereki/bin:/usr/local/bin:/usr/bin:/bin:/usr/lib/mit/sbin',
 JAVA_BINDIR: '/usr/lib64/jvm/jre/bin',
 KDE_SESSION_UID: '1000',
 KDE_SESSION_VERSION: '5',
 SDL_AUDIODRIVER: 'pulse',
 HISTSIZE: '1000',
 SESSION_MANAGER: 'local/linux:@/tmp/.ICE-unix/2202,unix/linux:/tmp/.ICE-
unix/2202',
 CPU: 'x86_64',
 CVS_RSH: 'ssh',
 LESSOPEN: 'lessopen.sh %s',
 GTK_IM_MODULE: 'ibus',
 NODE_VERSION: '9' }
```

Read more about `process.env` and its contents at https://nodejs.org/api/process.html#process_process_env.

There are two ways of taking advantage of this. We can either use an environment variable to check whether we are in development, in production, or in any other situation, and depending on that we can set some properties, or we can directly get the values for those properties from the environment itself. Any of these two solutions will help you unlink the code from the environment; let's see how this works in practice.

How it works...

Let's start by determining the environment. The standard is to set an environment variable called NODE_ENV with the name of the environment, before running the Node server itself. How to do that would depend on your actual machine, but in Linux, it would be something akin to the following, while in Windows the SET command would be required:

```
> export NODE_ENV=production
> echo $NODE_ENV
Production
```

In your code, you could set a isDev variable to true if you are running in development (and false otherwise) with just two lines. If no environment was specified, the first line makes it default to "development", which is most likely the safest choice:

```
// Source file: show_env.js

const dev = process.env.NODE_ENV || "development";
const isDev = dev === "development";
```

Then, for example, you could have set different logging levels easily: see the following code snippet, regarding how the level attribute gets its value, depending on the environment:

```
const logger = winston.createLogger({
    transports: [
        new winston.transports.Console({
            level: isDev ? "info" : "warn",
            format: winston.format.combine(
                winston.format.colorize({ all: true }),
                    .
                    .
                    .
```

Changing the log file would also be simple, along the same lines as the preceding code:

```
let loggingFile;
if (isDev) {
    loggingFile = "serv_http_errors.log";
} else {
    loggingFile = "/var/log/http_server.txt";
}

const morganStream = fs.createWriteStream(loggingFile, {
    flags: "a"
});
```

This style works, but it still has a couple of problems:

- Any change in the environment requires changing the (hardcoded) server
- The paths, tokens, passwords, and more, all reside in the source code, in a very viewable state

So, we can do even better by directly taking the values for our internal variables directly from the environment:

```
const DB_HOST = process.env.DB_HOST;
const DB_USER = process.env.DB_USER;
const DB_PASS = process.env.DB_PASS;
const DB_SCHEMA = process.env.DB_SCHEMA;
const SECRET_JWT_KEY = process.env.SECRET_JWT_KEY;
```

Alternatively, for logging, we could use the following:

```
const logger = winston.createLogger({
    transports: [
        new winston.transports.Console({
            level: process.env.WINSTON_LEVEL,
            format: winston.format.combine(
                winston.format.colorize({ all: true }),
                .
                .
                .
```

There's more...

If you want to simplify working in development, but also make it easy for others when pushing code to production or other environments, you may want to look into dotenv, an npm package that lets you work with environment variables in text files. Install the package with npm install dotenv --save, and then create a file at the root of your project with the .env extension, which contains the desired variables values:

```
DB_HOST=127.0.0.1
DB_USER=fkereki
DB_PASS=modernJS!!
DB_SCHEMA=world
SECRET_JWT_KEY=modernJSbook
```

Then, in your code, you only need to add a single line, and that will load and merge all the definitions in your .env file into process.env. Of course, if you only want to use this feature in development (as it was originally intended by the creator of dotenv) you could previously check the isDev variable, as we saw earlier:

```
if (isDev) {
    dotenv.load();
}
```

Environment files should never be uploaded to source control, so it makes sense to add a line with **/*.env to your .gitignore file. You can, however, upload a sample file (say, config.env.example), but without the actual values for the environment variables; this will help new developers get the necessary files, but preserve security.

 You can learn more about dotenv at https://github.com/motdotla/dotenv.

Unit testing your code

One of the best practices to ensure quality and to protect yourself from regression bugs (those that happen when you modify something, and reintroduce an earlier, previously corrected, bug) is to make sure that your code is *unit tested*. There are three types of testing:

- *Unit testing*, which applies to each component, on their own
- *Integration testing*, which applies to components working together
- ***End-to-end*** (**E2E**) *testing*, which applies to the system as a whole

Unit testing is good—not only because it helps try out your code, but because if done well, as in **Test-Driven Design** (TDD), in which you basically first set up the tests, and only then write the code—as it will help produce code of a better quality, and this will surely have an impact on reducing bugs all over your system. (Finding bugs even before any testing work begins is also a money saver; the earlier you find and fix bugs, the less costly it is.) So, let's focus on how you can use unit testing for your Node work.

 Of course, it's well-known that *testing can prove the existence of bugs, but not their absence,* so no matter how much testing you do, some bugs will fall through! And, when that happens, TDD will make you first create some new unit tests that pinpoint the bug, and only then work at actually fixing it; at least, that specific bug won't reappear, because it will be detected.

There are plenty of tools and frameworks for unit testing, and in this book we'll be using Jest, a modern tool for *Delightful JavaScript Testing* as its lemma goes, which was developed by Facebook. We'll have the additional advantage of being able to also use it with React or React Native. Installation is quite simple, requiring just `npm install jest --save-dev`. After doing that, we'll be able to write our tests; let's see how.

 You can read more about Jest at the official web page, at `https://facebook.github.io/jest/`.

In this recipe, we'll look at how to write unit tests for Node and get valid experience for future chapters.

How to do it...

Writing unit tests can be simpler or harder, depending on how you designed your code. If you work in a clear, side effects-free style, then writing functional tests will be quite simple. If you start adding complexities such as callbacks or promises and databases or filesystems, then you'll require more work, because you'll have to *mock* some of those elements; after all, you don't want to run tests on a production database, do you?

In the following sections, we'll look at how we can write unit tests and learn how to work with some specific concepts such as *mocks* or *spies*.

Doing functional tests

First, let's see a simple, basic set of functional tests, and for that, let's go back to the rounding library we wrote in the *Working with modules* section of `Chapter 3`, *Developing with Node*. When you test a module, you only test the exported functions to see if they perform according to their specs. The interesting part to test is, then, the following:

```
const addR = (x: number, y: number): number => roundToCents(x + y);

const subR = (x: number, y: number): number => addR(x, changeSign(y));

const multR = (x: number, y: number): number => roundToCents(x * y);

const divR = (x: number, y: number): number => {
    if (y === 0) {
        throw new Error("Divisor must be nonzero");
    } else {
        return roundToCents(x / y);
    }
};
```

These four functions are totally functional, insofar that their computed results depend only on their input parameters, and they have absolutely no side effects. Writing tests requires (1) defining groups of tests, and (2) including one or more tests in each group. Here, it makes sense to write a group for each function, so let's see how the code could go; we could start with the `addR()` function, and write something like this:

```
// Source file: src/roundmath.test.js

/* @flow */
"use strict";

const rm = require("./roundmath");

describe("addR", () => {
    it("should add first and round later", () => {
        expect(rm.addR(1.505, 2.505)).toBe(4.01);
    });

    it("should handle negatives", () => {
        expect(rm.addR(3.15, -2.149)).toBe(1.0);
    });
});

// continues...
```

The most usual style is naming the unit test file in the same way as the tested file, but adding "test" or "spec" before the file extension. In our case, for roundmath.js, we named the unit test file as roundmath.test.js. As for placement, Jest is able to find your tests no matter where you place them, so the usual practice is to place this new file alongside the original one so that it will be easy to find.

Each describe() call defines a group, and each it() call within defines a specific test. Should a test fail, Jest will report it, giving the group's and test's descriptions, as in "addR should add first and round later". Tests consist of (1) setting things up, if needed; (2) actually running the test by calling the function; and (3) checking whether the function did as we expected.

The first test we wrote verifies that, when adding numbers, addition should be done first, and only then rounding; rounding first and then adding wouldn't be right. We test this by calling addR(1.505, 2.505), and we expect the result to be 4.01; if the function had been rounded first, the result would have been 4.02. Each test should be good at verifying at least one property of the function; our second test checks that addR() can handle negative numbers.

The style in which you write your assumptions about the code is meant to be easy to read: *expect so-and-so to be such-value*. Methods such as toBe() or toThrow() (see our next example) are called matchers; see the quite long list at https://facebook.github.io/jest/docs/en/expect.html for more information.

Of course, just a couple of tests would probably not be enough for complex code, and you'll usually have more tests, but as an example, these will do. Note that we should write tests for all functions; for example, divR() could use something like this. While the first test is quite straightforward (similar to one for addR()), in the second one, we verify that calling divR() with a zero divisor should throw an exception:

```
// ...continued

describe("divR", () => {
    it("should divide first, then round", () => {
        expect(rm.divR(22.96, 0.001)).toBe(22960);
    });

    it("should not divide by zero", () =>
        expect(() => rm.divR(22, 0)).toThrow());
});
```

If you miss some functions or part of them, later in this chapter, we'll look at ways to detect that; don't worry just now. At this point in time, we'll keep writing tests, and then we'll run the complete suite.

Using spies

The functional tests we wrote are quite good, but just won't do for some situations, such as when you work with callbacks. Let's turn to another piece of code we wrote: the user validation routine we used for JWT. Basically, this function received a username, a password, and an error-first callback, which was used to signal whether the username really had that password or not. We wrote very basic validation code (a single user was accepted!), but that doesn't matter here; we want to look at how we can deal with the callback. The important parts we care about now are highlighted in the following code extract:

```
const validateUser = (
    userName: string,
    password: string,
    callback: (?string, ?string) => void) => {
    if (!userName || !password) {
        callback("Missing user/password", null);
    } else if (userName === "fkereki" && password === "modernjsbook") {
        callback(null, "fkereki"); // OK, send userName back
    } else {
        callback("Not valid user", null);
    }
};
```

Testing this would require actually passing a callback, and then trying to see how it was called; this can be done, but the details would be messy. Alternatively, we can have a spy—a dummy function, which we can later interrogate to see if it was called or not, with which parameters it was called, and more:

```
// Source file: validate_user.test.js

/* @flow */
"use strict";

const validateUser = require("./validate_user");

describe("validateUser", () => {
    let cb;
    beforeEach(() => {
        cb = jest.fn();
    });
```

```
    it("should reject a call with empty user", () => {
        validateUser("", "somepass", cb);
        expect(cb).toHaveBeenCalled();
        expect(cb).toHaveBeenCalledWith("Missing user/password", null);
    });

    it("should reject a wrong password", () => {
        validateUser("fkereki", "wrongpassword", cb);
        expect(cb).toHaveBeenCalledWith("Not valid user", null);
    });

    it("should accept a correct password", () => {
        validateUser("fkereki", "modernjsbook", cb);
        expect(cb).toHaveBeenCalledWith(null, "fkereki");
    });
});
```

We can create such a spy by calling jest.fn(). Since we'll need a new spy for each test we'll write, we can take advantage of a beforeEach() function, which Jest will call automatically before running each individual test; this will save some extra writing. There are actually four functions you can use, as follows:

- beforeAll() will be called only once, before starting with your tests; for example, you could set up a test database here and fill it with certain data
- beforeEach() will be called before each test, as we did in our example to create a spy
- afterEach() will be called after each test, to *clean up*
- afterAll() will be called after running all tests; for example, you could destroy a test database you had created for testing purposes only

All three tests are similar; we will pick the first one. We call the validation routine, but pass an empty parameter. In terms of the validation specification, that should create an error. By doing this, we can test that the callback was actually called, and that it was called by passing an error as the first parameter, and nothing as the second.

(Of course, the first test, using the .toHaveBeenCalled() matcher, is not needed given the second one that tests if it was called with specific values, but we just wanted to show a new pair of matchers.)

Using spies is quite practical if we only care about seeing if a given function was called or not, but what would happen if the function under test actually required some value back from our spy? We can also solve that; let's get into a more complex example.

Working with mocks

Let's finish by working with a more complex example—a part of the REST code that worked with regions, which requires a database and uses promises, among several complications. Let's take the `DELETE` method handler as an example:

```
const deleteRegion = async (
    res: any,
    dbConn: any,
    country: string,
    region: string
) => {
    try {
        const sqlCities = `
            SELECT 1 FROM cities
            WHERE countryCode="${country}"
            AND regionCode="${region}"
            LIMIT 1
        `;

        const cities = await dbConn.query(sqlCities);

        if (cities.length > 0) {
            res.status(405).send("Cannot delete a region with cities");
        } else {
            const deleteRegion = `
                DELETE FROM regions
                WHERE countryCode="${country}"
                AND regionCode="${region}"
            `;

            const result = await dbConn.query(deleteRegion);

            if (result.info.affectedRows > 0) {
                res.status(204).send();
            } else {
                res.status(404).send("Region not found");
            }
        }
    } catch (e) {
        res.status(500).send("Server error");
    }
};
```

We did something right by passing the database connection (dbConn) as a parameter to the function. This means that we can *mock* it—meaning, provide an alternative version that will behave as we may want it, but without actually using any database. Similarly, processing our request will need to simulate a response object (res) whose status code we'll want to check; we could code it by hand, but using the node-mocks-http package is simpler, so just install it with npm install node-mocks-http --save. Check out its documentation at https://github.com/howardabrams/node-mocks-http, for more information—it can do much more!

We know that the DELETE method should (1) confirm that the region to be deleted must have no cities, and (2) if true, then actually delete the region. How can we test if the first check works? Let's provide deleteRegion() with a mock that will say that the region we want to delete actually has some cities:

```
// Source file: src/restful_regions.test.js

/* @flow */
"use strict";

const { deleteRegion } = require("./restful_regions");
const mockRes = require("node-mocks-http");

describe("deleteRegion", () => {
    let mDb;
    let mRes;
    beforeEach(() => {
        mDb = { query: jest.fn() };
        mRes = new mockRes.createResponse();
    });

    it("should not delete a region with cities", async () => {
        mDb.query.mockReturnValueOnce(Promise.resolve([1]));
        await deleteRegion(mRes, mDb, "FK", "22");
        expect(mRes.statusCode).toBe(405);
    });

// continues...
```

We could program a complete mock database that would analyze the incoming query and then provide some expected answer, but in this case, a little knowledge about how the code checks for cities is good. We can create a mock database object with a query attribute (mDb.query) and set it so that when mDb.query() is called for the first time, it will return a promise resolved to an array with a single 1—for that's what the actual SQL statement would have produced when checking a region that actually includes some cities. We'll also create a mock response object (mRes) that will get the routine's answer.

What's left to do? You just have to call the `deleteRegion()` function with all the parameters, `await` its results, and verify that the response status code is 405, as expected; then, you're done!

The other tests are similar, but we have to simulate two SQL accesses, not one:

```
// ...continued

    it("should delete a region without cities", async () => {
        mDb.query
            .mockReturnValueOnce(Promise.resolve([]))
            .mockReturnValueOnce(
                Promise.resolve({
                    info: { affectedRows: 1 }
                })
            );
        await deleteRegion(mRes, mDb, "ST", "12");
        expect(mRes.statusCode).toBe(204);
    });

    it("should produce a 404 for non-existing region", async () => {
        mDb.query
            .mockReturnValueOnce(Promise.resolve([]))
            .mockReturnValueOnce(
                Promise.resolve({
                    info: { affectedRows: 0 }
                })
            );
        await deleteRegion(mRes, mDb, "IP", "24");
        expect(mRes.statusCode).toBe(404);
    });
});
```

The interesting thing is that we can set up a mock function to produce different answers each time it is called, according to what we need. Thus, in order to test whether `deleteRegion()` would correctly delete a region without cities, our mock DB object must do the following:

- First, return an empty array, showing that the region to be deleted has no cities
- Second, return an object with `affectedRows:1`, showing that the (supposed) DELETE SQL command was successful

After setting things up in this way, the rest of the code is like our first case; await the function and check the status code.

How it works...

To run the tests, we'll have to edit a script in `package.json`. Change the `"test"` script, which up till now had just an error message, so it will read as follows:

```
"test": "jest out/"
```

The `"test"` script can be run just by typing npm test. In our case, since our output code goes into the `out/` directory we are telling Jest to inspect that directory, and run all tests (`*.test.js` files, by default) that it can find. You can modify Jest's configuration for more specific cases, but in general, it works well with *zero configuration*. The output is short and practical, as shown in the following screenshot:

```
> npm test

> simpleproject@1.0.0 test /home/fkereki/MODERNJS/chapter05
> jest out/

 PASS  out/restful_regions.test.js
 PASS  out/validate_user.test.js
 PASS  out/roundmath.test.js

Test Suites: 3 passed, 3 total
Tests:       10 passed, 10 total
Snapshots:   0 total
Time:        0.647s, estimated 1s
Ran all test suites matching /out\//i.
>
```

The result of the npm test command is short and to the point

In our case, matching what we did, it shows that we ran three suites of tests, including a total of 10 tests, and they all passed. Had one or more tests produced a wrong result, we'd have gotten another sort of result, with lots of red. I modified a test on purpose so that it would fail, and the following output was the result:

```
> npm test

> simpleproject@1.0.0 test /home/fkereki/MODERNJS/chapter05
> jest out/

FAIL out/restful_regions.test.js
  ● deleteRegion > should produce a 404 for non-existing region

    expect(received).toBe(expected) // Object.is equality

    Expected: 204
    Received: 404

      41 |              );
      42 |          await deleteRegion(mRes, mDb, "IP", "24");
    > 43 |          expect(mRes.statusCode).toBe(204);
         |                                  ^
      44 |      });
      45 | });
      46 |

      at _callee3$ (out/restful_regions.test.js:43:33)
      at tryCatch (node_modules/regenerator-runtime/runtime.js:62
:40)
      at Generator.invoke [as _invoke] (node_modules/regenerator-
runtime/runtime.js:296:22)
      at Generator.prototype.(anonymous function) [as next] (node
_modules/regenerator-runtime/runtime.js:114:21)
      at step (out/restful_regions.test.js:4:191)
      at out/restful_regions.test.js:4:361

PASS out/validate_user.test.js
PASS out/roundmath.test.js

Test Suites: 1 failed, 2 passed, 3 total
Tests:       1 failed, 9 passed, 10 total
Snapshots:   0 total
Time:        1.11s
Ran all test suites matching /out\//i.
npm ERR! Test failed.  See above for more details.
> []
```

Modifying a test to make it fail, and running Jest, produces a listing including the missed expectations, the failed test, and more

In the preceding screenshot, we can see that one test failed, in the `restful_regions.test.js` file, showing that a 204 result was expected, but a 404 error was received instead. The file is marked with a red `FAIL` message; the other two files are marked with `PASS`, in green. In our case, it happened because we purposefully wrote a failing test, but in real life, if the test had been running fine before, and now failed, it would mean that someone messed with the code and accidentally introduced a bug. (To be fair, there also exists the possibility that the test was not totally correct then, and the tested function was actually right!) In any case, getting a red result means that the code cannot be considered ready, and more work is needed.

There's more....

Should you need to mock some package that you cannot (or won't) inject as a parameter into a function, you can provide Jest with a complete mocked version. Suppose you wanted to mock the `"fs"` package: you'd start by creating a `__mocks__` directory at the same level of the `node_modules` one, then you would write and place your manual mock code there, and finally you would specify `jest.mock("fs")` at the beginning of your test file so that `Jest` will use your module rather than the standard one.

All of this can become a chore, so you'd better try to provide all of the modules as parameters to your functions (as we did with `dbConn` when deleting regions) so that standard mocks can be used. However, if you can't do that, check out `https://facebook.github.io/jest/docs/en/manual-mocks.html` for more information.

Measuring your test coverage

OK, so you have written a lot of tests, but how much of your code base are you actually testing? This measure of the quality (breadth) of your testing is called *coverage*, and it's easy to determine; in this recipe, let's find out how to do this. Fortunately, given all the work that we have done, it will be a very simple recipe.

How to do it...

To have `Jest` produce a coverage report, showing what parts of your code were (and weren't) covered by your tests, all you have to do is add a pair of parameters to the corresponding script in the `package.json` file:

```
"test": "jest out/ --coverage --no-cache"
```

In the preceding line of code, the first parameter, `--coverage`, tells `Jest` to collect all of the necessary information, and the second parameter, `--no-cache`, ensures that all information will be fresh; in certain situations, not totally correct results have been produced when this parameter was omitted. How does this affect the testing? Let's see!

How it works...

The key difference when running `Jest` with coverage is that a different report is added at the console, and also a HTML page is built. First, let's check the former: check out the following screenshot —and once again, I accept that seeing colors in black and white is really hard!

```
> npm test

> simpleproject@1.0.0 test /home/fkereki/MODERNJS/chapter05
> jest out/ --coverage --no-cache

 PASS  out/validate_user.test.js
 PASS  out/roundmath.test.js
 PASS  out/restful_regions.test.js
----------------------|----------|----------|----------|----------|--------------------|
File                  | % Stmts  | % Branch | % Funcs  | % Lines  | Uncovered Line #s  |
----------------------|----------|----------|----------|----------|--------------------|
All files             |   45.12  |   38.89  |   45.45  |   45.45  |                    |
 restful_regions.js   |   26.32  |   15.38  |      25  |   26.32  |... 72,173,175,178  |
 roundmath.js         |   83.33  |     100  |      50  |     100  |                    |
 validate_user.js     |     100  |     100  |     100  |     100  |                    |
----------------------|----------|----------|----------|----------|--------------------|

Test Suites: 3 passed, 3 total
Tests:       10 passed, 10 total
Snapshots:   0 total
Time:        1.869s
Ran all test suites matching /out\//i.
>
```

Including coverage options when running Jest produces a more detailed analysis of your tests

For each file, you get the following information:

- `%Stmts`: The percentage of statements that were executed at least once because of your tests. Ideally, each and every statement should have been executed at least once; otherwise, whatever statement wasn't executed could be anything, and you wouldn't realize it.

- %Branch: The percentage of branches that were taken. The reasoning for this is similar to that of %Stmts—if there are some branches (for example, an else) that were never taken, that means that there are some paths in your code that could do anything.
- %Funcs: The percentage of functions in the file that were called.
- %Lines: The percentage of lines that were covered. Note that a line may have several statements, so %Lines will always be greater or equal to %Stmts.
- Uncovered Line #s: This is NOT the number of lines (several billion!?), but the numbers of specific lines that were never executed.

In our case, we find that all of the functions were tested in validate_user.js, but half the functions were missed in roundmath.js (we tested addR() and divR(), but forgot about subR() and multR(), so that's correct) and only one function (the DELETE handler) was tested in restful_regions.js. Getting better coverage numbers means more work, and it may not always be wise, in economic terms, to aim for 100% (80%-90% is common), but 25% or 50% is definitely too low, so more work is needed.

The more interesting part is that you can analyze in depth how tests ran by looking into the coverage/lcov_report/ directory of your project and opening index.html in a browser, as shown in the following screenshot:

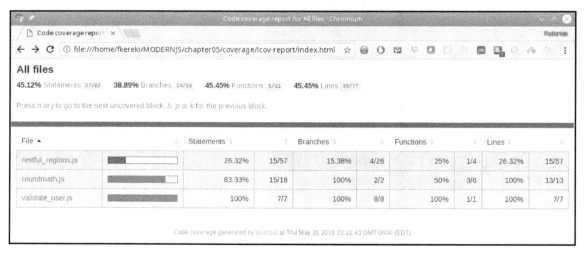

The main page of the web coverage report shows essentially the same data as the console run

First, you can see the files in different colors: as usual, red means a not-too-good result, and green is the best result. The interesting part is that if you click on a file, you'll get a detailed analysis, including each line, if it was executed or not, and more:

```
64
65  1x   const deleteRegion = async {
66            res        ,
67            dbConn     ,
68            country    ,
69            region
70        ) => {
71  3x       try {
72  3x           const sqlCities =
73                   SELECT 1 FROM cities
74                   WHERE countryCode="${country}"
75                   AND regionCode="${region}"
76                   LIMIT 1
77                   ;
78  3x           const cities = await dbConn.query(sqlCities);
79  3x           if (cities.length > 0) {
80  1x               res.status(405).send("Cannot delete a region with cities");
81              } else {
82  2x               const deleteRegion =
83                       DELETE FROM regions
84                       WHERE countryCode="${country}"
85                       AND regionCode="${region}"
86                       ;
87
88  2x               const result = await dbConn.query(deleteRegion);
89  2x               if (result.info.affectedRows > 0) {
90  1x                   res.status(204).send();
91                  } else {
92  1x                   res.status(404).send("Region not found");
93                  }
94              }
95          } catch (e) {
96              res.status(500).send("Server error");
97          }
98      };
99
```

You can see which lines were executed, and which were missed, and why 100% wasn't achieved

In our case, even if we thought we had covered all of the cases in `deleteRegion()`, the screen shows us that we missed a possible situation: the SQL server failing to answer. Of course, whether we include a specific test for this or not is a decision you'll have to take: at least we can see that all of the most important code was covered, but don't forget the other functions in the same file, which weren't tested at all!

Debugging your code

At some point or another, you'll have to debug your code. You might do well enough with just a bit of logging (using the console object, as we saw earlier at the beginning of the *Adding logging with Winston* section), but using a more powerful debugger is a great help. In this recipe, let's see how you can do real-time debugging with breakpoints, inspection of variables, and so on, so that you won't be limited to just trying to deduce what's wrong by looking at console logs.

How to do it...

There are two ways of doing debugging; let's see both methods here.

If you just want to stay in your IDE, Visual Studio Code lets you directly start a debugging session. Just click on the code you want to run (a reminder: pick the code in the out/ directory, and don't forget to use `npm run build`) and pick **Debug | Start Debugging** in the menu. The window will look as follows:

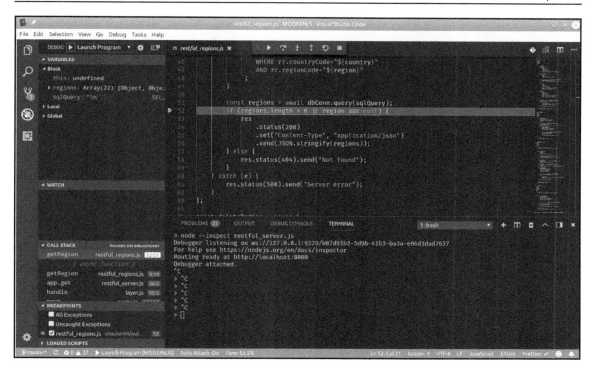

You can start a debugging session right in Visual Studio Code

Alternatively, if you'd rather keep using your favorite developer tools from Chrome, there's an alternative you can use. First, in Chrome, look for `N.I.M.`, the *Node.js V8 Inspector Manager*, which can be found at `https://chrome.google.com/webstore/detail/nodejs-v8-inspector-manag/gnhhdgbaldcilmgcpfddgdbkhjohddkj`, and add it to your browser.

After doing that, open the N.I.M. console by going to `about:inspect`, and you'll get something like what's shown in the following screenshot:

The N.I.M. extension lets you debug Node sessions using Chrome's developer tools

All you have to do now is go to VSC, or a shell session, and run your code. Before doing this, add the `--inspect` option, as in `node --inspect out/restful_server.js`. You will receive the following output:

To connect Node to Chrome's developer tools, you must run your code with an extra --inspect option

After that, a window will open, and you'll have full access to Chrome's debugger console, as shown in the following screenshot:

If you examine the URL in Chrome's debugger, you'll see something like `chrome-devtools://devtools/bundled/inspector.html?experiments=true&v8only=true&ws=...`, followed by a URL and a (long) hexadecimal number. These values are listed after running `Node` with `--inspect`, in the line starting with "Debugger listening on ws...".

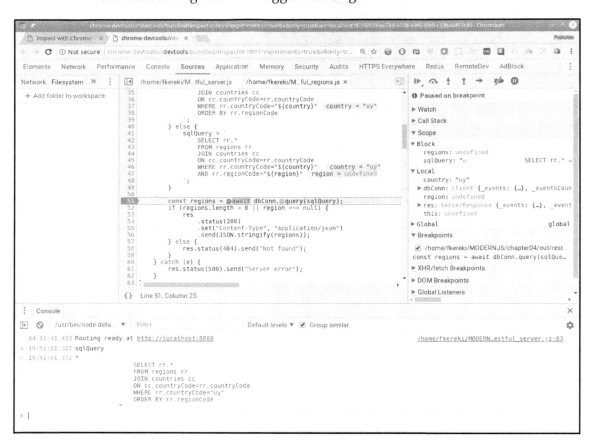

If N.I.M. is enabled, your Node session will connect to it, and you'll be able to debug your code from within Chrome

Finally, in any case, you are ready to start a serious debugging session; let's see what you can do.

 If you want to learn about how code inspection works, read the following article: `https://nodejs.org/en/docs/guides/debugging-getting-started/`. This also gives you tips for debugging with other IDEs.

How it works...

In the preceding screenshots, both with VSC and Chrome, I opened the `out/restful_regions.js` file and set a breakpoint at the place where a `SELECT` is done in order to get some regions. Doing a request for `/regions/uy` caused the run to pause at the point. You can then do the following:

- Examine all variables, including block, local, and global ones—this includes the possibility of modifying their values, if you want to
- Add some variables or expressions to watch; whenever execution pauses, you'll see their values
- See the call stack
- Set some specific breakpoints

As for program execution, you can do the following:

- Stop execution at any breakpoint
- Restart execution
- Step through your code, with the option of *drilling down* to analyze function calls

If you use Chrome, you'll be able to get some extra options, like memory usage analysis or code execution profiling, but clearly the web-specific options won't do any good. However, debugging your code by using the inspection option is a very good aid for bug chasing, so get used to it; you'll appreciate it a lot!

Testing simple services from the command line

Whenever you create services, you will need some way of testing them. So far, we have seen some examples of doing just that with curl. So, in this recipe, let's go a bit deeper and check out some options that you may find useful. Alternatively, you could opt for another tool, such as wget. For our purposes, both options are roughly equivalent, allowing us to do everything we need for RESTful services testing: they are scriptable, they can download things, and they can also send requests posting data, so what you use will be mostly a question of personal preference.

 If you want to read more about curl, check out its site at https://curl.haxx.se/, or the source code at https://github.com/curl/curl. You may also be interested in *Everything Curl*, a book that details all there is to know about this tool, and which is freely available at https://www.gitbook.com/download/pdf/book/bagder/everything-curl—however, do take into account that it's over 300 pages long!

Getting ready

How to install curl will depend on your operating system, but it's available for practically every platform you are likely to work with; just check out all the downloads at https://curl.haxx.se/download.html. The command has dozens of possible options, but for our intents, we will be looking at the following table. Note that most options have two versions: a short, single character one, and a longer one, intended to be clearer for understanding:

-K filename --config filename	Lets you specify the name of a file that has options in it so that your command is shorter. In the given file, each option will be in a different line.
-d key=value --data key=value	Allows you to send data in the body of the request. If you use this option several times, curl will use & as a separator, as standard.
--data-binary someData	Similar to --data, but used to send binary data. Most frequently it is followed by @filename, meaning that the contents of the named file will be sent.
-D filename --dump-header filename	Dumps the headers of the received data into a file.

-H "header:value" --header "header:value"	Allows you to set and send some header with a request. You can use this option several times to set many headers.
-i --include	Includes headers of the received data in the output.
-o filename --output filename	Stores the received data in the given file.
-s --silent	Minimizes output to the console.
-v --verbose	Maximizes output to the console.
-X method --request method	Specifies which HTTP method will be used, such as GET, POST, PUT, and so on.

Finally, if you need help, use `curl --help` or `curl --manual`, and you'll get a full description of the utility and its options. Now let's look at how we can use `curl` to test our services.

How to do it...

Let's do a complete set of tests for the RESTful server we created in the previous chapter, with all options enabled, including JWT—which, as you'll remember, we removed in order to simplify our code! Let's follow these steps:

Firstly, we may verify that the server is up and running; the / route had no token requirement. Remember that we are using `8443`, and actual HTTPS: requests will be sent to that port:

```
> curl localhost:8443/
Ready
```

Now, if we try to access some region, we'll be refused, because of the lack of an authorizing JWT:

```
> curl localhost:8443/regions/uy/10
No token specified
```

- If the line starts with *, it's some information from `curl` itself
- If the line starts with >, it's a header sent with the request
- If the line starts with <, it's a received header

In the following listing, I highlighted the incoming data:

```
> curl localhost:8443/regions/uy/10 --verbose
* Trying 127.0.0.1...
* TCP_NODELAY set
* Connected to localhost (127.0.0.1) port 8443 (#0)
> GET /regions/uy/10 HTTP/1.1
> Host: localhost:8443
> User-Agent: curl/7.59.0
> Accept: */*
>
< HTTP/1.1 401 Unauthorized
< X-Powered-By: Express
< Access-Control-Allow-Origin: *
< Connection: close
< Content-Type: text/html; charset=utf-8
< Content-Length: 18
< ETag: W/"12-s2+Ia/H9PDrgc59/6Z0mcWLfxuw"
< Date: Sun, 03 Jun 2018 21:00:40 GMT
<
* Closing connection 0
No token specified
```

We can get a token by using the /gettoken route and providing user and password values. Let's store the received token in a file to simplify future tests:

```
> curl localhost:8443/gettoken -d "user=fkereki" -d "password=modernjsbook"
-o token.txt
  % Total    % Received % Xferd  Average Speed   Time    Time     Time
Current
                                 Dload  Upload   Total   Spent    Left
Speed
100   187  100   153  100    34   149k  34000 --:--:-- --:--:-- --:--:--
182k

> cat token.txt
eyJhbGciOiJIUzI1NiIsInR5cCI6IkpXVCJ9.eyJ1c2VyaWQiOiJma2VyZWtpIiwiaWF0IjoxNT
I4MDU5Nzc0LCJleHAiOjE1MjgwNjMzNzR9.6tioV798HHqriOFkhUpf8xJc8wq5TY5g-jN-
XhgwaTs
```

Now we can try a simple GET. We can either cut-and-paste the token in a header, or use some shell features, at least in Linux-based systems, and take advantage of the back tick option to include the token file's contents in the request:

```
> curl localhost:8443/regions/uy/10 -H "Authorization: Bearer
eyJhbGciOiJIUzI1NiIsInR5cCI6IkpXVCJ9.eyJ1c2VyaWQiOiJma2VyZWtpIiwiaWF0IjoxNT
I4MDU5Nzc0LCJleHAiOjE1MjgwNjMzNzR9.6tioV798HHqriOFkhUpf8xJc8wq5TY5g-jN-
XhgwaTs"
```

```
[{"countryCode":"UY","regionCode":"10","regionName":"Montevideo"}]

> curl localhost:8443/regions/uy/10 -H "Authorization: Bearer `cat
token.txt`"
[{"countryCode":"UY","regionCode":"10","regionName":"Montevideo"}]
```

All we've got left is to try out the other routes and methods. Let's change the name of Montevideo to MVD, which actually is the IATA code for its international airport; we'll do a PUT first (which should produce a 204 status code) and then a GET to verify the update:

```
> curl localhost:8443/regions/uy/10 -H "Authorization: Bearer `cat
token.txt`" -X PUT -d "name=MVD" --verbose
*    Trying 127.0.0.1...
* TCP_NODELAY set
* Connected to localhost (127.0.0.1) port 8443 (#0)
> PUT /regions/uy/10 HTTP/1.1
> Host: localhost:8443
> User-Agent: curl/7.59.0
> Accept: */*
> Authorization: Bearer
eyJhbGciOiJIUzI1NiIsInR5cCI6IkpXVCJ9.eyJ1c2VyaWQiOiJma2VyZWtpIiwiaWF0IjoxNT
I4MDU5Nzc0LCJleHAiOjE1MjgwNjMzNzR9.6tioV798HHqriOFkhUpf8xJc8wq5TY5g-jN-
XhgwaTs
> Content-Length: 8
> Content-Type: application/x-www-form-urlencoded
>
* upload completely sent off: 8 out of 8 bytes
< HTTP/1.1 204 No Content
< X-Powered-By: Express
< Access-Control-Allow-Origin: *
< Connection: close
< Date: Sun, 03 Jun 2018 21:09:01 GMT
<
* Closing connection 0

> curl localhost:8443/regions/uy/10 -H "Authorization: Bearer `cat
token.txt`"
[{"countryCode":"UY","regionCode":"10","regionName":"MVD"}]
```

In one experiment, I created a new region, numbered 20. Let's delete it and verify that it's gone with yet another GET. The first request should get a 204 status, and the second should get a 404, because the region will no longer exist:

```
> curl localhost:8443/regions/uy/20 -H "Authorization: Bearer `cat
token.txt`" -X DELETE --verbose
*    Trying 127.0.0.1...
* TCP_NODELAY set
* Connected to localhost (127.0.0.1) port 8443 (#0)
```

```
> DELETE /regions/uy/20 HTTP/1.1
> Host: localhost:8443
> User-Agent: curl/7.59.0
> Accept: */*
> Authorization: Bearer
eyJhbGciOiJIUzI1NiIsInR5cCI6IkpXVCJ9.eyJ1c2VyaWQiOiJma2VyZWtpIiwiaWF0IjoxNT
I4MDU5NzcwLCJleHAiOjE1MjgwNjMzNzR9.6tioV798HHqriOFkhUpf8xJc8wq5TY5g-jN-
XhgwaTs
>
< HTTP/1.1 204 No Content
< X-Powered-By: Express
< Access-Control-Allow-Origin: *
< Connection: close
< Date: Sun, 03 Jun 2018 21:12:06 GMT
<
* Closing connection 0

> curl localhost:8443/regions/uy/20 -H "Authorization: Bearer `cat
token.txt`" -X DELETE --verbose
.
. several lines snipped out
.
< HTTP/1.1 404 Not Found
.
. more snipped lines
.
Region not found
```

Finally, let's invent a new region to verify that POST also works; a 201 status should be returned, as well as the new ID (which would be 20, after we deleted the previous invented 20th Uruguayan region):

```
> curl localhost:8443/regions/uy -H "Authorization: Bearer `cat token.txt`"
-X POST -d "name=Fictitious" --verbose
.
. lines snipped out
.
< HTTP/1.1 201 Created
< X-Powered-By: Express
< Access-Control-Allow-Origin: *
< Connection: close
< Location: /regions/uy/20
.
. snipped lines
.
Region created

> curl localhost:8443/regions/uy -H "Authorization: Bearer `cat token.txt`"
```

```
[{"countryCode":"UY","regionCode":"1","regionName":"Artigas"},{"countryCode
":"UY","regionCode":"10","regionName":"MVD"},
.
. snipped out lines
.
{"countryCode":"uy","regionCode":"20","regionName":"Fictitious"},
.
. more snipped out lines
.
{"countryCode":"UY","regionCode":"9","regionName":"Maldonado"}]
```

So, by using `curl` and some console work, we can set out to test any kind of services. However, at some point, you may need to work with more complex sequences of service calls, and doing all this work by hand could become a chore. Indeed, by careful scripting you may simplify your job, but let's consider another tool, Postman, that's more apt for that kind of work.

Testing more complex sequences of calls with Postman

Testing services manually, or even with a carefully crafted shell script, isn't really easy. Furthermore, if you require some kind of complex test, using scripting may prove to be just too hard. `Postman` can be used to write tests for services, to organize them into full testing suites, and to document the way your RESTful API works. You can also use it to mock services or as a help in development, but we won't be getting into that here. In this recipe, we'll focus on the testing aspects.

Getting ready

Download `Postman` from `https://www.getpostman.com/`, and install it according to the instructions for each platform. Remember to take a look at its documentation for more features that we won't be seeing here.

How to do it...

Postman lets you create requests that you can store in collections. Before and after each request, you may execute JavaScript code, either to set up the upcoming request, to process the resulting response, or to store some information for future requests in a test sequence. Let's take a look at the following sections.

Doing basic requests

First, we'll start with a simple test to get a JWT, which we'll then store so that we can use it in upcoming tests. Open the `Postman` application and click on **New** to create a request. Give it a name and a description, and either select or create a collection or folder to save it. Don't worry too much about the actual placement; you'll be able to move requests around, edit them, and more.

Then, to get a token, we need a `POST`, so set the method appropriately. Select the **BODY** tab, pick the `x-www-form-urlencoded` option, and add two values, `user` and `password`, which will be sent with the request. (For other situations, you might send raw data such as XML or JSON, or binary data such as a file.) Check out the following screenshot:

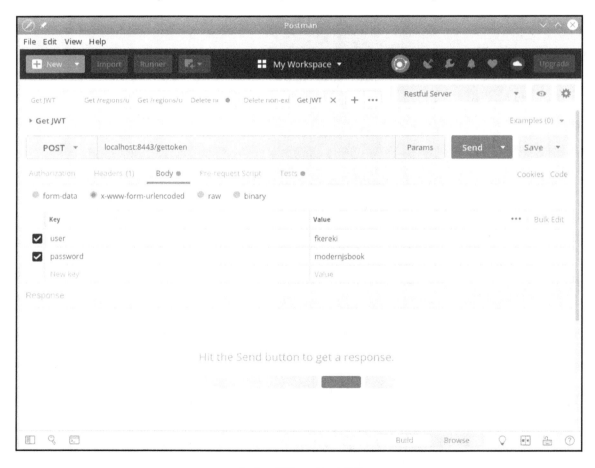

Creating a POST request to get a JWT

Now, if you test it out by clicking on **Send**, the request will go to your server, and the answer will appear at the bottom of the screen:

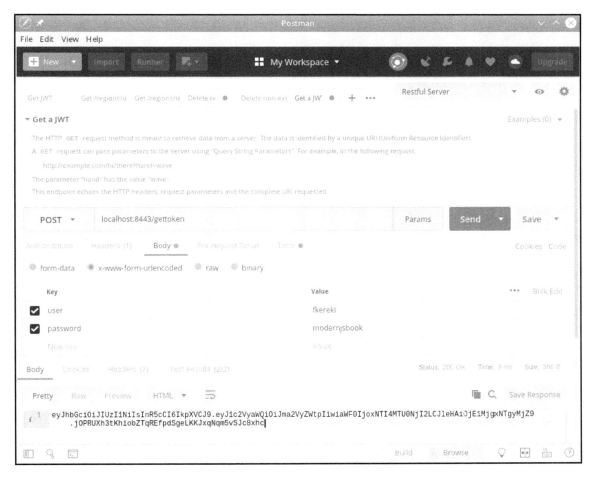

A test run of our request shows that everything is working fine

Adding some checks

However, that's not enough. We don't just want to check whether the `/gettoken` endpoint works—we'd like to test if the token looks right, and if so, store it so that later requests can use it. We will create an environment (click on the gear at the upper right corner) and add a `token` entry so that we can store and retrieve the value we got from the server:

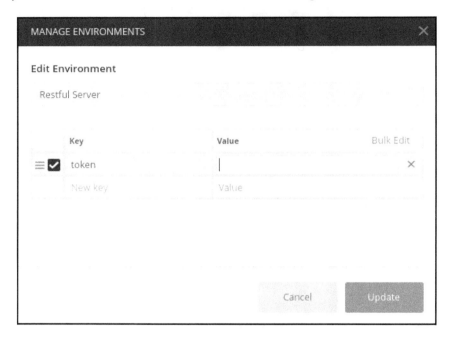

Creating an environment is one way you can share data between requests

Finally, let's write some tests for the token, and also store its value in the environment. Writing the tests themselves is sort of similar to what we already did, but you'll have to look into the documentation to see what objects and methods are available. As for the tests themselves, they use `Chai` (see `http://www.chaijs.com/`), which is similar to `Jest` when it comes to writing your expectations, but not exactly the same:

```
pm.test("Response is long enough", () =>
    pm.expect(pm.response.text()).to.have.lengthOf.above(40));

pm.test("Response has three parts", () =>
    pm.expect(pm.response.text().split(".")).to.have.lengthOf(3));
pm.environment.set("token", pm.response.text()); // for later scripts
```

First, we will test that the answer should be at least 40 bytes long; tokens have no special size limits, but 40 characters is on the low side. Then, a second test will check that the token is comprised of three parts, separated by periods. Finally, we will store the response itself in the environment, for future use. If you check the **TESTS** tab, you'll see that both our tests passed, as shown in the following screenshot:

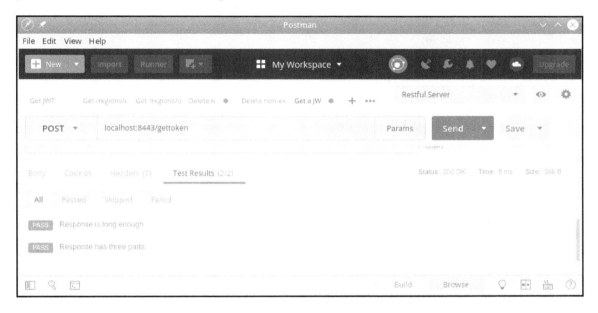

Both tests we created were successful

Chaining requests

If you check the environment, you'll see that the token was stored. Now let's write a second test, a `GET`, that will use the token. I went through a similar sequence by doing a request for `/regions/uy`, but I added a line in the headers, with the `Authorization` key and the `Bearer {{token}}` value, so that the previously stored token value would be replaced in the header. I also added a couple of tests to make sure (1) I got a successful JSON answer, and (2) the answer was an array of at least 19 regions. (Yes, I know my country, Uruguay, has exactly 19 regions, but sometimes, for test purposes, I may add some new ones!) The tests show some features we haven't seen before:

```
pm.test("Answer should be JSON", () => {
    pm.response.to.be.success;
    pm.response.to.have.jsonBody();
});

pm.test("Answer should have at least 19 regions", () => {
    const regions = JSON.parse(pm.response.text());
    pm.expect(regions).to.have.lengthOf.at.least(19);
});
```

In this fashion, you can create complete sequences of requests; make sure that getting the JWT is placed earlier in the list. In a collection, you can also have many folders, each with a distinct sequence of steps. (You may also change the sequence programatically, but we won't get into that here; check out `https://www.getpostman.com/docs/v6/postman/scripts/branching_and_looping` for more information.)

I created two folders to test some `GET`s and a `DELETE`—but, of course, you should be writing even more tests to verify every method, and as many different sequences as possible. Let's see how we can make them run.

How it works...

Once you have organized your requests in folders, you can run any given sequence by clicking on it at the sidebar on the left. If everything is OK, you'll get green marks for all tests; a red mark highlights an issue:

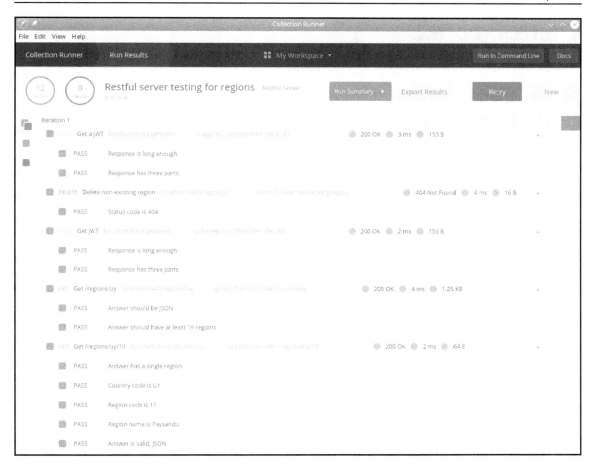

Running a collection runs every test in it. Green blocks show successes; red ones mark errors.

With this, you already have a good tool for documenting your API (make sure that every test and field has an explanation) and for making sure that it keeps working, going beyond the unit testing into full **end-to-end** (E2E) testing.

Depending on your `Postman` account, you can also set things up to get periodical monitoring of your API; check out `https://www.getpostman.com/docs/v6/postman/monitors/intro_monitors` for more information.

There's more...

By using the `newman` package (install it with `npm install newman --save-dev`), you can run your `Postman` tests from the command line, which could also allow you to include them in a continuous integration workflow. First, export your collection from `Postman` (uninspiredly, I called mine `postman_collection.json`), and then add a new script to your `package.json` file called `"newman":"newman run postman_collection.json"`. Using `npm run newman` will then produce an output like the one shown in the following code snippet. You could also test whether all of the tests ran satisfactorily or whether there was a problem:

```
> npm run newman

> simpleproject@1.0.0 newman /home/fkereki/MODERNJS/chapter05
> newman run postman_collection.json

newman

Restful server testing for regions

❏ Test Delete
↳ Get JWT
   POST localhost:8443/gettoken [200 OK, 386B, 14ms]
   ✓ Response is long enough
   ✓ Response has three parts

↳ Delete non-existing region
   DELETE localhost:8443/regions/zz/99 [404 Not Found, 255B, 4ms]
   ✓ Status code is 404 baby!!

❏ Test Get
↳ Get JWT
   POST localhost:8443/gettoken [200 OK, 386B, 2ms]
   ✓ Response is long enough
   ✓ Response has three parts

↳ Get /regions/uy
   GET localhost:8443/regions/uy [200 OK, 1.46KB, 2ms]
   ✓ Answer should be JSON
   ✓ Answer should have at least 19 regions

↳ Get /regions/uy/10
   GET localhost:8443/regions/uy/11 [200 OK, 303B, 2ms]
   ✓ Answer has a single region
   ✓ Country code is UY
   ✓ Region code is 11
```

```
✓ Region name is Paysandu
✓ Answer is valid, JSON
```

	executed	failed
iterations	1	0
requests	5	0
test-scripts	10	0
prerequest-scripts	5	0
assertions	12	0

```
total run duration: 212ms
```

```
total data received: 1.6KB (approx)
```

```
average response time: 4ms
```

Documenting and testing your REST API with Swagger

Now let's focus more on documentation and testing with a well-known tool: Swagger. This is a tool that's meant to help you design, model, and test APIs. The key idea is that you'll end up by having an online, interactive document that will describe in detail all of your API calls, the parameter types and restrictions, the required and optional values, and so on, even letting you try calls *on the fly* to better understand how the API is meant to be used.

How to do it...

The first—and hardest!—part of setting up `Swagger` is preparing the specification for your complete API. This is meant to be written in **YAML Ain't Markup Language (YAML)**, and can be difficult to get right. However, you can use a web editor, which you can run at your own server (go to `https://swagger.io/tools/swagger-editor/` for the necessary download) or online at `https://editor.swagger.io`. After writing that, however, setting everything up will be truly easy, needing just three lines of code!

 YAML is a recursive acronym that stands for *YAML Ain't Markup Language*. If you want to learn more about it, visit `http://yaml.org/`.

Writing our specs

We won't be able to introduce the full rules for writing API specs here, and also won't be able to include all of its features in our example. Furthermore, a complete description for any API can be hundreds of lines long, and that's another problem. So, let's just go over some basic definitions, as well as a couple of the services, to get a taste of what needs to be done. First, we'll need some basic data about our server:

```
swagger: "2.0"
info:
  description: "This is a RESTful API to access countries, regions, and
cities."
  version: "1.0.0"
  title: "World Data API"

host: "127.0.0.1:8443"
schemes:
- "http"
```

Then we must describe the tags (think *sections*) that our documentation will be divided into. We work with tokens (for security), plus countries, regions, and cities, so those seem to be the needed definitions:

```
tags:
- name: "token"
  description: "Get a JWT for authorization"
- name: "countries"
  description: "Access the world countries"
- name: "regions"
  description: "Access the regions of countries"
```

```
 - name: "cities"
   description: "Access the world cities"
```

Let's take a look at the /gettoken route. We define a POST request, which gets body encoded parameters, and returns plain text. Two string parameters, user and password, are required. The API may either return a 200 status if everything was OK, or 401 otherwise:

```
paths:
  /gettoken:
    post:
      tags:
      - "token"
      summary: "Get a token to authorize future requests"
      consumes:
        - "application/x-www-form-urlencoded"
      produces:
        - text/plain
      parameters:
        - in: formData
          name: user
          required: true
          type: string
        - in: formData
          name: password
          required: true
          type: string
      responses:
        200:
          description: A valid token to use for other requests
        401:
          description: "Wrong user/password"
```

Getting regions for a country would get a similar specification:

```
  /regions:
    get:
      tags:
      - "regions"
      summary: "Get all regions of all countries"
      produces:
        - application/json
      parameters:
        - in: header
          name: "Authorization"
          required: true
          type: string
          description: Authorization Token
```

```
responses:
  200:
    description: "OK"
  401:
    description: "No token provided"
```

Enabling Swagger

To enable the Swagger documentation, we need the swagger-ui-express package, and also need to load the JSON version of the YAML specs, so you'll need a couple of lines of code. First, install the package with the usual npm install swagger-ui-express --save, and then add the following lines to your server:

```
const swaggerUi = require("swagger-ui-express");
const swaggerDocument = require("../swagger.json");
```

In the server, we must also add a line for enabling the new route, at the beginning, after other app.use() statements. We are adding Swagger to our RESTful API, and without a token: you might prefer to set up a different server, only providing access to the API, and possibly also enabling authorization, but both changes will be easy to accomplish. So, let's go with the simpler version here:

```
app.use(cors());
app.use(bodyParser.urlencoded({ extended: false }));
app.use("/api-docs", swaggerUi.serve, swaggerUi.setup(swaggerDocument));
```

You're all set! After you rebuild the project and start the server, the new route will be available, providing online documentation for your server.

How it works...

If you start the server, accessing the /api-docs route will provide access to the main Swagger screen, as follows:

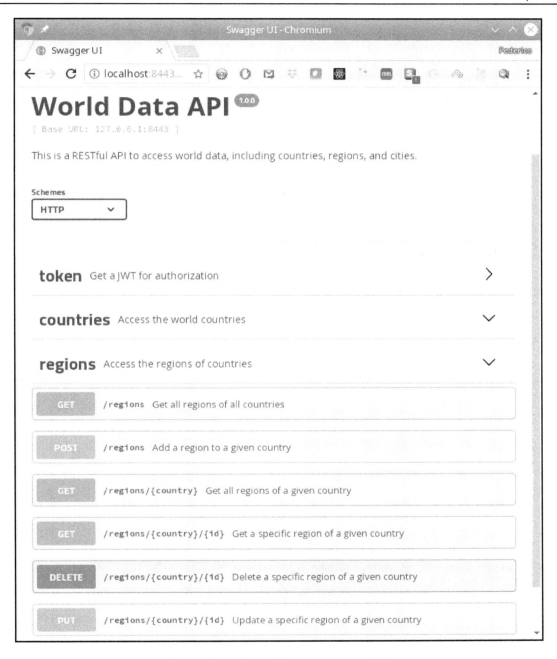

Swagger produces a main page, with access to every route you defined

Interaction is easy: select an area, click on a given request, and you'll get the list of all routes and operations. Let's see, for example, how to get the regions for Uruguay. First, we must get a token, so we want to open the token area and enter the necessary user and password, as shown in the following screenshot:

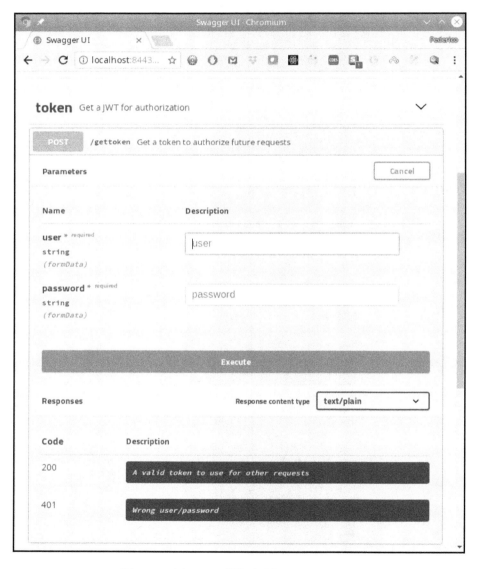

Doing a request is just a matter of filling the fields and executing the query

When the process runs, you'll get the answer, as shown in the following screenshot:

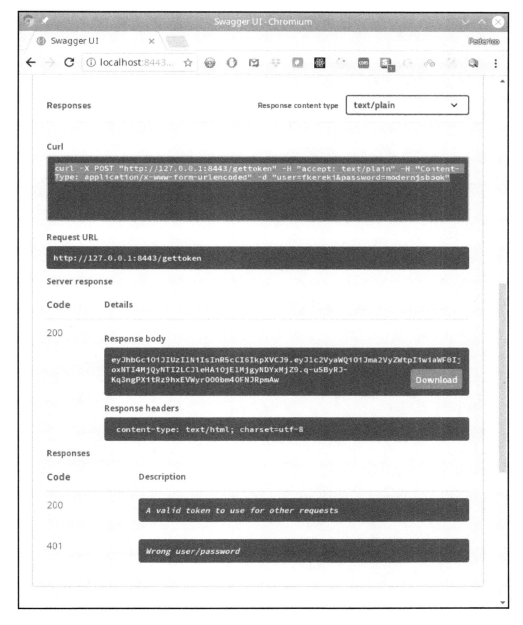

A successful request returned the security token

You can see the equivalent `curl` request at the top, which matches what we did earlier in this chapter, in the *Testing simple services from the command line* section. Now, copying that token and pasting it into the `/regions/uy` endpoint means that we're ready to do that query:

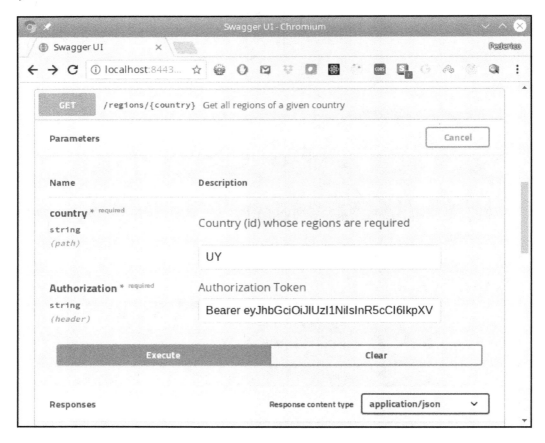

After getting a token, we can set up the query to get all of the regions of a country

All that's left to do is execute that query, and we'll get the desired results, as shown in the following screenshot:

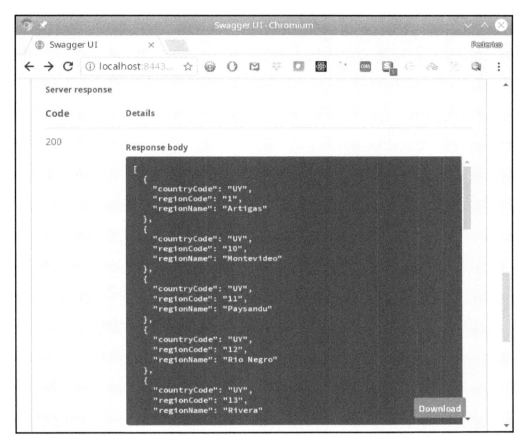

Doing sequences of calls is possible, and Swagger lets you experiment easily with different endpoints

What can we point out? First, obviously, Swagger is a very good tool, in terms of documentation. You can add descriptions to methods, parameters, results, and even include sample values and results. This means that developers who need to use your API will have a very good way of learning about how to use it. In terms of actually using your API, Swagger is simpler than curl or Postman, but it cannot chain operations, which you'll have to do on your own. You should really think about starting your development with this tool, and only moving forward with actual coding once you have everything documented; give it a try!

6
Developing with React

In this chapter, we will cover the following recipes:

- Starting out with React
- Reinstalling your tools
- Defining components
- Handling state
- Composing components
- Handling life cycle events
- Simplifying component development with Storybook

Introduction

In the last three chapters, we were developing a backend with Node, and now we'll turn to the frontend and build a web application: in particular, a **Single Page Application (SPA)** in the modern style users have gotten used to.

Starting out with React

Suppose you want to build a web application. How would you go about it? Unless you have been hiding away somewhere, you are probably aware that there are many frameworks out there that can help you construct and organize your web page. However, you might be wondering, if you already know HTML, CSS, and JS, why use a framework at all, instead of just keeping with vanilla JS, and possibly some library like jQuery or Lodash? After all, a framework imposes some rules and ways of working that you could consider to be offputting or bothersome.

You also have to *learn* how to use the framework, of course, and you probably won't benefit from it until you become proficient. So, there are several possible answers for the *why?* question – even including *Sure, don't use any framework!* – which could be just fine for a very small, simple project:

- Frameworks provide you with a well-tested, solid way, to organize your project
- Frameworks usually scale better for large size applications
- Frameworks let you work at a higher level of abstractions (for example, creating and using your own components) and deal with the nitty-gritty aspects of getting everything to work
- Ramping up new developers is usually simpler: if they know the framework, they already know where things are supposed to go and how they interact with each other

Of course, as I mentioned previously, all of these advantages do not apply for small projects, with a few developers.

There's one extra reason, however, that can be considered even more important. Frameworks help you with the difficult task of keeping state (data) and view in sync. With large applications, a change or event that happens in one *corner* of your application may have implications elsewhere, in other places of the same application. Trying to wire things up so that all of the changes are correctly propagated throughout your code isn't a simple endeavor.

Most frameworks automatically generate the view from the data, and whenever anything changes in the state, they do whatever's needed to update the screen in an optimal fashion. For example, say you had a list of doodads somewhere. Then, you call a webservice and you get an updated list—most doodads match, but some are added and some are missing. You could, of course, just recreate the list from zero, but that wouldn't look very good, and if you decide to regenerate the whole screen every time something changes, performance will suffer. Usually, what will happen is that the framework will compute the differences between the current list and the new one, and will correspondingly update the HTML code, adding or removing DOM elements, so that the list is once again correct. Doing all of this by hand, extending this to your whole application, would be a tad too much to do!

There are several well-known frameworks such as `Angular` (by Google), `Vue`, `Ember`, `Backbone`, `Knockout`, and so on. (Sometimes you feel that a new framework is born every day!) We'll be using `React` (by Facebook) in this book.

An admission: `React` is more correctly called a *library* than a framework, because it doesn't include everything you need to develop your application out of the box. However, all of the necessary packages are out there, so that won't impede us. By the way, this sort of criticism also applies to `Vue`, `Knockout`, and `Backbone`.

`React` also extends to doing mobile applications with `React-Native`, which we'll see later in this book in `Chapter 11`, *Creating Mobile Apps with React Native*.

An interesting article, *The Ultimate Guide to JavaScript Frameworks*, at `https://javascriptreport.com/the-ultimate-guide-to-javascript-frameworks/`, lists over fifty frameworks! Take a look, and see what pros and cons each framework has.

In this recipe, we'll install the necessary packages and build a very basic first web application of our own.

How to do it...

Let's go ahead and create our basic application. If you had to set up a project purely by hand, you'd find yourself having to deal with many different tools, such as `Babel` for transpiling, `ESLint` for code checks, `Jest` for testing, or `Webpack` in order to pack all of your application together, instead of having to send dozens or hundreds of individual files over the web. However, nowadays, there is a much simpler tool, `create-react-app`, that can deal with this chore and get you set up for `React` development in a jiffy. The key selling point is *zero configuration*, meaning that some reasonable good choices for both development and production builds have been selected, and you can directly move on to writing code, not really caring about myriad configuration details.

For people in the know, `create-react-app` is known as CRA, and that's the name we'll be using. By the way, CRA is not the only possible way to create a project; for example, `react-boilerplate` (at `https://github.com/react-boilerplate/react-boilerplate`) provides an alternate solution, but the chosen set of packages and tools are more suited to experienced `React` developers.

To create the basic structure (which we'll explain later on) we'll use npx to run the application creator tool, as shown in the following code. Since we are at Chapter 6, let's (imaginatively!) name our project chapter06!

```
> npx create-react-app chapter06
Creating a new React app in /home/fkereki/JS_BOOK/modernjs/chapter06.

Installing packages. This might take a couple minutes.
Installing react-scripts...

...many lines describing installed packages, snipped out...

Success! Created chapter06 at /home/fkereki/JS_BOOK/modernjs/chapter06
Inside that directory, you can run several commands:

  npm start
    Starts the development server.

  npm run build
    Bundles the app into static files for production.

  npm test
    Starts the test runner.

  npm run eject
    Removes this tool and copies build dependencies, configuration files
    and scripts into the app directory. If you do this, you can't go back!

We suggest that you begin by typing:

  cd chapter06
  npm start

Happy hacking!
```

If you are curious, npx is similar to npm, but it executes a *binary* command, which is either found in your node_modules directory, or at a central cache, even installing any packages it might need to run. For more information, go to its GitHub page at https://github.com/zkat/npx, or better yet, read an article by npx's creator, *Introducing npx: an npm package runner* at https://medium.com/@maybekatz/introducing-npx-an-npm-package-runner-55f7d4bd282b.

How it works...

Running the script will create a basic project structure, including the following:

- A package.json file, and a corresponding node_modules directory.
- A README.md file, essentially a copy of what you can find at https://github.com/wmonk/create-react-app-typescript/blob/master/packages/react-scripts/template/README.md. Pay particular attention to it, because it's full of tips, suggestions, and solutions to usual problems you may encounter.
- A public/ directory, with the index.html basic HTML code for your application, plus a favicon.ico icon file and a manifest.json file describing your app. (If you want to read more about the latter, check out https://developer.mozilla.org/en-US/Add-ons/WebExtensions/manifest.json.)
- A src/ directory with the index.js JS basic code for your application, index.css with CSS styles, and an App component that shows some welcome text, plus some basic instructions. All of your JS and CSS files should be placed in src/ or in subdirectories within it, otherwise they won't be included in the build.

Basically, you will want to edit the index.* and App.* files, and grow the project by expanding its structure to provide more components, styles, and so on. (Be careful: don't change the names of the index.* files, or your project won't run!) Before getting into writing code, and as shown in the preceding run, in the created project directory, you should try npm start.

By doing this, you'll be able to see the new application, as shown in the following screenshot:

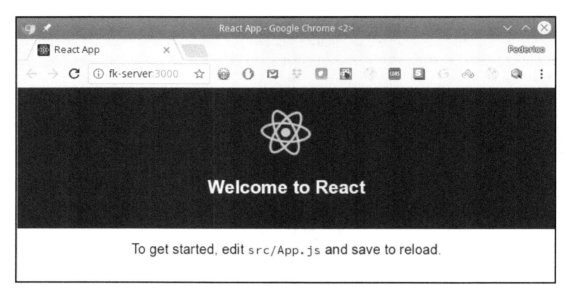

The created application, ready for you to start coding

If you wish, you can make any kind of minor change in App.js, save it, and notice the immediate change in the browser page. As to what features of JS you can use in your coding, the project is set to accept most modern options, from ES6 (full), ES7 (like the exponentiation operator, which you may probably never use!), and even newer (most interestingly, async and await), plus some *Stage 3* proposals; check https://github.com/facebook/create-react-app/blob/master/packages/react-scripts/template/README.md#supported-language-features-and-polyfills for an updated list. It's noteworthy that Flow is recognized, and also JSX, which we'll be using in later sections.

There's more...

It may happen, at some time, that you need to do some extra configuration that CRA hasn't considered, or that you are unable to add it otherwise. In this case, you can use the npm run eject command to move all of the configuration, scripts, and dependencies directly into your project so that you can start tweaking things in any way you want. Of course, this will be harder than using the *zero configuration* setup, but at least you won't be locked in, with no way out.

If you are curious to learn where all of those things are hidden away, possibly to study how everything is set up, the answer is "in the `node_modules/create_react_app`" directory; ejecting the project copies things from that directory to your project's.

Reinstalling your tools

We have been using `ESLint` for code quality checks, `Prettier` for formatting, and `Flow` for data types. In this recipe, we'll get these packages back to work, and we'll leave testing (`Jest`, plus more) for `Chapter 10`, *Testing your Application*. Doing this for two of our tools will be quite straightforward, but a tad more complex for the third.

How to do it...

With a fully manual installation, getting everything to work together will be quite difficult, but CRA already includes practically everything we need, so all you have to do is add some configuration details.

Reinstalling Flow and Prettier

Let's start with `Flow`. It's quite simple to do this: I just did the same as for `Node`, adding the same packages, scripts, `.flowconfig` file, and so on. (If you need to, check out the *Adding Flow for Data Types checks* section of `Chapter 1`, *Working with JavaScript Development Tools* for more information.)

Next, let's deal with `Prettier`. It also is a simple matter: I had to remove the following lines from `package.json` and put them in a separate `.prettierrc` file:

```
{
    "tabWidth": 4,
    "printWidth": 75
}
```

`Flow` already *knows* about `React` and CRA, so you won't need anything with regard to that. However, to use `PropTypes` (we'll get to that very soon), you'll need the appropriate flow-typed package, which is easy to install:

```
npm run addTypes prop-types@15
```

Reinstalling ESLint

Finally, our third tool will require a bit more work. For ESLint, we cannot use package.json either, and we need a .eslintrc file. But, even if you extract that part, you'll find that the configuration doesn't pay attention to your settings, and that's because CRA has its own set of ESLint rules, which you cannot change! Unless, of course, you decide to eject the project and start doing configuration by yourself, which you'll want to avoid for as long as possible. There's a package, react-app-rewired, that lets you change the internal configurations without ejection. Start by installing a couple of required packages:

```
npm install react-app-rewired react-app-rewire-eslint --save-dev
```

As for rules themselves, you'll want to have the following:

```
npm install eslint-plugin-flowtype eslint-config-recommended eslint-plugin-react --save-dev
```

Now you'll have to change a few scripts in package.json:

```
"scripts": {
    "start": "react-app-rewired start",
    "build": "react-app-rewired build",
    "test": "react-app-rewired test --env=jsdom",
    "eject": "react-app-rewired eject",
    .
    .
    .
```

Finally, create a config-overrides.js files, at the root of your project, at the same level of the package.json file. The /* global module */ comment is there to avoid an error that will pop up after ESLint gets to work, reporting that module isn't defined:

```
const rewireEslint = require("react-app-rewire-eslint");
function overrideEslintOptions(options) {
    // do stuff with the eslint options...
    return options;
}

/* global module */
module.exports = function override(config, env) {
    config = rewireEslint(config, env, overrideEslintOptions);
    return config;
};
```

You're all set! Your `.eslintrc` file should look as follows, with some additions and changes:

```
{
    "parser": "babel-eslint",
    "parserOptions": {
        "ecmaVersion": 2017,
        "sourceType": "module"
    },
    "env": {
        "node": true,
        "browser": true,
        "es6": true,
        "jest": true
    },
    "extends": [
        "eslint:recommended",
        "plugin:flowtype/recommended",
        "plugin:react/recommended"
    ],
    "plugins": ["babel", "flowtype", "react"],
    "rules": {
        "no-console": "off",
        "no-var": "error",
        "prefer-const": "error",
        "flowtype/no-types-missing-file-annotation": 0
    }
}
```

If you are wondering why I left the line for Node, it's because Storybook (which we'll see near the end of this chapter) uses a module variable, which would otherwise be marked as undefined.

How it works...

In this case, there's not too much to explain. The normal configuration of the project already includes all of the tools we need, so we are just configuring a bit instead of just going with the standard.

As for ESLint, when you now use npm start, the ESLint configuration will get *rewired* to work with your configuration instead of CRA's one. This means that all of your standard settings and checks will continue to run, and you'll apply the same quality checks for React than for other JS code—except, obviously, for the React-specific ones.

You can read more about `react-app-rewired` at `https://github.com/timarney/react-app-rewired`.

Defining components

The key idea behind working with `React` is that everything – and I mean, *everything* – is a component. Your whole web application will be a component, itself made of other components, which will themselves have smaller components, and so on. Components generate HTML, which is shown onscreen. The data for the HTML comes from externally assigned *props* (*properties*) and internally maintained *state*. Whenever there is a change in props or state, React takes care of refreshing the HTML so that the view (what the user sees) is always up to date.

Let's look at an example. Imagine that you want to create a screen that will let the user query data about regions of the world. How could you go about designing it? Check out the following screenshot for details:

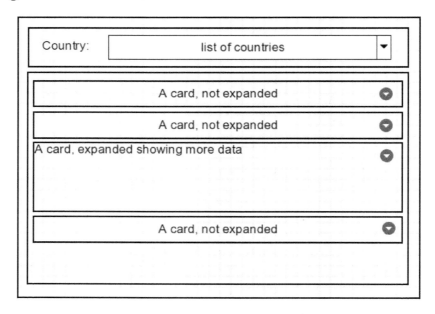

Whenever the user selects a country, we'll show several cards with information about its regions.
Note: I created this sketch at http://www.wireframes.com—but don't blame the tool for my poor sketching ability!

Your whole view would be a component, but it's fairly obvious that wouldn't help with coding or testing. A good design principle is that *each component should be responsible for a single duty,* and if it needs to do more, decompose it into smaller components. In our case, we'd have the following:

- The whole table is a `RegionsInformationTable`.
- The part at the top can be the `CountryFilterBar`, with a dropdown for countries
- At the bottom we have a `ResultsDataTable`, which shows a collection of `ExpandableCard` components, each with a title, a toggle, and space for more components. We could have designed a specific card for this situation, but having a generic card, whose components may be whatever we want, is more powerful.

A first rule involves events, such as clicks on elements, data being entered, and so on. They should be passed up until a component is able to fully process them: *events flow up.* For example, when the user clicks on the button, that component shouldn't (and couldn't) fully process it, at the very least because it couldn't access the table. So, the event will be passed up (by means of callbacks) until some component is able to deal with it. You may have options: for example, the `CountryFilterBar` component could handle calling a service and getting the data, but then it would pass the results up to the `RegionsInformationTable`, so that it can pass it to the `ResultsDataTable` component, which will itself produce the necessary `ExpandableCard` elements. Alternatives would be passing the `CountryFilterBar` value up to the `RegionsInformationTable`, which would do the search on its own, or passing it even higher, to some component to do the search and push the data down as props to our big table.

The preceding explanation helps us with a second decision. You should analyze your components hierarchy and decide where data (props or state) should be kept. A key rule is: if two (or more) components share data (or if one component produces data that other component needs). It should belong to a component higher up, which will pass it down as needed: *data flows down.* In our case, we already applied that rule when we decided that the regions data would be owned by the `CountryFilterBar`, which was then to be passed to the `RegionResults` table; each `ExpandableCard` would only work with the props it receives.

Even if we don't know how to handle web service requests to get the necessary data just yet (or, for example, to initialize the countries dropdown), we can build a static version of our components and see how it works.

It's better to start with these static aspects of web design, and only afterwards deal with the dynamic aspects, such as reacting to events or getting data. Let's get to that code.

How to do it...

We need to create several components, and that will allow us to find out how we can include components in other components, how to pass properties, how to define them, and more. Let's go component by component.

Creating the application

To start a React application, all we need is a basic HTML page, and CRA already provides one in `public/index.html`. Stripped down to the basics (check the book source code for the full version), it's something like the following, and the key part is the `<div>`, in which all of the React generated HTML code will be placed:

```
<!DOCTYPE html>
<html lang="en">
    <head>
        .
        .
        .
        <title>React App</title>
    </head>
    <body>
        <div id="root"></div>
    </body>
</html>
```

The entry point to our application will be `index.js`, which (we're dropping out some lines of code that are irrelevant here) boils down to the following code:

```
/* @flow */

import React from "react";
import ReactDOM from "react-dom";
import App from "./App";

const root = document.getElementById("root");
if (root) {
    ReactDOM.render(<App />, root);
}
```

Why do we need to define a `root` variable and `if`? The key is a `Flow` check: a `document.getElementById(...)` call may produce a web node, or may be null, and `Flow` reminds us to check for null before committing to work.

Now that we have our basic scaffolding, let's get to writing some actual `React` components!

Creating the basic App component

Let's start with the `App.js` file; we'll render a simple `RegionsInformationTable`. We are extending a `React` class called `PureComponent`; we'll explain what this implies later. Your own components should have names starting with upper case to distinguish them from HTML names, which should go in lower case. Every component should have a `.render()` method that produces whatever HTML is needed; there are more methods you can use for this, as we'll see:

```
/* @flow */

import React from "react";
import { RegionsInformationTable } from
"./components/regionsInformationTable";

class App extends React.PureComponent<{}> {
    render() {
        return <RegionsInformationTable />;
    }
}

export default App;
```

 The only method that must be specified when defining a component is `.render()`. Components also have many other methods, including several *life cycle* ones, that we'll see later in the *Handling life cycle events* section, but all of them are optional.

You may be asking yourself: why go to the bother of creating an `<App>` component that doesn't do anything but produce a `<RegionsInformationTable>` component? Why not use the latter directly? We'll get to the reason why in the upcoming sections; we'll want the `<App>` component to do more, such as defining routing, managing a store, and so on. So, even in this particular small example, it's overkill – it's a pattern we want to keep.

You'll also want to notice that we wrote `React.PureComponent<{}>`, and this was to let `Flow` know that our component doesn't need either properties or state. In later sections we'll look at more examples that require better type definitions.

Creating the RegionsInformationTable component

We can immediately see how the `RegionsInformationTable` component is rendered: it just depends on two more of the components we decided that we would create. Note that we are returning HTML code as if it were a valid JS value: this is JSX, and it provides a very simple way to intermingle JS code and HTML code. We'll have a list of countries (much reduced!) that supposedly comes from a web service, and a list of regions (also reduced, with fake data) that would come from a different service, after the user has selected a country. This data is the *state* of the component; whenever any of those lists changes, React will re-render the component and everything it includes. We'll look at that further in the *Handling State* section:

```
// Source file: src/components/regionsInformationTable/index.js

/* @flow */

import React from "react";

import { CountryFilterBar } from "../countryFilterBar";
import { ResultsDataTable } from "../resultsDataTable.2";

export class RegionsInformationTable extends React.PureComponent<
    {},
    {
        countries: Array<{
            code: string,
            name: string
        }>,
        regions: Array<{
            id: string,
            name: string,
            cities: number,
            pop: number
        }>
    }
> {
    state = {
        countries: [
            { code: "AR", name: "Argentine" },
            { code: "BR", name: "Brazil" },
            { code: "PY", name: "Paraguay" },
```

```
                    { code: "UY", name: "Uruguay" }
            ],

            regions: []
    };

    update = (country: string) => {
        console.log(`Country ... ${country}`);

        this.setState(() => ({
            regions: [
                {
                    id: "UY/5",
                    name: "Durazno",
                    cities: 8,
                    pop: 60000
                },
                {
                    id: "UY/7",
                    name: "Florida",
                    cities: 20,
                    pop: 67000
                },
                {
                    id: "UY/9",
                    name: "Maldonado",
                    cities: 17,
                    pop: 165000
                },
                {
                    id: "UY/10",
                    name: "Montevideo",
                    cities: 1,
                    pop: 1320000
                },
                {
                    id: "UY/11",
                    name: "Paysandu",
                    cities: 16,
                    pop: 114000
                }
            ]
        }));
    }

    render() {
        return (
            <div>
```

```
            <CountryFilterBar
                list={this.state.countries}
                onSelect={this.update}
            />
            <ResultsDataTable results={this.state.regions} />
        </div>
    );
  }
}
```

This component receives no props, but works with state, so for Flow's sake, we had to write `React.PureComponent<{},{countries:..., regions:...}>`, providing data types for the state elements. You could also define these data types in a separate file (see `https:/ /flow.org/en/docs/types/modules/` for more on this), but we'll let it be.

What about the list of countries? The `CountryFilterBar` should show some countries, so the parent will provide the list as a prop; let's see how it will receive and use that list. We'll also provide a callback, `onSelect`, that the child component will use to inform you whenever the user selects a country. Finally, we'll pass the list of (fake, hardcoded) regions to the `ResultsDataTable`.

A noteworthy comment: props are passed using a `name=...` syntax, as standard with HTML elements; your `React` elements are used in the same fashion as common, standard HTML ones. The only difference here is that you use braces, in template fashion, to include any expression.

By the way, note that our list of regions starts out empty; the results table will have to deal with that. When the user selects a country, the `.update()` method will run and load some regions by using the `.setState()` method, which we'll see in the following section. Later in this book, we'll also see how to use a web service to get that data, but for the time being, a fixed result will have to do.

Creating the CountryFilterBar component

The next component we need is more complex: it receives a pair of props, and that starts by providing `PropTypes` definitions for them:

```
// Source file: src/components/countryFilterBar.js

/* @flow */

import React from "react";
import PropTypes from "prop-types";
```

```
export class CountryFilterBar extends React.PureComponent<{
    list?: Array<{ code: string, name: string }>,
    onSelect: string => void
}> {
    static propTypes = {
        list: PropTypes.arrayOf(PropTypes.object),
        onSelect: PropTypes.func.isRequired
    };

    static defaultProps = {
        list: []
    };

// continued...
```

This is our first component that receives props. We'll have to provide a definition for `Flow`, which is easy: the component will receive `list`, an array of objects, and `onSelect`, a function with a single string parameter, that doesn't return anything.

`React` also lets you define a runtime check for parameters. We define a `propTypes` class property, with an element for each actual prop that our component will receive, and another `defaultProps` property, for default values should actual ones not be provided. Defining the data types is also needed (for example, `onSelect` is a function) if they are required or optional (both are required, in this case). In development (not in production), whenever you pass props to an object, they will be checked against their definitions and a warning will be produced if there is some mismatch; this is a good debugging technique.

 Why use both `Flow` and `PropTypes` if it seems that both do the same job? Basically, `Flow` is a static checker, while `PropTypes` is a dynamic, runtime checker. If you use `Flow` everywhere throughout your application, theoretically, you could get by without using `PropTypes`—but since this package, in testing, will catch anything you missed, it's an extra "safety net" for your code. I do agree that writing two sets of data types is a bother, though.

The valid types for this are as follows:

- `any`, if any type is acceptable – this is not a good practice
- `array`
- `arrayOf(someType)`, to specify the values of the array elements
- `bool`, for Booleans
- `element`, for a React element
- `func`, for functions

- `instanceOf(SomeClass)`, for an object that must be an instance of a given class
- `node`, for anything that can be rendered as HTML, such as numbers or strings
- `number`
- `object`
- `objectOf(SomeType)`, to specify an object with property values of a given type
- `oneOf([...an array of values...])`, to verify that a prop is limited to some values
- `oneOfType([...an array of types...])`, to specify that a prop will be one of a list of types
- `shape({...an object with types...})`, to completely define an object, including keys and value types
- `string`
- `symbol`

 You can go even further and define, for example, specific functions for type validation. For a complete explanation of all of the possibilities of PropTypes, read `https://reactjs.org/docs/typechecking-with-proptypes.html`.

Now, how would we generate the HTML for the filter? We need several `<option>` elements, and we can apply `.map()` to `this.props.list` (properties are accessed through `this.props`) as follows. Also note how we use the `onChange` callback to inform the parent component whenever a different country is selected:

```
// ...continues

onSelect(e) {
    this.props.onSelect(e.target.value);
}

render() {
    return (
        <div>
            Country: 
            <select onChange={this.onSelect}>
                <option value="">Select a country:</option>
                {this.props.list.map(x => (
                    <option key={x.code} value={x.code}>
                        {x.name}
                    </option>
                ))}
            </select>
```

```
            </div>
        );
    }
}
```

The input properties (`this.props`) should be considered read-only, and never modified. On the other hand, the component's state (`this.state`) is read-write and can be modified, though not directly but rather through `this.setState()`, as we'll see.

A special explanation is needed for the `key=` attribute. Whenever you define a list (with `<option>` or `<li>`, for example) and React needs to re-render it, the key attribute is used to recognize already available elements and avoid regenerating them, but rather reuse them. Keep in mind that the `CountryFilterBar` component will be called, over time, with different lists of countries to render, so React will optimize its performance by avoiding the creation of already existing list elements.

Creating the ResultsDataTable component

Building the results table is easy, and requires similar work to what we did with the countries selector. We only have to check the special case when we haven't got any regions to show:

```
// Source file: src/components/resultsDataTable.1/index.js

/* @flow */

import React from "react";
import PropTypes from "prop-types";

import { ExpandableCard } from "../expandableCard.1";
import "../general.css";

export class ResultsDataTable extends React.PureComponent<{
    results: Array<{
        id: string,
        name: string,
        cities: number,
        pop: number
    }>
}> {
    static propTypes = {
        results: PropTypes.arrayOf(PropTypes.object).isRequired
    };
```

```
        render() {
            if (this.props.results.length === 0) {
                return <div className="bordered">No regions.</div>;
            } else {
                return (
                    <div className="bordered">
                        {this.props.results.map(x => (
                            <ExpandableCard
                                key={x.id}
                                name={x.name}
                                cities={x.cities}
                                population={x.pop}
                            />
                        ))}
                    </div>
                );
            }
        }
    }
```

A side comment: `React` allows us to define props as optional (meaning that no
`isRequired` is included when defining `PropTypes`) and to provide default values instead.
In this case, if results could be *not* provided, you would have written the following code,
using `defaultProps` to provide the necessary default values:

```
    static propTypes = {
        results: PropTypes.arrayOf(PropTypes.object)
    };

    static defaultProps = {
        results: []
    }
```

In terms of `Flow` and `PropTypes`, the definition is very much similar to the previous ones.
The interesting part is using `.map()` to process all of the received objects, creating an
`ExpandableCard` for each; this is a very common pattern with React. So, all we need now
to finish our application is to provide an expandable card, so let's get to that.

Creating the ExpandableCard component

For starters, let's forget about expanding a card—even though that makes the name of the component a misnomer! Here, we'll just make a component that shows a few strings. In the *Composing Components* section, we'll see some interesting ways of achieving our original goal:

```
// Source file: src/components/expandableCard.1/index.js

/* @flow */

import React from "react";
import PropTypes from "prop-types";

import "../general.css";

export class ExpandableCard extends React.PureComponent<{
    name: string,
    cities: number,
    population: number
}> {
    static propTypes = {
        name: PropTypes.string.isRequired,
        cities: PropTypes.number.isRequired,
        population: PropTypes.number.isRequired
    };

    render() {
        return (
            <div className="bordered">
                NAME:{this.props.name}
                <br />
                CITIES:{this.props.cities}
                <br />
                POPULATION:{this.props.population}
            </div>
        );
    }
}
```

Everything is ready; let's see how and why it functions!

How it works...

When you start the application with `npm start`, you get our basic screen, showing the dropbox with the countries, and no cards, as shown in the following screenshot:

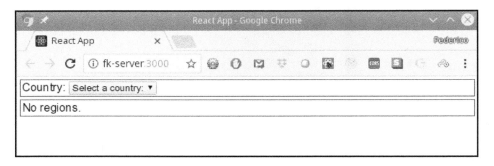

Our basic application, showing fixed, non-varying cards

Then, suppose you select a country; what will happen? Let's follow that, step by step:

1. In the `CountryFilterBar`, the `onChange` event will fire and will execute a callback (`this.props.onSelect()`), providing it with the selected country code.

2. In the `RegionsInformationTable`, the callback that was provided to the `CountryFilterBar` is `this.update()`, so that method will execute.

3. The update method will log the country (just for reference) and use `this.setState` (see the next section) to load some regions in the `RegionsInformationTable` state.

4. The change in state will cause `React` to re-render the component.

5. The `CountryFilterBar` won't need re-rendering because neither its props nor its state changed.

6. The `ResultsDataTable`, on the other hand, will be re-rendered because its props will change, receiving a new list of regions.

So, after all this is said and done, the new view will be as follows:

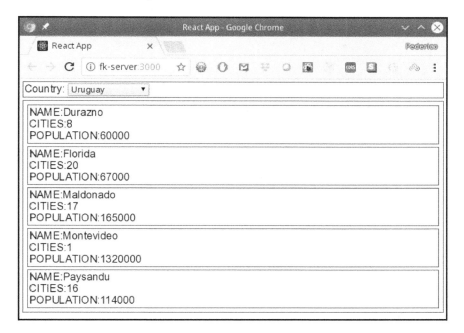

The updated view, after React handles all the necessary re-rendering

This is basically how your application will work: events are captured and handled, state is changed, props are passed, and React takes care of re-rendering whatever needs to be re-rendered.

There's more...

Let's go back to the CountryFilterBar component. We used the most recent JS ways to define it, but in many articles and books, you may find an older style that you should be aware of, if only to better understand the variant:

```
// Source file: src/components/countryFilterBar.old.style.js

/* @flow */

import React from "react";
import PropTypes from "prop-types";
import "../general.css";
```

```
export class CountryFilterBar extends React.PureComponent<{
    list: Array<{ code: string, name: string }>,
    onSelect: string => void
}> {
    constructor(props) {
        super(props);
        this.onSelect = this.onSelect.bind(this);
    }

    onSelect(e: { target: HTMLOptionElement }) {
        this.props.onSelect(e.target.value);
    }

    render() {
        return (
            <div className="bordered">
                Country: 
                <select onChange={this.onSelect}>
                    <option value="">Select a country:</option>
                    {this.props.list.map(x => (
                        <option key={x.code} value={x.code}>
                            {x.name}
                        </option>
                    ))}
                </select>
            </div>
        );
    }
}

CountryFilterBar.propTypes = {
    list: PropTypes.arrayOf(PropTypes.object).isRequired,
    onSelect: PropTypes.func.isRequired
};

CountryFilterBar.defaultProps = {
    list: []
};
```

We can sum up the differences as follows:

- The `propTypes` and `defaultProps` values are defined separately, by directly modifying the class
- We bind `this.onSelect` in the constructor, so when this method is called, the value of `this` will be the `window` object, not what we need.

With modern JS features, this is not needed, but be aware that in older JS code, you are likely to find these patterns.

Handling state

In the previous section, we saw the usage of *state* for the regions; let's delve a bit deeper into that. The concept of state is very similar to props, but with crucial differences: props are assigned from the outside and are read-only, and state is handled privately, and read-write. If a component needs to keep some information, which it can use to render itself, then using state is the solution.

How to do it...

Defining state is done by using class fields, a fairly new feature of JS, that's enabled via `Babel` since it isn't fully official yet. (See `https://github.com/tc39/proposal-class-fields` for the proposal, which is at Stage 3, meaning that it's one step away from being officially adopted.) With older JS versions, you would have had to create `this.state` in the class constructor, but this syntax is clearer. Let's remember what the code looked like, and let's drop the Flow definition.

First, let's modify the `RegionsInformationTable` component:

```
export class RegionsInformationTable extends React.PureComponent<...> {
    state = {
        countries: [
            { code: "AR", name: "Argentine" },
            { code: "BR", name: "Brazil" },
            { code: "PY", name: "Paraguay" },
            { code: "UY", name: "Uruguay" }
        ],

        regions: []
    };
```

Second, let's see what happens when a country changes. Rendering for an object can depend on both its props (which it cannot change, as we said) and its state (which it can change), but there is an important restriction on updating state. You cannot simply assign a new value to the component's state because it won't be detected by React, and then no rendering will be done. Instead, you must use the .setState() method. This method can be called in different ways, but *functional* .setState() is the safest way to do this. With this, you must pass a function that will receive both state and props and return whatever parts of the state need to be updated. In our earlier code, we would have written the following:

```
update(country: string) {
    .
    .
    .
    this.setState((state, props) => ({ regions: [
        .
        .
        .
    ]}));
```

If you check, you'll see that we didn't include the state and props parameters in the actual code, but that was in order to satisfy ESLint's rule about no unused arguments in functions.

How it works...

Why did we need to pass a function? There's a key point to understanding this: *state updates are asynchronous*. Whenever you call .setState(), React will update the component's state and start its reconciliation process to update the UI view. But what happens if there is more than one .setState() call? There lies the problem.

React is allowed to *queue* many such calls together into a single update to achieve better performance, and that has an important effect: state may have changed before .setState() is executed! (Even so, if batching is done, updates will be done in the order they are called.) So, you provide a function and React will call it with the appropriately updated state parameter. Don't do anything depending on this.state because it may be wrong; always work with the state parameter.

There is a shortcut that you should know, in any case. If (and only if) your update does not depend in any way on the state or props values, you can use an alternative call without requiring a function. For example, our update could have been simply written as follows, and `this.state.regions` would be changed, leaving the rest of the state unchanged; the key is that the new values for the `regions` attribute are not dependent in any way on state or props:

```
this.setState({ regions: [ ... ]});
```

Why would this work? Because in this case, even if the state had changed before, your update would still be the same. Be careful, though, and use this syntax only when your update is totally independent of state and props; otherwise, use the functional approach we showed first.

 Once you realize that the state updates are functions, you can move that logic out of components, for separate, independent coding and testing, this will be quite similar to things we'll be doing with Redux in Chapter 8, *Expanding your Application*. You would write `this.setState(someFunction)` and `someFunction()` would be defined separately; your code will have become more declarative in style.

There's more...

With what we have done here, you may realize that you have all you could need to handle state, for any application size – and you would be right! You could set up the general state for your whole application in the App component (remember we mentioned that App would have more responsibilities?) and you would be able to do the following:

- Pass it down to components by using props
- Update it in answer to events that the components send

This is a perfectly valid solution, and `App.state` could have all sorts of data for the whole page. App could handle, for example, calling a web service to get the regions for a given country, storing the results in its state, and passing it to our components so that they can be rendered. In our hardcoded version, `RegionsInformationTable` had the list of countries (where did it get it from?) and handled the requests for regions (by returning hardcoded data). In reality, as we'll see later in this book, getting this sort of information from a server would be handled differently, and at a higher level: `RegionsInformationTable` would handle rendering the table and leave data gathering to another part of your solution.

Even if you passed web services handling to `App`, as your application grows in size, this sort of solution may become unwieldy because of the number of data fields you may have to keep track of. We'll find a better scalable solution for this in Chapter 8, *Expanding your Application*, by adding a specific package to handle state updates in a more orderly, structured fashion.

Composing components

Let's go back to the `ExpandableCard`, which we didn't quite finish before. We could certainly do a regions-specific card, but it seems that the general concept of a card that can be expanded or condensed is useful enough that we could prefer a more general solution. React allows us to do that via *composition*, as we'll see in this section.

How to do it...

The component we want to create could have any kind of content. (The same idea would apply to generic dialog boxes, header sections, or sidebars, by the way.) Instead of creating a base class and using inheritance to create multiple derived classes, React allows you to pass a special children prop (`this.props.children`) so that you can pass children elements to the original component.

First, let's see how our `ResultsDataTable` code would change. First, the `render()` method would have to change:

```
render() {
    if (this.props.results.length === 0) {
        return <div className="bordered">No regions.</div>;
    } else {
        return (
            <div className="bordered">
                {this.props.results.map(x => (
                    <ExpandableCard key={x.id} title={x.name}>
                        <div>CITIES:{x.cities}</div>
                        <div>POPULATION:{x.pop}</div>
                    </ExpandableCard>
                ))}
            </div>
        );
    }
}
```

Second, let's define the component we are using. We are inserting an `ExpandableCard` component with a key and a title, and within it we are including a couple of `<div>` elements with data for cities and population. This content will be available as `this.prop.children`, as we'll see later. We also added a `title` prop and an internal state, `open`, which will be toggled when you expand or condense a card via the `.toggle()` method. First, let's look at the props, state, and types:

```
// Source file: src/comopnents/expandableCard.2/index.js

/* @flow */

import * as React from "react";
import PropTypes from "prop-types";

import "../general.css";
import "./expandableCard.css";

export class ExpandableCard extends React.PureComponent<
    {
        children: React.ChildrenArray<React.ChildrenArray<React.Node>>,
        title: string
    },
    { open: boolean }
> {
    static propTypes = {
        children: PropTypes.arrayOf(PropTypes.element).isRequired,
        title: PropTypes.string.isRequired
    };

    state = {
        open: false
    };

// continues...
```

For `React`, `Flow` predefines a lot of data types. (You can read more about this at `https://github.com/facebook/flow/blob/master/website/en/docs/react/types.md`.)

The few more usual ones you are likely to require are as follows, but read the aforementioned web page for a full list:

Data Types	Explanations
`React.ChildrenArray<T>`	An array of children, of type <T>, just as shown in the previous code.
`React.Element<typeof Component>`	A node of a specific type: for example, `React.Element<"div">` is an element that renders a `<div>`.
`React.Key`	The type of a prop that is used as key: essentially, either a number or a string.
`React.Node`	Any node that can be rendered, including React elements, numbers, strings, Booleans, undefined, null, or arrays of those types.

Finally, let's get to the functioning part of the component. Let's see how we show the children of the component when the state of the component shows that it should be expanded. Also of interest is looking at how clicking on the card calls the `.toggle()` method to change the component's `state.open` value:

```
// continued...

    toggle = () => {
        this.setState(state => ({ open: !state.open }));
    }

    render() {
        if (this.state.open) {
            return (
                <div className="bordered">
                    {this.props.title}
                    <div
                        className="toggle"
                        onClick={this.toggle}
                    >
                        △
                    </div>
                    <div>{this.props.children}</div>
                </div>
            );
        } else {
            return (
                <div className="bordered">
                    {this.props.title}
                    <div
                        className="toggle"
```

```
                        onClick={this.toggle}
                    >
                        ▽
                    </div>
                </div>
            );
        }
    }
}
```

We're done! Let's see how this all comes together.

How it works...

When this object is rendered for the first time, `this.state.open` is false, so the
`.render()` method will just produce the title of the card, plus a triangle pointing down, to
suggest that the card may be expanded by clicking on it. When the user clicks on the
triangle, `this.setState()` is called with a function that will take the current value of
`this.state.open`, and toggle it. React will decide whether the object needs to be re-
rendered (because of the change in state) and this time, since `this.state.open` will be
true, the expanded, complete version of the card will be rendered. In particular, the triangle
will be shown pointing up, so the user will understand that the card will be condensed if
they click there. Check out the following screenshot for a trial run, showing some expanded
and condensed cards:

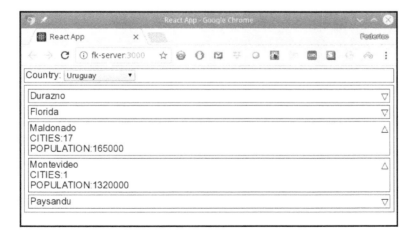

A run of our application; some cards are expanded and show their children

What's going to be the content of the expanded card? This is where `this.props.children` comes in. Whatever elements were provided as props will be rendered here. In this way, you can reuse your `ExpandableCard` with any type of content. The main characteristics (the title, the triangle to expand/condense the card) will always be there, but thanks to the use of composition, you'll be able to have as many versions of expandable cards as you may need.

Handling life cycle events

Components don't only have a `.render()` method – they can also implement many more *life cycle* events that can help you in specific situations. In this section, let's go over all of the available methods and provide ideas about when you will use them.

For a full description of all the available methods, go to `https://reactjs.org/docs/react-component.html` – but pay careful attention to some deprecated, legacy methods that should be avoided, and also read about the conditions and parameters for each method.

How to do it...

Let's go over the life of a component, in order from the time a component is created and placed into the DOM, during its life when it may be updated, up to the moment the component is removed from the DOM. We are going to hit only the main methods, and even so it's likely that you won't get to use all of them:

- `constructor()`: This method is called before the component is mounted for basic setup and initialization. This method is used for all kinds of initialization. The only key rule is that you should always start by calling `super(props)` before doing anything else, so `this.props` will be created and accessible.
- `componentDidMount()`: This method is called after the component is mounted.
- `shouldComponentUpdate(nextProps, nextState)`: This method is used by React to decide whether a component needs to be re-rendered or not.
- `render()`: This (mandatory) method produces HTML elements, ideally based only on `this.props` and `this.state`. If the function returns a `boolean` or `null` value, nothing will be rendered. The method should be pure, not attempting to modify the component's state (which can lead to nasty loops) or to use anything but state and props.

- `forceUpdate()`: This method is not really a life cycle one, and you can call it whenever you want to force a re-rendering to be done.
- `componentDidUpdate(previousProps, previousState)`: This method is called after a component has been updated.
- `componentWillUnmount()`: This method is called just before a component is going to be unmounted.

How it works...

We went over the methods in the previous section. Now let's go over some ideas about getting the less obvious of them to work:

Methods	Explanations
`componentDidMount()`	This is the usual place to start some action to get data from a web service. A usual trick for that is to have a state property like `this.state.loading` that you initialize to true when you ask for the data and reset to false after the data comes in. You can then make the `.render()` method produce different outputs, possibly a loading icon, until the data comes, and real data afterwards.
`shouldComponentUpdate(...)`	This method works as a performance optimization, allowing React to skip unnecessary updates. With `React.PureComponent`, this is implemented by a comparison between the current state and the next state, and the current props and the next props. For normal `React.Components` this method always returns `true`, forcing re-rendering. If your component is rendered based on anything extra (such as other than state and props), you should use a `Component` instead of a `PureComponent`.
`componentDidUpdate(...)`	You could use this method to do some animation, or to get data from a web service—but in the latter case, you might want to compare the current state and props with the previous values, because if there were no changes, the request may not be needed, or it might have already been done.
`componentWillUnmount()`	This is the usual place to do some cleanup tasks, like disabling timers or removing listeners, for example.

Simplifying component development with Storybook

When you are developing components, there is a basic, important question: how can you try them out? Of course, you could include them somewhere, in any page, but then whenever you want to see how they work, you must follow the full path through your application so that you can get to actually see the component.

`Storybook` is a UI development environment that lets you visualize your components in isolation, outside of your application, even making changes to them in an interactive way until you get them exactly right!

How to do it...

First, start by installing `Storybook` itself; we are going to use this version for `React`, but the tool can also be used with `Angular` and `Vue`:

```
npm install @storybook/react --save-dev
```

Then add a couple of scripts to `package.json`: one will launch `Storybook` (as we'll see later) and the other will build a standalone application that you can use to showcase your components in an independent fashion:

```
"scripts": {
    "storybook": "start-storybook -p 9001 -c .storybook",
    "build-storybook": "build-storybook -c .storybook -o out_sb",
    .
    .
    .
```

Now let's write a simple story for `ExpandableCard`. In the same directory where that component is (the final version, which actually allowed expanding and compressing, not the first version without that behavior), create a `ExpandableCard.story.js` file. What would you want to show about your component? You could display the following:

- An expandable card with a couple of lines within, as we used previously
- Another card with many lines, to show how the card stretches
- A card containing other cards, each of them with some minimal content

The code will look quite similar in style to the tests we wrote for `Node` back in `Chapter 5`, *Testing and Debugging your Server*. I'm assuming that you can figure out what each test does:

```
// Source file: src/components/expandableCard.2/expandableCard.story.js

import React from "react";
import { storiesOf } from "@storybook/react";

import { ExpandableCard } from "./";

storiesOf("Expandable Card", module)
    .add("with normal contents", () => (
        <ExpandableCard key={229} title={"Normal"}>
```

```
            <div>CITIES: 12</div>
            <div>POPULATION: 41956</div>
        </ExpandableCard>
    ))

    .add("with many lines of content", () => (
        <ExpandableCard key={229} title={"Long contents"}>
            Many, many lines<br />
            Many, many lines<br />
            Many, many lines<br />
            Many, many lines<br />
            Many, many lines<br />
            Many, many lines<br />
            Many, many lines<br />
            Many, many lines<br />
            Many, many lines<br />
            Many, many lines<br />
            Many, many lines<br />
            Many, many lines<br />
            Many, many lines<br />
            Many, many lines<br />
        </ExpandableCard>
    ))

    .add("with expandable cards inside", () => (
        <ExpandableCard key={229} title={"Out card"}>
            <ExpandableCard key={1} title={"First internal"}>
                A single 1
            </ExpandableCard>
            <ExpandableCard key={2} title={"Second internal"}>
                Some twos
            </ExpandableCard>
            <ExpandableCard key={3} title={"Third internal"}>
                Three threes: 333
            </ExpandableCard>
        </ExpandableCard>
    ));
```

So as not to have a single story, let's write a short one for the `CountryFilterBar` component; it will be in the same directory, named `countryFilterBar.story.js`. And, yes, I know this is a very simple component, but this is just for our example!

```
// Source file: src/components/countryFilterBar/countryFilterBar.story.js

import React from "react";
import { storiesOf } from "@storybook/react";

import { CountryFilterBar } from "./";
```

```
const countries = [
    { code: "AR", name: "Argentine" },
    { code: "BR", name: "Brazil" },
    { code: "PY", name: "Paraguay" },
    { code: "UY", name: "Uruguay" }
];

storiesOf("Country Filter Bar", module).add("with some countries", () => (
    <CountryFilterBar list={countries} onSelect={() => null} />
));
```

Finally, we need a launcher. Create a .storybook directory at the root of the project, and a config.js file within, as follows:

```
import { configure } from "@storybook/react";

configure(() => {
    const req = require.context("../src", true, /\.story\.js$/);
    req.keys().forEach(filename => req(filename));
}, module);

configure(loadStories, module);
```

Yes, it's sort of mysterious—but it basically says to scan the /src directory, and pick up all of the files whose names end with .story.js. Now we are set to see how this all comes together.

How it works...

We have written stories for just a couple of our components, but that will do for our purposes. To start the Storybook server, you'll have to run one of the scripts we created earlier in this section:

```
npm run storybook
```

After some work, you'll get the following screen:

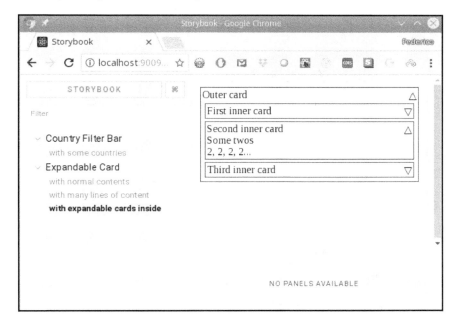

The Storybook, showing all of the available stories. You can interact with components, click on them, and even test out changes in source code.

You can select any component in the left sidebar (or even use the **Filter** text box), and you'll get the individual stories for it. Clicking on a story will show the corresponding component on the right. You can work with the component and see how it looks and performs... and if you are not satisfied, you can dynamically change its source code, and immediately see the results!

To finish, let's build a separate showcase application:

```
$ npm run build-storybook

> chapter06@0.1.0 build-storybook /home/fkereki/JS_BOOK/modernjs/chapter06
> build-storybook -s public -o out_sb

info @storybook/react v3.4.8
info
info => Loading custom addons config.
info => Using default webpack setup based on "Create React App".
info => Copying static files from: public
info Building storybook ...
info Building storybook completed.
```

After this, in the `/out_sb` directory, we will have a full standalone version of our showcase. To see how it works, we can use the **Web Server for Chrome** application (search for it in the Chrome extensions) and choose the output directory:

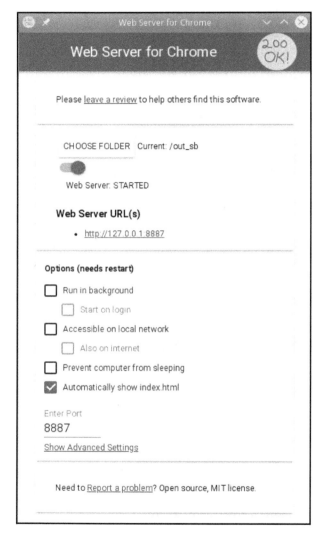

The Web Server for Chrome application is sufficient to let us see what the standalone Storybook would look like

If you open the web server URL that is shown onscreen, you'll get exactly the same output as earlier – but now you could copy the `out_sb` directory elsewhere, and use it as a showcase tool, with independence from the developers.

There's more...

You can expand Storybook with *add-ons*, which allow you to enhance your showcase. Out of the many available ones, we will install three of them and have a quick look at their usage:

- addon-actions lets you see the data received by event handlers to see what would happen, for example, when the user clicks on a component
- addon-notes allows you to add notes to a component, to explain how it works or to give insights on its usage
- addon-knobs lets you dynamically tweak a component's props to see how they change

 You can read more about add-ons at https://storybook.js.org/addons/ introduction/ and take a look at the gallery of available add-ons at https://storybook.js.org/addons/addon-gallery/.

Since add-ons are quite simple, let's look at an example where all of the aforementioned ones are used. First, we'll have to create an addons.js file in the .storybook directory, with a line for each add-on that we want to use:

```
import "@storybook/addon-actions/register";
import "@storybook/addon-knobs/register";
import "@storybook/addon-notes/register";
```

Now let's modify our stories so that CountryFilterBar will show what value it sends back with the onSelect event, and will also show some notes describing the component, so that ExpandableCard will let you tweak the props it receives:

```
// Source file:
src/components/expandableCard.2/expandableCardWithAddon.story.js

import React from "react";
import { storiesOf } from "@storybook/react";
import { action } from "@storybook/addon-actions";
import { withNotes } from "@storybook/addon-notes";

import { CountryFilterBar } from "./";
import markDownText from "./countryFilterBar.md";

const countries = [
    { code: "AR", name: "Argentine" },
    { code: "BR", name: "Brazil" },
    { code: "PY", name: "Paraguay" },
```

```
        { code: "UY", name: "Uruguay" }
];

storiesOf("Country Filter Bar (with addons)", module).add(
    "with some countries - with actions and notes",
    withNotes(markDownText)(() => (
        <CountryFilterBar
            list={countries}
            onSelect={action("change:country")}
        />
    ))
);
```

For the action, I provided an `action(...)` function, which will display its results in another tab, **ACTION LOGGER**, as follows:

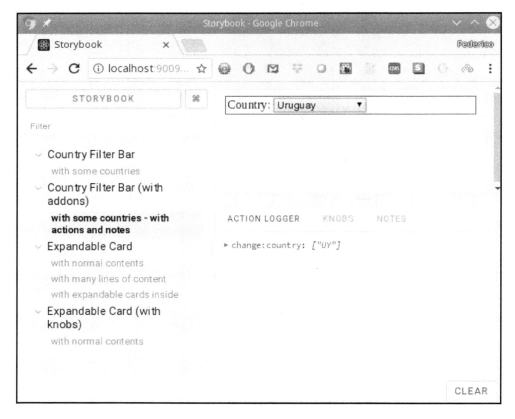

Whenever you select a country, the executed callback and its parameters are shown in the ACTIONS tab.
I clicked on my country, Uruguay, and I can see that "UY" is being sent.

I also added a `withNotes(...)` call, providing the text from a markdown file I created. The content of this will be shown in the **NOTES** tab, as shown in the following screenshot:

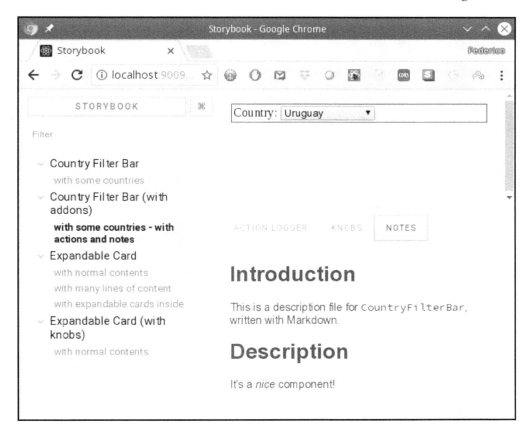

You can provide good documentation (not like mine!) for every component

Finally, we can add a few "knobs" that lets the user change parameters dynamically. Let's allow them to modify the card's title and the numbers shown inside it:

```
import React from "react";
import { storiesOf } from "@storybook/react";

import { withKnobs, text, number } from "@storybook/addon-knobs';

import { ExpandableCard } from "./";

storiesOf("Expandable Card (with knobs)", module)
    .addDecorator(withKnobs)
```

```
.add("with normal contents", () => (
    <ExpandableCard key={229} title={text("Card title", "XYZZY")}>
        <div>CITIES: {number("Number of cities", 12)}</div>
        <div>POPULATION: {number("Population", 54321)}</div>
    </ExpandableCard>
));
```

When the user sees this story, the **KNOBS** panel lets them type in some values that are immediately updated on screen, as follows:

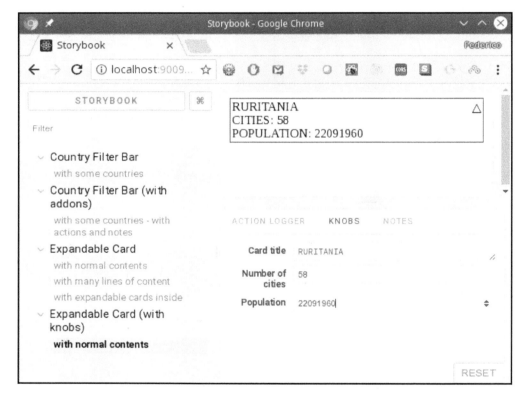

Adding knobs to a story lets users experiment with different settings. The values you enter in the Knobs panel are automatically reflected in the component.

We used only texts and numbers, but you can also provide knobs for Booleans, colors, dates, numbers within a given range, objects, string arrays, and options from a list.

Enhancing Your Application

7

In this chapter, we'll move forward and consider several tools that make for a better application. The recipes we'll be seeing include the following:

- Adding SASS for separate styling
- Creating StyledComponents for inline styling
- Making your application responsive to screen sizes
- Making your application adaptive for enhanced usability
- Making a global application with internationalization and localization
- Setting up for accessibility

Introduction

In the previous chapter, we started developing applications with React, and saw the basics of how to use it, how to create an application, and how to develop components.

We'll also be taking advantage of Storybook, which we used in the previous chapter, so we can demonstrate each tool separately, and so we don't have to waste time focusing on anything else.

Adding SASS for separate styling

Just about the very first thing we should add is some way to handle styling for our application. If you wish, you need learn nothing new, nor install anything extra, for you could go with plain old-fashioned CSS—as we already did! We used some CSS in the previous chapter (look for the `src/components/general.css` file), but we don't even need to go there. When we created our project then, an App.js file was created with the following code:

```
import React, { Component } from "react";
import logo from "./logo.svg";
import "./App.css";

class App extends Component {
    render() {
        return (
            <div className="App">
                <header className="App-header">
                    <img src={logo} className="App-logo"
                        alt="logo" />
                    <h1 className="App-title">Welcome to
                        React</h1>
                </header>
                <p className="App-intro">
                    To get started, edit <code>src/App.js</code>
                    and save to reload.
                </p>
            </div>
        );
    }
}

export default App;
```

By including the `import "./App.css"` line, you are getting the styles that were defined in the App.css file, and you can then use them everywhere, as shown in the code.

 This usage of `import` to deal with styling is not a JS thing, but rather is due to Webpack, which is used by `create-react-app` to generate the output code for your application.

So, if you wanted to get by with just CSS, you need to do but little, and you are set! However, there are many tools that can help you with styling, adding features that really come in handy, and in this section we will consider how to use SASS, one of the best-known CSS extension languages.

 If you want to fully learn SASS, I'd recommend browsing to `http://sass-lang.com/` and particularly check out the **LEARNING SASS** and **DOCUMENTATION** areas, at `http://sass-lang.com/guide` and `http://sass-lang.com/documentation/file.SASS_REFERENCE.html`, respectively.

How to do it...

SASS is a preprocessor that works with `.scss` (*Sassy CSS*) files and produces standard CSS files that browsers can work with. The preprocessing step is the key to using features that aren't (at least yet) available in CSS, such as variables, nested structures, inheritance, mixins, and many others. You can install and use SASS as a separate tool, but that isn't really too appealing; we'll aim to instead include it in the project, so all needed preprocessing will be done automatically. Let's see how to do that.

 SASS has two possible syntaxes: an older, indented one, plainly known as *the indented syntax*, and the newer SCSS. While the former is more concise, the latter has the advantage of being an extension of CSS, which means that any valid CSS file you might already have is automatically a valid SCSS file with the very same meaning. This is a very good help if you are migrating from CSS to SASS, so we'll only use SCSS in the text.

First, we need to install a tool. The developers of `create-react-app` didn't want to include a fixed CSS preprocessor, so you can really add whichever you want. There are several SASS tools, but the following one is recommended:

```
npm install node-sass-chokidar --save-dev
```

Second, we'll also have to add an extra line to the `.flowconfig` file, so `.scss` files will be properly recognized. The changed section would become as follows:

```
[options]
include_warnings=true
module.file_ext=.scss
.
.
.
```

Finally, we'll have to modify some scripts. SASS preprocessing will run in parallel to npm start, and for that we need a package that lets you run several commands in parallel:

```
npm install npm-run-all --save-dev
```

Now the changed scripts will be the following:

```
"build-scss": "node-sass-chokidar src/ -o src/",
"watch-scss": "npm run build-scss && node-sass-chokidar src/ -o src/ --
watch --recursive",
"start-js": "react-app-rewired start",
"build-js": "react-app-rewired build",
"storybook-js": "start-storybook -p 9001 -c .storybook",
"start": "npm-run-all -p watch-scss start-js",
"build": "npm-run-all build-scss build-js",
"storybook": "npm-run-all -p watch-scss storybook-js",
    .
    .
    .
```

Let's see what our new and updated processes do:

- build-scss converts .scss files in src/ to .css files; we'll be using the latter ones
- watch-scss does an initial conversion of SASS files, and then runs the conversion in *watch* mode, running whenever there are new or changed files to process
- start-js, build-js, and storybook-js are our old start, build, and storybook processes, which we won't be using directly
- start now runs both watch-scss and start-js, in parallel (because of the -p option)
- build now runs build-scss followed by build-js, so all SCSS will have been converted before building the application
- storybook runs both watch-scss and storybook-js, also in parallel

You are set! From now on, .scss files will be properly processed, and converted to .css files; let's see how we can make this work for us now.

How it works...

Let's create and style a basic component, a colored button, trying to take advantage of as many SASS features as possible. This will be an extreme example, because it's not very likely you'll have such a complex way of creating simple code, but we want to highlight SASS here.

First, the code for the button itself, which we will call SassButton. It has three props: normal (if true, will show *normal* colors; if false, *alert* ones); buttonText, which will be displayed by the button; and onSelect, a callback for clicks. I highlighted the CSS-related lines in the following code snippet:

```
// Source file: /src/components/sassButton/sassButton.js

/* @flow */

import React from "react";
import PropTypes from "prop-types";
import "./styles.css";

export class SassButton extends React.PureComponent<{
    normal: boolean,
    buttonText: string,
    onSelect: void => void
}> {
    static propTypes = {
        normal: PropTypes.bool.isRequired,
        buttonText: PropTypes.string.isRequired,
        onSelect: PropTypes.func.isRequired
    };

    render() {
        return (
            <div
                className={
                    this.props.normal ? "normalButton" : "alertButton"
                }
                onClick={this.props.onSelect}
            >
                <span>{this.props.buttonText}</span>
            </div>
        );
    }
}
```

Even if working with SASS and .scss files, you'll be importing the preprocessed .css output files, not the .scss original ones. Be careful not to import a .scss file by mistake.

We assume that CSS classes .normalButton and .alertButton do exist; let's now get to creating them. First, let's define a *partial* SCSS file, _constants.scss, which will define some variables with colors. The filenames of partial files always start with an underscore, and they won't be converted into CSS; rather, they are assumed to be an @import from other SCSS files:

```
$normalColor: green;
$normalText: yellow;

$alertColor: red;
$alertText: white;
```

Variables' names start with a dollar sign, and are a very good way to set standard definitions, such as for fonts or colors. If I were to decide that I want to change my normal color to be blue, I would have to change it in just a single place, and it would be replaced everywhere. Note that I could use $normalColor in many places, for backgrounds, texts, and more, and all would be updated with a single edit.

Let's now define some *mixins* that can be used to include CSS code, even working with parameters. Our darkenBackground() mixin will produce code to set the background-color to a value, and to change the :hover attribute of whatever element it's used in to a 25% darker version. Note the ampersand in &:hover, which stands for the parent element, and also the darken() function, which is just one of many functions that SASS provides, for working with colors, sizes, and so on.

See http://sass-lang.com/documentation/file.SASS_REFERENCE.html#operations for more on this:

```
@mixin darkenBackground($color) {
    background-color: $color;
    &:hover {
        background-color: darken($color, 25%);
        transition: all 0.5s ease;
    }
}

@mixin coloredBoldText($color) {
    color: $color;
    font-weight: bold;
}
```

Finally, we can build our styles in a `styles.scss` file. First, we import our partials:

```
@import "_constants.scss";
@import "_mixins.scss";
```

Then, to show off other SASS features, let's define a basic placeholder class, `%baseButton`, that will be extended. The initial `%` character (similar to class or ID initial characters) means that this code is not meant to be directly used:

```
%baseButton {
    display: inline-block;
    text-decoration: none;
    padding: 5px 10px;
    border-radius: 3px;
}
```

Now let's extend this base class to create our buttons: we'll use `@extend` for that, and also `@include` to add the output of our mixins to the resulting code. We also included some `/* ... */` comments, but you can also use `//` for single-line comments:

```
/*
    A simple button for normal situations
*/
.normalButton {
    @extend %baseButton;
    @include darkenBackground($normalColor);

    span {
        @include coloredBoldText($normalText);
    }
}

/*
    An alert button for warnings or errors
*/
.alertButton {
    @extend %baseButton;
    @include darkenBackground($alertColor);

    span {
        @include coloredBoldText($alertText);
    }
}
```

If you are wondering what eventually comes out of all that, the produced `styles.css` file is as follows: check it out carefully, and you'll see the translated mixins and constants, and also how extended styles are defined, how `:hover` is used, and so on:

```css
.normalButton, .alertButton {
  display: inline-block;
  text-decoration: none;
  padding: 5px 10px;
  border-radius: 3px; }

.normalButton {
  background-color: green; }
  .normalButton:hover {
    background-color: #000100;
    transition: all 0.5s ease; }
  .normalButton span {
    color: yellow;
    font-weight: bold; }

.alertButton {
  background-color: red; }
  .alertButton:hover {
    background-color: maroon;
    transition: all 0.5s ease; }
  .alertButton span {
    color: white;
    font-weight: bold; }
```

All we need now is to write a story and check out our buttons in `Storybook`:

```jsx
// Source file: /src/components/sassButton/sassButton.story.js

import React from "react";
import { storiesOf } from "@storybook/react";
import { action } from "@storybook/addon-actions";

import { SassButton } from "./";

storiesOf("SASS buttons", module)
    .add("normal style", () => (
        <SassButton
            normal
            buttonText={"A normal SASSy button!"}
            onSelect={action("click:normal")}
        />
    ))
    .add("alert style", () => (
        <SassButton
```

```
        normal={false}
        buttonText={"An alert SASSy button!"}
        onSelect={action("click:alert")}
    />
));
```

When a prop is meant to be `true` or `false`, just including its name makes it true. See how in the first story we can just write `normal` instead of `normal={true}`; both are equivalent.

We can see the normal button in the following screenshot:

Our normal button, shown in Storybook

The alert button, with a hovering cursor, is seen in the following screenshot:

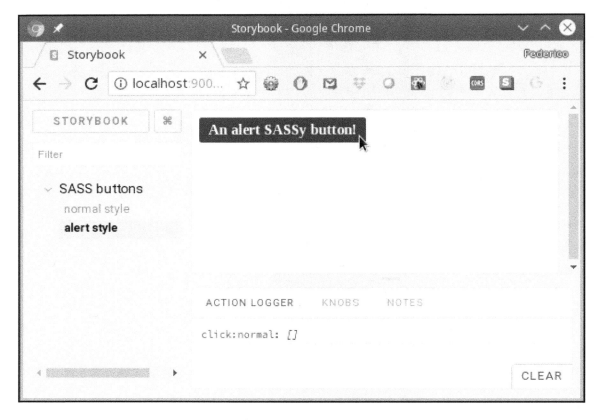

Our alert button, with hovering colors

So, here we have seen a common solution: using SASS to create CSS. In the next section, let's get into a more original way of working, by having the CSS code right within our JS code rather than separated from it!

Creating StyledComponents for inline styling

CSS-in-JS is a sometimes controversial topic. Before `React`, it was almost mandatory that you'd have a trio of sets of JS, HTML, and CSS separate files. When `React` introduced JSX, that was a shot against the trio, because we started placing HTML in the JS code. CSS-in-JS is the natural extension of that idea, because now we want to also include styling within the same JS files.

A first reaction to this is: *Isn't that just going back to inline styles?* This is a valid question, but inline styles aren't just powerful enough. While you can manage lots of styling by inlining styles, the fact is that there are several features that aren't accessible in this way: keyframes animation, media queries, pseudo selectors, and more.

The idea of going with CSS-in-JS is writing styles by using JS, but then injecting those styles in a `<style>` tag within the DOM, so you'll have the full power of CSS for your code. Furthermore, this is also well-aligned with component-based approaches such as React's, because you manage to pack everything you need together in a properly encapsulated way instead of depending on global style files and having to deal with CSS's single namespace.

There are many packages that promote this way of styling, and out of those, we are going to pick `styled-components`, which is one of the best-regarded packages for CSS-in-JS styling. Its philosophy is interesting: instead of adding styles to components, you create components that incorporate those styles and use them everywhere. Let's start by seeing how to add this package to our code, and then move on to using it.

 For the original talk on CSS-in-JS, by Christopher *vjeux* Chedeau, in which he gives the reasons for working with styling done in JS, see `https://speakerdeck.com/vjeux/react-css-in-js`.

How to do it...

Installing `styled-components` is quite simple—and note this is not a development dependency, because you'll be actually using the package in your production code, not as a separate preprocessing step or anything like that:

```
npm install styled-components --save
```

We will be using tagged template literals (which we earlier saw in the *Working with strings* section of `Chapter 2`, *Using Modern JavaScript features*), so you may want to refresh that part of the book.

Working with `Flow` won't be a problem, because `styled-components` is well supported by it, so we won't have to do anything in particular. Finally, for VSC you might want to use the `vscode-styled-components` extension to add syntax highlighting.

Read the full documentation for `styled-components` at `https://www.styled-components.com/docs`.

How it works...

Let's try to recreate the button we build with `SASS`, but through using our new tool. We won't try to mimic the `SASS` code, but we'll try to apply some of the same concepts like defining constants in a separate file, having functions work as mixins, and extending a class as we did earlier. We have a problem, because `styled-components` doesn't provide color functions as `SASS` does, so we'll add a new library to take care of that, `color`:

This package provides you with lots of methods to create and manipulate colors, so you'll do well by taking a look at its documentation, at `https://github.com/qix-/color`.

```
npm install color --save
```

Now, we are set. First, we'll have some basic color constants, in file `constants.js`, that could be used everywhere:

```
export const NORMAL_COLOR = "green";
export const NORMAL_TEXT = "yellow";

export const ALERT_COLOR = "red";
export const ALERT_TEXT = "white";
```

There's an alternative way of sharing global style data, by means of theming; if you are interested, check it out at `https://www.styled-components.com/docs/advanced#theming`.

Now we'll directly get to defining our component, since all styling will also be there. First, we'll need some imports:

```
// Source file: /src/components/styledButton/styledButton.js

/* @flow */

import React from "react";
import PropTypes from "prop-types";
import styled from "styled-components";
import Color from "color";

import {
    NORMAL_TEXT,
    NORMAL_COLOR,
    ALERT_TEXT,
    ALERT_COLOR
} from "./constants";

// continues...
```

Given this, we can get to the main code. We'll have a makeSpan() function that will work as a mixin; we'll get to use it very shortly, and we'll see what props means:

```
// ...continued

const makeSpan = props => `
    span {
        color: ${props.normal ? NORMAL_TEXT : ALERT_TEXT};
        font-weight: bold;
    }
`;

// continues...
```

Then, we'll define a BasicStyledDiv component, with some basic styling, that will do as a base class for our button. (Remember, we are working in this unneedlessly complex way, just to highlight several features you may want to use in problems that really need it!) This component will roughly be the equivalent of our %baseButton declaration in SASS, from the previous section:

```
// ...continued

const BasicStyledDiv = styled.div`
    display: inline-block;
    text-decoration: none;
    padding: 5px 10px;
```

```
        border-radius: 3px;
`;

// continues...
```

After, we can create a `StyledDiv` component by extending the previous one. Since `styled-component` lets us use functions and expressions, we won't have to create two distinct styles, as we did with SASS when we built `.normalButton` and `.alertButton`. Also, note that we can use `&` here, meaning a reference to the class, just as in SASS:

```
// ...continued

const StyledDiv = BasicStyledDiv.extend`
    background-color: ${props =>
        props.normal ? NORMAL_COLOR : ALERT_COLOR};
    &:hover {
        background-color: ${props =>
            Color(props.normal ? NORMAL_COLOR : ALERT_COLOR)
                .darken(0.25)
                .string()};
        transition: all 0.5s ease;
    }
    ${props => makeSpan(props)};
`;

// continues...
```

What is this `props` parameter we see? When creating a style, the component's props will be passed to our code, so we can tweak our style. In this case, if the component's `this.props.normal` value is `true`, NORMAL_COLOR will be used; otherwise, ALERT_COLOR will apply. This simplifies our code a lot, because we won't have to create styles in a fixed fashion; we can make them adjust to whatever we want.

After all of this, the code for our button itself is very simple:

```
// ...continued

export class StyledButton extends React.PureComponent<{
    normal: boolean,
    buttonText: string,
    onSelect: void => void
}> {
    static propTypes = {
        normal: PropTypes.bool.isRequired,
        buttonText: PropTypes.string.isRequired,
        onSelect: PropTypes.func.isRequired
    };
```

```
    render() {
        return (
            <StyledDiv
                normal={this.props.normal}
                onClick={this.props.onSelect}
            >
                <span>{this.props.buttonText}</span>
            </StyledDiv>
        );
    }
}

// continues...
```

Writing a story to check this is actually trivial, because we only need to copy the previous one we wrote for the SASS style button and substitute StyledButton for SassButton; no need for anything else. (OK, I also changed some strings for clarity, but those edits are trivial.) If we launch Storybook, we can quickly verify that our new button works in the same way as our previous one; see following screenshot for evidence of that:

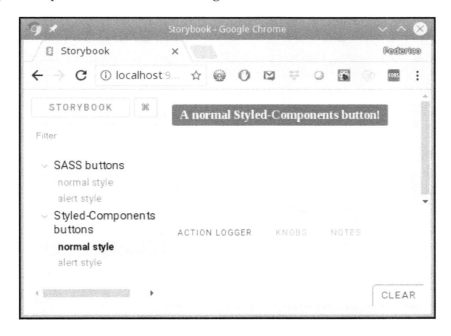

Using styled-components is as successful as SASS, and more "JavaScripty"

If you want to get some specific tips, and learn some new tricks, check out `https://github.com/styled-components/styled-components/blob/master/docs/tips-and-tricks.md`.

Making your application responsive to screen sizes

Creating a web application means that you cannot assume any given display size. In fact, the user may change the browser's window size, and your application should somehow respond to that, rearranging whatever is shown on screen to better work with the current screen dimensions. If your web application is capable of this reorganization, it's said to be *responsive*. Today, given the extreme range of devices with browsers (ranging from small phone handsets to very large flat screens), doing responsive design is really a must, so in this section we'll see how to work with this. I'll assume you are already aware of CSS concepts such as grids and columnar designs; please read up on them if not.

To allay a common, fairly obvious question, if you are aware of current trends in CSS, you may ask why aren't we using Flexbox or CSS Grids, both of which easily allow responsive designs. The answer lies in availability: if you check places such as `https://www.caniuse.com/`, you'll find out that both those features are only recently available, and thus users may not yet have access to them. To sum it up, note the following:

- Internet Explorer has partial support of both features, with many bugs
- Edge supports them only since version 17, dated April 2018
- FireFox supports them since version 60, dated May 2018
- Safari supports them since version 11.1, dated March 2018
- Chrome supported FlexBox since version 49, from March 2016, but CSS Grid only since version 66, dated April 2018

As you can see, if you want to use these features, as of today (December 2018), only a few of your users may have access to them, and for the vast majority, scrambled up displays would be the result. So, even if it means working with a larger library than need be, we'll go with a current-day standard, as we'll see in the next section.

How to do it...

One of the most popular frontend libraries for the design of websites and web applications, is Bootstrap, which has been available since August 2011; it's about seven years old. It has included responsive design handling since version 2. *Mobile First Design* (so you should first get your design to work in smaller devices, and only afterwards worry about adding handling for larger screens) was included in version 3, and SASS support appeared in version 4. Apart from responsive design support, Bootstrap also offers other features, such as components, typography, and more utilities, so you should probably not miss checking the whole documentation at https://getbootstrap.com/docs/4.1/getting-started/introduction/.

 Bootstrap is currently GitHub's second most starred project, following FreeCodeCamp's first place. And if you wonder, React is practically tied at third place with another framework, Vue, and with EBook's Foundation set of free programming books. You can check the results by yourself at https://github.com/search?o=desc&q=stars%3A%3E1&s=starstype= Repositories.

To install Bootstrap, we just need the usual npm command:

```
npm install bootstrap --save
```

 You can save your work by downloading pre-build images, both for CSS and JS; see https://getbootstrap.com/docs/4.1/getting-started/download/ for those options. Alternatively, there exists a React package at https://react-bootstrap.github.io/, react-bootstrap, which today only supports Bootstrap version 3, but promises forthcoming full support for Bootstrap version 4. Yet another possible option you may want to look into is reactstrap, at https:// reactstrap.github.io/.

Bootstrap provides lots of features, including:

- *Components*, such as alerts, buttons, dropdowns, navigation bars, and much more; see https://getbootstrap.com/docs/4.1/components for a complete list
- *Tables*, a common third-party component, with many configuration possibilities; see https://getbootstrap.com/docs/4.1/content/tables for more

- *Typography-related elements*, dealing with the many fonts you'll use in your design; check out `https://getbootstrap.com/docs/4.1/content/typography/S`
- *Styling details*, such as borders, colors, shadows, sizing, and more; read `https://getbootstrap.com/docs/4.1/utilities/`

In any case, we won't be specifically dealing with the preceding list, since it's basically just a matter of styling, and we've already done that. We are going to focus, instead, on positioning elements, changing their sizes, and even hiding or showing them according to the current screen size; let's move on to that now.

How it works...

`Bootstrap` uses a grid system, based on 12 columns, with breakpoints for several device sizes, based on media queries:

- `xs`: very small, such as portrait phones, less than 576 pixels wide
- `sm`: small, like landscape phones, up to 768 pixels
- `md`: medium, like tablets, up to 992 pixels
- `lg`: large, like desktops, up to 1200 pixels
- `xl`: extra large, over 1200 pixels

 These limits aren't hardcoded, and may be changed. Other common values are 1024 and 1440, instead of 992 and 1200. Yet another possibility is considering HD devices (1920x1080) and 4K devices, with a resolution of 2560x1600.

Whenever you place elements, you specify their width in terms of columns, and positions will be arranged depending on the available row space, moving to new rows if need be. You can also allow for different sizing and ordering of elements depending on screen dimensions, and even hide or show components (in full, or partially) depending on available space.

Resizing elements

By using `col-xx-yy` classes (such as `col-sm-3` or `col-md-5`) you can decide the size of elements depending on the current screen width. The following code example shows that—and notice I avoided a separate style sheet, just to simplify:

```
// Source file: /src/App.1.js

/* @flow */

import React, { Component } from "react";

class App extends Component<{}> {
    render() {
        const cl = "border border-dark p-2 bg-warning ";

        return (
            <div className="container mw-100">
                <div className="row border">
                    <div className={cl + "col-sm-2 col-md-6"}>2/6</div>
                    <div className={cl + "col-sm-4"}>4</div>
                    <div className={cl + "col-sm-1"}>1</div>
                    <div className={cl + "col-sm-1"}>1</div>
                    <div className={cl + "col-sm-1"}>1</div>
                    <div className={cl + "col-sm-1 col-md-5"}>1/5</div>
                    <div className={cl + "col-sm-2 "}>2</div>
                    <div className={cl + "col-sm-7 col-md-3"}>7/3</div>
                    <div className={cl + "col-sm-4 "}>4</div>
                    <div className={cl + "col-sm-1 col-md-3"}>1/3</div>
                </div>
            </div>
        );
    }
}

export default App;
```

We can see how rendering changes with screen size; see following image:

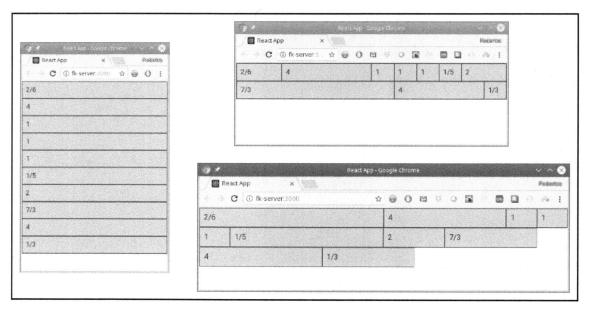

The same elements, rendered at different screen widths

At the smallest screen size, all elements are rendered at the same size vertically; this would suit, logically, a very small device. As we enlarge the window size, the 7/3 element now takes up 7 columns, while the 2/6, 1/5, and 1/3 elements are narrow. When we increase the window width even more, note the 7/3 element takes only three columns, and the 3 other elements become wide.

Of course, it's highly unlikely you'd ever come up with this weird design, with so many different widths and such peculiar resizing rules, but the point here is that by using the Bootstrap grid, elements can vary in size and gracefully flow to different rows, without having to do anything special.

Reordering elements

In the previous example, we saw how components resized themselves, and flowed across lines. However, there are other requirements: for instance, you could want a component to appear at a different position for a given screen size. Fortunately, Bootstrap also allows for that. Let's have an element that will change its place among the rest:

```
// Source file: /src/App.2.js

/* @flow */

import React, { Component } from "react";

class App extends Component<{}> {
    render() {
        const cl = "border border-dark p-2 bg-warning ";
        const ch = "border border-dark p-2 bg-dark text-white ";

        return (
            <div className="container mw-100">
                <div className="row border">
                    <div className={cl + "col-sm-2 col-md-6"}>2/6</div>
                    <div className={cl + "col-sm-4"}>4</div>
                    <div className={cl + "col-sm-1"}>1</div>
                    <div
                        className={
                            ch + "col-sm-1 order-sm-first order-md-
                            last"
                        }
                    >
                        1
                    </div>
                    <div className={cl + "col-sm-1 col-md-5"}>1/5</div>
                    <div className={cl + "col-sm-3 "}>3</div>
                </div>
            </div>
        );
    }
}

export default App;
```

For small devices, our special component should be the first, and for medium ones, it should move to the end. For very small devices (for which we haven't provided any special rules) it should appear at its normal place. See the following images:

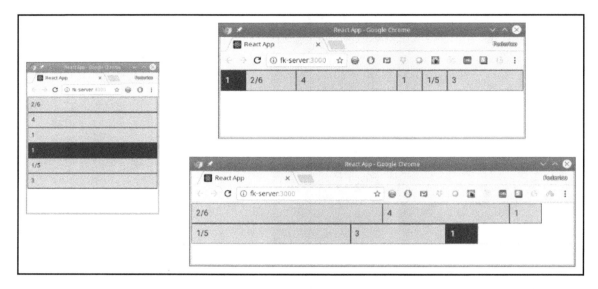

Components can also change their relative positions.

This takes care of a common second set of requirements, letting you vary at will the sequence in which components appear on screen. We only have one more case, which we'll see in the next section.

Hiding or showing elements

Our final type of design rule is that some components (or parts of them) should possibly not be displayed at given screen sizes. For instance, if you were providing information about a movie, in large screens you could include a still from a scene, plus pictures of the main actors, in addition to the movie title and a full description, but in small screens you could make do with just the movie title and basic information. Let's show this kind of requirement with a couple of components: one will be fully hidden, while the other will just hide part of its contents:

```
// Source file: /src/App.3.js

/* @flow */

import React, { Component } from "react";
```

```
class App extends Component<{}> {
    render() {
        const cl = "border border-dark p-2 bg-warning ";
        const ch = "border border-dark p-2 bg-dark text-white ";

        return (
            <div className="container mw-100">
                <div className="row border">
                    <div className={cl + "col-sm-2 col-md-6"}>2/6</div>
                    <div className={ch + "d-none d-sm-block col-sm-4"}>
                        0/4
                    </div>
                    <div className={cl + "col-sm-2"}>2</div>
                    <div className={cl + "col-sm-2"}>2</div>
                    <div className={cl + "col-sm-1 col-md-5'"}>1/5</div>
                    <div className={cl + "col-sm-3 "}>3</div>
                    <div className={ch + "col-sm-7 "}>
                        <div>TOP</div>
                        <div className="d-none d-sm-block">(MIDDLE)
                        </div>
                        <div>BOTTOM</div>
                    </div>
                    <div className={cl + "col-sm-4 "}>4</div>
                </div>
            </div>
        );
    }
}

export default App;
```

To see this in action, check out the following image:

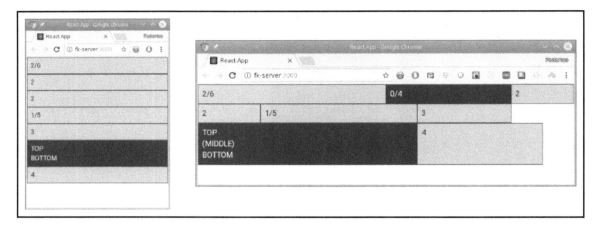

A component fully disappears in small screens, while others show different contents

The 0/4 component is set to be shown only at small screens and more, so in the left side screenshot it just disappears. The other component shows two lines in the smaller screen, but fuller contents (OK, three lines instead of two) in bigger screens.

Making your application adaptive for enhanced usability

By using grids and all the styles we saw in the previous section, in many cases you won't need anything extra in order to build a responsive website. However, in some cases moving components around, resizing them, or even hiding part or all of them, isn't enough. For example, you may actually want to show totally different components for small and large screens—say, a screen with three tabs for a phone, showing only one tab at a time, but a three-column display for a desktop, showing everything simultaneously. Changes could be even more drastic: you might decide that some functionality isn't going to be available on mobile devices, but only included in large screens. So, instead of doing responsive design, you are delving into adaptive design, meaning that the actual design and functions of the screen will change, and then we need to be able to handle internal changes in code.

How to do it...

If you wanted to do adaptive design on your own, you could certainly set things up to listen for screen size or orientation changes, and then produce some components or other. While there's nothing wrong with this approach, it can be made far simpler by installing `react-responsive`, a package that takes care of all that—you just specify the conditions under which some components will be rendered, and whenever they are satisfied, those components will be rendered. On any size or orientation change, the package will take care of whatever re-rendering is needed.

Installation requires the usual `npm` command:

`npm install react-responsive --save`

The key component in this package is called `<MediaQuery>`, and lets you work with either media queries, or by using props, in a fashion more like `React`; I prefer the latter, but check out the documentation if you are interested about the more CSS-y option. Let's now see how it is used.

 Read more about `react-responsive` at `https://github.com/contra/react-responsive`. There are many more features than I'll be showing in this text.

How it works...

Basically, all you have to do in order to detect any size changes is to produce one or more `<MediaQuery>` components when rendering, and those whose requirements are met will actually be rendered, and the rest won't appear on the page.

Let's write a very basic example with plenty of media queries, to see the coding style you'll be using. The following is an example given in the react-responsive GitHub page; we'll just try to detect some aspects of the current device and window:

```
// Source file: /src/App.4.js

/* @flow */

import React, { Component } from "react";
import MediaQuery from "react-responsive";

const XS = 576; // phone
const SM = 768; // tablet
```

```
const MD = 992; // desktop
const LG = 1200; // large desktop

class App extends Component<{}> {
    render() {
        return (
            <div>
                <MediaQuery minDeviceWidth={MD + 1}>
                    <div>Device: desktop or laptop</div>

                    <MediaQuery maxWidth={XS}>
                        <div>Current Size: small phone </div>
                    </MediaQuery>

                    <MediaQuery minWidth={XS + 1} maxWidth={SM}>
                        <div>Current Size: normal phone</div>
                    </MediaQuery>

                    <MediaQuery minWidth={SM + 1} maxWidth={MD}>
                        <div>Current Size: tablet</div>
                    </MediaQuery>

                    <MediaQuery minWidth={MD + 1} maxWidth={LG}>
                        <div>Current Size: normal desktop</div>
                    </MediaQuery>

                    <MediaQuery minWidth={LG + 1}>
                        <div>Current Size: large desktop</div>
                    </MediaQuery>
                </MediaQuery>

                <MediaQuery maxDeviceWidth={MD}>
                    <div>Device: tablet or phone</div>
                    <MediaQuery orientation="portrait">
                        <div>Orientation: portrait</div>
                    </MediaQuery>
                    <MediaQuery orientation="landscape">
                        <div>Orientation: landscape</div>
                    </MediaQuery>
                </MediaQuery>
            </div>
        );
    }
}

export default App;
```

I defined the four size constants (XS, SM, MD, and LG) to match the values used by Bootstrap, but you could certainly work with other sizes.

> You can also modify the values in Bootstrap, so it will work with different breakpoints: see https://getbootstrap.com/docs/4.1/layout/grid/#grid-tiers for more on this.

Whenever our App component is rendered, the media queries are executed, and depending on their result, components will or won't be rendered. In our case, we are just producing some <div> instances with text, but it should be obvious that you could actually produce any other kind of components.

We can run this application in Chrome, and see how it produces different contents as we resize the window: see the following image :

Our component automatically reacts to any screen size changes, and produces different components, even if our example lacks variety!

Alternatively, you could use the device toggle in the toolbar, and then you'd be also able to see your application as it would look in a phone or tablet; take a look at the following screenshot for a sample of this:

Chrome's Developer Tools include a device toggle that lets you simulate multiple kinds of devices, including phones and tablets as well

Working with `Bootstrap` for simple adjustments, and `react-responsive` for more complex work, you can ensure your application will fit whatever device it's run on. Let's now move on to a different kind of situation: running in different countries or regions!

Making a global application with internationalization and localization

With the growing globalization levels, it's most likely that any website you write may be required to be in two or more languages. In Canada, English and French would be mandatory; in Switzerland, four languages could be asked for; and even in a (supposedly single-language) country like the United States, a Spanish version of the site could well be added to the English one. Of course, translation isn't enough: dates and currency amounts also require different formatting depending on the country, so we'll have to take care of that too.

Some definitions, now: being able to adapt your software to different languages is called *internationalization*, usually abbreviated as *i18n*—the 18 stands for the 18 letters between the initial *i* and the final *n*. Then, the specific process of configuring the system for a specific area is called *localization*, abbreviated as *l10n* for similar reasons as in i18n. Finally, if you really are into these *numeronyms*, the combination of internationalization and localization is also known as *globalization*, shortened to *g11n*.

This pair of definitions is based upon a document by the W3C, at `https://www.w3.org/International/questions/qa-i18n`. There, they define that "Internationalization is the design and development [...] that enables easy localization for target audiences that vary in culture, region, or language" and "Localization refers to the adaptation [...] to meet the language, cultural and other requirements of a specific target market (a locale)."

Fortunately, handling these aspects is simple in `React`, and only requires some planning ahead, as we'll see in this recipe.

How to do it...

A good package for handling all i18n concerns is `i18next`. We can install it, together with a package for detecting the browser language, with the following command:

```
npm install i18next i18next-browser-languagedetector --save
```

You'll also have to decide on a fallback language (probably "en", for English), and provide translations for all strings used in your application. To get a taste of this, for a fictitious data entry form (in a really very small application; usually, you'd have hundreds of translations!) you could have the following `translations.en.json` file for English:

```json
{
    "details": "Details",
    "number": "How many things?",
    "color": "Thing Color",
    "send it before": "Send the thing before",
    "please enter details": "Please, enter details for your thing:",
    "summary": "Your only thing will be there before {{date,
    AS_DATE}}",
    "summary_plural":
        "Your {{count}} things will be there before {{date, AS_DATE}}",
    "colors": {
        "none": "None",
        "steel": "Steel",
        "sand": "Sand"
    }
}
```

If you decided to also provide Spanish ("es") translations, you'd add another file, `translations.es.json`. (Note: you can name your files in any way you wish, and you don't have to follow my examples.) This new JSON file has the very same keys, but translated into Spanish:

```json
{
    "details": "Detalles",
    "number": "¿Cuántas cosas?",
    "color": "Color de la cosa",
    "send it before": "Enviar antes de",
    "please enter details": "Por favor, ingrese detalles para su
    cosa:",
    "summary": "Su única cosa llegará antes de la fecha {{date,
    AS_DATE}}",
    "summary_plural":
        "Sus {{count}} cosas llegarán antes del {{date, AS_DATE}}",
    "colors": {
        "none": "Ninguno",
        "steel": "Acero",
        "sand": "Arena"
    }
}
```

The idea is that, whenever you want to display some text, you'll refer to it by its key (such as `"details"` or `"number"`), eventually providing extra parameters (as in `"summary"`), and the translation package will pick the correct string to display; let's see how it works by completing an example.

The `i18next` package can also deal with plurals and specific formatting rules. You'll first have to initialize it, as follows; we are creating a `i18n` file:

```javascript
// Source file: /src/components/i18nform/i18n.js

import i18n from "i18next";
import LanguageDetector from "i18next-browser-languagedetector";

import EN_TEXTS from "./translations.en.json";
import ES_TEXTS from "./translations.es.json";

i18n.use(LanguageDetector).init({
    resources: {
        en: { translations: EN_TEXTS },
        es: { translations: ES_TEXTS }
    },
    fallbackLng: "en",
    ns: ["translations"],
    defaultNS: "translations",
    debug: true,
    interpolation: {
        escapeValue: false,
        format: function(value, format, lang = i18n.language) {
            if (format === "AS_DATE") {
                try {
                    const dd = new Date(value);
                    return new Intl.DateTimeFormat(lang).format(
                        new Date(
                            dd.getTime() + dd.getTimezoneCffset() *
                            60000
                        )
                    );
                } catch (e) {
                    return "???";
                }
            } else {
                return value;
            }
        }
    }
});
```

```
const t = i18n.t.bind(i18n); // to allow using t(...) instead of
i18n.t(...)

export { i18n, t };
```

Some details about the code should be noted:

- The `use(...)` method tells `i18next` to use the browser language detector package.
- In the `resources` attribute, you have to provide the set of translations for each language, which we imported from our JSON files.
- `fallbackLng` specifies that English (`"en"`) will be the default language.
- `ns` and `defaultNS` define the namespace for translations, usually just *translations* as we used in the `resources` attribute.
- `debug` is a good tool, for it will log to the console any keys you want to translate, but that haven't been defined in the resources.
- `interpolation.escapeValue` gives you the option to escape all values: you could use it to display unchecked user-entered values, but we don't need it here.
- `interpolation.format` lets you define a special formatting function that should produce whatever output you desire for a given value, in a specific format, for a given language. In our case, we used it with the `summary` and `summary_plural` keys to format dates in the proper style: month/day/year for English, day/month/year for Spanish. You could also use this function to format numbers as currency, for example.

 You can check the full documentation for `i18next` at `https://www.i18next.com/`.

How it works...

Imagine we are defining an input form that lets you order some things, picking their color and deciding a top date for delivery. Our `<I18nForm>` component could be coded as follows—and note that we are just focusing on the input form, paying no attention to actually *doing* anything with the user data! Also, pay no attention to the poor UI design; once again, we care about translation here, so I wanted as little extra JSX code as possible:

```
// Source file: /src/components/i18nform/i18nform.js
```

```
/* @flow */

import React from "react";

import "./styles.css";

import { i18n, t } from "./i18n";

export class I18nForm extends React.PureComponent<
    {},
    {
        delivery: String,
        howMany: Number,
        thingColor: String
    }
> {
    state = {
        delivery: "2018-09-22",
        howMany: 1,
        thingColor: "NC"
    };

    constructor(props) {
        super(props);
        this.rerender = () => this.forceUpdate();
    }

    componentDidMount() {
        i18n.on("languageChanged", this.rerender);
    }

    componentWillUnmount() {
        i18n.off("languageChanged", this.rerender);
    }

    render() {
        return (
            <div>
                <div>
                    <h2>{t("details")}</h2>
                    <button onClick={() => i18n.changeLanguage("es")}>
                        ES
                    </button>
                    <button onClick={() => i18n.changeLanguage("en")}>
                        EN
                    </button>
                </div>
                <br />
```

```jsx
            <div>{t("please enter details")}</div>
            <br />
            <div>
                {t("send it before")}:
                <input
                    type="date"
                    value={this.state.delivery}
                    onChange={e =>
                        this.setState({ delivery: e.target.value })
                    }
                />
            </div>
            <div>
                {t("number")}:
                <input
                    type="number"
                    min="1"
                    value={this.state.howMany}
                    onChange={e =>
                        this.setState({
                            howMany: Number(e.target.value)
                        })
                    }
                />
            </div>
            <div>
                {t("color")}:
                <select
                    onChange={e =>
                        this.setState({ thingColor: e.target.value })
                    }
                >
                    <option value="NC">{t("colors.none")}</option>
                    <option value="ST">{t("colors.steel")}</option>
                    <option value="SD">{t("colors.sand")}</option>
                </select>
            </div>
            <br />
            <div>
                {t("summary", {
                    count: this.state.howMany,
                    date: this.state.delivery
                })}
            </div>
        </div>
    );
  }
}
```

Some details about the code should be noted:

- Passing extra parameters for interpolation (as with the "summary" key) is done via an object, with the desired parameters
- If you want to have distinct lines for singular and plural versions, you have to define two keys as we did here: summary for singular, and summary_plural for plural, and then i18next will decide which to used based on the value of the count parameter

How can we deal with dynamic language changes? We provided two buttons to call i18n.changeLanguage(...), but how do we re-render components? There are (at least) three ways of doing so:

- You can listen to the "languageChanged" event and force an update, which was what we did here. (We use .on(...) to set our component to listen, and .off(...) to stop it later, when unmounting.)
- Another solution would be to include the currently selected language in the application state (we'll be looking into this in the next chapter) and you could supply it to components via props, so React will re-render everything on a language change.
- And, finally, you could use the react-i18next framework package at https:// github.com/i18next/react-i18next to provide an even more seamless integration.

We can test our translations with a very simple story:

```
// Source file: /src/components/i18nform/i18nform.story.js

/* @flow */

import React from "react";
import { storiesOf } from "@storybook/react";

import { I18nForm } from "./";

storiesOf("i18n form", module).add("standard", () => <I18nForm />);
```

When the story is loaded, it looks as seen in the following screenshot:

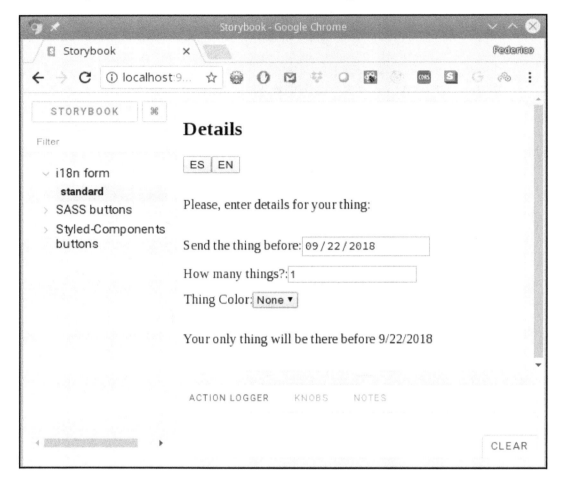

Our input form, with initial values, displayed in English

If you change the quantity, the text at the bottom will be updated accordingly; see the following screenshot:

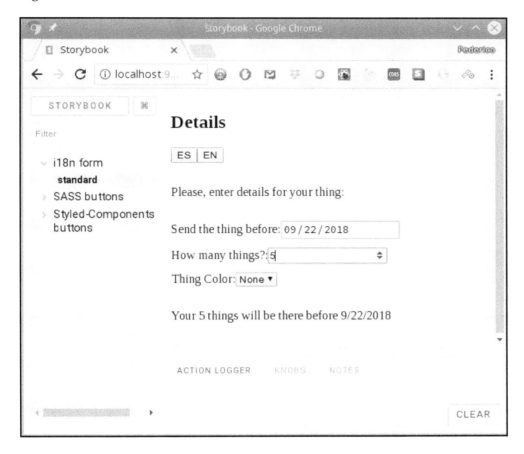

If we order more than one thing, the plural translation is used

And, if you change the language to Spanish, all texts will be automatically translated; take a look at the following screenshot:

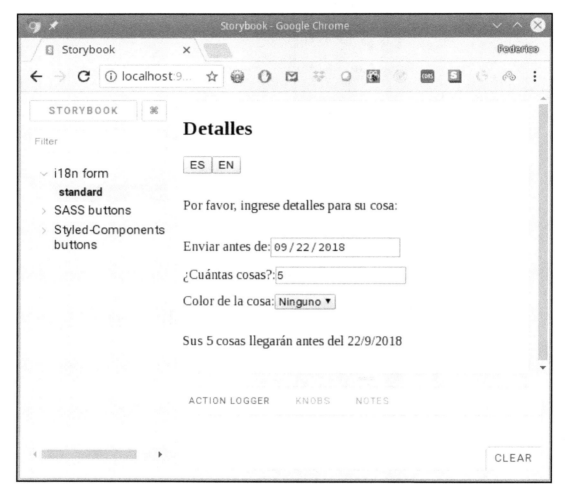

By listening to the language change event, we can force the component to re-render itself and show translations for the newly chosen language

A small detail: whenever you use a date `<input>` element, dates are formatted according to your computer's locale, so the displayed value doesn't change for Spanish. However, the element's value is always the same, in ISO format: in our case, `2018-09-22`. You can solve this by using a special handcrafted component, but we won't be doing that, since what we cared about was showing how translations work.

As we saw, preparing an application for international usage isn't really a very hard problem. Even if you don't plan on doing it at the beginning, it will pay to work in this way; having to retrofit translations in existing code can be harder.

Setting up for accessibility (a11y)

When designing a web page, the term "accessibility" refers to providing support so everyone, including people with disabilities, can use your page. There are then many needs that have to be considered, including, for instance, the following:

- *Vision limitations*, varying from poor eyesight, through color vision problems, all the way up to total blindness
- *Hearing limitations*, which require some fallback method for hearing impaired users
- *Mobility limitations*, which may imply difficulty or impossibility of using the hands or controlling a mouse
- *Cognitive limitations*, which may complicate understanding the information shown on screen

There are many tools that can assist disabled users, such as screen zooming, speech recognition, screen readers, braille terminals, closed captioning, and more, but even those tools need some extra information in order to work properly. The **Web Content Accessibility Guidelines (WCAG)** are a set of guidelines, published by the **Web Accessibility Initiative (WAI)** of the **World Wide Web Consortium (W3C)**. The current version, 2.1, available online at `https://www.w3.org/TR/WCAG21/`, is based on four principles, known as POUR as an acronym:

- *Perceivable*: Information and user interface components must be presentable to users in ways they can perceive
- *Operable*: User interface components and navigation must be operable

- *Understandable*: Information and the operation of user interface must be understandable
- *Robust*: Content must be robust enough that it can be interpreted by by a wide variety of user agents, including assistive technologies

These principles, quoted from the cited page, include *guidelines* for use of color, working with a keyboard, providing information for screen readers, having enough contrast, displaying errors, and more; *sufficient and advisory techniques*, that can help follow the guidelines; and *success criteria*, meaning testable conditions to be used for conformance testing. The latter criteria are also used to define three levels of conformance: *A*, the minimum; *AA*, medium, including all of *A* and *AA* success criteria, and *AAA*, the hardest to attain, fulfilling all existing criteria—but it is acknowledged that it may be impossible to achieve for some sites.

Trying to make sure that your web application follows all guidelines and applies all techniques is not easy, so we'll see how we can add some tools to React in order to make your task a bit easier.

How to do it...

In order to check our work for accessibility, we'll install a couple of packages, so let's follow the procedure mentioned: one for static checks when writing code, using ESLint, and another for dynamic checks when running our application. And, if you ask yourself *Why two tools instead of only one?*, the answer is that a static tool cannot check everything: for example, if you assign a variable's value to a title, will that value not be empty at run time? On the other hand, since all your code is linted, you got a chance to detect some things that could be missed during normal tests, so by using two tools you are not doing redundant work, but rather increasing the odds of finding accessibility problems.

Installing the ESLint module is quite simple. First, we'll use npm to add the package:

```
npm install eslint-plugin-jsx-a11y --save-dev
```

Then, we'll have to modify our `.eslintrc` file a bit, adding the new plugin, and specifying what rules we want to enforce:

```
{
    .
    .
    .
    "extends": [
        "eslint:recommended",
        "plugin:flowtype/recommended",
        "plugin:react/recommended",
        "plugin:jsx-a11y/recommended"
    ],
    "plugins": ["babel", "flowtype", "react", "jsx-a11y"],
    .
    .
    .
}
```

If you don't want to use all rules (as we did here) you can specify the rules you care for in the `"rules"` part of the file: see https://github.com/evcohen/eslint-plugin-jsx-a11y for details on this, and inspect the complete set of available rules at https://github.com/evcohen/eslint-plugin-jsx-a11y/tree/master/docs/rules.

The second addition we want is `react-a11y`, a package that modifies React rendering functions internally, so accessibility problems can be detected at runtime. Installation is simple:

```
npm install react-a11y --save
```

Then, at the start of your application, you'll have to initialize the `a11y` module, along with the rules you want to check. The format of the rules is the same as `ESLint` uses. Check https://github.com/reactjs/react-a11y/tree/master/docs/rules for the complete list, because new rules may be added. (You'll also have to see that list in order to learn which rules, if any, have special options.) By default, all rules are `"off"`, so you must explicitly turn them on to `"warn"` or `"error"`. A full configuration would be as follows, as of December 2018:

```
import React from "react";
import ReactDOM from "react-dom";
import a11y from "react-a11y";

a11y(React, ReactDOM, {
    rules: {
        "avoid-positive-tabindex": "warn",
```

```
            "button-role-space": "warn",
            "hidden-uses-tabindex": "warn",
            "img-uses-alt": "warn",
            "label-uses-for": "warn",
            "mouse-events-map-to-key-events": "warn",
            "no-access-key": "warn",
            "no-hash-ref": "warn",
            "no-unsupported-elements-use-aria": "warn",
            "onclick-uses-role": "warn",
            "onclick-uses-tabindex": "warn",
            "redundant-alt": ["warn", ["picture", "image", "photo", "foto",
            "bild"]],
            "tabindex-uses-button": "warn",
            "use-onblur-not-onchange": "warn",
            "valid-aria-role": "warn"
        }
});

// a11y.restoreAll() would undo all changes
```

You might want to not enable a11y in production, to avoid a needless slowdown.

We have everything set up; let's now see how all of this comes together.

How it works...

First, let's see what happens with the errors that are detected via ESLint, and then we'll move to the runtime problems.

Solving static problems

Our first *victim* of bad a11y coding is our SASS button; see the following screenshot:

```
 8   export class SassButton extends React.PureComponent<{
 9       normal: boolean,
10       buttonText: string,
11       onSelect
12   }> {         [eslint] Visible, non-interactive elements with click handlers must
13       static p   have at least one keyboard listener. (jsx-a11y/click-events-have-ke
14           norm   y-events)
15           butt [eslint] Static HTML elements with event handlers require a role. (j
16           onSe sx-a11y/no-static-element-interactions)
17       };
18               (property) JSX.IntrinsicElements.div:
19       render() React.DetailedHTMLProps<React.HTMLAttributes<HTMLDivElement>, HTMLDi
20           retu vElement>
21           <div
22               className={
23                   this.props.normal ? "normalButton" : "alertButton"
24               }
25               onClick={this.props.onSelect}
26               >
27               <span>{this.props.buttonText}</span>
28           </div>
29           );
30       }
31   }
```

Our SASS button has (at least) two accessibility-related problems

One a11y rule is that you should be able to use the application with only the keyboard, so we need to be able to tab our way to the button (this requires using a tabIndex) and providing a keyboard listener (onKeyPress or onKeyDown). Furthermore, the role of our element (which works as a button) must be specified. The corrected JSX code would be as follows:

```
<div
    className={
        this.props.normal ? "normalButton" : "alertButton"
    }
    onClick={this.props.onSelect}
    onKeyPress={this.keyDownAsClick}
    tabIndex="0"
    role="button"
>
    <span>{this.props.buttonText}</span>
</div>
```

The new method, `.keyDownAsClick()`, would check if the user pressed the spacebar (ASCII code 32) or the *ENTER* key (ASCII code 13), and if so, call the same logic as the `onClick` handler:

```
keyDownAsClick = (e: { keyCode: number }) => {
    if (e.keyCode === 32 || e.keyCode === 13) {
        this.props.onSelect();
    }
}
```

Our input form also has a problem, albeit a simpler one. See the following screenshot:

```
</di  [eslint] onBlur must be used instead of onchange, unless absolutely
<div  necessary and it causes no negative consequences for keyboard only
      or screen reader users. (jsx-a11y/no-onchange)
    <select
        onChange={e =>
            this.setState({ thingColor: e.target.value })
        }
    >
        <option value="NC">{t("colors.none")}</option>
        <option value="ST">{t("colors.steel")}</option>
        <option value="SD">{t("colors.sand")}</option>
    </select>
```

Our things ordering form only has a small a11y problem

The problem and its solution are clear: instead of using `onChange`, the suggestion is to substitute `onBlur`, which effectively has no consequences for users. We won't show the edited code, given how small the required change is, and just edit the file to replace the method.

We could try adding an image to our form, just for the sake of getting another, different warning. Try adding a Packt logo to the form, as follows:

```
<img
src="http://d1ldz4te4covpm.cloudfront.net/sites/all/themes/packt_v4/images/
packt-logo.svg"
    style={{ width: "50px", height: "25px" }}
/>
```

In this case, we'd get a warning about the need for an `alt` attribute (adding `alt="Packt logo"` to the `img` tag would do) to describe the image; take a look at the following screenshot:

```
[eslint] img elements must have an alt prop, either with meaningful
  text, or an empty string for decorative images. (jsx-a11y/alt-text)
<img
  src="http://d1ldz4te4covpm.cloudfront.net/sites/all/themes/packt_v4/images/packt-logo.svg"
  style={{ width: "50px", height: "25px" }}
/>
<br />
<div>{t("please enter details")}</div>
```

Another a11y rule requires images to have an alt attribute to describe them

Finally, let's see a case in which our tool fails! The button we created with `styled-components` has basically the same problems as our SASS button, but nothing is reported; why? The reason is simple: if you examine the code (see the *Adding SASS for separate styling* section earlier in this chapter) we aren't using `<div>` or `<button>` instances or any other recognizable HTML tags, but rather `<StyledDiv>` and `<StyledButton>`, which our a11y `eslint` plugin doesn't understand. So far, the only workaround for this is to manually change our styled components back to their original tags, solve whatever problems may pop up, and then go back to the styled version not a very good solution, admittedly!

Solving runtime problems

If we now try our fixed components in `Storybook`, `react-a11y` won't say anything about them, but it will report some problems with the `styled-components` one, which we couldn't solve beforehand; see the following screenshot:

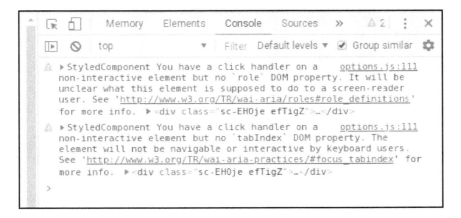

The react-a11y runtime tests show some problems in our component

Of course, given that we build our component to match the previous SASS one, it won't be a surprise that the solution to the accessibility problems are the same: adding `onKeyDown`, `tabIndex`, `role`, and a key-handling method. The relevant parts of the corrected code would be as follows:

```
keyDownAsClick = (e: { keyCode: number }) => {
    if (e.keyCode === 32 || e.keyCode === 13) {
        this.props.onSelect();
    }
};

render() {
    return (
        <StyledDiv
            normal={this.props.normal}
            onClick={this.props.onSelect}
            onKeyDown={this.keyDownAsClick}
            tabIndex="0"
            role="button"
        >
            <span>{this.props.buttonText}</span>
        </StyledDiv>
    );
}
```

Of course, we have just seen the tip of the iceberg as to all the problems that can appear, and their solutions—but what really matters is that you have some tools to help you with the development of a11y-enabled applications, as we have shown.

There is more

What can we do to ensure a fully compliant a11y application? Unfortunately, you won't be able to manage it with just some tools. For instance, none of the tools we selected pointed out that we should add a name to the input fields, as pointed out by an ARIA rule (see https://w3c.github.io/using-aria/#fifth for more on it). Also, there are some conditions that cannot be tested in code. For example, guidelines say that error or mandatory fields should not be highlighted just with color (because of color blindness) but should have some external text or mark; how would you test for that in an automated way? take a look at the following screenshot for an example, taken from https://govuk-elements.herokuapp.com/errors/example-form-validation-multiple-questions, with enhanced visibility for errors:

Your personal details

Full name

As shown on your birth certificate or passport

Error message about full name goes here

National Insurance number

It's on your National Insurance card, benefit letter, payslip or P60.
For example, 'QQ 12 34 56 C'.

FK 22 09 60 B

Continue

A sample input form from a UK government site that shows good a11y practices for errors

It's not possible to get an A, AA, or AAA level without an audit, but you can add more tools to help out with that:

- The W3C Web Accessibility Initiative provides an extensive list of tools (113, as of today!) at `https://www.w3.org/WAI/ER/tools/`
- The A11Y Project provides a community effort to simplify web accessibility, showing several useful techniques, at `https://a11yproject.com/`
- MDN has a full overview of ARIA, a spec from the W3C geared to providing extra information for screen readers by way of the usage of HTML attributes, at `https://developer.mozilla.org/en-US/docs/Web/Accessibility/ARIA/ARIA_Techniques`
- The W3C also provides many suggestions for using ARIA, including samples of code, at `https://w3c.github.io/using-aria/`
- There are several accessibility checkers, for all main browsers, which can diagnose a page *on the go*, so just search for them; some work as browser extensions, while others are code meant to be added to your website, to detect and report possible problems

Even if no single tool or set of tools can ensure `a11y` compliance, you will be able to build yourself a good starting lot of tools; experiment a bit!

Expanding Your Application

In this chapter, we are going to focus on larger, more complex applications, adding recipes such as the following:

- Managing state with Redux
- Doing async actions with redux-thunk
- Adding routing with react-router
- Adding authorization to routes
- Code splitting for performance

Introduction

In the previous two chapters, we saw how to develop web applications with `React`, and endeavored to make them internationally usable, accessible for everybody, and nicely styled to boot. In this chapter, we'll add some more features, which are typical of most applications.

Managing state with Redux

What's difficult about building an application? Obviously, you can do anything with plain, vanilla JS, but things start getting hairy when you try to keep the UI and the state of the application in sync. You call services, you get data. Data must be reflected in several places, HTML elements must be changed, added, or removed, and so on—this is where the complexity lies.

So far, we've been working only with state in components, and you could very well keep doing so: your top level component's state will include everything you need, and you'd be able to manage by passing everything you need as props to the components below. Of course, as your application grows, this won't scale very well. What's the tipping point? Redux is a tool to manage state, but its own developers suggest that you should use their package if and only if you fulfill the following conditions, and I quote from `https://redux.js.org/#before-proceeding-further`:

- *"You have reasonable amounts of data changing over time."*

- *"You need a single source of truth for your state."*

- *"You find that keeping all your state in a top-level component is no longer sufficient."*

Of course, these rules are not really precise, and allow for subjectivity, so there's no clear-cut point at which you'll *have* to use Redux. However, for most modern large scale applications, it's quite safe to say that Redux will probably come in handy, so let's assume that for the rest of this chapter.

In this recipe, we'll install Redux, and start to see how to work with it in React.

Getting ready

Before anything else, we must install a couple of packages: redux, the state-managing package itself, and the react-redux bindings for using Redux with React. (You can use Redux with other frameworks or libraries, but this is not covered in this book.) Installation is simple, just use npm, as we have done several times before:

```
npm install redux react-redux --save
```

We'll have to learn several concepts in order to use `Redux`:

- *Store*: The only place ("single source of truth") where you hold the application state. You create the store globally, at the beginning of your application, and then you *connect* components to it. Connected components will get re-rendered when the state changes, and everything they need to render themselves should come from the store. The store can only be updated through actions.
- *Actions*: Objects that your components *dispatch* with any new data you wish. Actions always have a `type` attribute to distinguish different types, and any other data, with no restriction. Actions are usually created by *action creators* to simplify coding, and after being dispatched they are processed by reducers.
- *Reducers*: Pure functions (meaning, no side effects!) that change the application's state, depending on the data received in actions. The state is never modified; rather, a new state must be produced with whichever changes were necessary. The reducer produces a new state as a function of the old state and the data received in the action.

This is shown in the following diagram:

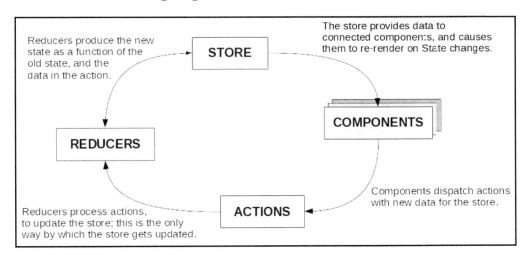

Data flow in Redux is strictly uni-directional, always following a circular pattern

Using this flow cycle helps keep the state and the view in sync—since the latter is produced in terms of the former, and all updates to the state immediately cause the view to be updated. We have installed the necessary tools to use, and we know what we have to do; now, let's get to an actual example.

You may want to look at `eslint-plugin-redux`, which gives you some rules for how to get the best out of `Redux`. Check it out at `https://github.com/DianaSuvorova/eslint-plugin-react-redux`, and if you're interested, add some or all of its rules to your `ESLint` configuration; by default, they are all disabled.

In this recipe, let's do a simple example to show most of the concepts in the previous section. After reading multiple articles and tutorials on the web, I think it's mandatory to provide some kind of example involving a counter, and let's not break that tradition and do it here too! We want to have a counter that we can modify by clicking on some buttons, and we also want to know how many clicks we've made.

How to do it...

Before we start writing the code, let's have it in the open: we'll be writing too many lines of code for what could have been easily solved *without* `Redux`—we won't have a *reasonable amount of data changing over time* but only a couple of counts, and we certainly won't *find that keeping all your state in a top-level component* isn't good enough, but since we want a simple initial example, we'll use `Redux` anyway.

Defining actions

First, we need some actions. We'll want to increment and decrement the counter, and we'll also want to reset it to zero. The first two requirements can be achieved with a single action (decrementing is just incrementing by a negative amount), so we'll need two actions, each identified by a constant:

```
// Source file: src/counterApp/counter.actions.js

/* @flow */

export const COUNTER_INCREMENT = "counter:increment";
export const COUNTER_RESET = "counter:reset";

export type CounterAction = {
    type: string,
    value?: number
};

export const reset = () =>
    ({
        type: COUNTER_RESET
```

```
    }: CounterAction);

export const increment = (inc: number) =>
    ({
        type: COUNTER_INCREMENT,
        value: inc
    }: CounterAction);

export const decrement = (dec: number) =>
    ({
        type: COUNTER_INCREMENT,
        value: -dec
    }: CounterAction);

// returning increment(-dec) would have worked as well
```

In fact, we should say that increment(), decrement(), and reset() are action creators; the actual actions are the values returned by those functions.

Writing a reducer

Then, after defining our actions, we need a reducer to process them. Of course, this also means that we have to define the shape of our state, and its initial value:

```
// Source file: src/counterApp/counter.reducer.js

/* @flow */

import : COUNTER_INCREMENT, COUNTER_RESET } from "./counter.actions";

import type { CounterAction } from "./counter.actions.js";

export const reducer = (
    state = {
        // initial state
        count: 0,
        clicks: 0
    },
    action: CounterAction
) => {
    switch (action.type) {
        case COUNTER_INCREMENT:
            return {
                count: state.count + action.value,
                clicks: state.clicks + 1
            };
```

```
        case COUNTER_RESET:
            return { count: 0, clicks: state.clicks + 1 };

        default:
            return state;
    }
};
```

Our reducer is basically a switch statement; when the right type is found, a new state is returned. This pattern is very important, and key to Redux. We don't simply update the state, but rather we produce a new state object every time. We need a default case because actions are passed to all reducers (not in our case, since we have a single one), so it's possible that a reducer will ignore an action.

 In our example, we have a single reducer and a single set of actions, so it can be argued that they could all be placed together in the same file, but that's not likely with most applications. Furthermore, if your state grows too large, check out combineReducers() at https://redux.js.org/api/combinereducers, and you'll be able to work in a more organized way, with multiple reducers and a store divided into logical pieces.

Defining the store

Then, after all the previous definitions, we can define our store:

```
// Source file: src/counterApp/store.js

/* @flow */

import { createStore } from "redux";

import { reducer } from "./counter.reducer.js";

export const store = createStore(reducer);
```

By the way, it's also possible to define the initial value for the state by passing it as a second parameter to createStore().

Building our components

Finally, having fully defined our store plus the actions that will be dispatched and the reducer that will process them, we can finish quickly by defining our components. Our `Counter` component will have text, the counter value, and a few buttons. Note that we are receiving count (the counter value) as a prop, and we also have a `dispatch()` function as yet another prop:

```
// Source file: src/counterApp/counter.component.js

/* @flow */

import React from "react";
import { PropTypes } from "prop-types";

import {
    increment,
    decrement,
    reset,
    CounterAction
} from "./counter.actions.js";

export class Counter extends React.PureComponent<{
    count: number,
    dispatch: CounterAction => any
}> {
    static propTypes = {
        count: PropTypes.number.isRequired,
        dispatch: PropTypes.func.isRequired
    };

    onAdd1 = () => this.props.dispatch(increment(1));
    onSub2 = () => this.props.dispatch(decrement(2));
    onReset = () => this.props.dispatch(reset());

    render() {
        return (
            <div>
                Value: {this.props.count}
                <br />
                <button onClick={this.onAdd1}>Add 1</button>
                <button onClick={this.onSub2}>Subtract 2</button>
                <button onClick={this.onReset}>Reset</button>
            </div>
        );
    }
}
```

Each button dispatches an action that was created by the action creators that we saw earlier.

We need a second component. The `ClicksDisplay` component is even simpler! We receive the total number of `clicks` as a prop, and we simply display it:

```
// Source file: src/counterApp/clicksDisplay.component.js

/* @flow */

import React from "react";
import { PropTypes } from "prop-types";

export class ClicksDisplay extends React.PureComponent<{
    clicks: number
}> {
    static propTypes = {
        clicks: PropTypes.number.isRequired
    };

    render() {
        return <div>Clicks so far: {this.props.clicks}</div>;
    }
}
```

Connecting components to the store

A good design rule, separating concerns, says that you shouldn't directly connect a component to the store, but rather create a new component, a connected one, that will get whatever is needed from the store and pass it on to the original component. This rule will simplify, for example, all of our testing: our basic components will still receive everything via props, and we won't have to do any mocking of the store or anything like that in order to test them.

A good article on defining components, by Dan Abramov, is *Presentational and Container Components*, at https://medium.com/@dan_abramov/smart-and-dumb-components-7ca2f9a7c7d0. More on this can be found in *Container Components*, at https://medium.com/@learnreact/container-components-c0e67432e005.

So, following that rule, for each component we want to connect, we'll add a new connected version. In our case, the connected version of the count will be the following, so the `count` prop of the component will receive the `state.count` value:

```
// Source file: src/counterApp/counter.connected.js

/* @flow */

import { connect } from "react-redux";

import { Counter } from "./counter.component";

const getProps = state => ({ count: state.count });

export const ConnectedCounter = connect(getProps)(Counter);
```

Similarly, the component to display the total number of clicks will be connected in a similar fashion:

```
// Source file: src/counterApp/clicksDisplay.connected.js

/* @flow */

import { connect } from "react-redux";

import { ClicksDisplay } from "./clicksDisplay.component";

const getProps = state => ({
    clicks: state.clicks
});

export const ConnectedClicksDisplay = connect(getProps)(ClicksDisplay);
```

We will place those connected components in our main code, and they will get the values from the store, and pass them on to our original components, which will be totally unchanged.

Defining the main page

Our last piece of code is based on the standard App.js file that's produced by create-react-app; the App class is imported by index.js:

```
// Source file: src/App.counter.js

/* @flow */

import React, { Component, Fragment } from "react";
import { Provider } from "react-redux";

import { store } from "./counterApp/store";
import { ConnectedCounter, ConnectedClicksDisplay } from "./counterApp";

class App extends Component<{}> {
    render() {
        return (
            <Provider store={store}>
                <Fragment>
                    <ConnectedCounter />
                    <hr />
                    <ConnectedClicksDisplay />
                </Fragment>
            </Provider>
        );
    }
}
```

The key part here is the <Provider> component. This is a part of React's latest Context feature (see https://reactjs.org/docs/context.html for more on it), and it gives access to the store object to any of the following components; the connect() function (that we used in the previous section) uses it to provide props to those components, and to subscribe them to changes. By the way, we are using Fragment here, just because Provider expects a single element. In addition to this, <div> could have worked as well.

With everything together, let's see how this works!

How it works...

When we start the application, the current state count is zero, and so is the number of clicks, so the screen looks like the following:

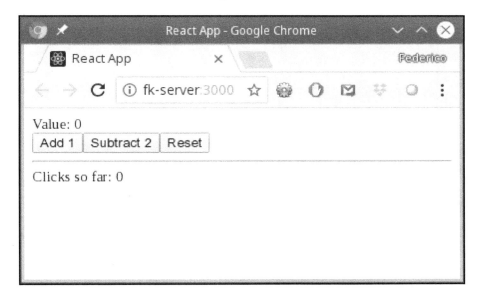

Our counter application in its initial state.

After some clicks on the following buttons, the value and clicks count get updated, and the view automatically reflects those changes as they happen; see the following screenshot. Be sure to understand how everything happens:

- Whenever you click a button, an action is dispatched.
- When the reducer processes the action, it creates a new state.

- When `React` sees the state change, it redraws your application. Take a look at the following screenshot:

After every click, the counter value and the number of clicks get automatically updated, and the view is re-rendered

So, we have seen that we can work with `Redux` in order to keep a global state and have the view re-rendered whenever it's needed, without extra work on our part. Now, let's consider a common problem: how would we deal with asynchronous changes, for example, when we do Ajax calls?

See also

`Redux` is not the only state management package that you can use with `React`. The most favored one is surely `MobX`, which adds reactive programming concepts, such as observable objects and arrays; check it out at `https://github.com/mobxjs/mobx`. Its basic paradigm is quite different from the `Redux` one, simpler in many ways, and more akin to a spreadsheet; be ready, however, to change your way of thinking before using it!

Doing async actions with redux-thunk

How can we do async actions, such as calling a web service? This kind of call requires some different processing: you cannot just dispatch an action, if we are still waiting for the results of an Ajax call. The `Redux` *thunk* middleware lets you write an action creator that returns a function instead of an action; the function is given access to the store contents and to the dispatch function itself, and can then do async calls, dispatch other functions, and so on.

 It seems that the origin of the **thunk** word comes from a very late programming session, in which, after many hours of work, a solution to a problem was found that had been *thought before*, and *thunk* became its name as a derivative of *think*, make of it what you will!

This sound a bit mysterious, so let's dive in and see how it works by doing a variation on the country/region components we built in the *Defining components* section in Chapter 6, *Developing with React*, only that this time we'll be working with actual API calls—for which we already have our Node server, which we created in Chapter 4, *Implementing RESTful Services with Node*.

How to do it...

Let's modify our region application so that it will connect to the backend service.

First of all, to use `redux-thunk`, we will have to install the package:

```
npm install redux-thunk --save
```

Then, we must modify the store to use the new middleware. (We'll be seeing more middleware later in this chapter, and in the next one as well.) This change is very small, as the following code shows:

```
// Source file: src/regionsApp/store.js

/* @flow */

import { createStore, applyMiddleware } from "redux";
import thunk from "redux-thunk";

import { reducer } from "./worlds.reducer.js";

export const store = createStore(reducer, applyMiddleware(thunk));
```

Defining the actions

Whenever you try to get data from a service, a common pattern is as follows:

- *Fire an action when you do the request*; this action may set some flag, which will in turn be used by some component to display a "Loading..." text or a spinning icon to show that something's going on, and the user should wait
- *If the service request was successful*, fire an action signaling this success, resetting the *Loading...* flag, and also providing the new data that must be added to the store
- *If the service request failed*, reset the *Loading...* flag, but signal error in some way

The actions we'll need for our application have to do with, firstly, getting the list of countries for the country drop-down list, and, secondly, getting the list of regions for a given country. The actions are as follows; first, here are the country-related ones:

```
// Source file: src/regionsApp/world.actions.js

/* @flow */

// Countries actions

export const COUNTRIES_REQUEST = "countries:request";
export const COUNTRIES_SUCCESS = "countries:success";
export const COUNTRIES_FAILURE = "countries:failure";

export type CountriesAction = {
    type: string,
    country?: string,
    listOfCountries?: [object]
};

export const countriesRequest = () =>
    ({
        type: COUNTRIES_REQUEST
    }: CountriesActions);

export const countriesSuccess = (listOfCountries: []) =>
    ({
        type: COUNTRIES_SUCCESS,
        listOfCountries
    }: CountriesActions);

export const countriesFailure = () =>
    ({
        type: COUNTRIES_FAILURE
```

```
    }: CountriesActions);
```

```
// continues...
```

For regions, we have a similar set:

```
// ...continued
```

```
// Regions actions
```

```
export const REGIONS_REQUEST = "regions:request";
export const REGIONS_SUCCESS = "regions:success";
export const REGIONS_FAILURE = "regions:failure";
```

```
export type RegionsAction = {
    type: string,
    listOfRegions?: [object]
};
```

```
export const regionsRequest = (country: string) =>
    ({
        type: REGIONS_REQUEST,
        country
    }: RegionsActions);
```

```
export const regionsSuccess = (listOfRegions: [{}]) =>
    ({
        type: REGIONS_SUCCESS,
        listOfRegions
    }: RegionsActions);
```

```
export const regionsFailure = () =>
    ({
        type: REGIONS_FAILURE
    }: RegionsActions);
```

Note the style of the action constants—we are using `"countries"` and `"regions"` as a sort of namespacing (as in `"countries:success"` versus `"regions:success"`) to avoid possible name duplications.

Writing the reducer

We have actions; now, we need a reducer. Its code is also not complex:

```
// Source file: src/regionsApp/world.reducer.js

/* @flow */

import {
    COUNTRIES_REQUEST,
    COUNTRIES_SUCCESS,
    COUNTRIES_FAILURE,
    REGIONS_REQUEST,
    REGIONS_SUCCESS,
    REGIONS_FAILURE
} from "./world.actions";

import type { CountriesAction, RegionsAction } from "./world.actions";

// import type { CounterAction } from "./world.actions.js";

export const reducer = (
    state: object = {
        // initial state
        loadingCountries: false,
        currentCountry: "",
        countries: [],
        loadingRegions: false,
        regions: []
    },
    action: CountriesAction | RegionsAction
) => {
    switch (action.type) {
        case COUNTRIES_REQUEST:
            return {
                ...state,
                loadingCountries: true,
                countries: []
            };

        case COUNTRIES_SUCCESS:
            return {
                ...state,
                loadingCountries: false,
                countries: action.listOfCountries
            };

        case COUNTRIES_FAILURE:
```

```
            return {
                ...state,
                loadingCountries: false,
                countries: []
            };

        case REGIONS_REQUEST:
            return {
                ...state,
                loadingRegions: true,
                currentCountry: action.country,
                regions: []
            };

        case REGIONS_SUCCESS:
            return {
                ...state,
                loadingRegions: false,
                regions: action.listOfRegions
            };

        case REGIONS_FAILURE:
            return {
                ...state,
                loadingRegions: false,
                regions: []
            };

        default:
            return state;
    }
};
```

The only thing that needs to be remarked upon is the following style of code, using the spread operator in a way you may not have seen before:

```
return {
    ...state,
    loadingCountries: true,
    currentCountry: "",
    countries: []
};
```

We must be careful when returning the new state to not lose part of the old state, so starting the object with ...state is a very common coding pattern.

To avoid accidentally changing the state, a good solution is to handle state with packages such as immutable-js (at https://github.com/facebook/immutable-js/) or seamless-immutable (at https://github.com/rtfeldman/seamless-immutable), because then you aren't able to modify the state object; you are forced to produce a new one, avoiding many hard-to-find mistakes.

Modifying the country drop-down list

We earlier had a country drop-down list that received a list of countries. Let's rewrite it so that if no such list is provided, it will use a function to call a thunk, and get the countries from our server:

```
// Source file: src/regionsApp/countrySelect.component.js

/* @flow */

import React from "react";
import PropTypes from "prop-types";

import "../general.css";

export class CountrySelect extends React.PureComponent<{
    dispatch: ({}) => any
}> {
    static propTypes = {
        loading: PropTypes.bool.isRequired,
        list: PropTypes.arrayOf(PropTypes.object).isRequired,
        onSelect: PropTypes.func.isRequired,
        getCountries: PropTypes.func.isRequired
    };

    componentDidMount() {
        if (this.props.list.length === 0) {
            this.props.getCountries();
        }
    }

    onSelect = (e: { target: HTMLOptionElement }) =>
        this.props.onSelect(e.target.value);

    render() {
        if (this.props.loading) {
            return <div className="bordered">Loading countries...</div>;
        } else {
```

```
        const sortedCountries = [...this.props.list].sort(
            (a, b) => (a.countryName < b.countryName ? -1 : 1)
        );

        return (
            <div className="bordered">
                Country: 
                <select
                    onChange={this.onSelect}
                    onBlur={this.onSelect}
                >
                    <option value="">Select a country:</option>
                    {sortedCountries.map(x => (
                        <option
                            key={x.countryCode}
                            value={x.countryCode}
                        >
                            {x.countryName}
                        </option>
                    ))}
                </select>
            </div>
        );
    }
    }
}
```

As we can see in the `.componentDidMount()` method, if no list is available, we call a function (which we'll see soon) to get that list, and put it in the store. A `loading` attribute will be used, so while we wait for the countries to arrive, a `Loading countries...` text will be shown instead of an empty `<select>` component. You'll also notice that I sorted the countries, because the service sends them ordered by country code.

The connected version of this component is not as short as before, because we'll have to connect props to the store, and also to actions to be dispatched; I highlighted those parts of the code in the following snippet:

```
// Source file: src/regionsApp/countrySelect.connected.js

/* @flow */

import { connect } from "react-redux";

import { CountrySelect } from "./countrySelect.component";
import { getCountries, getRegions } from "./world.actions";

const getProps = state => ({
```

```
        list: state.countries,
        loading: state.loadingCountries
});

const getDispatch = dispatch => ({
        getCountries: () => dispatch(getCountries()),
        onSelect: c => dispatch(getRegions(c))
});

export const ConnectedCountrySelect = connect(
        getProps,
        getDispatch
)(CountrySelect);
```

Modifying the region table

Since most of the new behavior will occur in the country drop-down component, we can make do with a very simple table:

```
// Source file: src/regionsApp/regionsTable.component.js

/* @flow */

import React from "react";
import PropTypes from "prop-types";

import "../general.css";

export class RegionsTable extends React.PureComponent<{
    list: Array<{
        regionCode: string,
        regionName: string
    }>
}> {
    static propTypes = {
        list: PropTypes.arrayOf(PropTypes.object).isRequired
    };

    static defaultProps = {
        list: []
    };

    render() {
        if (this.props.list.length === 0) {
            return <div className="bordered">No regions.</div>;
        } else {
            const ordered = [...this.props.list].sort(
```

```
            (a, b) => (a.regionName < b.regionName ? -1 : 1)
        );

        return (
            <div className="bordered">
                {ordered.map(x => (
                    <div key={x.countryCode + "-" + x.regionCode}>
                        {x.regionName}
                    </div>
                ))}
            </div>
        );
    }
  }
}
```

We also sort the regions in alphabetic order, and we just create a plain list of `<div>`, each with a single region's name. The connected component gets access to the list of regions and to a loading flag so that it can show something while the list of regions is being fetched from the server:

```
// Source file: src/regionsApp/regionsTable.connected.js

/* @flow */

import { connect } from "react-redux";

import { RegionsTable } from "./regionsTable.component";

const getProps = state => ({
    list: state.regions,
    loading: state.loadingRegions
});

export const ConnectedRegionsTable = connect(getProps)(RegionsTable);
```

Setting up the main application

We have all the necessary components, so we can now produce our application. (And, no, I haven't forgotten the promised functions!) Our main code will be as follows:

```
// Source file: src/App.regions.js

/* @flow */

import React, { Component, Fragment } from "react";
```

```
import { Provider } from "react-redux";

import {
    ConnectedCountrySelect,
    ConnectedRegionsTable
} from "./regionsApp";

import { store } from "./regionsApp/store";

class App extends Component<{}> {
    render() {
        return (
            <Provider store={store}>
                <Fragment>
                    <ConnectedCountrySelect />
                    <ConnectedRegionsTable />
                </Fragment>
            </Provider>
        );
    }
}

export default App;
```

Using thunks

Now, things start getting interesting. We are providing two functions to the country drop-down list, both of which will work with thunks in order to connect to the server. Let's see them!

We'll need two functions: one will deal with getting the list of countries, and the other will be used to get the regions for the currently selected country. Let's just begin with the former, and keep in mind that this code is to be added to the action file we saw earlier:

```
// Source file: src/regionsApp/world.actions.js

import axios from "axios";

export const getCountries = () => async dispatch => {
    try {
        dispatch(countriesRequest());
        const result = await axios.get(`http://fk-server:8080/countries`);
        dispatch(countriesSuccess(result.data));
    } catch (e) {
```

```
            dispatch(countriesFailure());
        }
};
```

First, the signature for our `getCountries()` function is a bit weird (a function that returns an async function, with a `dispatch` parameter), but this is what `redux-thunk` requires. The logic is more interesting:

- To start, we dispatch the results of the `countriesRequest()` action creator, so the state of the application will show that we are waiting for some results.
- Then, we use the `axios()` package, as used earlier in our Node work, to call our server and get the list of countries.
- If the call is successful, we dispatch a `countriesSuccess()` action, passing it the list of countries that we received.
- If the call failed, we dispatch a `countriesFailure()` action, to show that failure.

As you can see, our code is able to dispatch many actions, but waiting until the right moment to do so.

To work with regions, we'll have similar code:

```
// Source file: src/regionsApp/world.actions.js

export const getRegions = (country: string) => async dispatch => {
    if (country) {
        try {
            dispatch(regionsRequest());
            const result = await axios.get(
                `http://fk-server:8080/regions/${country}`
            );
            dispatch(regionsSuccess(result.data));
        } catch (e) {
            dispatch(regionsFailure());
        }
    } else {
        dispatch(regionsFailure());
    }
};
```

The code is quite similar to what we had before, so we don't need to do much analysis.

How it works...

When we `npm start` our application, we see a very plain design; see the following screenshot. Let's understand how did we get here:

1. The main page was displayed.
2. The countries drop-down list, on receiving an empty list of countries, used a thunk to get all countries.
3. A `getCountries()` action was dispatched.
4. The reducer updated the store to set the `loadingCountries` flag to true
5. The page was redrawn, and a `"Loading countries..."` text was shown instead of the drop-down list.
6. When the countries list came back, a `countriesSuccess()` action was dispatched, with the received list of countries.
7. The reducer updated the store to include all countries and to reset `loadingCountries` to false.
8. The page was redrawn, and now the country drop-down list has a list of countries to show as shown, in the following screenshot:

Our initial screen

If we select a country, the service will be called, and results will be shown; see the following screenshot. The logic for this is also interesting:

1. When the region table is drawn without any regions, some `"No regions"` text is displayed.
2. When the user selects a country, the drop-down list uses a thunk to get its regions.
3. A `regionsRequest()` action was dispatched.

4. When the regions came back, a `regionsSuccess()` action was dispatched,

5. The page was redrawn after the reducer created a new state, showing the regions' list. Refer to the following screenshot:

The results of calling our restful server

You could be wondering, however, where is the `"Loading countries..."` text? The problem (if you want to call it that!) is that the service response comes too quickly, so the message flashes by and disappears. We can get to see it a bit longer if we cheat and add some delay in the `getCountries()` function. Include the following line before calling `axios()` to delay execution for five seconds:

```
await new Promise(resolve => setTimeout(resolve, 5000));
```

Now, you'll have time to see the missing state, as shown in the following screenshot:

Adding some delay lets us see what's displayed while waiting for the list of countries

So, now we can see that our state handling was correct, and that everything is displayed the way we wanted it to be!

There's more...

When you write your action creator, it actually gets passed not only dispatch() but also the getState() function. This function can be used to access the current state value. We didn't use this, but, for example, you could do so for caching or other similar ideas. Our getRegions() function could be as follows, to detect whether you are requesting the same country's regions again:

```
// Source file: src/regionsApp/world.actions.js

export const getRegions2 = (country: string) => async (
    dispatch,
    getState
) => {
    if (country === getState().currentCountry) {
        console.log("Hey! You are getting the same country as before!");
    }

    if (country) {
        .
        .
        . everything as earlier
        .
        .
    }
};
```

In our case, we aren't doing anything other than logging a message, but you could use the received parameters plus the current state contents in order to do some more complex logic.

Adding routing with react-router

When you work with `React` (as with other frontend frameworks, such as `Angular` or `Vue`, to name just a couple) you usually develop **Single Page Applications** (**SPAs**) that never do a full-page reload when you access a different part of them; rather, new content is swapped into view, but staying put on the original page. Even if this kind of navigational experience is modern and fluid, some aspects of more traditional routing are expected: the *back* and *forward* buttons should move you, depending on your browsing story, and you should also be able to bookmark a specific part of your application to be able to quickly return to it later.

As usual, with `React`, there are many ways to handle routing, but `react-router` is currently by far the most used library, probably because it really fits the `React` paradigm: routes are just components that you render and work as expected! Let's start by building a simple application to show how routes work, and in the next section we'll add a bit of complexity by requiring authentication before allowing access to certain routes.

Getting started

The `react-router` library is practically a standard for handling routing within `React` applications. Installing it requires a subtle distinction: instead of directly getting that package, you must pick a different package, `react-router-dom`, which will itself take care of getting `react-router`:

```
npm install react-router-dom --save
```

We can easily build an application with several links, a router that will take care of rendering whichever view is correct, and even a 404 page for wrong links. Of course, we'll focus on the routing aspects, so in other terms, our application will be more of a skeleton than an actual usable web page—and don't get started on its very plain styling!

How to do it...

In this recipe, we'll be creating a basic application but with several routes; let's see how.

To begin with, we'll need to import some packages and create a few components that will represent the different pages in our application. For the latter, since we aren't going to include any actual logic or contents, we'll make do with very simple functional components that render a single H1 heading... I told you our application would be quite bare!

```
// Source file: src/App.routing.js

/* @flow */

import React, { Component } from "react";
import { Provider } from "react-redux";
import { BrowserRouter, Switch, Route, Link } from "react-router-dom";

import { store } from "./routingApp/store";

const Home = () => <h1>Home Sweet Home</h1>;
const Help = () => <h1>Help! SOS!</h1>;
const Alpha = () => <h1>Alpha</h1>;
const Bravo = () => <h1>Bravo</h1>;
const Charlie = () => <h1>Charlie</h1>;
const Zulu = () => <h1>Zulu</h1>;
const Error404 = () => <h1>404 Error!</h1>;

// continued...
```

Now, to continue, we must plan our application. We'll have <header> with a <nav> bar, in which we'll include links to the parts of our application. Below that, we'll have a common area in which the right component will be rendered. Our <App> component could be as follows—though in real life, you'd probably define all routes in separate files; I'm placing everything here for brevity:

```
// ...continued

class App extends Component<{}> {
    render() {
        return (
            <Provider store={store}>
                <BrowserRouter>
                    <div>
                        <header>
                            <nav>
                                <Link to="/">Home</Link> 
```

```
                    <Link to="/about/routing">
                        About Routing
                    </Link> 
                    <Link to="/alpha">Alpha...</Link> 
                    <Link to="/bravo">Bravo...</Link> 
                    <Link to="/charlie">Charlie...
                    </Link> 
                    <Link to="/wrong">...Wrong...
                    </Link> 
                    <Link to="/zulu">Zulu</Link> 
                    <Link to="/help">Help</Link> 
                </nav>
            </header>

            <Switch>
                <Route path="/" component={Home} />
                <Route path="/help" component={Help} />
                <Route
                    path="/about/:something"
                    render={props => (
                        <div>
                            <h1>About...</h1>
                            {props.match.params.something}
                        </div>
                    )}
                />
                <Route path="/alpha" component={Alpha} />
                <Route path="/bravo" component={Bravo} />
                <Route path="/charlie" component={Charlie}
                />
                <Route path="/zulu" component={Zulu} />
                <Route component={Error404} />
            </Switch>
        </div>
    </BrowserRouter>
    </Provider>
    );
    }
}

export default App;
```

I've highlighted several parts of the code; let's see why:

- <BrowserRouter> is a component based on the HTML5 "History" API, and takes care of keeping your view synchronized with the URL; a change in the latter will be reflected by a new view.

- `<Link ...>` is the component you must use instead of the usual `<a ...>` HTML tags, and `to=` points to the desired route.
- `<Switch>` is a component that renders the first child `<Route>` or `<Redirect>` component (we'll using `<Redirect>` soon) that happens to match the current location.
- `<Route ...>` defines which component must be rendered when the path is matched. Note that you could have to specify exactly to avoid false coincidences; otherwise, visiting `"/alpha"` would be matched by the first route, `"/"`, and the wrong component would be displayed. You may specify what is to be rendered by using `component=` or by providing a `render()` function; the latter is useful when you need to display several components or take some parameters. In particular, we used this for `"/about/:something"`; when this route is matched, in a way similar to `Express` (check the *Adding Routes* section, in Chapter 4, *Implementing RESTful Services with Node*) a new prop will be provided, with attributes coinciding with the colon-starting parts of the URL. You can omit this by specifying `path=`, and then you'll have a *catch-all*, which is useful for 404 errors, as we did here.

So, we have the code; let's see it in action.

How it works...

If you `npm start` the application and then navigate to it, you'll get the home page, as in the following screenshot:

Our routing application, showing the component for the basic "/" route

If you select any valid route (that is, don't pick the **Wrong** one, at least not yet!), the matching route will be activated, and the corresponding component will be displayed, as shown in the following screenshot:

Picking a valid route gets you the corresponding component

Finally, if you pick a wrong route, the default component will be shown, as follows:

The last route in our <Switch> is a catch-all for undefined routes

There's more...

There's something we haven't used yet: the possibility of directly navigating to a given route or going back to the previous location and more. Whenever a `<Route>` is matched, the rendered component gets some special props, which you can use:

- `this.props.history`, providing access to the browser history, with several methods like `.goBack()` to return to the previous page, or `.push("someURL")` to navigate to a different page; see `https://developer.mozilla.org/en-US/docs/Web/API/History_API` and especially `https://github.com/ReactTraining/react-router/blob/master/packages/react-router/docs/api/history.md` for more on this

- `this.props.location`, with several properties related to the current location and its URL; see `https://github.com/ReactTraining/react-router/blob/master/packages/react-router/docs/api/location.md` for extra data

- `this.props.match`, which tells you how the current route was matched; see `https://github.com/ReactTraining/react-router/blob/master/packages/react-router/docs/api/match.md`

So, we are now able to work with routes; let's move on to routes needing authorization.

Adding authorization to routes

Our previous routing example worked very well, but in some applications, you might need authorization so that only logged-in users may access parts of your website. (You would also need the user to be identified, if you were using an API such as the one we developed in Chapter 4, *Implementing RESTful Services with Node*, which required **JSON Web Token (JWT)**. So, let's see what extra work we need in order to have both restricted and unrestricted routes on our page.

How to do it...

Let's add authorization to our application by protecting some routes and requiring a previous successful login.

We can find a very `React`-like solution. We will have some unprotected routes that anybody may access without restriction, and protected routes that require having a login. We'll need two components for that.

Creating a login component

First, let's create a `<Login>` component that we'll call our RESTful server, passing a username and a password to it, and (if the values are right) getting back a JWT:

```
// Source file: src/routingApp/login.component.js

/* @flow */

import React from "react";
import PropTypes from "prop-types";
import { Redirect } from "react-router-dom";

export class Login extends React.PureComponent<{
    logging: boolean
}> {
    static propTypes = {
        onLogin: PropTypes.func.isRequired,
        logging: PropTypes.bool.isRequired,
        token: PropTypes.string.isRequired,
        location: PropTypes.object
    };

    state = {
        userName: "",
        password: ""
    };

    onUserNameBlur = e => this.setState({ userName: e.target.value });

    onPasswordBlur = e => this.setState({ password: e.target.value });

    onLoginClick = () =>
        this.props.onLogin(this.state.userName, this.state.password);

    render() {
        if (
            this.state.userName &&
            this.state.password &&
            this.props.token
        ) {
            return (
                <Redirect to={this.props.location.state.from.pathname} />
            );
        } else {
            return (
                <div>
                    <h1>Login Form</h1>
```

```
                        <div>
                            User:<input
                                type="text"
                                onBlur={this.onUserNameBlur}
                            />
                        </div>
                        <div>
                            Password:
                            <input
                                type="password"
                                onBlur={this.onPasswordBlur}
                            />
                        </div>
                        <button
                            onClick={this.onLoginClick}
                            disabled={this.props.logging}
                        >
                            Login
                        </button>
                    </div>
                );
            }
        }
    }
```

Defining actions and the reducer

Before getting into the details, let's see the reducer and actions we'll have. The former is quite simple, since basically all we care about is having a token and a logging flag:

```
// Source file: src/routingApp/login.reducer.js

/* @flow */

import {
    LOGIN_REQUEST,
    LOGIN_SUCCESS,
    LOGIN_FAILURE
} from "./login.actions";

export const reducer = (
    state: object = {
        // initial state
        logging: false,
        token: ""
    },
    action
```

```
) => {
    switch (action.type) {
        case LOGIN_REQUEST:
            return {
                ...state,
                logging: true,
                token: ""
            };

        case LOGIN_SUCCESS:
            return {
                ...state,
                logging: false,
                token: action.token
            };

        case LOGIN_FAILURE:
            return {
                ...state,
                logging: false
            };

        default:
            return state;
    }
};
```

We will have some action creators that will help us understand the rest. The important one is `attemptLogin()` that tries connecting to the server, and if successful stores the token that will mark that the user is logged in:

```
// Source file: src/routingApp/login.actions.js

/* @flow */

import { loginService } from "./serviceApi";

export const LOGIN_REQUEST = "login:request";
export const LOGIN_SUCCESS = "login:success";
export const LOGIN_FAILURE = "login:failure";

export const loginRequest = () => ({
    type: LOGIN_REQUEST
});

export const loginSuccess = (token: string) => ({
    type: LOGIN_SUCCESS,
    token
```

```
});

export const loginFailure = () => ({
    type: LOGIN_FAILURE
});

// Complex actions:

export const attemptLogin = (
    user: string,
    password: string
) => async dispatch => {
    try {
        dispatch(loginRequest());
        // the next line delays execution for 5 seconds:
        // await new Promise(resolve => setTimeout(resolve, 5000));
        const result = await loginService(user, password);
        dispatch(loginSuccess(result.data));
    } catch (e) {
        dispatch(loginFailure());
    }
};
```

 We'll leave it as an exercise to you to write a `<LogOut>` component that will provide a button, which when clicked will just call an action to delete the current token.

Creating a component to protect a route

To protect a route, let's create a new component that will check whether a user is logged in or not. In the first case, the route will be shown, with no further ado. However, in the second case, instead of the original route's component, `<Redirect>` will be produced, redirecting the user to the login page:

```
// Source file: src/routingApp/authRoute.component.js

/* @flow */

import React from "react";
import { Route, Redirect } from "react-router-dom";
import PropTypes from "prop-types";

export class Auth extends React.Component<{
    loginRoute: string,
    token: string,
```

```
      location: object
}> {
    static propTypes = {
        loginRoute: PropTypes.string.isRequired,
        token: PropTypes.string.isRequired,
        location: PropTypes.object
    };

    render() {
        const myProps = { ...this.props };
        if (!myProps.token) {
            delete myProps.component;
            myProps.render = () => (
                <Redirect
                    to={{
                        pathname: this.props.loginRoute,
                        state: { from: this.props.location }
                    }}
                />
            );
        }
        return <Route {...myProps} />;
    }
}
```

We will connect this component to the store so that it can access the current token plus the path to the login page:

```
// Source file: src/routingApp/authRoute.connected.js

/* @flow */

import { connect } from "react-redux";

import { Auth } from "./authRoute.component";
export const AuthRoute = connect(state => ({
    token: state.token,
    loginRoute: "/login"
}))(Auth);
```

Now, we have everything we need; let's make it work!

How it works...

To use our new component, we'll change something in our original routes from earlier in this chapter. Let's protect a few of the routes. All it will take is changing `Route` to `AuthRoute`:

```
// Source file: src/App.routing.auth.js

<AuthRoute path="/alpha" component={Alpha} />
<AuthRoute path="/bravo" component={Bravo} />
<AuthRoute path="/charlie" component={Charlie} />
<AuthRoute path="/zulu" component={Zulu} />
<AuthRoute component={Error404} />
```

All the changed routes will require a previous login—and if the user enters a wrong route, we won't even tell them about the 404 error; we'll force them to first log in, and if they won't do it, they won't be able to even learn that the route existed or not.

Now, if we open the application and try to access the normal unprotected routes, everything will work as before. However, if you try to get to some of the protected routes, such as `"/charlie"`, you will be redirected to the login page, as in the following screenshot:

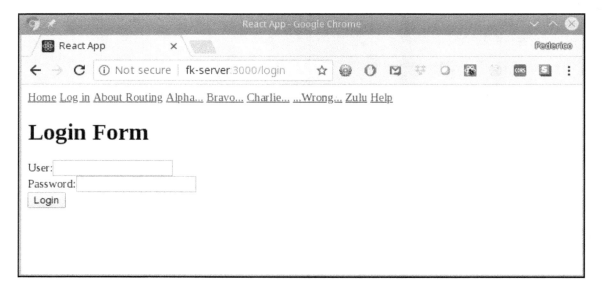

Trying to go to a protected route will redirect you to the login screen

After logging in, the `<Login>` component will produce a `<Redirect>` of its own that will send the user back to the originally requested page. See the following screenshot:

After a successful login process, you'll be redirected again to the page you had first requested; the URL now points to the page we wanted to access

So, now you have a way to handle all kinds of routes, and in a very React-ish way, too!

There's more...

In usual web development, you use cookies or possibly local storage for access information, but in a React application, storing the token (or whatever you use) in the state is good enough. If you need to provide the token for API calls, remember that actions are defined as follows:

```
const anActionCreator =
    (...parameters...) =>
        (dispatch, getState) =>
            { ...your action... }
```

So, you can access the token via the `getState()` function, and pass it back to the server as needed; go back to the `getRegions2()` code, where we saw how to do async actions, to see an example of using this function.

Code splitting for performance

As your application grows in size, it will progressively be slower to load, and that will be off-putting to your users. (And, remember that not everybody has access to high-speed connections, especially in mobile devices!) Furthermore, users shouldn't have to download the whole code if they only need a small part of it: for example, if a user wants to browse products, why should the sign-up view be downloaded?

The solution to this space and speed problem is *code splitting*, which implies that your application will be broken down into smaller chunks that will be loaded only if needed. Fortunately, there are very good tools for this, which don't involve many changes to your existing code, so it's a win all around.

Getting ready

When you import a module, it's a static thing, and the code for the desired module gets included in the general source code pack. However, you can work with *dynamic* import() calls to load code at runtime. You could work with that by yourself, but there's already a simple package you can import, react-loadable, that will take care of most situations. Let's install it in the usual way:

```
npm install react-loadable --save
```

We will be using a few of all the features of this package, so you should take a look at https://github.com/jamiebuilds/react-loadable to get ideas about more ways to enhance your dynamic code loading features.

 As of December 2018, import() is at stage 3, meaning that it's a candidate for acceptance, expecting only few a (if any) changes and is well on its way to stage 4, which means that it will be included in the formal ECMAScript standard. However, as with other JS extensions, you can already use them in your code, and it's supported by Babel and Webpack. You can read more about import() at https://tc39.github.io/proposal-dynamic-import/.

How to do it...

Let's modify our routing application—even if it's quite small!—to try out code splitting.

First, let's see what our main code will look like:

```
// Source file: src/App.splitting.js

/* @flow */

/* eslint-disable */

import React, { Component } from "react";
import { BrowserRouter, Switch, Route, Link } from "react-router-dom";

import {
    AsyncAlpha,
    AsyncBravo,
    AsyncCharlie,
    AsyncZulu,
    AsyncHelp
} from "./splittingApp";

const Home = () => <h1>Home Sweet Home</h1>;
const Error404 = () => <h1>404 Error!</h1>;

class App extends Component<{}> {
    render() {
        return (
            <BrowserRouter>
                <div>
                    <header>
                        <nav>
                            <Link to="/">Home</Link> 
                            <Link to="/alpha">Alpha...</Link> 
                            <Link to="/bravo">Bravo...</Link> 
                            <Link to="/charlie">Charlie...</Link> 
                            <Link to="/wrong">...Wrong...</Link> 
                            <Link to="/zulu">Zulu</Link> 
                            <Link to="/help">Help</Link> 
                        </nav>
                    </header>

                    <Switch>
                        <Route exact path="/" component={Home} />
                        <Route path="/help" component={AsyncHelp} />
                        <Route path="/alpha" component={AsyncAlpha} />
                        <Route path="/bravo" component={AsyncBravo} />
```

```
                            <Route path="/charlie" component={AsyncCharlie}
                            />
                            <Route path="/zulu" component={AsyncZulu} />
                            <Route component={Error404} />
                        </Switch>
                    </div>
                </BrowserRouter>
            );
        }
    }

    export default App;
```

We have separated the `Alpha`, `Bravo`, and other components so that we can load them dynamically. Seeing the code for one of them will be enough:

```
    // Source file: src/splittingApp/alpha.component.js

    /* @flow */

    import React from "react";

    const Alpha = () => <h1>Alpha</h1>;

    export default Alpha;
```

But what about `AsyncAlpha`, `AsyncBravo`, and the rest? These components are dynamically loaded versions of their normal counterparts, which we can get using `react-loadable`:

```
    // Source file: src/splittingApp/alpha.loadable.js

    /* @flow */

    import Loadable from "react-loadable";

    import { LoadingStatus } from "./loadingStatus.component";

    export const AsyncAlpha = Loadable({
        loader: () => import("./alpha.component"),
        loading: LoadingStatus
    });
```

The `AsyncAlpha` component can be loaded dynamically, and while it's being loaded, its contents will be provided by the `LoadingStatus` component; you can make it as fancy as you want but I went with a very simple thing:

```
// Source file: src/splittingApp/loadingStatus.component.js

/* @flow */

import React from "react";
import PropTypes from "prop-types";

export class LoadingStatus extends React.Component<{
    isLoading: boolean,
    error: boolean
}> {
    static propTypes = {
        isLoading: PropTypes.bool,
        error: PropTypes.bool
    };

    render() {
        if (this.props.isLoading) {
            return <div>Loading...</div>;
        } else if (this.props.error) {
            return <div>ERROR: the component could not be loaded.</div>;
        } else {
            return null;
        }
    }
}
```

So, now that we know how we can get any component to load dynamically, let's see how it works.

 Being able to load components dynamically, instead of whole routes as usual with web applications, is a great plus. For example, your application could have a large, heavy component in a tab, but why load it unless the user actually goes to that tab? Deferred loading can also help show a page faster; you could endeavor to first show components at the top, and use dynamic imports for the components at the bottom.

How it works...

We will use the web developer tools to look at the network transfers. When we start the application, we get the home page and just a few transfers, including `bundle.js`, the main source block. This is the file that will grow heavily in size as your application becomes larger. See the following screenshot:

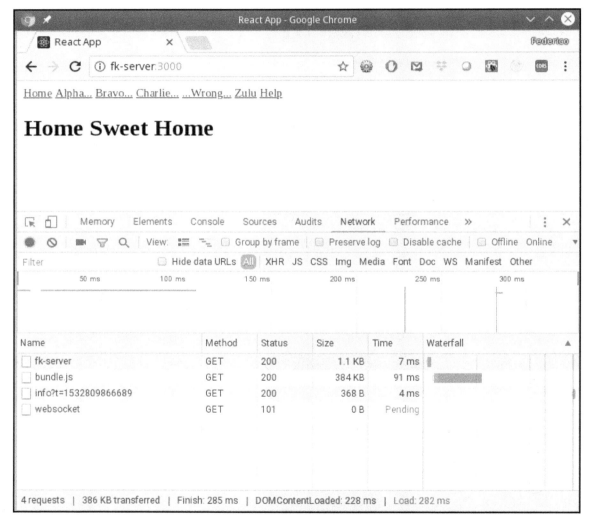

The initial load of the page shows that only bundle.js was sent over the net

If we click on a link, the corresponding chunk of split code will be transferred. After accessing several of the links, you'd get something like the following:

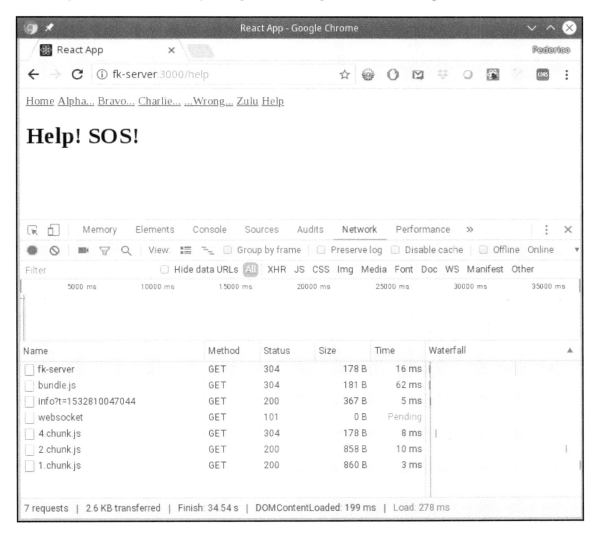

As you go to different links, chunks will get loaded, but only as needed

Even if our example is really tiny, you can see that you could easily partition the application to work in several smaller chunks. We can give no rules to suggest when you should start applying this technique, but, as we've seen, changing any component into an asynchronously loaded equivalent takes little effort, so you could start using the technique, even with all of your application already written.

There's more...

The components created by Loadable() include a .preload() method that you can use to start the importing process before the components are actually needed. We can quickly test it. For example, let's set things up so that if the user moves the mouse over the Alpha link, the component will be preloaded:

```
<Link to="/alpha">
    <span onMouseOver={() => AsyncAlpha.preload()}>Alpha...</span>
</Link>
```

We can quickly verify that this works. When you load the updated version of the code, if you hover over the **Alpha** link, you'll see that a chunk of code gets downloaded—though nothing changes onscreen, as the following screenshot shows:

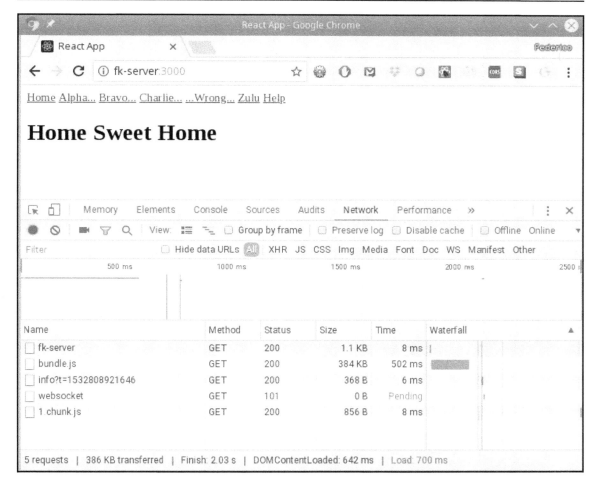

Preloading works in the background and lets you download a component in advance: a chunk (1.chunk.js) has been loaded, though it hasn't been shown onscreen

Give it some time, and note that when you actually click the **Alpha** link, the component will be shown immediately, with no further downloads. There are more usages for preloading: you could use `setTimeout()` after the initial page load, for instance, or you could do predictive downloading, trying to foresee what the user will want next, based on what they've been doing.

Debugging Your Application

9

The recipes we'll see here are:

- Logging with style
- Debugging with the React Developer Tools
- Debugging with the standalone tool
- Logging Redux with redux-logger
- Debugging Redux with the Redux Developer Tools
- Connecting routing for debugging

Introduction

In the previous chapters, we saw how to develop a basic `React` application, how to enhance it for a better user experience, and how to expand it, making it more scalable for complex and large application scopes. All this development, however, is sure to require both testing and debugging, so in this chapter, we'll be touching upon debugging recipes, and in the following chapter, we'll cover testing.

Logging with style

Logging is still a very good tool, but you cannot just depend on using tools such as `console.log()` or `console.error()`. Even though they do the work for a short debugging run, if you plan to include logging more seriously and want to disable it in production, you'll have a lot of work chasing down every logging call—or *monkey patching* the console object so `.log()` or `.error()` won't do their thing, and that's even worse!

Back in the *Adding logging with Winston* section of `Chapter 5`, *Testing and Debugging Your Server*, we used `Winston` for logging (and also `Morgan`, but that was specific for HTTP logging, so it doesn't count) and that library had features that enabled us to easily start or stop logging. There's no version of `Winston` for browsers, but we can fall back to `debug`, an old standard (we referred to in the *There's more...* section at the end of the chapter we just mentioned) that happens to work on the web as well.

 You can find the complete documentation for debug at `https://github.com/visionmedia/debug`. Note that if you wish, you could also use it with `Node`, though we think our earlier choice is better.

Getting ready

You install `debug` in the same way as if you wanted to use it with `Node`.

```
npm install debug --save
```

You will also have to decide how to *namespace* your logs because with debug you have an easy way to select which messages (if any) get shown and which are not displayed. Some possible ideas are to have names like `MYAPP:SERVICE:LOGIN`, `MYAPP:SERVICE:COUNTRIES`, `MYAPP_SERVICE:PDF_INVOICE`, and so on for each service in your application, or `MYAPP_FORM:NEW_USER`, `MYAPP:FORM:DISPLAY_CART`, `MYAPP:FORM:PAY_WITH_CARD`, and so on for each form, or `MYAPP:COMPONENT:PERSONAL_DATA`, `MYAPP:COMPONENT_CART`, and the like for specific components; the list can go on for actions, reducers, and so on, as you wish.

There's a way to select afterwards which logs will be shown, by storing a value in `LocalStorage` (we'll get to this) so you can set:

- `MYAPP:*` to display all logs from my app
- `MYAPP:SERVICE:*` to display all service-related logs
- `MYAPP:FORM:` and `MYAPP:COMPONENT:*` to display logs related to some forms or components, but omit others
- `MYAPP:SERVICE:COUNTRIES,MYAPP:FORM:NEW_USER` and `MYAPP:FORM:PAY_WITH_CARD` to display logs related to those three items

You can also prefix a string with `"-"` to exclude it. `MYAPP:ACTIONS:*,-MYAPP:ACTIONS:LOADING` will enable all actions, but not the `LOADING` one.

You may wonder: why include a fixed text such as MYAPP: everywhere? The key is that many of the libraries you may use actually also use debug for logging. If you were to say to display everything (*) instead of MYAPP:*, you would get in the console every single message from all those libraries, and that's not what you expected!

You are free to decide the naming of your logs, but setting up a well-structured list will make it possible for you to pick and choose later which logs to display, meaning that you won't have to start messing around with the code to enable or disable any given set of messages.

How to do it...

Let's aim to replicate what we had in Winston, at least in part, so it will be easier for you if you do full stack work, both client- and server-side. We want to have a logger object with methods such as .warn() and .info() that will display a given message in an appropriate color. Also, we don't want logs to be displayed in production. This leads us to the code as follows:

```
// Source file: src/logging/index.js

/* @flow */

import debug from "debug";

const WHAT_TO_LOG = "myapp:SERVICE:*"; // change this to suit your needs
const MIN_LEVEL_TO_LOG = "info"; // error, warn, info, verbose, or debug

const log = {
 error() {},
    warn() {},
    info() {},
    verbose() {},
    debug() {}
};

const logMessage = (
    color: string,
    topic: string,
    message: any = "--",
    ...rest: any
) => {
    const logger = debug(topic);
    logger.color = color;
```

```
        logger(message, ...rest);
    };

    if (process.env.NODE_ENV === "development") {
        localStorage.setItem("debug", WHAT_TO_LOG);

        /* eslint-disable no-fallthrough */
        switch (MIN_LEVEL_TO_LOG) {
            case "debug":
                log.debug = (topic: string, ...args: any) =>
                    logMessage("gray", topic, ...args);

            case "verbose":
                log.verbose = (topic: string, ...args: any) =>
                    logMessage("green", topic, ...args);

            case "info":
                log.info = (topic: string, ...args: any) =>
                    logMessage("blue", topic, ...args);

            case "warn":
                log.warn = (topic: string, ...args: any) =>
                    logMessage("brown", topic, ...args);

            case "error":
            default:
                log.error = (topic: string, ...args: any) =>
                    logMessage("red", topic, ...args);
        }
    }

    export { log };
```

Some important details:

- The `WHAT_TO_LOG` constant lets you select which messages should be shown.
- The `MIN_LEVEL_TO_LOG` constant defines the lowest level that will be logged.
- The log object has a method for each severity level, as in Winston.
- Finally, a non-operative `log` object is returned if we are not in development mode; all calls to logging methods will produce exactly nothing.

Note that we used fallthrough in the `switch` statement (no `break` statements in it!) to correctly build up the `log` object. It's not often that you can do this in a good way, and we had to shut up ESLint about it!

We have the code we need; let's see an example of its usage.

How it works...

Given that logging is not a complex concept and we have already seen it for the server, let's go with a very short example. We could change the index.js file for our application to include a few example logs:

```
// Source file: src/index.js

.
.
.

import { log } from "./logging";

log.error("myapp:SERVICE:LOGIN", `Attempt`, { user: "FK", pass: "who?" });

log.error("myapp:FORM:INITIAL", "Doing render");

log.info(
    "myapp:SERVICE:ERROR_STORE",
    "Reporting problem",
    "Something wrong",
    404
);

log.warn("myapp:SERVICE:LOGIN");

log.debug("myapp:SERVICE:INFO", "This won't be logged... low level");

log.info("myapp:SERVICE:GETDATE", "Success", {
    day: 22,
    month: 9,
    year: 60
});

log.verbose("myapp:SERVICE:LOGIN", "Successful login");
```

Running our application will produce the following output in the console; see the next screenshot. You should verify that only the correct messages were logged: `info` level and above, and only if they matched `myapp:SERVICE:*`:

Using debug produces clear, understandable output in the console

Note that, according to our specification, only the `myapp:SERVICE` related messages were shown.

Debugging with the React Developer Tools

When we worked with `Node` (in `Chapter 5`, *Testing and Debugging Your Server*) we saw how to do basic debugging, but now we are going to focus on a `React`-specific tool, the **React Developer Tools** (**RDT**), which are attuned to working with components and props. In this recipe, let's see how to install and use the package.

Getting Ready

The RDT are an extension for Chrome or Firefox that let you inspect components in the standard web developer tools. We are going to work with the Chrome version here, but usage is similar for Firefox. You can install the extension by going to the **Chrome Web Store** at `https://chrome.google.com/webstore/category/extensions` and searching for RDT; the extension you want is authored by Facebook. Click the **Add to Chrome** button, and when you open the Chrome Developer Tools, you'll find a new tab, **React**.

 If you don't use Chrome or Firefox, or if you have to test a `React` application that will be shown in an iframe, you'll want to look at the standalone version of the tools; we'll get to them in the *Debugging with the standalone tool* section, just after this one.

How to do it...

Let's see how to use RDT with the counter application we developed in the *Managing state with Redux* section in the previous chapter. That application was simple, so we'll be able to see easily how to use the tool, but of course you can apply it to very complex, full-of-components pages as well. Start the application, open the web developer tools, select the **React** tab, and if you expand every component, you'll see something like the following screenshot:

The **React** tab in the web developer tools let you access the whole component hierarchy for your application

By the way, you can use the tool with any `React`-developed application. The small tool's icon will change color when it can be used, and if you click on it you'll get information on whether you are running a development (red-colored icon) or production (green-colored icon); this screenshot shows our specific situation:

Our new tool will detect and work with any React-developed application

How it works...

We have installed our debugging tool, and we have applied it to our application; let's now see how it works, and what we can do with it.

If you select any specific component by clicking on it, you can see which components and HTML elements it generates. You can also select a component in a more traditional way by selecting a component directly onscreen (click on the leftmost icon, to the left of the **Memory** tab) and then click on the **React** tab; the element you clicked on will be selected. You can also use the **Search** function to look for a specific component; this will be useful with large applications to avoid having to manually scroll through lots and lots of HTML.

The triangle next to each component may have two different colors, depending on whether it's an actual `React` component (such as `<Counter>` or `<ClicksDisplay>`, in our case) or a `Redux` connection to the store. HTML elements don't have any triangles.

In the third panel, you can see the current props. If you edit one (try setting the `count` prop to a different value, for example), you'll immediately see changes on the left. Also, if you click on a button, you'll see how the prop values change; experiment a bit with the three buttons on your application.

If you want to interact with any component, you may notice that the currently selected one has == $r next to it. This means that there is a special JS variable, which points to the selected component in our case, <Counter>. If you open the **Console** tab, you can examine its props, by typing in $r.props, or experiment with calling the diverse methods available, such as $r.onAdd1(), as shown in the next screenshot:

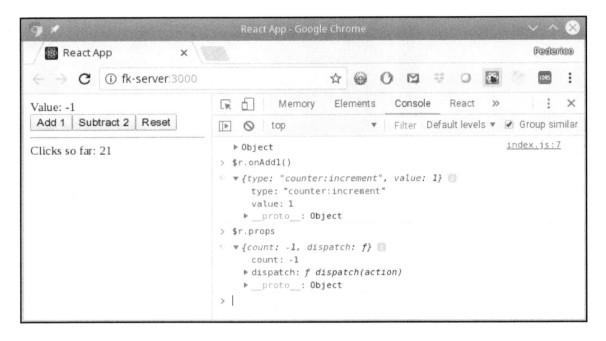

The $r variable lets you work (and experiment) with the currently selected component

Interestingly, in our application, as we coded it, the .onAdd1() method actually dispatches an action, and we can see it in the screenshot: an object with type:"counter:increment" and value:1, just as we coded it; see the *Defining Actions* section in the previous chapter to check.

If you select the <Provider> component, you can inspect the current state of the application. First you'll have to select it (so $r points to it) and then, in the **Console** tab, you'll need to enter $r.store.getState() to get results as in the next screenshot:

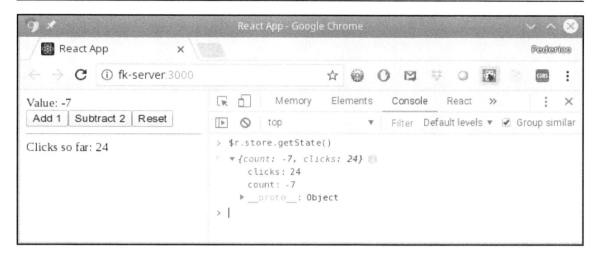

By selecting the <Provider> component, you can inspect the application's state

In fact, you can even fire actions if you want; by entering something like `$r.store.dispatch({type:"counter:increment", value:11})`, you have full control over the application state.

Debugging with the standalone tool

If you are working with other browsers such as Safari or Internet Explorer, or if you cannot use Chrome or Firefox for some reason, there's a standalone version of the tool, which you can find at `https://github.com/facebook/react-devtools/tree/master/packages/react-devtools`. Be warned, though, that for web development, you won't be getting the full functionality, so you'll probably be better off keeping to a supported browser!

Getting ready

We want to use the standalone tool; let's see how to set it up. To start with, obviously, we need to install the package. You can do it globally, but I prefer working locally within the project itself:

```
npm install react-devtools --save-dev
```

In order to be able to run the new command, you could use `npx` (as we saw a couple of times in the book), but it's easier to just define a new script in `package.json`. Add something like the following to it, and you'll be able to open the standalone app with `npm run devtools`:

```
"scripts": {
    .
    .
    .
    "devtools": "react-devtools"
}
```

Now you are set up; let's see how to use the tool.

 In case you are curious, this standalone application is itself written in JS and converted to a desktop application with `Electron`, as we'll be seeing later in the book in `Chapter 13`, *Creating a Desktop Application with Electron*.

How to do it...

We got the standalone tool; let's see how to use it. In order to use the RDT in a standalone fashion, you'll have to add a single line at the top of your HTML code.

```
<!DOCTYPE html>
<html lang="en">

<head>
    <script src="http://192.168.1.200:8097"></script>
    .
    .
    .
```

Then start the application normally, and after it's up and running, start the standalone app. You'll get something like the next screenshot. Note that we are seeing two separate windows: one with the RDT, and the other with the application (for variety) in Opera; in the same way I could have used Safari or IE or any other browser:

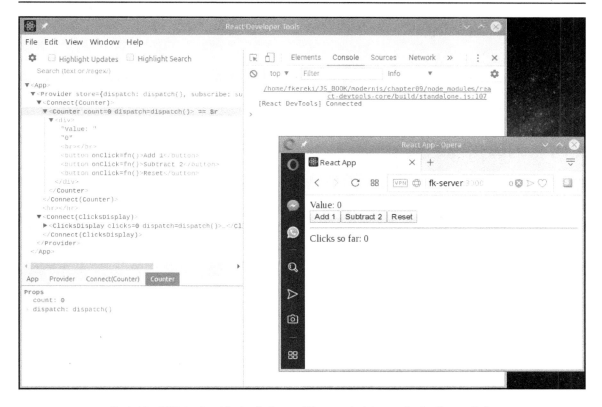

The standalone RDT let you inspect React applications even if they are running in browsers other than Chrome or Firefox

Now you are really set to go; let's finish this section by seeing what we can (and cannot) do.

For more details on how to configure the standalone application, in particular, if you need to use a different port, check out the official documentation at `https://github.com/facebook/react-devtools/tree/master/packages/react-devtools`. For complicated cases, you may end up using a different package, `react-devtools-core`, over at `https://github.com/facebook/react-devtools/tree/master/packages/react-devtools-core`.

How it works...

This version of the developer tools lets you interact with the application and see components and props, but you'll be restricted as to interacting with them through the console, as we'll see.

First, start by checking that if you click on the buttons in the Opera window, you'll automatically see the changes in the RDT, as before see the next screenshot for the results after some **Add 1** clicks:

Whatever you do in the React application will be shown in the Developer Tools. In this example, I clicked six times on **Add 1**, and the updated component tree shows the new values

Most functions work the same way as in Chrome. You can search for a component by name, and if you right-click on a component, you get several options, including showing all the occurrences of the component's name (as with the search) or copying its props; see the following screenshot:

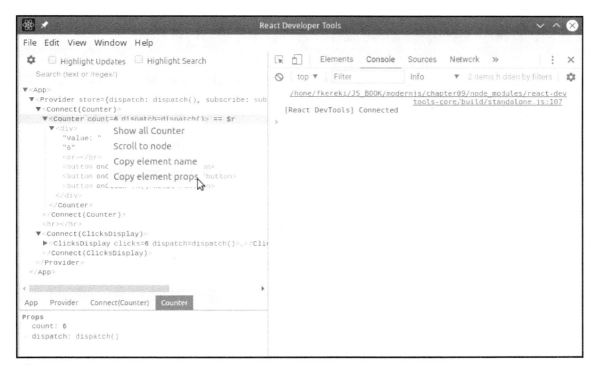

The RDT let you get full information about any component

However, note that you won't get *complete* values. For instance, in the preceding example, the copied props were as in the following code snippet; instead of a function, I got a string description:

```
{
  "count": 6,
  "dispatch": "[function dispatch]"
}
```

Another restriction is that you won't be able to use $r to directly access an object; this is beyond the tools' capabilities. However, if you are out of solutions for debugging, at least you'll be able to see the internal workings of your app, nothing to be dismissed out of hand!

Logging Redux with redux-logger

One basic tool for debugging is the use of a logger. While JS already has enough logging features available (we already mentioned the `window.console` functions in the *Adding logging with Winston* section in `Chapter 5`, *Testing and Debugging Your Server*, you will require some help in order to log the `Redux` actions, a key requirement. Certainly, you could add code before dispatching any action, but that would become too long-winded. Rather, we'll consider adding some middleware that will log all actions; even if we'll see better tools in the next *Debugging Redux with the Redux Developer Tools* section, this kind of log will prove quite useful. In this recipe, let's see how to add `redux-logger`.

 We have used middleware for thunks, but if you want to write your own middleware, you can find several examples (including a logging function) at `https://redux.js.org/advanced/middleware`.

Getting ready

Our first step, as always, is to get the new tool. Installation is simple and straightforward, along the same lines we seen in most of the text:

```
npm install redux-logger --save
```

This will install the new package, but you'll have to manually add it to your store creation code; by itself, the package won't have any effect.

 If you want to read more about the `redux-logger` features and capabilities, check out `https://github.com/evgenyrodionov/redux-logger`.

How to do it...

Setting up `redux-logger` requires first creating a logger with the `createLogger()` function, which lets you select many options to customize the logged output, and then include the generated logger as middleware for `Redux`.

Out of the many available options, these are the most interesting:

- `colors` : If you wish to change how the output looks.

- `diff:` : A Boolean flag to decide if you want to display the difference between the old state and the new state; there's also a `diffPredicate(getState, action)` function that you can use to decide whether to display the differences.

- `duration` : A Boolean flag to print how long it took to process an action; this would be interesting mainly in async actions

- `predicate(getState, action)` : Can inspect the action and the current state, and return true or false to define whether the action should be logged or not; this is quite useful to restrict logging to, say, just a few action types.

- `titleFormatter()`, `stateTransformer()`, `actionTransformer()`, and several other formatter functions.

 For the complete set of options, check out `https://github.com/ evgenyrodionov/redux-logger`.

Setting up our counter application

We'll see how to use this logger with our counter application for the simplest possible case, and then with the regions browser, which will add thunks to the mix. You have to use the `applyMiddleware()` function (which we already saw in the *Doing async actions: redux-thunk* section in Chapter 8, *Expanding Your Application,* when we started using `redux-thunk`) to add the logger to the process:

```
// Source file: src/counterApp/store.js

/* @flow */

import { createStore, applyMiddleware } from "redux";
import { createLogger } from "redux-logger";

import { reducer } from "./counter.reducer.js";

const logger = createLogger({ diff: true, duration: true });
export const store = createStore(reducer, applyMiddleware(logger));
    .
    .
    .
```

Of course, you would probably want to enable this only for development, so the last line in the preceding snippet should rather be something like the following:

```
export const store =
    process.env.NODE_ENV === "development"
        ? createStore(reducer, applyMiddleware(logger))
        : createStore(reducer);
    .
    .
    .
```

This sets the logger to access every single action that gets dispatched, and to log it including the differences between states and the processing time. We'll get to see how this works soon, but first let's take a look at our second application, which already had some middleware.

Setting up our region application

When you want to apply two or more pieces of middleware, you have to specify in which order they will be applied. In our case, remembering that a thunk could either be an object (fine to list) or a function (that will get called to eventually produce an object) we have to place our logger right at the end of all possible middleware:

```
// Source file: src/regionsApp/store.js

/* @flow */

import { createStore, applyMiddleware } from "redux";
import thunk from "redux-thunk";
import { createLogger } from "redux-logger";

import { reducer } from "./worlds.reducer.js";

const logger = createLogger({ duration: true });

export const store = createStore(reducer, applyMiddleware(thunk, logger));
.
.
.
```

I decided to skip listing differences because we'd be getting lists that are a bit long (over 200 countries, for example) so output would have become too large. Let's now get to see how this logging works in practice.

How it works...

We set both our applications to log all actions, with no filtering; all we have to do is npm start, and the logger's output will appear in the web developer tools console.

Logging the counter application

The counter application is quite simple: the whole state had just two pieces of data (the current counter value and the number of clicks so far) so it's easy to follow what happens during a test run; see the next screenshot:

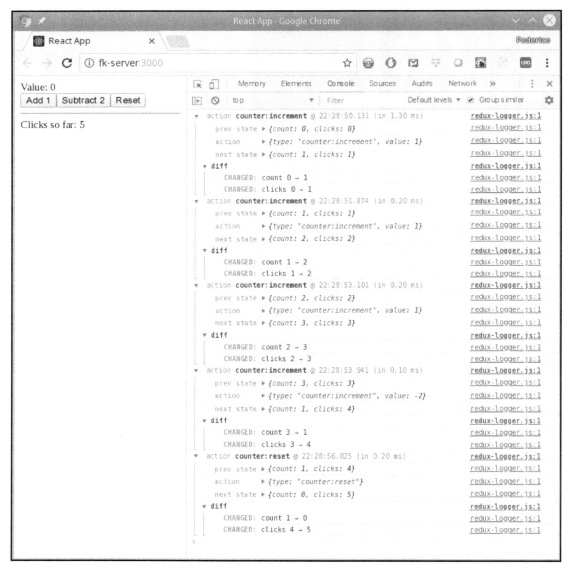

A sample run of the counter application, but logging all actions with redux-logger

You can easily follow the test run, and you'll be able to see when we clicked each of the buttons which action was dispatched and the successive values of the store—if there were any problems with the reducer's logic, you'd probably find them easy to detect, given all the information that appears onscreen.

Logging the region application

Our second application is more interesting, given that we are doing actual async requests, the amount of data to process is larger, and the screen display, while still a bit simple, is at least more complex than the counter display. When we start the application, the dropdown used an action to request the whole list of countries, as you can see in this screenshot:

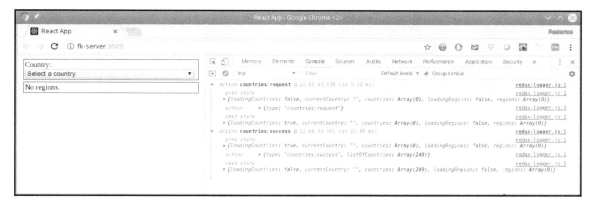

The drop-down component dispatched an action to get the countries (countries:request), and it proved successful (countries:success) returning a list with 249 countries

After the countries were loaded, I decided to pick **France** (a very small homage to the FIFA Soccer World champions of 2018!), and some new actions were fired, as shown in the next screenshot:

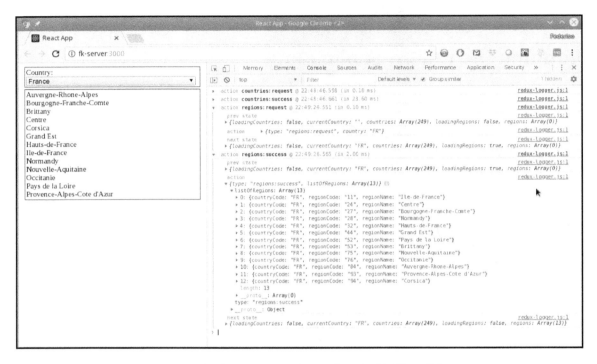

The results of picking a country: several actions were dispatched and the API was called

For the sake of a smaller display, I compacted the two first actions, and I could then expand the last one, showing the answer that was received from our own server. You can check that all regions are correctly displayed, though in alphabetic order, as we had sorted the list by name.

With this logger, you have already a good tool to see what happens in the React+Redux applications—but we'll add yet another tool for a even better way of working.

Debugging Redux with the Redux Developer Tools

One of the best things to have if you are working with React+Redux are the Redux Developer Tools (or DevTools), which provide a console that lets you look into actions and, states, and even provide a "time machine" mode that allows you to go back and forth in time, so you can carefully check if everything's as it should be. In this recipe, let's see how to use this very powerful tool to help debug our code.

 If you want to see Dan Abramov's demonstration of this tool, check out his talk at React Europe in 2015 at https://www.youtube.com/watch?v= xsSnOQynTHs.

Getting ready

Installing the required redux-devtools-extension is easy, but be careful! Don't confuse the redux-devtools-extension package, at https://github.com/zalnoxisus/redux-devtools-extension, with redux-devtools, a similar but different package at https://github.com/reduxjs/redux-devtools. The latter is more of a "DIY" package, which requires plenty of configuration, though it will let you create a totally custom monitor for Redux, if you care to. For ourselves, this is what we need:

```
npm install redux-devtools-extension --save-dev
```

You will also want to install a Chrome extension, Redux Devtools, which works together with the package we just installed. This extension will add a new option to the web developer tools, as we'll see.

How to do it...

In order to enable the tool, once again we must change the creation of the store. Let's do it for the region application, which already had a couple of middleware functions in it. On the plus side, we won't have to worry about development or production environments: the Redux DevTools will only work in the former. The modified store code can be as seen in the following snippet; the composeWithDevTools() added function will take care of the necessary connections to make everything work:

```
// Source file: src/regionsApp/store.js

/* @flow */

import { createStore, applyMiddleware } from "redux";
import thunk from "redux-thunk";
import { createLogger } from "redux-logger";
import { composeWithDevTools } from "redux-devtools-extension";

import { reducer } from "./worlds.reducer.js";

const logger = createLogger({ duration: true });

export const store = createStore(
    reducer,
    composeWithDevTools(applyMiddleware(thunk, logger))
);
```

If you run the code, it will work exactly as before, but let's see how the added debugging functions work.

How it works...

Let's fire up our region application, and then open the web developer tools and pick the **Redux** tab. You'll get something like in the following screenshot:

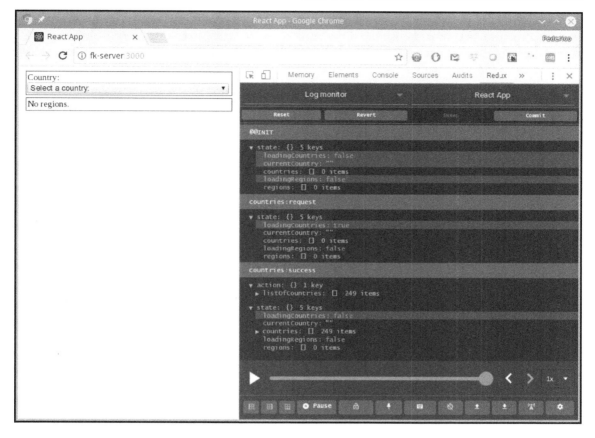

Loading the application shows the initial state plus a couple of actions: the request for countries and the success of that request

There are many features here. The following slider (you will have to click the clock icon on the bottom bar to see it) is probably the most interesting one, because it lets you go back and forth; try sliding it, and you'll see how the application changes.

For example, you could easily see how the screen looked when the country request action had been dispatched, but before the data came back; see the next screenshot. You'll remember that in order to check this out, we had to add an artificial time delay before; now, you can examine the situation at will, with no need to add any special code:

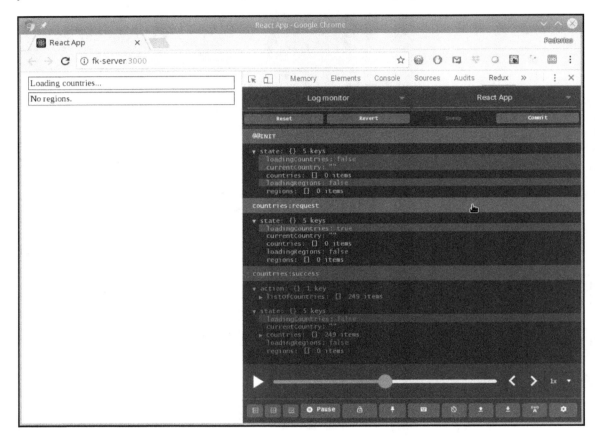

By using the slider, you can see how the application looked at any previous moment

If you select the **Inspector** option in the drop-down list at the top, you can examine actions and states. For example in the next screenshot, you can examine the action that was dispatched when the list of countries was retrieved from the server with all its data. You'll notice that this kind of information is very similar to what the Redux logger package produced, but you can work with it in a more dynamic way:

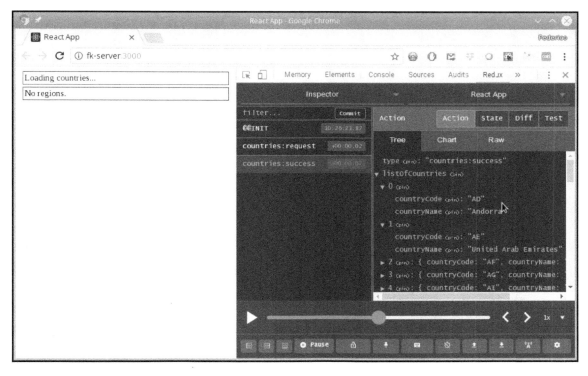

The Inspector feature lets you view actions (as here) and states, so you can inspect everything that happened

Let's advance a bit; select **France** again, and we'll see how the state changed after those regions came in. The **Diff** tab shows you only the differences in the state: in our case, the `loadingRegions` value was reset to false (it had been set to true when the request for region action was dispatched), and the list of regions got its values (all the regions of France). See the following screenshot:

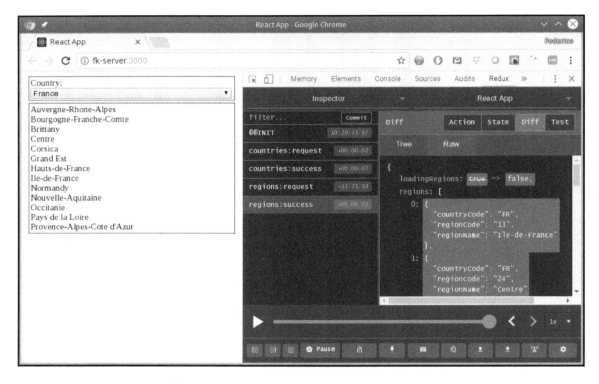

The **Diff** tab lets you quickly see just the state changed attributes for a faster, simpler analysis

We haven't gone through all functions, so go ahead and click everywhere to find what else is available. For example, the buttons on the left in the bottom bar let you open a separate window for debugging, so your screen won't get so cramped; another button lets you create and dispatch any action, so go ahead, try everything out!

You really should experiment with the tool to get a clear perspective on what you can achieve with it—and, in particular, try out the `time machine` function. You'll appreciate the fact that this kind of result is possible only because of the way in which `React` creates the view as a function of the state, but then you will eventually come to notice that something is missing; let's find out what is it, and how to fix it?

Connecting routing for debugging

What did we miss? The simple applications we tried out in previous sections of this chapter didn't include routing—but what would have happened if they did? The problem now is visible: whenever the user navigates to a new route, nothing in the state would keep track of that change, so the time machine functions wouldn't really work. To solve this, we need to keep the router information in sync with the store, and that will restore full functionality to our debugging; let's see here how to do that.

Getting ready

With previous versions of `react-router`, a `react-router-redux` package took care of linking the router and the state, but that package was recently deprecated and replaced by `connected-react-router`, which we'll install. I'm mentioning this because there are many articles on the web that still show the usage of the former package; be careful:

```
npm install --save connected-react-router
```

This is half the solution; getting the package to work will (once more!) require changes in the store and in the structure of your application; let's see that.

How to do it...

We want to modify our code so that the Redux time machine functionality will work. Let's use again the basic routing application we saw in the *Adding routing with react-router* section in Chapter 8, *Expanding Your Application*; we had routing and also a login form that dispatched some actions, so we'll be able to see (on a very small scale, agreed!) all the kinds of things we find in a normal application.

There will be changes in two places: first, we'll have to connect our store with a `history` object related to the router, and, second, we'll have to add a component to our main code. The store changes are as follows—observe that we also added here our other debugging tools to match those in the rest of the chapter:

```
// Source file: src/routingApp/store.js

/* @flow */

import { createStore, applyMiddleware } from "redux";
import thunk from "redux-thunk";
import { createLogger } from "redux-logger";
import { composeWithDevTools } from "redux-devtools-extension";
import { connectRouter, routerMiddleware } from "connected-react-router";
import { createBrowserHistory } from "history";

import { reducer } from "./login.reducer";

const logger = createLogger({ duration: true });

export const history = createBrowserHistory();

export const store = createStore(
    connectRouter(history)(reducer),
    composeWithDevTools(
        applyMiddleware(routerMiddleware(history), thunk, logger)
    )
);
```

The code is sort of obscure-looking, but basically:

- We create a `history` object, which we'll have to export because we'll need it later
- We wrap our original `reducer` with `connectRouter()` to produce a new reducer that will be aware of the router state
- We add `routerMiddleware(history)` to allow for routing methods like `push()`

Then we'll have to add a `<ConnectedRouter>` component to our main JSX; this will require the history object that we created before:

```
// Source file: src/App.routing.auth.js

import React, { Component } from "react";
import { Provider } from "react-redux";
import { BrowserRouter, Switch, Route, Link } from "react-rcuter-dom";
import { ConnectedRouter } from "connected-react-router";

import {
    ConnectedLogin,
    AuthRoute
} from "./routingApp";
import { history, store } from "./routingApp/store";

const Home = () => <h1>Home Sweet Home</h1>;
const Help = () => <h1>Help! SOS!</h1>;
.
.
.

class App extends Component<{}> {
    render() {
        return (
            <Provider store={store}>
                <BrowserRouter>
                    <ConnectedRouter history={history}>
                        <div>
                            <header>
                                <nav>
                                    <Link to="/">Home</Link> 
                                    <Link to="/login">Log
                                     in</Link> 
                                    .
                                    .
                                    .
                                </nav>
                            </header>
```

```
                                <Switch>
                                  <Route exact path="/" component={Home} />
                                  <Route path="/help" component={Help} />
                                         .
                                         .
                                         .
                                </Switch>
                            </div>
                      </ConnectedRouter>
                  </BrowserRouter>
              </Provider>
          );
      }
  }

  export default App;
```

Everything's set now; let's see how this works.

 For a fuller description of connected-react-router, check out its GitHub page at https://github.com/supasate/connected-react-router; in particular, you may be interested in the many articles listed near the bottom of the page with diverse tips and suggestions.

How it works...

Let's start our application now, and don't forget to run our server from Chapter 4, *Implementing RESTful Services with Node*, as we did before. Opening the Redux DevTools, we see a single new action, @@INIT, and the state now includes a new router attribute; see the following screenshot:

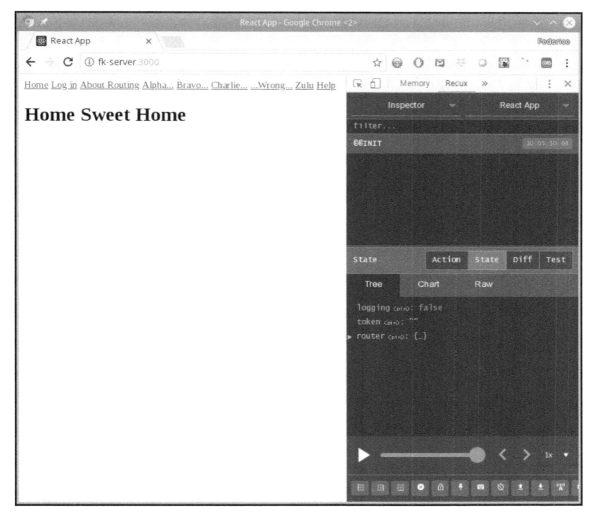

After connecting routing to the store, some new actions and state attributes appear

If we click on **Alpha...**, we'll see that two actions were dispatched: the first attempted to access /alpha, and the second was our redirection to the /login page, as shown in this screenshot:

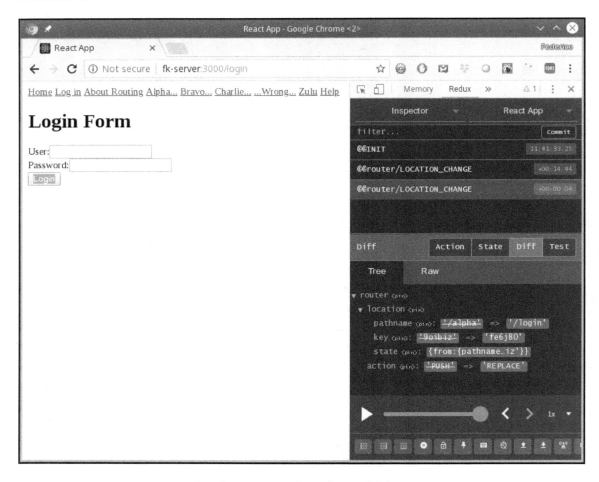

Attempting to access a protected route redirects us to the login page

After entering user and password, we see our **login:request** and **login:success** actions—as we have seen since we enabled the `Redux` Developer Tools—followed by another action, corresponding to the redirection to the `/alpha` page appears after as shown in the following screenshot:

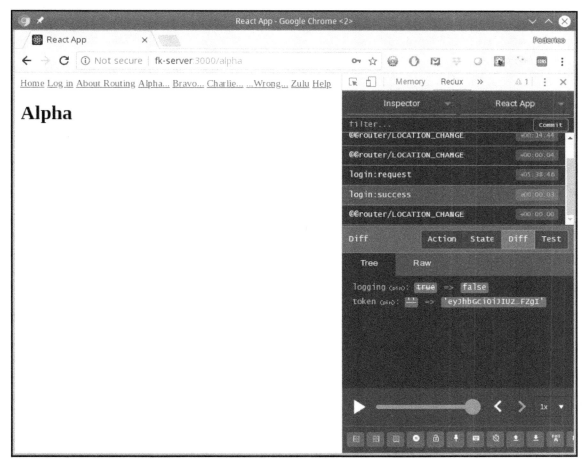

Our own actions are intermixed with the router actions

But, now the time machine functionality is enabled for routing as well; for example, if you move the slider back to the beginning, you'll see the home page again, and you can go back and forth, and the view will appropriately reflect everything you had earlier seen; check the next screenshot:

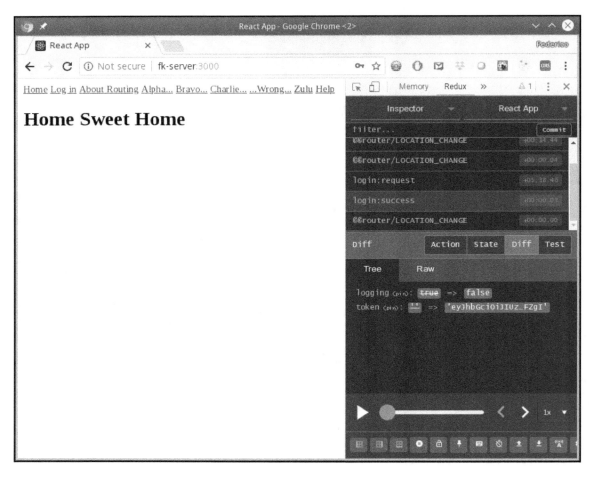

Having connected the router to the state, now we can use the slider to go back and see the correct pages every time

We now have a good set of debugging tools; let's move on to do automatic testing, as we earlier did with `Node`.

Testing Your Application **10**

In this chapter, we will cover the following recipes:

- Testing components with Jest and Enzyme
- Testing reducers and mappings
- Testing actions and thunks
- Testing changes with snapshots
- Measuring test coverage

Introduction

In the previous chapter, we dealt with debugging. Now let's add some unit testing recipes to round out all we'll need for development. As we've seen before, having good unit testing helps not only with development, but also as a preventive tool to avoid regression bugs.

Testing components with Jest and Enzyme

Back in `Chapter 5`, *Testing and Debugging Your Server*, we did unit testing for our `Node` code, and we used `Jest` for it. As we said there, an advantage of this package is that we can also use it with `React` (or `React Native`, which we'll be looking at in `Chapter 11`, *Creating Mobile Apps with React Native*), so everything we learned about earlier in this book still holds; give it a quick look over if you will, so we won't have to repeat ourselves here.

What shall we test? Obviously, we'll have to write unit tests for our components, but since we've been using `Redux`, we'll also require tests for reducers, actions, and thunks; we'll cover all of these topics in this section and the following ones. Some of these tests will be quite simple to write, and for others, some more work will be needed. Let's get started, then!

Getting ready

For Node, we had to install Jest on our own, but create-react-app already does that for us, so it's one less thing to worry about. (If you created the React application on your own, by writing your own configuration files then you should take a look at https://jestjs.io/docs/en/getting-started to see how to proceed.) We will, however, also use Enzyme, a package that will simplify making assertions about, or manipulating, the HTML that your components produce in a way that is quite similar to jQuery.

 If you want to learn more about these functions, or if you haven't used jQuery for a while (my own case!), read about cheerio, the package that's used by Enzyme, at https://github.com/cheeriojs/cheerio. For Enzyme itself, including its configuration, you can visit its GitHub site at https://github.com/airbnb/enzyme.

Since we are using version 16 of React, the current way to install the package is as follows; the enzyme-adapter-react-16 additional package is needed to link Enzyme with React:

```
npm install enzyme enzyme-adapter-react-16 --save-dev
```

Another nice thing is that we won't need to do any particular configuration, because create-react-app also takes care of setting everything up. However, should you decide that you need something special, react-app-rewired will help: check out https://github.com/timarney/react-app-rewired for more on that.

We have everything we need; let's get testing!

How to do it...

What components should we test? We have worked with connected and unconnected components already, but we'll focus on the latter here. Why? Connected components get their props and dispatch logic from the mapStateToProps() and mapDispatchToProps() functions; we can trust this is so, and therefore we don't actually have to test it. If you want, you could set up a store and verify that those two functions do their job—but those test are trivial to write, and I wouldn't suggest that you actually need them. Instead, we'll focus on the unconnected version of the components and fully test them. We'll set up all of the tests here, and then we'll look at how to run them, and what output to expect.

Testing a component without events

We want to test a component, so let's pick up a suitable one. For our first unit testing, let's work with the `<RegionsTable>` component, which didn't process any events; it was just a display component. Tests are usually named the same way as the component, but changing the extension from `.js` to `.test.js`—or to `.spec.js`, but I like `.test.js` better. Pick whatever you want, and just be consistent about it.

First, let's start by considering what should we test. The specification for our component says that it works differently depending on whether it receives an empty or non-empty list of countries. In the first case, we can test that the produced HTML text includes *No regions*, and in the second case, we should verify that all of the provided regions do appear in the output. Of course, you can think up more detailed, specific cases, but try not to make your tests too *brittle*, meaning that the slightest change in implementation will make your tests fail. The tests that I described may not cover all cases, but it's pretty certain that even if you were to implement the component in a different way, the tests should still be successful.

Starting out with the actual tests, all of them will start in a similar way: with us needing to import to necessary libraries, plus the component to test, and setting up Enzyme and its adapter. In the following code, I'll highlight the related lines:

```
// Source file: src/regionsApp/regionsTable.test.js

/* @flow */

import React from "react";
import Enzyme from "enzyme";
import Adapter from "enzyme-adapter-react-16";

import { RegionsTable } from "./regionsTable.component";

Enzyme.configure({ adapter: new Adapter() });

// continued...
```

Like we did earlier, we'll start using `describe()` and `it()` to set up different test cases. To check the empty regions list case, we can just use a few lines of code:

```
// ...continues

describe("RegionsTable", () => {
    it("renders correctly an empty list", () => {
        const wrapper = Enzyme.render(<RegionsTable list={[]} />);
        expect(wrapper.text()).toContain("No regions.");
    });

// continued...
```

We use `Enzyme.render()` to generate the DOM for our component, and the `.text()` method to generate a text version of it. With the latter, we just need to verify that the desired text appears so that the whole test is really short.

We also had a second use case, in which we provided a non-empty list of regions. The code is similar, but obviously longer; let's check out the code first, and we'll explain it after:

```
// ...continues

    it("renders correctly a list", () => {
        const wrapper = Enzyme.render(
            <RegionsTable
                list={[
                    {
                        countryCode: "UY",
                        regionCode: "10",
                        regionName: "Montevideo"
                    },
                    {
                        countryCode: "UY",
                        regionCode: "9",
                        regionName: "Maldonado"
                    },
                    {
                        countryCode: "UY",
                        regionCode: "5",
                        regionName: "Cerro Largo"
                    }
                ]}
            />
        );
        expect(wrapper.text()).toContain("Montevideo");
        expect(wrapper.text()).toContain("Maldonado");
        expect(wrapper.text()).toContain("Cerro Largo");
```

```
    });
});
```

The logic is pretty similar: render the components, produce text, check that the right content is there. As we said, you could also verify if each region is within a `<li>` element, and if they have keys, and so on; keep in mind, however, what we wrote about brittle tests, and avoid over-specifying the tests, so that only one possible, specific, given implementation of the component could pass them!

Testing a component with events

Now we want to test a component with events. For this, the `<CountrySelect>` component will come in handy, because it can process some events, and it will call some callbacks accordingly.

First of all, let's see the initial setup, including a list of countries that we'll be using for different tests:

```
// Source file: src/regionsApp/countrySelect.test.js

/* @flow */

import React from "react";
import Enzyme from "enzyme";
import Adapter from "enzyme-adapter-react-16";

import { CountrySelect } from "./countrySelect.component";

Enzyme.configure({ adapter: new Adapter() });

const threeCountries = [
    {
        countryCode: "UY",
        countryName: "Uruguay"
    },
    {
        countryCode: "AR",
        countryName: "Argentina"
    },
    {
        countryCode: "BR",
        countryName: "Brazil"
    }
];

// continued...
```

Now, what cases will we write unit tests for? Let's start with the case in which no list of countries is given: according to what we wanted, in that case, the component would have to use a prop, such as `getCountries()`, to get the necessary data. We'll use *spies* again (we saw them in the *Using spies* section of `Chapter 5`, *Testing and Debugging Your Server*) to simulate and test the necessary behavior:

```
// ...continues

describe("CountrySelect", () => {
    it("renders correctly when loading, with no countries", () => {
        const mockGetCountries = jest.fn();
        const mockOnSelect = jest.fn();

        const wrapper = Enzyme.mount(
            <CountrySelect
                loading={true}
                onSelect={mockOnSelect}
                getCountries={mockGetCountries}
                list={[]}
            />
        );
        expect(wrapper.text()).toContain("Loading countries");

        expect(mockGetCountries).toHaveBeenCalledTimes(1);
        expect(mockOnSelect).not.toHaveBeenCalled();
    });

// continued...
```

We are creating two spies: one for the `onSelect` event handler, and one to get the list of countries. Testing that the output of the component includes the `"Loading countries"` text is simple; let's focus on the spies instead. We expect that the component should have called the function to get the list of countries (but only once!) and that the event handler should not have been called: the last two checks take care of this.

Now, what should happen if a list had been provided? We can write a similar test, and just verify, for a difference, that the component didn't call the function to get the (already given) countries; I have highlighted the related code:

```
// ...continues

    it("renders correctly a countries dropdown", () => {
        const mockGetCountries = jest.fn();
        const mockOnSelect = jest.fn();

        const wrapper = Enzyme.mount(
            <CountrySelect
                loading={false}
                onSelect={mockOnSelect}
                getCountries={mockGetCountries}
                list={threeCountries}
            />
        );

        expect(wrapper.text()).toContain("Uruguay");
        expect(wrapper.text()).toContain("Argentina");
        expect(wrapper.text()).toContain("Brazil");

        expect(mockGetCountries).not.toHaveBeenCalled();
        expect(mockOnSelect).not.toHaveBeenCalled();
    });

// continued...
```

Given the tests we have already written, this part of the code should have been easy to understand: we have already seen similar tests before, so we don't have anything new to explain here.

Let's get to the final, more interesting, situation: how do we simulate that the user selected something? For this, we'll have to detect the `<select>` element within our `<CountrySelect>` component, and for that I decided to provide a name attribute: I changed a single line in the component's original `render()` method and changed it from `<select onChange={this.onSelect}>` to `<select onChange={this.onSelect} name="selectCountry">`, so that I have a way to get at the element. Of course, you could object to changing the original component code in any way, and you could also very correctly add that this makes the test somewhat brittler than before; should the component be re-coded in a different way, without using a `<select>` element, the test would automatically fail, and you'd be right. This is a judgment call as to how far to go in the tests, and what extra baggage is needed.

To finish our suite of tests, we want to verify that the correct event handler is called:

```
// ...continues

it("correctly calls onSelect", () => {
    const mockGetCountries = jest.fn();
    const mockOnSelect = jest.fn();

    const wrapper = Enzyme.mount(
        <CountrySelect
            loading={false}
            onSelect={mockOnSelect}
            getCountries={mockGetCountries}
            list={threeCountries}
        />
    );

    wrapper
        .find("[name='selectCountry']")
        .at(0)
        .simulate("change", { target: { value: "UY" } });

    expect(mockGetCountries).not.toHaveBeenCalled();
    expect(mockOnSelect).toHaveBeenCalledTimes(1);
    expect(mockOnSelect).toHaveBeenCalledWith("UY");
});
});
```

We have to use some DOM traversal to find the desired element, and then use
.simulate() to fire an event. Since no actual event is really fired, we'll have to provide the
values it would include, which in our case is .target.value. Then we can finish our test
by verifying that the event handler was called once with the right value ("UY").

We have written our component tests; let's see how they work.

How it works...

Running the tests is simple: you just need to use npm test, in the same way that we did for
Node, as follows:

```
PASS   src/regionsApp/regionsTable.test.js
PASS   src/regionsApp/countrySelect.test.js

Test Suites: 2 passed, 2 total
Tests:       5 passed, 5 total
Snapshots:   0 total
Time:        1.031s, estimated 2s
Ran all test suites related to changed files.

Watch Usage
 › Press a to run all tests.
 › Press p to filter by a filename regex pattern.
 › Press t to filter by a test name regex pattern.
 › Press q to quit watch mode.
 › Press Enter to trigger a test run.
```

The Jest output is in the same style as we saw for Node; the Snapshots total will be explained later

Jest is set up to automatically watch for changes, so if you modify any file, testing will proceed again – the q command will stop the watch mode, and you'll have to use a to run all tests, or p and t to filter some tests to run.

We have now seen how to test components. However, some extra work is needed, because in our examples, we haven't dealt with any Redux-related matters, such as dispatching actions or thunks; let's move on to other kinds of tests.

Testing reducers and mappings

After testing the components, we are now moving on to a simpler set of tests: first, reducers; and then mappings such as mapStateToProps() and mapDispatchToProps(). Why are these tests easier to write? Because in all of these cases, we are dealing with pure functions, without side effects, that produce their output based only on their inputs. We already dealt with these sort of functions earlier in this book when we did testing for Node, so now we'll make do with a short section. The only particular care we'll have is to verify that no function (for example, a reducer) attempts to modify the state, but other than that, it's simple to test all the way. In this recipe, let's look at the different kind of tests we'll need for reducers and mappings.

How to do it...

We'll have to test the reducers and mappings, so let's start by thinking about how you would test a reducer. There are two key things to verify: first, that given an input state, it produces a correct output state, and second, that the reducer doesn't modify the original state. The first condition is pretty obvious, but the second can easily be missed – and a reducer that modifies the current state can produce hard-to-find bugs.

Let's look at how we could test our countries and regions application's reducer. First, since all tests are analog, we'll just see a couple of them, for two of all the possible actions – but of course, you want to test *all* of the actions, right? We'll also include another test to verify that for unknown actions, the reducer just returns the initial state, unchanged in every way:

```
// Source file: src/regionsApp/world.reducer.test.js

/* @flow */

import { reducer } from "./world.reducer.js";
import { countriesRequest, regionsSuccess } from "./world.actions.js";

describe("The countries and regions reducer", () => {
    it("should process countryRequest actions", () => {
        const initialState = {
            loadingCountries: false,
            currentCountry: "whatever",
            countries: [{}, {}, {}],
            loadingRegions: false,
            regions: [{}, {}]
        };

        const initialJSON = JSON.stringify(initialState);

        expect(reducer(initialState, countriesRequest())).toEqual({
            loadingCountries: true,
            currentCountry: "whatever",
            countries: [],
            loadingRegions: false,
            regions: [{}, {}]
        });

        expect(JSON.stringify(initialState)).toBe(initialJSON);
    });

    it("should process regionsSuccess actions", () => {
        const initialState = {
            loadingCountries: false,
```

```
            currentCountry: "whatever",
            countries: [{}, {}, {}],
            loadingRegions: true,
            regions: []
        };

        const initialJSON = JSON.stringify(initialState);

        expect(
            reducer(
                initialState,
                regionsSuccess([
                    { something: 1 },
                    { something: 2 },
                    { something: 3 }
                ])
            )
        ).toEqual({
            loadingCountries: false,
            currentCountry: "whatever",
            countries: [{}, {}, {}],
            loadingRegions: false,
            regions: [{ something: 1 }, { something: 2 }, { something: 3 }]
        });

        expect(JSON.stringify(initialState)).toBe(initialJSCN);
    });

    it("should return the initial state for unknown actions", () => {
        const initialState = {
            loadingCountries: false,
            currentCountry: "whatever",
            countries: [{}, {}, {}],
            loadingRegions: true,
            regions: []
        };
        const initialJSON = JSON.stringify(initialState);

        expect(
            JSON.stringify(reducer(initialState, { actionType: "other" }))
        ).toBe(initialJSON);
        expect(JSON.stringify(initialState)).toBe(initialⅭSON);
    });
});
```

Are you wondering about `Enzyme`, and why we skipped it? We only need it when we are rendering components, so for testing reducers or actions (as we'll be doing soon), it's not required at all.

Each test for the reducer will be the same, and follow these steps:

1. Define an `initialState` and use `JSON.stringify()` to save its original string representation.
2. Invoke the reducer and use `.toEqual()` (a `Jest` method that does deep, recursive, equality comparison between objects) to verify that the new state fully matches what you expect it to be.
3. Check that the `initialState` JSON representation still matches the original value.

I used dummy values for countries and regions, but if you want to be even more careful, you could specify complete, correct values instead of things like `{ something:2 }` or `"whatever"`; it's up to you.

 You may want to take a look at `redux-testkit` at `https://github.com/wix/redux-testkit`; this package can help you write reducer tests, automatically checking whether the state has been modified.

After writing these tests, it should be fairly obvious that writing a test for a mapping function is the same thing. For example, when we set up the `<ConnectedRegionsTable>` component, we wrote a `getProps()` function:

```
const getProps = state => ({
    list: state.regions,
    loading: state.loadingRegions
});
```

We would have to export the function (we didn't at the time, because it wasn't going to be used elsewhere) and then a test could be performed, as follows:

```
// Source file: src/regionsApp/regionsTable.connected.test.js

/* @flow */

import { getProps } from "./regionsTable.connected.js";

describe("getProps for RegionsTable", () => {
    it("should extract regions and loading", () => {
        const initialState = {
            loadingCountries: false,
            currentCountry: "whatever",
            countries: [{ other: 1 }, { other: 2 }, { other: 3 }],
            loadingRegions: false,
            regions: [{ something: 1 }, { something: 2 }]
        };
        const initialJSON = JSON.stringify(initialState);

        expect(getProps(initialState)).toEqual({
            list: [{ something: 1 }, { something: 2 }],
            loading: false
        });
        expect(JSON.stringify(initialState)).toBe(initialJSCN);
    });
});
```

How does this work? Let's see what happens when we run these tests.

How it works...

Using npm test will produce a nice *all green* output, meaning that all of the tests have passed, as in the previous section; no need to see that again. In each individual test, we apply the technique that was described earlier: set up state, save a string version of it, apply the reducer or the mapper function, check it matches what you wanted it to produce, and check that the original state still matches the saved version.

Imagine that somebody accidentally modified the getProps() function that we tested so that instead of returning the regions, it returned the countries list, like so:

```
FAIL  src/regionsApp/regionsTable.connected.test.js
  ● getProps for RegionsTable › should extract regions and loading

    expect(received).toEqual(expected)

    Expected value to equal:
      {"list": [{"something": 1}, {"something": 2}], "loading": false}
    Received:
      {"list": [{"other": 1}, {"other": 2}, {"other": 3}], "loading": false}

    Difference:

    - Expected
    + Received

      Object {
        "list": Array [
          Object {
    -       "something": 1,
    +       "other": 1,
          },
          Object {
    -       "something": 2,
    +       "other": 2,
          },
    +     Object {
    +       "other": 3,
    +     },
        ],
        "loading": false,
      }
```

Any unexpected change in a mapping (or reducer) function would be detected by our usage of the .toEqual() method, which does a deep comparison of the produced and expected values

So, these simple tests can help you be safe against accidental changes – including the addition, removal, or modification of the expected values. This is a good safety net!

Testing actions and thunks

To finish our testing goals, we have to look at how we can test actions and thunks. Testing the former is really trivial after everything we've done so far, because it's just a matter of calling an action creator and checking the fields on the produced action, but testing thunks, which will surely involve an asynchronous service call and will surely dispatch several – OK, that's interesting!

We'll skip the simpler action tests (though we'll get to test them, anyway, as you'll see) and we'll dive in directly to writing unit tests for our thunks.

Getting ready

A good tool that we'll need here is `redux-mock-store`, a small package that lets us work with a fake store, aping all its functionality, and providing with some calls, such as `.getActions()`, to inspect which actions were dispatched, in what order, with which data, and so on. The installation is simple, as usual:

```
npm install redux-mock-store --save-dev
```

You may be wondering how we'll manage to mock the API service calls. Depending on your architecture, if you have thunks directly using things like `axios()` or `fetch()` to contact a service, then you will certainly need a corresponding mock package. However, since we spirited away those API calls in separate packages, we can do very well by mocking the whole call so that no AJAX calls will ever be done; we'll get to this soon.

 Check out the full documentation for `redux-mock-store` at its GitHub site, over at `https://github.com/dmitry-zaets/redux-mock-store`.

How to do it...

We want to test actions. Let's take a look at how we can execute those tests.

Since we've been working with our countries-and-regions example a lot, let's finish by testing (at least some of) its actions and thunks: `getCountries()` is a good example, and quite similar to `getRegions()`. It will be good to remember that particular code here, so let's take a look:

```
export const getCountries = () => async dispatch => {
    try {
        dispatch(countriesRequest());
        const result = await getCountriesAPI();
        dispatch(countriesSuccess(result.data));
    } catch (e) {
        dispatch(countriesFailure());
    }
};
```

To begin with, it dispatches an action to mark that a request is being done. Then it waits for the result of a web service call; this will require mocking! Finally, if the call was successful, an action is dispatched, including the received list of countries. On a failed call, a different action is dispatched, but showing the failure.

Now let's consider the following—how can we deal with the API call? The `world.actions.js` source code directly imports `getCountriesAPI()` from a module, but `Jest` has a feature just for that: we can mock a full module, providing mocks or spies for whichever functions we desire, as follows:

```
// Source file: src/regionsApp/world.actions.test.js

/* @flow */

import configureMockStore from "redux-mock-store";
import thunk from "redux-thunk";

import {
    getCountries,
    COUNTRIES_REQUEST,
    COUNTRIES_SUCCESS,
    COUNTRIES_FAILURE
} from "./world.actions.js";

import { getCountriesAPI } from "./serviceApi";

let mockPromise;
```

```
jest.mock("./serviceApi", () => {
    return {
        getCountriesAPI: jest.fn().mockImplementation(() => mockPromise)
    };

// continues...
```

Whenever the getCountries() function calls getCountriesAPI(), our mocked module will be used and a promise (mockPromise) will be returned; it's up to us to appropriately decide what should that promise be, and we'll make that choice depending on whether we want a test to fail or succeed.

Now that we have a way to intercept API calls and have them produce any result we want, we can move on to writing the actual tests.

Let's deal with the *happy path* first, in which the API call for countries is successful, with no problems. A test can be written in the following way:

```
// ...continued

describe("getCountries", () => {
    it("on API success", async () => {
        const fakeCountries = {
            data: [{ code: "UY" }, { code: "AR" }, { code: "BR" }]
        };
        mockPromise = Promise.resolve(fakeCountries);

        const store = configureMockStore([thunk])({});

        await store.dispatch(getCountries());

        const dispatchedActions = store.getActions();

        expect(getCountriesAPI).toHaveBeenCalledWith();
        expect(dispatchedActions.length).toBe(2);
        expect(dispatchedActions[0].type).toBe(COUNTRIES_REQUEST);
        expect(dispatchedActions[1].type).toBe(COUNTRIES_SUCCESS);
        expect(dispatchedActions[1].listOfCountries).toEqual(
            fakeCountries.data
        );
    });
});

// continues...
```

How is this code structured?

1. We initially define some data (`fakeCountries`) that will be returned by our `mockPromise`.

2. Then we create a mock store, according to the `redux-mock-store` documentation; we are only using the `thunk` middleware in our case, but you may add more. In fact, in our original code, we followed `thunk` with `logger`, but that's not relevant for our testing.

3. After that, we `store.dispatch()` the `getCountries()` thunk and await its results.

4. Once everything is done, we use `store.getActions()` to get the list of actions that were actually dispatched.

5. We test that our `getCountriesAPI()` function was called; if it hasn't been, we'll be in deep trouble!

6. Finally, we test all of the dispatched actions, checking their `type` and other attributes. This is, in fact, an indirect test on the action creators themselves!

Now that we've looked at a successful case, let's simulate that the API call somehow failed. To simulate this, all we have to do is define a different promise for the `getCountriesAPI()` call to return:

```
// ...continued

    it("on API failure", async () => {
        mockPromise = Promise.reject(new Error("failure!"));

        const store = configureMockStore([thunk])({});

        await store.dispatch(getCountries());

        const dispatchedActions = store.getActions();

        expect(getCountriesAPI).toHaveBeenCalledWith();
        expect(dispatchedActions.length).toBe(2);
        expect(dispatchedActions[0].type).toBe(COUNTRIES_REQUEST);
        expect(dispatchedActions[1].type).toBe(COUNTRIES_FAILURE);
    });
});

// continues...
```

What's different in this case? Our `mockPromise` is now set to fail, so the tests for the second dispatched actions vary: in this case, instead of success and a list of countries, we just get a failure—but the rest of the test is essentially the same.

Let's finish with an extra case. When we coded our thunks, we saw that we could access the current state by means of a `getState()` function and act differently depending on its contents. We could have coded our `getCountries()` function to avoid doing an API call if the list of countries had already been obtained, for a small optimization; the key part would have been as follows:

```
// ...continued

export const getCountries = () => async (dispatch, getState) => {
    if (getState().countries.length) {
        // no need to do anything!
    } else {
        try {
            dispatch(countriesRequest());
            const result = await getCountriesAPI();
            dispatch(countriesSuccess(result.data));
        } catch (e) {
            dispatch(countriesFailure());
        }
    }
};

// continues...
```

How could we test this case? The difference would be in how we set up the store, and what actions actually get dispatched:

```
// ...continued

describe("optimized getCountries", () => {
    it("doesn't do unneeded calls", async () => {
        const store = configureMockStore([thunk])({
            countries: [{ land: 1 }, { land: 2 }]
        });

        jest.resetAllMocks();

        await store.dispatch(getCountries());

        expect(getCountriesAPI).not.toHaveBeenCalled();
        expect(store.getActions().length).toBe(0);
    });
});
```

When we set up the store, we can provide it with initial values, as in this case, in which we make believe that some countries (fake data!) are already loaded. A special requirement: we must use `jest.resetAllMocks()`, because otherwise we won't be able to check that `getCountriesAPI()` wasn't called – because it *was* called, but by the *previous* tests. Then, after dispatching the thunk, we just check that the API wasn't called and that zero actions were dispatched: everything's OK!

How it works...

There isn't much to running these tests, and `npm test` is all we need. We can see the results for both our tests (the original and the optimized `getCountries()` functions), and the passing result shows that everything is as expected. The output, when you run a single test, is more detailed, showing each individual test:

```
PASS  src/regionsApp/world.actions.test.js
  getCountries
    ✓ on API success (5ms)
    ✓ on API failure (1ms)
  optimized getCountries
    ✓ doesn't do unneeded calls (1ms)


Test Suites: 1 passed, 1 total
Tests:       3 passed, 3 total
Snapshots:   0 total
Time:        0.608s, estimated 1s
Ran all test suites related to changed files.


Watch Usage
 › Press a to run all tests.
 › Press p to filter by a filename regex pattern.
 › Press t to filter by a test name regex pattern.
 › Press q to quit watch mode.
 › Press Enter to trigger a test run.
```

The tests for actions and thunks require a bit more setup, but run in the same way. We're getting a more detailed output because we're running a single test this time.

Testing changes with Snapshots

So far, we've been looking at automatic tests for components, events, and actions, so let's end this chapter by considering a testing tool that isn't really a part of TDD, but rather a safeguard against unwanted or unexpected changes after the fact: *snapshots*. (In TDD, tests would be written before coding the component, but you'll see that this is impossible here.) Snapshot tests work like this: you render a UI component, capture what HTML was produced, and then that is compared to a reference capture that was previously stored. If both captures do not match, either somebody made an unexpected change or the change was actually expected. If this is the case, you'll have to verify that the new capture is correct and then drop the old one.

How to do it...

We can use snapshot testing for all of our components, but it's more interesting for those whose output varies in terms of their props, so different behaviors are to be expected. We will be using a different way of rendering: instead of producing HTML elements, we'll use renderers that produce text output that can be stored and compared in a easy way.

First, the simplest cases are for components with a standard, fixed kind of output. We have some examples of that: for our `<ClicksDisplay>` component, the test would be written as follows:

```
// Source file: src/counterApp/clicksDisplay.test.js

import React from "react";
import TestRenderer from "react-test-renderer";

import { ClicksDisplay } from "./";

describe("clicksDisplay", () => {
    it("renders correctly", () => {
        const tree = TestRenderer
            .create(<ClicksDisplay clicks={22} />)
            .toJSON();
        expect(tree).toMatchSnapshot();
    });
});
```

Basically, we import the special `TestRenderer` renderer function, use it to produce output for our component, and then compare that with the stored snapshot; we'll see how this looks soon. Tests are pretty much always the same: for our `<Counter>` component, the test code would be totally analog:

```
// Source file: src/counterApp/counter.test.js

import React from "react";
import TestRenderer from "react-test-renderer";

import { Counter } from "./counter.component";

describe("clicksDisplay", () => {
    it("renders correctly", () => {
        const tree = TestRenderer
            .create(<Counter count={9} dispatch={() => null} />)
            .toJSON();
        expect(tree).toMatchSnapshot();
    });
});
```

The differences are minimal; it's just a matter of providing the correct expected props, and nothing more. Let's move on to more interesting cases.

 Should you have to render an object with prop values that cannot be predetermined (not the most likely case), you'll have to use special *Property Matchers*; you can read more about them at https://jestjs.io/docs/en/snapshot-testing#property-matchers.

When you have components whose output varies depending on their props, snapshot tests become more interesting because they let you verify that different results are produced as expected. With our countries and regions code, we had these kind of cases: for example, the `<RegionsTable>` component was expected to display a list of regions (if any were provided) or a "No regions" text (if none were available). We should write these tests, then. Let's proceed:

```
// Source file: src/regionsApp/regionsTable.snapshot.test.js

import React from "react";
import TestRenderer from "react-test-renderer";

import { RegionsTable } from "./regionsTable.component";

describe("RegionsTable", () => {
    it("renders correctly an empty list", () => {
        const tree = TestRenderer.create(<RegionsTable list={[]}
```

```
    />).toJSON();
        expect(tree).toMatchSnapshot();
    });

    it("renders correctly a list", () => {
        const tree = TestRenderer
            .create(
                <RegionsTable
                    list={[
                        {
                            countryCode: "UY",
                            regionCode: "10",
                            regionName: "Montevideo"
                        },
                        .
                        .
                        .
                    ]}
                />
            )
            .toJSON();
        expect(tree).toMatchSnapshot();
    });
});
```

We have two distinct cases, just like we described previously: one snapshot will match the *no regions* case, and the other will match what's expected if some regions were given. For the <CountrySelect> component, the code would be similar:

```
// Source file: src/regionsApp/countrySelect.snapshot.test.js

import React from "react";
import TestRenderer from "react-test-renderer";

import { CountrySelect } from "./countrySelect.component";

describe("CountrySelect", () => {
    it("renders correctly when loading, with no countries", () => {
        const tree = TestRenderer
            .create(
                <CountrySelect
                    loading={true}
                    onSelect={() => null}
                    getCountries={() => null}
                    list={[]}
                />
            )
            .toJSON();
```

```
            expect (tree).toMatchSnapshot();
        });

        it("renders correctly a countries dropdown", () => {
            const tree = TestRenderer
                .create(
                    <CountrySelect
                        loading={false}
                        onSelect={() => null}
                        getCountries={() => null}
                        list={[
                            {
                                countryCode: "UY",
                                countryName: "Uruguay"
                            },
                            .
                            .
                            .
                        ]}
                    />
                )
                .toJSON();
            expect (tree).toMatchSnapshot();
        });
    });
```

So, testing components with more than one possible output isn't hard at all, and only requires you to write more than one snapshot test; a simple solution.

Finally, in order to simplify tests, when you have components that themselves have more components, using shallow rendering helps concentrate on the main, high level aspects, and leave the details of the inner components' rendering to other tests. We could whip up something like this, with an invented <CountryAndRegions> component that shows both our countries' drop-down and regions table:

```
// Source file: src/regionsApp/countryAndRegions.test.js

import React from "react";
import ShallowRenderer from "react-test-renderer/shallow";

import { CountrySelect } from "./countrySelect.component";
import { RegionsTable } from "./regionsTable.component";

class CountryAndRegions extends React.Component {
    render() {
        return (
            <div>
```

```
                    <div>
                        Select:
                        <CountrySelect
                            loading={true}
                            onSelect={() => null}
                            getCountries={() => null}
                            list={[]}
                        />
                    </div>
                    <div>
                        Display: <RegionsTable list={[]} />
                    </div>
                </div>
            );
        }
    }

    describe("App for Regions and Countries", () => {
        it("renders correctly", () => {
            const tree = new ShallowRenderer().render(<CountryAndRegions />);
            expect(tree).toMatchSnapshot();
        });
    });
```

Note that the way to use the `ShallowRenderer` differs from the other renderer: you must create a new object, call its `.render()` method, and not use `.toJSON()` anymore. We'll look at how this new test differs from the previous ones soon.

How it works...

Running snapshots is no different from running other tests: you run the `Jest` test script, and all the tests run together.

Running the tests

If you run `npm test`, like we did earlier, you'll now get an output similar to the following listing:

```
PASS src/regionsApp/countryAndRegions.test.js
PASS src/counterApp/counter.test.js
PASS src/regionsApp/countrySelect.test.js
PASS src/regionsApp/regionsTable.test.js
PASS src/counterApp/clicksDisplay.test.js
```

```
Test Suites: 5 passed, 5 total
Tests:       7 passed, 7 total
Snapshots:   7 passed, 7 total
Time:        0.743s, estimated 1s
Ran all test suites related to changed files.

Watch Usage
 › Press a to run all tests.
 › Press p to filter by a filename regex pattern.
 › Press t to filter by a test name regex pattern.
 › Press q to quit watch mode.
 › Press Enter to trigger a test run.
```

The only visible difference is that you get a specific count of snapshots (seven, in this case), but there's something more.

The produced snapshot files

If you check the source code directories, you'll find some new __snapshots__ directories, with some .snap files in it. For example, in the /regionsApp directory, you'd find this:

```
> dir
-rw-r--r-- 1 fkereki users 956 Aug 10 20:48 countryAndRegions.test.js
-rw-r--r-- 1 fkereki users 1578 Jul 28 13:02 countrySelect.component.js
-rw-r--r-- 1 fkereki users 498 Jul 25 23:16 countrySelect.connected.js
-rw-r--r-- 1 fkereki users 1301 Aug 10 20:31 countrySelect.test.js
-rw-r--r-- 1 fkereki users 212 Jul 22 21:07 index.js
-rw-r--r-- 1 fkereki users 985 Aug 9 23:45 regionsTable.component.js
-rw-r--r-- 1 fkereki users 274 Jul 22 21:17 regionsTable.connected.js
-rw-r--r-- 1 fkereki users 1142 Aug 10 20:32 regionsTable.test.js
-rw-r--r-- 1 fkereki users 228 Jul 25 23:16 serviceApi.js
drwxr-xr-x 1 fkereki users 162 Aug 10 20:44 __snapshots__
-rw-r--r-- 1 fkereki users 614 Aug 3 22:22 store.js
-rw-r--r-- 1 fkereki users 2679 Aug 3 21:33 world.actions.js
```

For each .test.js file that includes snapshots, you'll find a corresponding .snap file:

```
> dir __snapshots__/
-rw-r--r-- 1 fkereki users 361 Aug 10 20:44 countryAndRegions.test.js.snap
-rw-r--r-- 1 fkereki users 625 Aug 10 20:32 countrySelect.test.js.snap
-rw-r--r-- 1 fkereki users 352 Aug 10 20:01 regionsTable.test.js.snap
```

The contents of those files show the snapshots that were taken at runtime. For example, the countrySelect.test.js.snap file includes the following code:

```
// Jest Snapshot v1, https://goo.gl/fbAQLP

exports[`CountrySelect renders correctly a countries dropdcwn 1`] = `
<div
  className="bordered"
>
  Country:
  <select
    onChange={[Function]}
  >
    <option
      value=""
    >
      Select a country:
    </option>
    <option
      value="AR"
    >
      Argentina
    </option>
    <option
      value="BR"
    >
      Brazil
    </option>
    <option
      value="UY"
    >
      Uruguay
    </option>
  </select>
</div>
`;

exports[`CountrySelect renders correctly when loading, with no countries
1`] = `
<div
  className="bordered"
>
  Loading countries...
</div>
`;
```

You can see the output for both our cases: one with a full list of countries, and another for when the countries were being loaded, waiting for the service response to arrive.

We can also see a shallow test in the `countryAndRegions.test.js.snap` file:

```
// Jest Snapshot v1, https://goo.gl/fbAQLP

exports[`App for Regions and Countries renders correctly 1`] = `
<div>
  <div>
    Select:
    <CountrySelect
      getCountries={[Function]}
      list={Array []}
      loading={true}
      onSelect={[Function]}
    />
  </div>
  <div>
    Display:
    <RegionsTable
      list={Array []}
    />
  </div>
</div>
`;
```

In this case, note that the `<CountrySelect>` and `<RegionsTable>` components weren't expanded; this means that you are testing only the high level snapshot here, as desired.

Regenerating snapshots

What happens if a component has changed? Just for the sake of it, I made a pretty small change to a component. Upon running the tests, I got a **FAIL** message, with a comparison, that was produced by the usual `diff` command:

```
FAIL src/regionsApp/countryAndRegions.test.js
  ● App for Regions and Countries › renders correctly

    expect(value).toMatchSnapshot()
    Received value does not match stored snapshot 1.
    - Snapshot
    + Received
    @@ -7,11 +7,11 @@
            loading={true}
            onSelect={[Function]}
```

```
            />
          </div>
          <div>
  -       Display:
  +       Displays:
            <RegionsTable
              list={Array []}
            />
          </div>
        </div>
        at Object.it (src/regionsApp/countryAndRegions.test.js:31:22)
            at new Promise (<anonymous>)
        at Promise.resolve.then.el (node_modules/p-map/index.js:46:16)
```

What should you do, then? You should first verify whether the change is correct or not, and in the former case, you could either delete the .snap file (so that it will get regenerated next time) or you can press u, as shown in the test summary:

```
Snapshot Summary
 › 1 snapshot test failed in 1 test suite. Inspect your code changes or
press `u` to update them.
```

Be careful! If you just regenerate the snapshot without verifying that the output is correct, the tests will be worthless; a very bad result!

Measuring test coverage

We already saw how to get coverage for Jest tests back in the *Measuring your test coverage* section of Chapter 5, *Testing and Debugging Your Server*, so in this recipe, we'll just go over some small changes that we'll be making to the test.

How to do it...

We want to measure how thorough our testing is, so let's look at the necessary steps. When working with `Node`, we directly invoked the `jest` command. Here, however, as the application was built by `create-react-app`, we'll have to work a bit differently. We'll have to add a new script to `package.json` that will invoke our tests with extra parameters:

```
"scripts": {
    .
    .
    .
    "test": "react-app-rewired test --env=jsdom",
    "coverage": "react-app-rewired test --env=jsdom --coverage --no-cache",
    .
    .
    .
}
```

The `--coverage` option will produce a coverage report, and also generate a `/coverage` directory, in the same way as with `Node`, and the `--no-cache` option will force Jest to regenerate all results instead of depending on previously, possibly no longer valid, cached values.

 Our `.gitignore` file includes a line reading `/coverage`, so the generated files won't be pushed to the Git server.

How it works...

If you run `npm run coverage`, you'll get both a text output and a HTML one. The former looks like what's shown in the following screenshot; you'll have to accept that in reality, lines are colored green, yellow, or red, depending on the achieved degree of coverage.

In our case, we got quite a lot of red since we only wrote a few tests, instead of going for a full test suite; you may work on completing it on your own, as an *exercise for the reader*!

```
                            chapter09 : bash — Konsole
  File    Edit    View    Bookmarks    Settings    Help

Test Suites: 10 passed, 10 total
Tests:       19 passed, 19 total
Snapshots:   7 passed, 7 total
Time:        2.43s
Ran all test suites.
```

File	% Stmts	% Branch	% Funcs	% Lines	Uncovered Line #s
All files	13.22	10.08	18.87	17.07	
src	0	0	0	0	
App.counter.js	0	0	0	0	1,3,4,6,7,11,20
App.regions.js	0	0	0	0	1,3,4,6,11,15,23
App.routing.auth.js	0	0	0	0	... 22,23,27,58,88
index.js	0	0	0	0	... 17,18,23,25,26
index.without.logging.js	0	0	0	0	1,2,4,5,7,8
registerServiceWorker.js	0	0	0	0	... 36,137,138,139
src/counterApp	13.21	0	18.18	15.56	
clicksDisplay.component.js	100	100	100	100	
clicksDisplay.connected.js	0	100	0	0	1,3,5,7,11
counter.actions.js	62.5	100	0	62.5	13,18,24
counter.component.js	25	100	25	25	22,23,24
counter.connected.js	0	100	0	0	1,3,5,7,9
counter.reducer.js	0	0	0	0	1,3,7,15,17,23,26
index.js	0	100	100	0	1,3,4,6,7,10,11,12
store.js	0	100	100	0	1,3,4,5,7,9,24
src/logging	0	0	0	0	
index.js	0	0	0	0	... 45,46,50,51,53
index.without.level.js	0	0	0	0	... 14,15,16,20,62
src/regionsApp	46.9	43.33	58.06	50	
countrySelect.component.js	100	100	100	100	
countrySelect.connected.js	0	100	0	0	... ,8,13,14,15,18
index.js	0	100	100	0	1,3,4,6
regionsTable.component.js	100	75	100	100	27
regionsTable.connected.js	100	100	100	100	
serviceApi.js	50	100	0	50	6,9
store.js	0	0	0	0	1,3,4,5,6,8,10,19
world.actions.js	52.83	12.5	57.14	53.06	... 14,115,117,120
world.reducer.js	55.56	37.5	100	55.56	36,43,50,65
src/routingApp	0	0	0	0	
authRoute.component.js	0	0	0	0	... 21,22,23,31,32
authRoute.connected.js	0	100	0	0	1,3,5,6
index.js	0	100	100	0	1,3,4,5,7
login.actions.js	0	100	0	0	... 28,29,32,33,35
login.component.js	0	0	0	0	... 30,33,38,42,67
login.connected.js	0	100	0	0	1,3,5,6,8,9,13,15
login.reducer.js	0	0	0	0	... 17,19,26,33,39
protectedRoutes.component.js	0	0	0	0	1,3,4,5,19,29
protectedRoutes.connected.js	0	100	0	0	1,3,5,7
serviceApi.js	0	0	0	0	1,3,5,6
store.js	0	0	0	0	... ,8,10,12,14,16

The colored ASCII output shows the coverage evaluations for all of our source code files; green means good coverage, yellow a medium one, and red means a poor result. Since we only wrote a few tests, we are getting plenty of red!

If you open the `/coverage/lcov-report/index.html` file in a browser, you'll get the same sort of result as in the `Node` chapter, as follows:

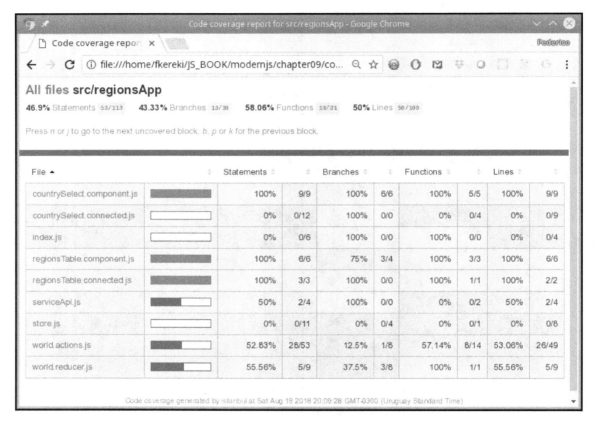

All files src/regionsApp

46.9% Statements 53/113   **43.33%** Branches 13/30   **58.06%** Functions 18/31   **50%** Lines 50/100

Press *n* or *j* to go to the next uncovered block, *b*, *p* or *k* for the previous block.

File ▲		Statements		Branches		Functions		Lines	
countrySelect.component.js		100%	9/9	100%	6/6	100%	5/5	100%	9/9
countrySelect.connected.js		0%	0/12	100%	0/0	0%	0/4	0%	0/9
index.js		0%	0/6	100%	0/0	100%	0/0	0%	0/4
regionsTable.component.js		100%	6/6	75%	3/4	100%	3/3	100%	6/6
regionsTable.connected.js		100%	3/3	100%	0/0	100%	1/1	100%	2/2
serviceApi.js		50%	2/4	100%	0/0	0%	0/2	50%	2/4
store.js		0%	0/11	0%	0/4	0%	0/1	0%	0/8
world.actions.js		52.83%	28/53	12.5%	1/8	57.14%	8/14	53.06%	26/49
world.reducer.js		55.56%	5/9	37.5%	3/8	100%	1/1	55.56%	5/9

Code coverage generated by istanbul at Sat Aug 18 2018 20:09:28 GMT-0300 (Uruguay Standard Time)

The HTML output lets you browse the directories and files of your project. If you click on a specific file, you can even see which lines and functions were executed, and which were skipped by your tests.

 If you want, you can even use the `coverageThreshold` configuration object to specify coverage levels that must be reached, in order for the tests to be considered sufficient; see `https://jestjs.io/docs/en/configuration.html#coveragethreshold-object` for more on this.

We have now finished working with `React` and `Redux`, we've looked at how to build web applications, and we've used our previously developed `Node` server backend. Let's move on to other types of development, starting with mobile applications, also with JS!

11
Creating Mobile Apps with React Native

n this chapter, we'll look at the following recipes:

- Setting things up
- Adding development tools
- Using native components
- Adapting to devices and orientation
- Styling and laying out your components
- Adding platform-specific code
- Routing and navigation

Introduction

In the last few chapters, we showed you how to use React to build web applications, and in this chapter, we'll use a close relative, React Native, to develop native apps that you can run on Android and iOS (Apple) phones.

Setting things up

For development of mobile apps, there are several possible approaches:

- *Use native languages*, with possibilities such as Java or Kotlin for Android, or Objective C or Swift for iOS, using the native development tools for each platform. This can make sure that your app has the best fit for different phones, but will require multiple teams of developers, each with experience of a specific platform.
- *Use a pure website* that the user can visit with the phone's browser. This is the simplest solution, but the application will have limitations, such as not being able to access most of the phone's features because they cannot be used in HTML. Also, running with a wireless connection, which may vary in strength, can sometimes prove hard. You can use any framework for this development, such as React.
- *Develop a hybrid application*, which is a web page, bundled with a browser that includes a set of extensions so that you can use the phone's internal features. For the user, this is a single standalone application, which runs even without a web connection, and that can use most of the phone's features. These applications frequently use Apache Cordova, or a derived product, PhoneGap.

There's a fourth style, provided by React Native, which was developed by Facebook, along the lines of the existing React. Instead of rendering components to a browser's DOM, React Native (which, from now on, we'll shorten to *RN*) invokes native APIs to create internal components that are handled through your JS code. There are some differences between the usual HTML elements and RN's components, but they are not too hard to overcome. With this tool, you are actually building a native app that looks and behaves exactly as any other native application, except that you use a single language, JS, for both Android and iOS development.

In this recipe, we'll set up a RN application so that we can start trying our hand at developing apps for mobile phones.

How to do it...

There are three ways to set up a RN application: completely manually, which you won't want to do; secondly, with packages, using the `react-native-cli` command-line interface; or lastly, by using a package very similar to what we already used for `React`, `create-react-native-app` (from now on, we'll refer to this as *CRAN*). A key difference between the two packages is that with the latter, you cannot include custom native modules, and if you need to do so, you'll have to *eject* the project, which will also require setting up several other tools.

 You can read more about the two latter methods at `https://facebook.github.io/react-native/docs/getting-started.html`, and if you want to be prepared for ejecting, go to `https://github.com/react-community/create-react-native-app/blob/master/EJECTING.md`.

We start by getting a command-line utility, which will include plenty of other packages:

```
npm install create-react-native-app -g
```

Afterwards, we can create and run a simple project with just three commands:

```
create-react-native-app yourprojectname
cd yourprojectname
npm start
```

You're set! Let's see how it works—and yes, we still have some more configuration to do, but it's good to check whether things are going well so far.

How it works...

When you run your app, it starts a server at your machine, at port `19000` or `19001`, to which you will connect using the `Expo` application, which you can find at `https://expo.io/learn`, available for both Android or iOS. Install it by following the instructions onscreen:

The initial screen you get when you fire up your app

When you open the Expo app for the first time, it will look like the following screenshot. Note that both the phone and your machine must be in the same local network, and your machine must also allow connections to ports 19000 and 19001; you may have to modify your firewall for this to work:

On loading the Expo app, you'll have to scan the QR code in order to connect to the server

After you use the **Scan QR Code** option, there will be some synchronization, and soon you'll get to see your basic code running with no problems:

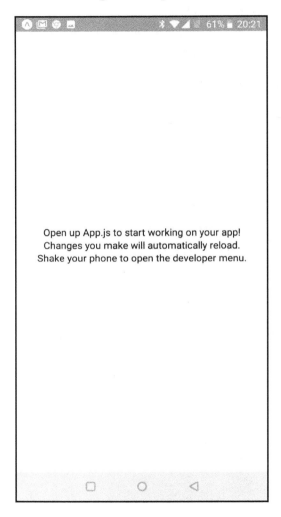

Success—your code is up and running!

Furthermore, if you modify the `App.js` source code, the changes will be immediately reflected in your device, which means all is well! To make sure this happens, shake the phone to enable the debugging menu, and make sure that **Live Reload** and **Hot Reloading** are enabled. You'll also require **Remote JS Debugging** for later. Your phone should look as follows:

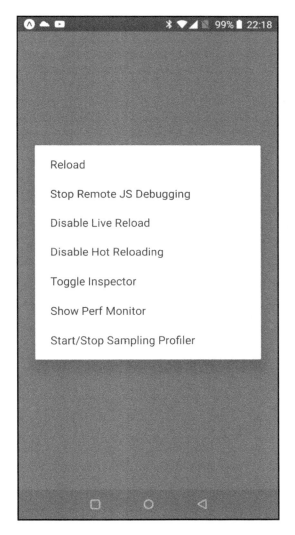

These settings enable reloading and debugging

There's more...

By using the Expo client, CRAN lets you develop for iOS, even if you don't own an Apple computer. (You cannot develop for Apple systems if you have a Windows or Linux machine; you must have a MacBook or similar; this is a restriction of Apple's.) Also, working on an actual device is better in some ways, because you can actually see what the final user will see—no question about it.

However, there may be a couple of reasons why you would want to work differently, perhaps with an emulator on your computer that simulates real-life devices. Firstly, it may be difficult for you to get a dozen or so of the most popular devices in order to test your application on each of them. Secondly, it's more convenient to work on your own machine only, where you can easily debug, take screenshots, copy and paste, and so on. So, you could install Xcode or the Android SDK to enable yourself to work with emulated machines.

We won't be going into details here, because there are a lot of combinations depending on your development OS and the target OS; rather, let's point you to the documentation at https://facebook.github.io/react-native/docs/getting-started.html, where you should click on **Building Projects with Native Code**, and see what's needed in order to work with emulators. After having installed them, you will need the Expo client (as for your actual device) and then you'll be able to run your code on your own machine.

For instance, take a look at the Android emulator simulating a Nexus 5 in the following screenshot:

An emulated Nexus 5 running Android, directly on your screen

With this emulator, you have exactly the same functionality as with an actual device. For example, you can also get the debugging menu, though opening it will be different; for example, on my Linux machine, I needed to press *Ctrl + M*:

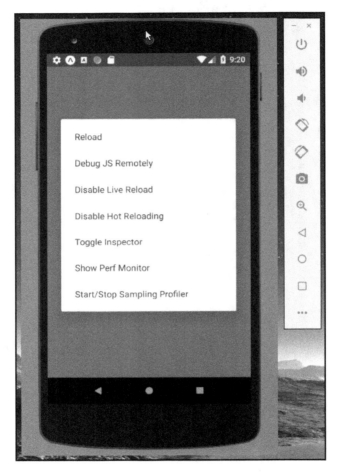

All the functionality that is available on your phone is also available with emulated devices

Using the **Android Virtual Device** (**AVD**) manager, you can create lots of different emulators for phones and tablets; you get similar functionality with Xcode, though that will only work on macOS computers.

Adding development tools

Now, let's now get a better configuration going. As in previous chapters, we want to have ESLint for code checking, `Prettier` for formatting, and `Flow` for data types. CRAN takes care of including `Babel` and `Jest`, so we won't have to do anything for those two.

How to do it...

As opposed to what happened with `React`, where we had to add a special `rewiring` package in order to work with specific configurations, in RN, we can just add some packages and configuration files, and we'll be ready to go.

Adding ESLint

For ESLint, we'll have quite a list of packages we want. We used most of them in `React`, but there's a special addition, `eslint-plugin-react-native`, which adds a few RN-specific rules:

```
npm install --save-dev \
  eslint eslint-config-recommended eslint-plugin-babel \
  eslint-plugin-flowtype eslint-plugin-react eslint-plugin-react-native
```

 If you want to learn more about the (actually few) extra rules added by `eslint-plugin-react-native`, check out its GitHub page at `https://github.com/Intellicode/eslint-plugin-react-native`. Most of them have to do with styles, and one is applied for platform-specific code, but we'll get to this later.

We'll require a separate `.eslintrc` file, as we did with `React`. The appropriate contents includes the following, and I've highlighted the RN-specific additions:

```
{
    "parser": "babel-eslint",
    "parserOptions": {
        "ecmaVersion": 2017,
        "sourceType": "module",
```

```
            "ecmaFeatures": {
                "jsx": true
            }
        },
        "env": {
            "node": true,
            "browser": true,
            "es6": true,
            "jest": true,
            "react-native/react-native": true
        },
        "extends": [
            "eslint:recommended",
            "plugin:flowtype/recommended",
            "plugin:react/recommended",
            "plugin:react-native/all"
        ],
        "plugins": ["babel", "flowtype", "react", "react-native"],
        "rules": {
            "no-console": "off",
            "no-var": "error",
            "prefer-const": "error",
            "flowtype/no-types-missing-file-annotation": 0
        }
    }
```

Adding Flow

Having completed that, ESLint is set to recognize our code, but we have to configure Flow as well:

```
npm install --save-dev flow flow-bin flow-coverage-report flow-typed
```

We'll have to add a couple of lines to the scripts section of package.json:

```
"scripts": {
    "start": "react-native-scripts start",
    .
    .
    .
    "flow": "flow",
    "addTypes": "flow-typed install"
},
```

Then, we have to initialize the working directories of `Flow`:

```
npm run flow init
```

Finally, we can use the same `.flowconfig` files that we used earlier for React:

```
[ignore]
.*/node_modules/.*

[include]

[libs]

[lints]
all=warn
untyped-type-import=off
unsafe-getters-setters=off

[options]
include_warnings=true

[strict]
```

We are now set to use `Flow`, so we can keep working in the style we were accustomed to—we just have to add `Prettier` to format our code, and we'll be on our way!

Adding Prettier

There's not much to re-installing `Prettier`, and all we need is a `npm` command, plus the `.prettierrc` file we've been working with. For the former, just use the following command:

```
npm install --save-dev prettier
```

For configuration, we can use the contents of this `.prettierrc` file:

```
{
    "tabWidth": 4,
    "printWidth": 75
}
```

Now, we are set! We can check it's working; let's do that.

How it works...

Let's check that everything is OK. We'll start by looking at the App.js file that was created by CRAN, and we can immediately verify that the tools work—because a problem is detected! Have a look at the following screenshot:

We can verify that ESLint integration is working, because it highlights a problem

The rule that fails is a new one, from `eslint-plugin-react-native`: `no-color-literals`, because we are using constants in styling, which could prove to be a maintenance headache in the future. We can solve that by adding a variable, and we'll use a type declaration to make sure `Flow` is also running. The new code should be as follows—I've highlighted the required changes:

```
// Source file: App.original.fixed.js

/* @flow */

import React from "react";
import { StyleSheet, Text, View } from "react-native";

export default class App extends React.Component<> {
    render() {
        return (
            <View style={styles.container}>
                <Text>Open up App.js to start working on your app!</Text>
                <Text>Changes you make will automatically reload.</Text>
                <Text>Shake your phone to open the developer menu.</Text>
            </View>
        );
    }
}

const white: string = "#fff";
```

```
const styles = StyleSheet.create({
    container: {
        flex: 1,
        backgroundColor: white,
        alignItems: "center",
        justifyContent: "center"
    }
});
```

So, now that we have restored all our tools, we can get started with actual code!

Using native components

Working with RN is very much like working with React—there are components, state, props, life cycle events, and so on—but there is a key difference: your own components won't be based on HTML, but on specific RN ones. For instance, you won't be using `<div>` elements, but rather `<View>` ones, which will be then mapped by RN to a `UIView` for iOS, or to an `Android.View` for Android. Views can be nested inside views, just as `<div>` tags can be. Views support layout and styling, they respond to touch events and more, so they are basically equivalent to `<div>` tags, leaving aside the mobile environment behaviors and specifics.

There are more differences: components also have different properties than the HTML ones, and you'll have to go through the documentation (at `https://facebook.github.io/react-native/docs/components-and-apis`) to learn about all the possibilities for each specific component.

 You are not limited to using the components that RN provides you with. You can extend your project by using native components developed by other people; for this, a top notch source is the **Awesome React Native** list, at `http://www.awesome-react-native.com/`. Note that it's likely that you'll have to eject your project in order to do this, so check `https://github.com/react-community/create-react-native-app/blob/master/EJECTING.md` for more.

Getting ready

Let's start by going over the list of RN components and APIs you may want to use, and afterward, we'll move to some actual code:

RN Component	Replaces...	Objective
ActivityIndicator	animated GIF	A component to display a circular loading indicator
Button	button	A component to handle touches (clicks)
DatePickerAndroid TimePickerAndroid	input type="date" input type="time"	An API that shows a popup where you can enter a date and a time; for Android
DatePickerIOS	input type="date" input type="datetime-local" input type="time"	A component where the user can enter a date and time; for iOS
FlatList	-	A list component that only renders elements that are visible; used for performance gains
Image	img	A component to display an image
Picker	select	A component to pick a value from a list
Picker.Item	option	A component to define values for the list
ProgressBarAndroid	-	A component to show activity; for Android only
ProgressViewIOS	-	A component to show activity; for iOS only
ScrollView	-	Scrolling container that may contain multiple components and views
SectionList	-	Similar to FlatList, but allows for sectioned lists
Slider	input type="number"	A component to select a value from a range of values
StatusBar	-	A component to manage the app status bar
StyleSheet	CSS	Apply styling to your app
Switch	input type="checkbox"	A component to accept a Boolean value
Text	-	A component to display text
TextInput	input type="text"	A component to enter text using the keyboard
TouchableHighlight TouchableOpacity	-	Wrapper to make views respond to touches
View	div	A basic structural feature for your app
VirtualizedList	-	An even more flexible version of FlatList
WebView	iframe	A component to render web content

There are also many APIs that you may be interested in; some of them are as follows:

API	Description
Alert	Displays an alert dialog with the given title and text
Animated	Simplifies creating animations
AsyncStorage	An alternative to LocalStorage
Clipboard	Provides access for getting and setting clipboard content
Dimensions	Provides access to the device dimensions and orientation changes
Geolocation	Provides access to geolocation; available only for ejected projects
Keyboard	Allows control of keyboard events
Modal	Displays content above a view
PixelRatio	Provides access to the device pixel density
Vibration	Allows control of device vibration

 To have as few problems as possible, you might prefer to eschew platform-specific components and APIs, and make do with the generic, compatible components. However, if you are determined to use some Android or iOS-specific elements, have a look at https://facebook. github.io/react-native/docs/platform-specific-code for details on how to do it; it's not complex. Remember, however, that this will become harder to maintain, and will probably change some interactions or screen designs.

Now, let's revisit an example we wrote for React in Chapter 6, *Developing with React*, the countries and regions page, which will also let us use Redux and async calls, as in Chapter 8, *Expanding Your Application*. Since we are using PropTypes, we'll need that package. Install it with the following command:

```
npm install prop-types --save
```

Then, we'll have to reinstall some packages, starting with Redux and relatives. Actually, CRAN already includes redux and react-redux, so we don't need those, but redux-thunk isn't included. If you had created the project in a different fashion, without using CRAN, you would have needed to install all three packages manually. In both cases, the following command would do, because npm won't install an already installed package:

```
npm install react react-redux redux-thunk --save
```

We'll also be using axios for async calls, as we did earlier in this book:

```
npm install axios --save
```

By default, RN provides `fetch` instead of `axios`. However, RN includes the `XMLHttpRequest` API, which allows us to install `axios` with no problems. For more on network handling, check out `https://facebook.github.io/react-native/docs/network`.

Our final step will be to run the server code that we wrote back in Chapter 4, *Implementing RESTful Services with Node*, so that our app will be able to do async calls. Go to the directory for that chapter, and just enter the following command:

```
node out/restful_server.js.
```

Now, we're set! Let's now see how we can modify our code to make it appropriate for RN.

How to do it...

Since RN uses its own components, your HTML experience will be of little use. Here, we'll see some changes, but in order to derive the full benefits of all of RN's possibilities, you'll have to study its components on your own. Let's start with the `<RegionsTable>` component, which was rather simple. We saw its original code in the *Defining Components* section of Chapter 6, *Developing with React*; here, let's focus on the differences, which are all constrained to the `render()` method. Earlier, we use `<div>` tags and displayed texts in them; here, with RN, we're required to use the `<View>` and `<Text>` elements:

```
// Source file: src/regionsApp/regionsTable.component.js

    .
    .
    .

render() {
    if (this.props.list.length === 0) {
        return (
            <View>
                <Text>No regions.</Text>
            </View>
        );
    } else {
        const ordered = [...this.props.list].sort(
            (a, b) => (a.regionName < b.regionName ? -1 : 1)
        );

        return (
            <View>
```

```
                {ordered.map(x => (
                    <View key={x.countryCode + "-" + x.regionCode}>
                        <Text>{x.regionName}</Text>
                    </View>
                ))}
            </View>
        );
    }
}
```

Notice that there are no changes in the rest of the component, and all your React knowledge is still valid; you just have to adjust the output of your rendering method.

Next, we'll change the `<CountrySelect>` component to use `<Picker>`, which is sort of similar, but we'll require some extra modifications. Let's take a look at our component, highlighting the parts where changes are needed:

```
// Source file: src/regionsApp/countrySelect.component.js

/* @flow */

import React from "react";
import PropTypes from "prop-types";
import { View, Text, Picker } from "react-native";

export class CountrySelect extends React.PureComponent<{
    dispatch: ({}) => any
}> {
    static propTypes = {
        loading: PropTypes.bool.isRequired,
        currentCountry: PropTypes.string.isRequired,
        list: PropTypes.arrayOf(PropTypes.object).isRequired,
        onSelect: PropTypes.func.isRequired,
        getCountries: PropTypes.func.isRequired
    };

    componentDidMount() {
        if (this.props.list.length === 0) {
            this.props.getCountries();
        }
    }

    onSelect = value => this.props.onSelect(value);

    render() {
        if (this.props.loading) {
            return (
                <View>
```

```
                <Text>Loading countries...</Text>
            </View>
        );
    } else {
        const sortedCountries = [...this.props.list].sort(
            (a, b) => (a.countryName < b.countryName ? -1 : 1)
        );

        return (
            <View>
                <Text>Country:</Text>
                <Picker
                    onValueChange={this.onSelect}
                    prompt="Country"
                    selectedValue={this.props.currentCountry}
                >
                    <Picker.Item
                        key={"00"}
                        label={"Select a country:"}
                        value={""}
                    />
                    {sortedCountries.map(x => (
                        <Picker.Item
                            key={x.countryCode}
                            label={x.countryName}
                            value={x.countryCode}
                        />
                    ))}
                </Picker>
            </View>
        );
    }
  }
}
```

Lots of changes! Let's go through them in the order they occur:

- An unexpected change: if you want a `<Picker>` component to display its current value, you must set its `selectedValue` property; otherwise, even if the user selects a country, the change won't be seen onscreen. We'll have to provide an extra prop, `currentCountry`, which we'll get from the store, so we can use it as the `selectedValue` for our list.

- The fired event when the user selects a value is also different; the event handler will be called directly with the chosen value, instead of with an event from which to work with `event.target.value`.

- We have to replace the `<select>` element with `<Picker>`, and provide a `prompt` text prop that will be used when the expanded list is shown onscreen.
- We have to use `<Item>` elements for the individual options, noting that the `label` to be displayed is now a prop.

Let's not forget the change when connecting the list of countries to the store; we'll only have to add an extra property to the `getProps()` function:

```
// Source file: src/regionsApp/countrySelect.connected.js

const getProps = state => ({
    list: state.countries,
    currentCountry: state.currentCountry,
    loading: state.loadingCountries
});
```

Now, all we need to do is see how the main app is set up. Our `App.js` code will be quite simple:

```
// Source file: App.js

/* @flow */

import React from "react";
import { Provider } from "react-redux";

import { store } from "./src/regionsApp/store";
import { Main } from "./src/regionsApp/main";

export default class App extends React.PureComponent<> {
    render() {
        return (
            <Provider store={store}>
                <Main />
            </Provider>
        );
    }
}
```

This is pretty straightforward. The rest of the setup will be in the `main.js` file, which has some interesting details:

```
// Source file: src/regionsApp/main.js

/* @flow */

import React from "react";
import { View, StatusBar } from "react-native";

import {
    ConnectedCountrySelect,
    ConnectedRegionsTable
} from ".";

export class Main extends React.PureComponent<> {
    render() {
        return (
            <View>
                <StatusBar hidden />
                <ConnectedCountrySelect />
                <ConnectedRegionsTable />
            </View>
        );
    }
}
```

Apart from the usage of `<View>` wherever we would previously have used `<div>` (a change to which you should already have gotten used to), there's an added detail: we don't want the status bar to show, so we use the `<StatusBar>` element, and make sure to hide it.

OK, that's it! When writing code for RN, at first you'll have to make some effort to remember what elements are the equivalent of your old and familiar HTML ones, and which props or events change, but aside from that, all your previous knowledge will still be valid. To finish, let's see our app running.

How it works...

Just for variety, instead of using my mobile phone, as I did earlier in this chapter, I decided to use an emulated device. After starting the application with `npm start`, I started my device, and soon got the following:

Our application, just loaded, waiting for the user to select a country

If the user touches the `<Picker>` element, a popup will be displayed, listing the countries that were received from our Node server, as shown in the following screenshot:

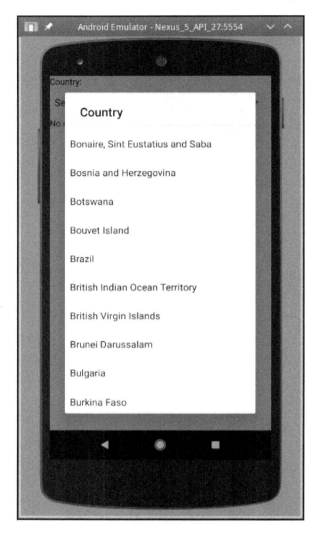

Upon touching on the list of countries, a popup shows up so that the user can select the desired country

When the user actually taps on a country, the `onValueChange` event is fired, and after calling the server, the list of regions is displayed, as follows:

After picking a country, the list of its regions is displayed, as in our earlier HTML React version

Everything works, and is using native components; great! By the way, if you were not very sure about the `selectedValue` problem we described, just omit that prop, and when the user picks on a country, you'll get a bad result:

There are some differences, such as requiring the selectedValue prop to be present, or otherwise the currently picked value won't be updated—even though Brazil was selected, the picker doesn't show it

Here, we went through an example of writing RN code, and as we have seen, it doesn't differ much from simple `React` code, other from the fact that we don't get to use HTML, having us instead depending on different elements.

 We have seen two ways of running our code: with the `Expo` client on our mobile device, and with emulators on our computer. To experiment with RN, there are a couple of online playgrounds you may want to look at Snack, at `https://snack.expo.io/`, and `Repl.it`, at `https://repl.it/ languages/react_native`. In both of these environments, you can create files, edit code, and see the results of your experiments online.

There's more...

One final step, after getting your app to run, is to create a standalone package that you could ideally distribute via the Apple and Google app stores. If you created your application manually, then the process can get a bit complicated, and you'll even require an actual macOS computer, because you won't be able to build for iOS otherwise: you'll have to read how to produce an app with `Xcode` or the Android developers' kit, which can be a bit complicated. With CRAN apps, instead, the process can be simplified, because `Expo` provides an app building capability so that you won't have to. Check out `https://docs. expo.io/versions/latest/guides/building-standalone-apps.html` for specific instructions.

 In any case, no matter which way you decide to proceed for your build process, check out some of the suggestions to help ensure your app will be approved and well received at `https://docs.expo.io/versions/latest/ guides/app-stores.html`.

Adapting to devices and orientation

When we developed a responsive and adaptive web page back in the *Making your application adaptive for enhanced usability* section in `Chapter 7`, *Enhancing Your Application*, we had to deal with the possibility that the window size could be changed at any moment, and our page's contents had to relocate itself properly. With mobile devices, the screen size won't change, but you still have the possibility of a rotation (changing from portrait mode to landscape, and vice versa), so you still have to deal with at least one change. And, of course, if you want to make your app look good on all devices, it's probable that you'll have to take into account the screen size in order to decide how to accommodate your contents.

In this recipe, we'll look at a simple technique to make your application aware of different device types. This technique can be easily upgraded to also cover specific screen dimensions.

 We'll look more at styling later; for the time being, we'll focus on getting the app to recognize the device type and orientation, and then in the next section, we'll follow up with specific style examples.

How to do it...

If we want our app to adapt, we have to be able to answer several questions in our code:

- How can we tell if the device is a tablet or a handset?
- How can we learn if it's in the portrait or landscape modes?
- How do we code a component that will render differently depending on the device type?
- How can we make a component redraw itself automatically upon a screen orientation change?

Let's go over all these questions now. Let's first look at how we can learn about the device type and orientation. RN includes an API, `Dimensions`, that provides data that's necessary to render the app, such as the screen dimensions. How can we, then, learn the device type and orientation? The second question is easier: since there are no square devices (at least so far!), it's enough to see which of the two dimensions is bigger—if the height is bigger, then the device is in portrait mode, and otherwise it's in landscape mode.

The first question, however, is harder. There's no strict rule that defines, in terms of screen sizes, where handsets end and where tablets start, but if we look at information on devices and calculate form factors (the ratio of the longest side to the shortest side), a simple rule appears: if the calculated ratio is 1.6 or below, it's more likely a tablet, and higher ratios suggest handsets.

 If you need more specific data, check `http://iosres.com/` for information on iOS devices, or `https://material.io/tools/devices` and `http://screensiz.es` for a larger variety of devices, in particular for Android, which is used on devices with a much greater variety of screen sizes.

With the following code, we basically return all the information provided by `Dimensions`, plus a couple of attributes (`.isTablet` and `.isPortrait`) to simplify the coding:

```
// Source file: src/adaptiveApp/device.js

/* @flow */

import { Dimensions } from "react-native";

export type deviceDataType = {
    isTablet: boolean,
    isPortrait: boolean,
    height: number,
    width: number,
    scale: number,
    fontScale: number
};

export const getDeviceData = (): deviceDataType => {
    const { height, width, scale, fontScale } = Dimensions.get("screen");

    return {
        isTablet: Math.max(height, width) / Math.min(height, width) <= 1.6,
        isPortrait: height > width,
        height,
        width,
        scale,
        fontScale
    };
};
```

Using the preceding code, we have all we'd need to draw a view in a manner that is suitable for all kinds of devices, sizes, and both possible orientations—but how would we use this data? Let's look at this now, and make our app adjust properly in all cases.

For more on the `Dimensions` API, read `https://facebook.github.io/react-native/docs/dimensions`.

We could directly use the information provided by `getDeviceData()` in our components, but that would pose some problems:

- The components would not be as functional as before, because they would have a hidden dependency in the function
- As a result, testing components would then become a bit harder, because we'd have to mock the function
- Most importantly, it wouldn't be so easy to set the components to re-render themselves when the orientation changes

The solution for all of this is simple: let's put the device data in the store, and then the relevant components (meaning those that need to change their way of rendering) can be connected to the data. We can create a simple component to do this:

```js
// Source file: src/adaptiveApp/deviceHandler.component.js

/* @flow */

import React from "react";
import PropTypes from "prop-types";
import { View } from "react-native";

class DeviceHandler extends React.PureComponent<{
    setDevice: () => any
}> {
    static propTypes = {
        setDevice: PropTypes.func.isRequired
    };

    onLayoutHandler = () => this.props.setDevice();

    render() {
        return <View hidden onLayout={this.onLayoutHandler} />;
    }
}

export { DeviceHandler };
```

The component won't be seen onscreen, so we can add it to our main view anywhere. Connecting the component is the other necessary step; when the `onLayout` event fires (meaning the device's orientation has changed), we'll have to dispatch an action:

```js
// Source file: src/adaptiveApp/deviceHandler.connected.js

/* @flow */
```

```
import { connect } from "react-redux";

import { DeviceHandler } from "./deviceHandler.component";
import { setDevice } from "./actions";

const getDispatch = dispatch => ({
    setDevice: () => dispatch(setDevice())
});

export const ConnectedDeviceHandler = connect(
    null,
    getDispatch
)(DeviceHandler);
```

Of course, we need to define both the actions and the reducer, as well as the store. Let's look at how to do this—we'll begin with the actions. The very minimum we'd need (apart from other actions needed by our hypothetical app) would be as follows:

```
// Source file: src/adaptiveApp/actions.js

/* @flow */

import { getDeviceData } from "./device";

import type { deviceDataType } from "./device"

export const DEVICE_DATA = "device:data";

export type deviceDataAction = {
    type: string,
    deviceData: deviceDataType
};

export const setDevice = (deviceData?: object) =>
    ({
        type: DEVICE_DATA,
        deviceData: deviceData || getDeviceData()
    }: deviceDataAction);

/*
    A real app would have many more actions!
*/
```

We are exporting a thunk that will include the deviceData in it. Note that by allowing it to be provided as a parameter (or a default value being used instead, created by getDeviceData()), we will simplify testing; if we wanted to simulate a landscape tablet, we'd just provide an appropriate deviceData object.

Finally, the reducer would look like the following (obviously, for a real app, there would be many more actions!):

```
// Source file: src/adaptiveApp/reducer.js

/* @flow */

import { getDeviceData } from "./device";

import { DEVICE_DATA } from "./actions";

import type { deviceAction } from "./actions";

export const reducer = (
    state: object = {
        // initial state: more app data, plus:
        deviceData: getDeviceData()
    },
    action: deviceAction
) => {
    switch (action.type) {
        case DEVICE_DATA:
            return {
                ...state,
                deviceData: action.deviceData
            };

        /*
            In a real app, here there would
            be plenty more "case"s
        */

        default:
            return state;
    }
};
```

So, now that we have our device information in the store, we can study how to code adaptive, responsive components.

We can see how to code adaptive and responsive components by using a very basic component that simply displays whether it's a handset or a tablet, and its current orientation. Having access to all of the deviceData objects means that we can take any kind of decisions: what to show, how many elements to display, what size to make them, and so on. We'll be making this example short, but it should be clear how to expand it:

```
// Source file: src/adaptiveApp/adaptiveView.component.js

/* @flow */

import React from "react";
import PropTypes from "prop-types";
import { View, Text, StyleSheet } from "react-native";

import type { deviceDataType } from "./device";

const textStyle = StyleSheet.create({
    bigText: {
        fontWeight: "bold",
        fontSize: 24
    }
});

export class AdaptiveView extends React.PureComponent<{
    deviceData: deviceDataType
}> {
    static propTypes = {
        deviceData: PropTypes.object.isRequired
    };

    renderHandset() {
        return (
            <View>
                <Text style={textStyle.bigText}>
                    I believe I am a HANDSET currently in
                    {this.props.deviceData.isPortrait
                        ? " PORTRAIT "
                        : " LANDSCAPE "}
                    orientation
                </Text>
            </View>
        );
    }

    renderTablet() {
        return (
            <View>
```

```
                    <Text style={textStyle.bigText}>
                        I think I am a
                        {this.props.deviceData.isPortrait
                            ? " PORTRAIT "
                            : " LANDSCAPE "}
                        TABLET
                    </Text>
                </View>
            );
    }


    render() {
        return this.props.deviceData.isTablet
            ? this.renderTablet()
            : this.renderHandset();
    }
}
```

 Don't worry about the textStyle definition—soon we'll be getting into how it works, but for now I think it should be easy to accept that it defines bold, largish, text.

Given this.props.deviceData, we can use the .isTablet prop to decide which method to call (.renderTablet() or .renderHandset()). In those methods, we can then use .isPortrait to decide what layout to use: portrait or landscape. Finally—although we don't show this in our example—we could use .width or .height to show more or fewer components, or to calculate the components' sizes, and so on. We only need to connect the component to the store as follows, and we'll be set:

```
// Source file: src/adaptiveApp/adaptiveView.connected.js

/* @flow */

import { connect } from "react-redux";

import { AdaptiveView } from "./adaptiveView.component";

const getProps = state => ({
    deviceData: state.deviceData
});

export const ConnectedAdaptiveView = connect(getProps)(AdaptiveView);
```

We have everything we need now; let's see it working!

How it works...

We have prepared a (hidden) component that responds to orientation changes by dispatching an action to update the store, and we know how to code a component that will use the device information. Our main page could look as follows:

```
// Source file: src/adaptiveApp/main.js

/* @flow */

import React from "react";
import { View, StatusBar } from "react-native";

import { ConnectedAdaptiveView } from "./adaptiveView.connected";
import { ConnectedDeviceHandler } from "./deviceHandler.connected";

export class Main extends React.PureComponent<> {
    render() {
        return (
            <View>
                <StatusBar hidden />
                <ConnectedDeviceHandler />
                <ConnectedAdaptiveView />
            </View>
        );
    }
}
```

If I run the app on a (simulated) Nexus 5 device in portrait mode, we'd see something like the following:

Our device is recognized as a handset, currently in portrait (vertical) orientation

Rotating the device would produce a different view:

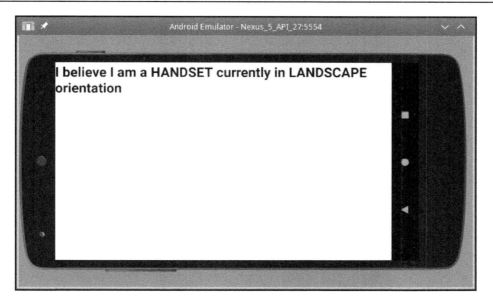

When the orientation changes, the store is updated and the app re-renders itself appropriately

In our design, components never use the `Dimension` API by themselves—since they get the device information from the store, testing the components' behavior for different devices and orientations could be done functionally, without needing to mock anything.

There's more...

In our component, we included everything in a single class, but that could prove not to be great for complex situations. In that case, we could opt to use classes and inheritance, as follows. To start with, create a basic `something.base.js` file, which will contain the base class that you will extend for handsets and tablets. In particular, your `.render()` method should be coded as in the following code snippet, in order to make the class behave as an abstract one that isn't meant to be used directly. You'll need to disable the `ESLint` `react/require-render-return` rule to make `.render()` not to return anything:

```
import React from "react";
import PropTypes from "prop-types";

// eslint-disable-next-line react/require-render-return
class SomethingBase extends React.PureComponent<{
    deviceData: deviceDataType
}> {
    static propTypes = {
```

```
            deviceData: PropTypes.object.isRequired
        };

        render() {
            throw new Error("MUST IMPLEMENT ABSTRACT render() METHOD");
        }
    }

    export { SomethingBase };
```

To continue, write separate `something.handset.js` and `something.tablet.js` files
that extend `SomethingBase` to define the `SomethingHandset` and `SomethingTablet`
components. And, to finish, set up the `something.component.js` file that will be used to
check whether the device is a handset or a tablet, and return either a
`<SomethingHandset>` component or a `<SomethingTablet>` one:

```
    import { SomethingTablet } from "./something.tablet";
    import { SomethingHandset } from "./something.handset";
    import { getDeviceData } from "./device";

    export const Something = getDeviceData().isTablet ? SomethingTablet
    : SomethingHandset;
```

With this style, you'd use and connect `<Something>` components in your code, which,
internally, would really be the appropriate version for the current device's type.

 In computer science terms, this is called the *Factory* design pattern, where
you are able to create an object without actually specifying its class.

Styling and laying out your components

Applying CSS styles to your app is not difficult, but you'll have to un-learn and re-learn
some of the following concepts that are just plain different in RN, when compared to
HTML:

- In web pages, CSS style is global, and applies to all tags; in RN, styling is done
  locally on a component-by-component basis; there is no global styling. Also, you
  don't need *selectors*, because styles are directly associated to components.

- There is no inheritance of styles: in HTML, children inherit some of their parent's style by default, but in RN, if you want this to happen, you'll have to provide the specific desired style to the children. However, if you wish, you can `export` styles and `import` them elsewhere.

- RN styles are completely dynamic: you can use all JS functions to compute whichever values you wish to apply. You could even alter styles on the fly, so an app background color could be lighter during the day, gradually changing to darker colors at night, as time goes by. You won't need anything like SASS or LESS; you can do math and use constants, because that's pure JS.

There are some other minor differences as well:

- RN uses *camelCase* style (such as `fontFamily`) instead of CSS's *kebab-case* style (for example, `font-family`); that's easy enough to get used to. Also, not all usual CSS properties may be present (it depends on specific components), and some may be restricted as to their possible values.

- RN has only two possible measurements: either percentages, or **density independent pixels (DP)**. DP aren't the classic screen pixels from the web; rather, they work well with every device, independently of their pixel density or **pixels per inch (ppi)**, thus guaranteeing a common look for all screens.

- The layout is done with flex, so positioning elements is simpler. You may not have the full set of options that are available for web pages, but what you get is absolutely enough for any kind of layout.

There's much to read about styling in RN (for starters, see `https://facebook.github.io/react-native/docs/style` for an introduction, and `https://facebook.github.io/react-native/docs/height-and-width` and `https://facebook.github.io/react-native/docs/flexbox` for sizing and positioning elements), so here, in this recipe, we'll look at some specific examples by styling our countries-and-regions app.

How to do it...

Let's try to enhance our app a bit. And, to complete what we earlier saw about adaptive and responsive displays, we are going to provide a different layout for portrait and landscape orientations. We won't need media queries or column based layouts; we'll make do with simple styling.

Let's begin by creating styles for the `<Main>` component. We'll be using the `<DeviceHandler>` we developed earlier; both components will be connected to the store. I didn't want to do specific versions for tablets and handsets, but I wanted to display a different layout for portrait and landscape orientations. For the former, I basically used what I had developed earlier, but for the latter, I decided to split the screen in half, displaying the countries selector on the left and the regions list on the right. Oh, and you may notice that I opted to use inline styles, even if it's not the preferred option; since components are usually short, you may place styles right in the JSX code without losing clarity. It's up to you to decide whether you like it or not:

```js
// Source file: src/regionsStyledApp/main.component.js

/* @flow */

import React from "react";
import { View, StatusBar } from "react-native";

import {
    ConnectedCountrySelect,
    ConnectedRegionsTable,
    ConnectedDeviceHandler
} from ".";
import type { deviceDataType } from "./device";

/* eslint-disable react-native/no-inline-styles */

export class Main extends React.PureComponent<{
    deviceData: deviceDataType
}> {
    render() {
        if (this.props.deviceData.isPortrait) {
            .
            . // portrait view
            .
        } else {
            .
            . // landscape view
            .
        }
    }
}
```

When the device is in portrait orientation, I created a `<View>`, occupying all the screen (`flex:1`) and setting its components vertically using `flexDirection:"column"`, although this is actually the default value, so I could have omitted this. I didn't specify a size for the `<CountrySelect>` component, but I set the `<RegionsTable>` to occupy all possible (remaining) space. The detailed code is as follows:

```
// Source file: src/regionsStyledApp/main.component.js

        return (
            <View style={{ flex: 1 }}>
                <StatusBar hidden />
                <ConnectedDeviceHandler />
                <View style={{ flex: 1, flexDirection: "column" }}>
                    <View>
                        <ConnectedCountrySelect />
                    </View>
                    <View style={{ flex: 1 }}>
                        <ConnectedRegionsTable />
                    </View>
                </View>
            </View>
        );
```

For the landscape orientation, some changes were required. I set the direction for the contents of the main view to horizontal (`flexDirection:"row"`) and I added two equal-sized views within. For the first, with the country list, I set its contents vertically and centered, because I thought it looked better that way, instead of appearing at the top. I didn't do anything in particular for the regions list that occupies the right side of the screen:

```
// Source file: src/regionsStyledApp/main.component.js

        return (
            <View style={{ flex: 1 }}>
                <StatusBar hidden />
                <ConnectedDeviceHandler />
                <View style={{ flex: 1, flexDirection: "row" }}>
                    <View
                        style={{
                            flex: 1,
                            flexDirection: "column",
                            justifyContent: "center"
                        }}
                    >
                        <ConnectedCountrySelect />
                    </View>
                    <View style={{ flex: 1 }}>
                        <ConnectedRegionsTable />
```

```
          </View>
        </View>
      </View>
   );
```

If you want a component to occupy a larger piece of space, increase its flex value; *flex* implies that components will flexibly expand or shrink according to the available space, which is shared among all components in direct proportion to their flex values. If I had wanted the countries list to occupy one third of the screen, leaving the other two thirds to the regions list, I would have set `flex:1` for it, and `flex:2` for the regions. Of course, you could also set heights and widths directly (in either DIP values or as percentages), as you could have done with CSS.

As for distributing children in a view, apart from `"center"`, which centers all children in the parent view, you also have several other options:

- `"flex-start"` places them together, at the start of the parent view; here, it's top, given the vertical alignment
- `"flex-end"` would have behaved similarly, but placed the children at the end (here, the bottom) of the parent view
- `"space-between"` splits the extra space equally between the children components
- `"space-around"` also splits extra space equally, but includes space at the start and at the end of the parent view
- `"space-evenly"` splits all space equally between children and dividing spaces

After setting how the components will be laid out in the main flex direction, you can use `alignItems` to specify how the children will be aligned along the secondary flex direction (if `flexDirection` is `"row"`, then the secondary direction will be `"column"`, and vice versa). Possible values are `"flex-start"`, `"center"`, and `"flex-end"`, with similar meaning to what was just given, or you could use `"stretch"`, which will occupy all possible space.

 If you want to experiment with these options, go to `https://facebook.github.io/react-native/docs/flexbox` and modify the code examples. You'll immediately see the effects of your changes, which is the easiest way to understand the effects and implications of each option.

Now, let's style the regions table. For this, I had to make some changes, starting with the need for a `<ScrollView>` instead of a plain `<View>`, given that the list may be too long to fit in the screen. Also, to show you some styles and constants, I decided to go with separate style files. I started by creating a `styleConstants.js` file, which defines a color constant and a simple, full-sized style:

```
// Source file: src/regionsStyledApp/styleConstants.js

/* @flow */

import { StyleSheet } from "react-native";

export const styles = StyleSheet.create({
    fullSize: {
        flex: 1
    }
});

export const lowColor = "lightgray";
```

The interesting thing here, rather than the (assumedly quite Spartan) `fullSize` style, is the fact that you can export styles, or define simple JS constants that will be used elsewhere. In the regions list, I imported both the style and the color:

```
// Source file: src/regionsStyledApp/regionsTable.component.js

/* @flow */

import React from "react";
import PropTypes from "prop-types";
import { View, ScrollView, Text, StyleSheet } from "react-native";

import type { deviceDataType } from "./device";

import { lowColor, fullSizeStyle } from "./styleConstants";

const ownStyle = StyleSheet.create({
    grayish: {
        backgroundColor: lowColor
    }
});

export class RegionsTable extends React.PureComponent<{
    deviceData: deviceDataType,
    list: Array<{
        regionCode: string,
        regionName: string
```

```
        }>
    }> {
        static propTypes = {
            deviceData: PropTypes.object.isRequired,
            list: PropTypes.arrayOf(PropTypes.object).isRequired
        };

        static defaultProps = {
            list: []
        };

        render() {
            if (this.props.list.length === 0) {
                return (
                    <View style={ownStyle.fullSize}>
                        <Text>No regions.</Text>
                    </View>
                );
            } else {
                const ordered = [...this.props.list].sort(
                    (a, b) => (a.regionName < b.regionName ? -1 : 1)
                );

                return (
                    <ScrollView style={[fullSizeStyle, ownStyle.grayish]}>
                        {ordered.map(x => (
                            <View key={`${x.countryCode}-${x.regionCode}`}>
                                <Text>{x.regionName}</Text>
                            </View>
                        ))}
                    </ScrollView>
                );
            }
        }
    }
}
```

There are some interesting details here in the preceding block of code:

- As I said before, I'm using a `<ScrollView>` component to enable the user can browse through lists that are longer than the available space. A `<FlatList>` component would also have been a possibility, though for relatively short and simple lists as here, it wouldn't have made much of a difference.

- I used the imported color to create a local style, `grayish`, which I used later.
- I directly applied the imported `fullSize` style to the regions' `<ScrollView>`.
- I applied more than one style to the second `<ScrollView>`; if you provide an array of styles, they get applied in the order of appearance. In this case, I got a full-sized gray area. Note that the color is only applied if some regions are present; otherwise, the color is unchanged.

Note that the style can be created dynamically, and that allows for interesting effects. To use an example based upon one in RN's documentation at `https://facebook.github.io/react-native/docs/stylesheet`, you could have a title changing style depending on a prop. In the following code, the style for the title would change depending on `this.props.isActive`:

```
<View>
    <Text
        style={[
            styles.title,
            this.props.isActive
                ? styles.activeTitle
                : styles.inactiveTitle
        ]}
    >
        {this.props.mainTitle}
    </Text>
</View>
```

You could produce even more interesting results; remember that you have the full power of JS available to you, and that a style sheet can be created on the fly, so you actually have limitless possibilities.

How it works...

I fired up the emulator, and tried out the code. When in portrait orientation, the view is as shown in the following screenshot; note that I scrolled down, and the app correctly handles it:

Our styled application, showing colors, styles, and a scrollable view

If you change the device's orientation, our device handler logic captures the event, and the app is rendered differently. Here, we can see the split screen, with centered elements on the left and the scrollable view on the right, with its grayish background:

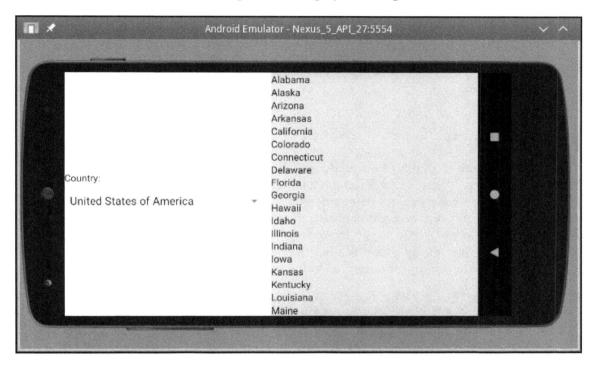

The landscape view gets a different layout, courtesy of new styling rules

As we've seen—and this was only an introduction to the many styling features provided by RN—you can get the same kind of results as with HTML and CSS, though here you are assuredly working with different elements and styles. The possibility of applying the full extent of JS to the definition of styles lets you forget about using tools such as SASS, because all the extra functionality that it would bring is already available through JS itself. Let's look at a further example of styling, this time for text, as we consider how to write code that's been specifically oriented to a given platform.

Adding platform-specific code

Working with the generic components is good enough for most development, but you may want to utilize some platform-specific feature, and RN provides a way to do so. Obviously, if you start along this trend, you may end with a bigger job, and it will be harder to maintain your code, but done judiciously, it can add some extra *pizzazz* to your app.

In this recipe, we'll look at how to adapt your app so that it will fit in better for whatever platform it runs on.

How to do it...

The simplest way to recognize your platform is by using the Platform module, which includes a property, Platform.OS, which tells you whether you are running Android or iOS. Let's go for a simple example. Imagine you wanted to use some monospaced font in your app. It happens that the right name for the relevant font family varies between platforms: it would be "monospace" in Android, but "AmericanTypewriter" (among others) on Apple devices. By checking Platform.OS, we can set the .fontFamily attribute of a style sheet appropriately, as in the following screenshot:

```
const styles = StyleSheet.create({
  container: {
    alignItems: 'center',
    justifyContent: 'center',
  },
  paragraph: {
    fontFamily: Platform.OS === "android" ? "monospace" : "AmericanTypewriter",
    margin: 24,
    marginTop: 0,
    fontSize: 22,
    fontWeight: 'bold',
    textAlign: 'center',
    color: '#34495e',
  },
```

Using Platform.OS is the simplest way to detect the platform of the device

If you wanted to pick several attributes differently, you might want to use `Platform.select()` instead:

```
const headings = Platform.select({
    android: { title: "An Android App", subtitle: "directly from Google" },
    ios: { title: "A iOS APP", subtitle: "directly from Apple" }
});
```

In this case, `headings.title` and `headings.subtitle` will get the values appropriate to the current platform, either Android or iOS. Obviously, you could have managed this using `Platform.OS`, but this style may be shorter.

 For more on the available font families in both Android and iOS devices, you may want to check the lists at `https://github.com/react-native-training/react-native-fonts`. Take into account, however, that the list may change from version to version.

How it works...

Just for variety, I decided to try out platform detection in Snack (at `https://snack.expo.io/`; we mentioned this tool earlier in this chapter) because it would be much faster and simpler than running code on two actual devices.

I opened the page, and in the sample application that is provided, I just added the
.fontFamily change I showed earlier, and tested the results for both platforms:

The Snack emulators show the different look of my app, with distinct fonts for Android (left) and iOS (right)

As we can see, issues with platform differences can be easily solved, and the end users of
your app will get something that more closely match their expectations regarding colors,
fonts, components, APIs, and whatnot.

There's more...

The changes we saw in this recipe are rather small in scope. If you wanted some radically bigger differences, such as, for example, getting a date by using a `DatePickerIOS` component for iOS, but the `DatePickerAndroid` API for Android, there's another feature you should consider.

Let's say your own component was named `AppropriateDatePicker`. If you create two files, respectively named `appropriateDatePicker.component.ios.js` and `appropriateDatePicker.component.android.js`, then when you import your component with `import { AppropriateDatePicker } from "AppropriateDatePicker"`, the `.ios.js` version will be used for Apple, and the `.android.js` version for Android: simple!

> For a complete description of the `Platform` module and the platform-specific options, read `https://facebook.github.io/react-native/docs/platform-specific-code`.

Routing and navigating

With the `React` router, you just used a `<Link>` component to navigate from one page to another, or used methods to programmatically open a different page. In RN, there is a different way of working, and the `react-navigation` package is practically the de facto standard. Here, you define a navigator (there are several kinds to pick from) and provide it with the screens (views) that it should handle, and then forget about it! The navigator will handle everything on its own, showing and hiding screens, adding tabs or a sliding drawer, or whatever it needs, and you don't have to do anything extra!

In this recipe, we'll revisit an example from earlier pages of this book, and show how the router is written differently, to highlight differences in style.

> There's more to navigation than what we'll see here. Check out the API documentation at `https://reactnavigation.org/docs/en/api-reference.html` for more, and beware if you Google around, because the `react-navigation` package has evolved, and many sites have references to old methods that are currently deprecated.

How to do it...

In the `React` part of this book, we built a complete routing solution, including public and protected routes, using a login view to enter the user's name and password. In a mobile application, since the user is more restricted, we can just make do by enabling a login at the beginning, and enabling the normal navigation afterward. All the work with usernames, passwords, and tokens is basically the same as before, so for now, let's only worry about navigation, which is different in RN, and forget the common details.

For starters, let's have some views—a empty screen with some centered text will do:

```
// Source file: src/routingApp/screens.js

/* @flow */

import React, { Component } from "react";
import {
    Button,
    Image,
    StyleSheet,
    Text,
    TouchableOpacity,
    View
} from "react-native";

const myStyles = StyleSheet.create({
    fullSize: {
        flex: 1
    },
    fullCenteredView: {
        flex: 1,
        flexDirection: "column",
        justifyContent: "center",
        alignItems: "center"
    },
    bigText: {
        fontSize: 24,
        fontWeight: "bold"
    },
    hamburger: {
        width: 22,
        height: 22,
        alignSelf: "flex-end"
    }
});

// continues...
```

Then, to simplify creating all the needed views, let's have a `makeSimpleView()` function that will produce a component. We'll include a *hamburger* icon at the top right, which will open and close the navigation drawer; we'll see more on this later. We'll use this function to create most of our views, and we'll add a `SomeJumps` extra view, with three buttons that allow you to navigate directly to another view:

```
// ...continued

const makeSimpleView = text =>
    class extends Component<{ navigation: object }> {
        displayName = `View:${text}`;

        render() {
            return (
                <View style={myStyles.fullSize}>
                    <TouchableOpacity
                        onPress={this.props.navigation.toggleDrawer}
                    >
                        <Image
                            source={require("./hamburger.png")}
                            style={myStyles.hamburger}
                        />
                    </TouchableOpacity>
                    <View style={myStyles.fullCenteredView}>
                        <Text style={myStyles.bigText}>{text}</Text>
                    </View>
                </View>
            );
        }
    };

export const Home = makeSimpleView("Home");
export const Alpha = makeSimpleView("Alpha");
export const Bravo = makeSimpleView("Bravo");
export const Charlie = makeSimpleView("Charlie");
export const Zulu = makeSimpleView("Zulu");
export const Help = makeSimpleView("Help!");

export const SomeJumps = (props: object) => (
    <View style={myStyles.fullSize}>
        <Button
            onPress={() => props.navigation.navigate("Alpha")}
            title="Go to Alpha"
        />
        <Button
            onPress={() => props.navigation.navigate("Bravo")}
            title="Leap to Bravo"
```

```
        />
        <Button
            onPress={() => props.navigation.navigate("Charlie")}
            title="Jump to Charlie"
        />
    </View>
);
```

 Here, for simplicity, and given that we weren't using props or state, and that the view was simple enough, I used a functional definition for the `SomeJumps` component, instead of using a class, as in most other examples. If you want to revisit the concept, have a look at `https://reactjs.org/docs/components-and-props.html`.

Where does the `navigation` prop come from? We'll see more in the next section, but some explanation can be given here. Whenever you create a navigator, you provide it with a set of views to handle. All those views will get an extra prop, `navigation`, which has a set of methods you can use, such as toggling the visibility of the drawer, navigating to a given screen, and more. Read about this object at `https://reactnavigation.org/docs/en/navigation-prop.html`.

Now, let's create the drawer itself. This will handle the sidebar menu and show whatever view is needed. The `createDrawerNavigator()` function gets an object with the screens that will be handled, and a set of options; here, we just specified the color of the drawer itself and its width (there are plenty more possibilities, which are detailed at `https://reactnavigation.org/docs/en/drawer-navigator.html`):

```
// Source file: src/routingApp/drawer.js

/* @flow */

import { createDrawerNavigator } from "react-navigation";

import {
    Home,
    Alpha,
    Bravo,
    Charlie,
    Zulu,
    Help,
    SomeJumps
} from "./screens";

export const MyDrawer = createDrawerNavigator(
    {
        Home: { screen: Home },
```

```
            Alpha: { screen: Alpha },
            Bravo: { screen: Bravo },
            Charlie: { screen: Charlie },
            Zulu: { screen: Zulu },
            ["Get Help"]: { screen: Help },
            ["Some jumps"]: { screen: SomeJumps }
        },
        {
            drawerBackgroundColor: "lightcyan",
            drawerWidth: 140
        }
    );
```

The result of createDrawerNavigation() is itself a component that will take care of
showing whatever view is selected, showing and hiding the drawer menu, and so on. We
only need to create the main application itself.

Next, let's creating our navigable application, since we now have a set of views and a
drawer navigator to handle them. The main view for our application is then quite
simple—check out its .render() method, and you'll have to agree:

```
// Source file: App.routing.js

/* @flow */

import React from "react";
import { StatusBar } from "react-native";

import { MyDrawer } from "./src/routingApp/drawer";

class App extends React.Component {
    render() {
        return (
            <React.Fragment>
                <StatusBar hidden />
                <MyDrawer />
            </React.Fragment>
        );
    }
}

export default App;
```

An interesting point: since navigators are components. If you so wish, you can have a navigator within another navigator! For example, you could create a `TabNavigator`, and include it in a drawer navigator: when the corresponding option is selected, you'll get a tabbed view onscreen, now governed by the tab navigator. You can compose navigators in any way you wish, allowing for very complex navigation structures, if you want.

How it works...

When you open the application, the initial route is shown. There are several options you can provide, such as `initialRouteName` to specify which should be the first shown view, `order` to rearrange the drawer items, and even a custom `contentComponent` if you want to draw the contents of the drawer by yourself; all in all, there is lots of flexibility. Your first screen should look like the following:

Our drawer navigator showing the initial screen

The usual way to open a drawer is by sliding from the left (although you can also set the drawer to slide in from the right). We also provided the hamburger icon to toggle the drawer open and shut. Opening the drawer should look like the following screenshot:

The opened drawer shows the menu, with the current screen highlighted, and the rest of the screen darkened

Clicking on any menu item will hide the current view, and show the selected view instead. For instance, we could select the `Some jumps` screen, as shown here:

After selecting an option, the drawer menu slides close on its own, and the selected screen is shown

In this particular screen, we show three buttons, all of which use the `props.navigation.navigate()` method to show a different screen. This shows that your navigation is not restricted to using the drawer, but that you can also directly browse in any way you want.

There's more...

You'll notice we didn't make any reference to `Redux`, as we did in the `React` chapters. While use of this is possible, the `react-navigation` authors are tending toward *not* enabling this, and at `https://reactnavigation.org/docs/en/redux-integration.html`, you can read the following:

> *"Warning: in the next major version of React Navigation, to be released in Fall 2018, we will no longer provide any information about how to integrate with Redux and it may cease to work. Issues related to Redux that are posted on the React Navigation issue tracker will be immediately closed. Redux integration may continue to work, but it will not be tested against or considered when making any design decisions for the library."*

This warning suggests that it wouldn't be a good idea to devote space to an integration that might just go away and stop working without notice. If you want to integrate `Redux`, read the preceding page I mentioned, but be careful when you update the navigation package, just in case something stops working. You have been warned!

Testing and Debugging Your Mobile App

12

In this chapter, we'll be looking into the following recipes:

- Writing unit tests with Jest
- Adding snapshot testing
- Measuring test coverage
- Using Storybook to preview components
- Debugging your app with react-native-debugger
- Debugging in an alternative way with Reactotron

Introduction

In the previous chapter, we saw how to develop a `React Native` (RN) mobile app, and along the same lines of what we did with `Node` and `React`, here let's complete the development process for mobile apps by looking at testing and debugging our app.

Writing unit tests with Jest

Doing unit testing for RN won't be too much of a surprise, because it happens that we'll be able to reuse most of what we learned before (for example, using `Jest` also with snapshots, or how to test `Redux`), except for some small details that must be taken care of, as we'll see.

In this recipe, we'll look at how to set up unit tests for RN, along the lines of what we already did for `Node` and `React`.

Getting ready

Whether you create the mobile app with CRAN (as we did) or with `react-native init`, support for `Jest` is baked in; otherwise, you'd have to install it on your own, as we saw in the *Unit testing your code* section of `Chapter 5`, *Testing and Debugging Your Server*. Depending on how you create the project, there's a difference in the `Jest` configuration in `package.json`; we won't have to do anything, but see `https://jestjs.io/docs/en/tutorial-react-native.html#setup` for the alternative. We'll have to add a few packages that we used earlier, but that's about it:

```
npm install enzyme enzyme-adapter-react-16 react-test-renderer redux-mock-store --save
```

After doing this, we can write tests as before. Let's look at an example.

How to do it...

Earlier in this book, we wrote some tests for the countries and regions application, and since we have already rewritten that in RN, why not also rewrite the tests? That will allow us to verify that writing unit tests for RN isn't that different from writing them for plain `React`. We had already written tests for the `<RegionsTable>` component; let's check them here:

```
// Source file: src/regionsStyledApp/regionsTable.test.js

/* @flow */

import React from "react";
import Enzyme from "enzyme";
import Adapter from "enzyme-adapter-react-16";

import { RegionsTable } from "./regionsTable.component";

Enzyme.configure({ adapter: new Adapter() });

const fakeDeviceData = {
    isTablet: false,
    isPortrait: true,
    height: 1000,
    width: 720,
    scale: 1,
    fontScale: 1
};
```

```
describe("RegionsTable", () => {
    it("renders correctly an empty list", () => {
        const wrapper = Enzyme.shallow(
            <RegionsTable deviceData={fakeDeviceData} list={[]} />
        );
        expect(wrapper.contains("No regions."));
    });

    it("renders correctly a list", () => {
        const wrapper = Enzyme.shallow(
            <RegionsTable
                deviceData={fakeDeviceData}
                list={[
                    {
                        countryCode: "UY",
                        regionCode: "10",
                        regionName: "Montevideo"
                    },
                    {
                        countryCode: "UY",
                        regionCode: "9",
                        regionName: "Maldonado"
                    },
                    {
                        countryCode: "UY",
                        regionCode: "5",
                        regionName: "Cerro Largo"
                    }
                ]}
            />
        );

        expect(wrapper.contains("Montevideo"));
        expect(wrapper.contains("Maldonado"));
        expect(wrapper.contains("Cerro Largo"));
    });
});
```

The differences are really minor, and mostly it's the same code:

- We had to add fakeDeviceData, but that was only because our RN component required it
- We changed Enzyme.render() to Enzyme.shallow()
- We changed the way we use the wrapper object to check for included text directly, using wrapper.contains()

For a complete (and long!) list of all the available wrapper methods, check out `https://github.com/airbnb/enzyme/blob/master/docs/api/shallow.md`.

We can also have a look at the `<CountrySelect>` tests, which involved simulating events. We can skip the tests that are practically identical to the `React` versions; let's focus on the last one of our original tests:

```
// Source file: src/regionsStyledApp/countrySelect.test.js

/* @flow */
import React from "react";
import Enzyme from "enzyme";
import Adapter from "enzyme-adapter-react-16";

import { CountrySelect } from "./countrySelect.component";

Enzyme.configure({ adapter: new Adapter() });

const threeCountries = [
    {
        countryCode: "UY",
        countryName: "Uruguay"
    },
    {
        countryCode: "AR",
        countryName: "Argentina"
    },
    {
        countryCode: "BR",
        countryName: "Brazil"
    }
];

const fakeDeviceData = {
    isTablet: false,
    isPortrait: true,
    height: 1000,
    width: 720,
    scale: 1,
    fontScale: 1
}

describe("CountrySelect", () => {
    //
    // some tests omitted
```

```
        //

    it("correctly calls onSelect", () => {
        const mockGetCountries = jest.fn();
        const mockOnSelect = jest.fn();

        const wrapper = Enzyme.shallow(
            <CountrySelect
                deviceData={fakeDeviceData}
                loading={false}
                currentCountry={""}
                onSelect={mockOnSelect}
                getCountries={mockGetCountries}
                list={threeCountries}
            />
        );

        wrapper.find("Picker").simulate("ValueChange", "UY");

        expect(mockGetCountries).not.toHaveBeenCalled();
        expect(mockOnSelect).toHaveBeenCalledTimes(1);
        expect(mockOnSelect).toHaveBeenCalledWith("UY");
    });
});
```

The key difference between how we wrote the tests for React and for RN is in the way we
.find() the element to click (RN uses a Picker component, instead of a group of option
elements), and the event we simulate ("ValueChange" instead of "change"). Other than
that, though, the code is the same as earlier.

 For native modules, you may have to use mocks in order to simulate the
expected behaviors. We haven't used such modules in our code, but
should you require any of them, use the same mocking styles we saw in
Chapter 5, *Testing and Debugging Your Server*, and for React itself in
Chapter 10, *Testing Your Application*.

Having gone over some of the differences in RN components testing, we are done, because
there are no differences in the code when testing actions or reducers. These use the same
style of functional unit testing that doesn't involve any particular RN features, so we have
nothing more to say. In the next section, we'll look at our test run.

How it works...

Running the tests is achieved with a single command, as before:

```
npm test
```

The output is as shown in the following screenshot—note that we also ran some tests we had copied from the `React` chapter, without any changes, and they also performed perfectly:

```
fkereki@fk-server:~/JS_BOOK/modernjs/chapter12> npm test

> chapter12b@0.1.0 test /home/fkereki/JS_BOOK/modernjs/chapter12
> jest

 PASS  src/regionsStyledApp/regionsTable.test.js
 PASS  src/regionsStyledApp/regionsTable.connected.test.js
 PASS  src/regionsStyledApp/countrySelect.test.js
 PASS  src/regionsStyledApp/world.reducer.test.js
 PASS  src/regionsStyledApp/world.actions.test.js

Test Suites: 5 passed, 5 total
Tests:       11 passed, 11 total
Snapshots:   0 total
Time:        1.395s
Ran all test suites.
```

All our components' tests run OK

So, apart from the need to use shallow rendering, and possibly some changes in the way we access elements or simulate events, coding unit tests for RN is pretty much the same as for `React`, which is good news. We are forgetting something, however – what about snapshot testing? Let's move on to that.

Adding snapshot testing

Snapshot testing with RN is a nice surprise, because you won't have to change anything in the way you worked before. Let's just look at a few examples, and you'll be convinced.

How to do it...

We had already seen snapshot testing in the *Testing changes with snapshots* section of Chapter 10, *Testing Your Application*. It so happens that the very same code will work perfectly with RN apps, without demanding any specific changes, other than those depending on variations in the code. Let's consider the following example. The `<RegionsTable>` component we had developed earlier has an extra prop in RN: `deviceData`. So, we can copy the original snapshot test code and just add the new prop, as follows:

```
// Source file: src/regionsStyledApp/regionsTable.snapshot.test.js

/* @flow */

import React from "react";
import TestRenderer from "react-test-renderer";

import { RegionsTable } from "./regionsTable.component";

const fakeDeviceData = {
    isTablet: false,
    isPortrait: true,
    height: 1000,
    width: 720,
    scale: 1,
    fontScale: 1
};

describe("RegionsTable", () => {
    it("renders correctly an empty list", () => {
        const tree = TestRenderer.create(
            <RegionsTable deviceData={fakeDeviceData} list={[]} />
        ).toJSON();
        expect(tree).toMatchSnapshot();
    });

    it("renders correctly a list", () => {
        const tree = TestRenderer.create(
            <RegionsTable
                deviceData={fakeDeviceData}
                list={[
                    {
                        countryCode: "UY",
                        regionCode: "10",
                        regionName: "Montevideo"
                    },
                    {
```

```
                              countryCode: "UY",
                              regionCode: "9",
                              regionName: "Maldonado"
                          },
                          {
                              countryCode: "UY",
                              regionCode: "5",
                              regionName: "Cerro Largo"
                          }
                      ]}
                  />
             ).toJSON();
             expect(tree).toMatchSnapshot();
         });
    });
```

If you bother to compare versions, you'll see that the only changed parts are the ones I highlighted in bold text, and they have to do with the different components, not with any RN-specific thing. If you write a snapshot test for the <CountrySelect> component, you'll find exactly the same result: the only necessary changes have to do with its new props (deviceData, currentCountry), but pose no other difficulty.

For variety, let's add snapshot testing to our <Main> component. We'll have two interesting details here:

- Since our component rendered itself differently in portrait or landscape mode, we should have two tests; and
- As the component includes connected components, we must not forget to add a <Provider> component, lest the connections cannot be made.

The code would be as follows; in particular, notice the varying device data, and the <Provider> inclusion:

```
// Source file: src/regionsStyledApp/main.snapshot.test.js

/* @flow */

import React from "react";
import { Provider } from "react-redux";
import TestRenderer from "react-test-renderer";

import { Main } from "./main.component";
import { store } from "./store";

const fakeDeviceData = {
    isTablet: false,
```

```
        isPortrait: true,
        height: 1000,
        width: 720,
        scale: 1,
        fontScale: 1
};

describe("Main component", () => {
    it("renders in portrait mode", () => {
        const tree = TestRenderer.create(
            <Provider store={store}>
                <Main
                    deviceData={{ ...fakeDeviceData, isPortrait: true }}
                />
            </Provider>
        ).toJSON();
        expect(tree).toMatchSnapshot();
    });

    it("renders in landscape mode", () => {
        const tree = TestRenderer.create(
            <Provider store={store}>
                <Main
                    deviceData={{ ...fakeDeviceData, isPortrait: false }}
                />
            </Provider>
        ).toJSON();
        expect(tree).toMatchSnapshot();
    });
});
```

How it works...

Since all our snapshot tests' filenames end with `.snapshot.js`, we can run all the snapshot tests with a single command:

```
npm test snapshot
```

The first time you run the tests, as before, the snapshots will be created:

```
fkereki@fk-server:~/JS_BOOK/modernjs/chapter12> npm test snapshot

> chapter12b@0.1.0 test /home/fkereki/JS_BOOK/modernjs/chapter12
> jest "snapshot"

 PASS  src/regionsStyledApp/main.snapshot.test.js
  › 2 snapshots written.
 PASS  src/regionsStyledApp/regionsTable.snapshot.test.js
  › 2 snapshots written.
 PASS  src/regionsStyledApp/countrySelect.snapshot.test.js
  › 2 snapshots written.

Snapshot Summary
 › 6 snapshots written in 3 test suites.

Test Suites: 3 passed, 3 total
Tests:       6 passed, 6 total
Snapshots:   6 added, 6 total
Time:        0.844s, estimated 1s
Ran all test suites matching /snapshot/i.
```

As with React, the first run will create snapshots for components

If we check the __snapshots__ directory, we will find the three produced .snap files within. Their format is the same as with the React examples that we developed earlier. Let's just have a look at the <RegionsTable> one, which we showed earlier:

```
// Jest Snapshot v1, https://goo.gl/fbAQLP

exports[`RegionsTable renders correctly a list 1`] = `
<RCTScrollView
  style={
    Array [
      undefined,
      Object {
        "backgroundColor": "lightgray",
      },
    ]
  }
>
  <View>
    <View>
      <Text
        accessible={true}
```

```
          allowFontScaling={true}
          ellipsizeMode="tail"
        >
          Cerro Largo
        </Text>
      </View>
      <View>
        <Text
          accessible={true}
          allowFontScaling={true}
          ellipsizeMode="tail"
        >
          Maldonado
        </Text>
      </View>
      <View>
        <Text
          accessible={true}
          allowFontScaling={true}
          ellipsizeMode="tail"
        >
          Montevideo
        </Text>
      </View>
    </View>
  </View>
</RCTScrollView>
`;

exports[`RegionsTable renders correctly an empty list 1`] = `
<View
  style={undefined}
>
  <Text
    accessible={true}
    allowFontScaling={true}
    ellipsizeMode="tail"
  >
    No regions.
  </Text>
</View>
`;
```

If in the future you run the tests again and nothing has been changed, then the results will be three **PASS** green messages:

```
fkereki@fk-server:~/JS_BOOK/modernjs/chapter12> npm test snapshot

> chapter12b@0.1.0 test /home/fkereki/JS_BOOK/modernjs/chapter12
> jest "snapshot"

PASS  src/regionsStyledApp/main.snapshot.test.js
PASS  src/regionsStyledApp/regionsTable.snapshot.test.js
PASS  src/regionsStyledApp/countrySelect.snapshot.test.js

Test Suites: 3 passed, 3 total
Tests:       6 passed, 6 total
Snapshots:   6 passed, 6 total
Time:        0.893s, estimated 1s
Ran all test suites matching /snapshot/i.
```

Our snapshot tests were all successful

Everything is working fine, so we can aver that writing snapshot tests doesn't add any complications to RN testing, and can be carried out without difficulty.

Measuring test coverage

In the same way we did for `Node` and `React`, back in `Chapter 5`, *Testing and Debugging Your Server*, and `Chapter 10`, *Testing Your Application*, we would like to have a measure of the coverage of our tests to see how thorough we have been, and to be able to detect pieces of code that need more work. Fortunately, we'll be able to manage with the same tools that we did before, so this recipe will prove easy to implement.

How to do it...

The setup for the application done by CRAN included `Jest`, as we saw, and `Jest` provides us with the coverage option we need. To start, we'll have to add a simple script, to run our suite of tests with a couple of extra parameters:

```
"scripts": {
    .
    .
    .
```

```
    "test": "jest",
    "coverage": "jest --coverage --no-cache",
},
```

That's all, we don't have anything else to do; let's just see it work!

How it works...

Running the tests is simple; we just have to use the new script:

```
npm run coverage
```

All of the suite will be run in the same fashion as in the previous sections of this chapter, but at the end, a text summary will be produced. As earlier, colors will be used: green for well-covered (in terms of testing) source files, yellow for intermediate coverage, and red for low or no coverage:

File	% Stmts	% Branch	% Funcs	% Lines	Uncovered Line #s
All files	78.57	62.96	74.29	78.1	
chapter12	100	100	100	100	
App.js	100	100	100	100	
chapter12/src/regionsStyledApp	78.38	62.96	73.53	77.88	
countrySelect.component.js	100	100	100	100	
countrySelect.connected.js	85.71	100	75	80	17
device.js	100	100	100	100	
deviceHandler.component.js	33.33	100	50	33.33	15,16
deviceHandler.connected.js	75	100	50	66.67	9
index.js	100	100	100	100	
main.component.js	100	100	100	100	
main.connected.js	100	100	100	100	
regionsTable.component.js	100	75	100	100	47
regionsTable.connected.js	100	100	100	100	
serviceApi.js	75	100	50	75	9
store.js	100	100	100	100	
styleConstants.js	100	100	100	100	
world.actions.js	66.67	0	54.55	67.5	... 99,100,103,104
world.reducer.js	50	44.44	100	50	30,43,50,57,72

```
Test Suites: 9 passed, 9 total
Tests:       18 passed, 18 total
Snapshots:   6 passed, 6 total
Time:        8.733s
Ran all test suites.
```

Running Jest with the coverage option enabled produces the same type of result we saw for Node and React

We can also examine the HTML-produced files, which can be found at `/coverage/lcov-report`. Open the `index.html` file there, and you'll get an interactive version of the report, as in the following screenshot:

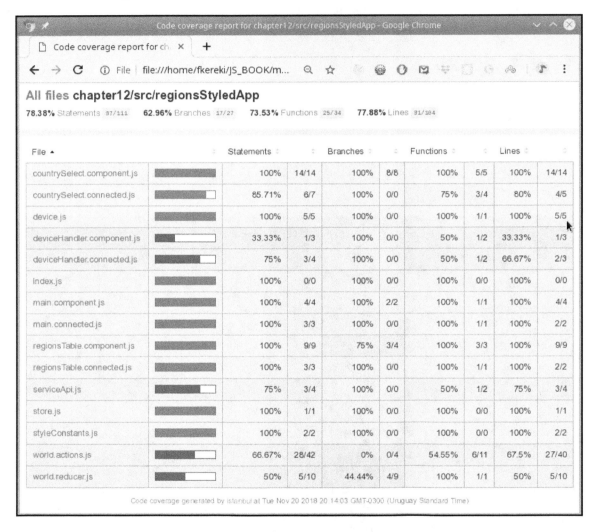

File ▲		Statements		Branches		Functions		Lines	
countrySelect.component.js		100%	14/14	100%	8/8	100%	5/5	100%	14/14
countrySelect.connected.js		85.71%	6/7	100%	0/0	75%	3/4	80%	4/5
device.js		100%	5/5	100%	0/0	100%	1/1	100%	5/5
deviceHandler.component.js		33.33%	1/3	100%	0/0	50%	1/2	33.33%	1/3
deviceHandler.connected.js		75%	3/4	100%	0/0	50%	1/2	66.67%	2/3
index.js		100%	0/0	100%	0/0	100%	0/0	100%	0/0
main.component.js		100%	4/4	100%	2/2	100%	1/1	100%	4/4
main.connected.js		100%	3/3	100%	0/0	100%	1/1	100%	2/2
regionsTable.component.js		100%	9/9	75%	3/4	100%	3/3	100%	9/9
regionsTable.connected.js		100%	3/3	100%	0/0	100%	1/1	100%	2/2
serviceApi.js		75%	3/4	100%	0/0	50%	1/2	75%	3/4
store.js		100%	1/1	100%	0/0	100%	0/0	100%	1/1
styleConstants.js		100%	2/2	100%	0/0	100%	0/0	100%	2/2
world.actions.js		66.67%	28/42	0%	0/4	54.55%	6/11	67.5%	27/40
world.reducer.js		50%	5/10	44.44%	4/9	100%	1/1	50%	5/10

All files chapter12/src/regionsStyledApp

78.38% Statements 87/111   **62.96%** Branches 17/27   **73.53%** Functions 25/34   **77.88%** Lines 91/184

Code coverage generated by istanbul at Tue Nov 20 2018 20:14:03 GMT-0300 (Uruguay Standard Time)

The produced HTML report is interactive, and lets you see what you missed in your tests

For example, if you wondered why the `deviceHandler.component.js` file got such a low value (and never mind that you didn't write a test for it; all code should be covered, if possible), you can click on it and see the reason. In our case, the `onLayoutHandler` code was (logically) never called, thus lowering the coverage for the file:

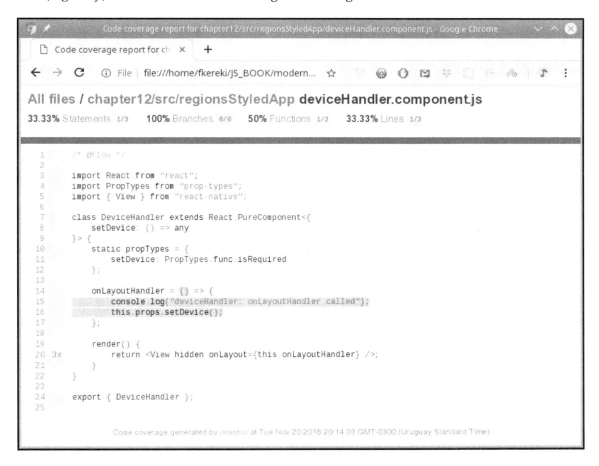

Clicking on a file shows what lines were executed and which ones (red background) were missed

 To see some ways to disable reporting lines that aren't covered, or for cases you don't want to consider, look at `https://github.com/gotwarlost/istanbul/blob/master/ignoring-code-for-coverage.md`.

Using Storybook to preview components

Storybook, our React tool from the *Simplifying component development with Storybook* section of Chapter 6, *Developing with React*, can also be used to help with the development of components, so in this recipe, let's look at how to use it in order to simplify our work.

Getting ready

Installing Storybook is simple, and similar to what we did before; the react-native-storybook-loader package will let us place our *.story.js files wherever we want, and find them anyway. The second command will take a while, installing many packages; be warned! Also, a storybook directory will be created, at the root of your directory. Install Storybook with the following command:

```
npm install @storybook/cli react-native-storybook-loader --save-dev
npx storybook init
```

> The storybook/Stories directory can be safely deleted, as we'll place our stories elsewhere, along with the components being demonstrated, as we did earlier in this book.

Running Storybook within an RN app created with CRNA requires an extra step: providing an appropriate App.js file. The simplest way to achieve this is with a one-liner file:

```
export default from './storybook';
```

However, this is a problem—how will you run your app? You could, of course, have two different App.storybook.js and App.standard.js files, and copy one or another to App.js, but that would quickly become boring if done manually. Of course, you could make do with some npm scripts. The following would work for Linux or macOS machines by using the cp command to copy files, but would require small changes for Windows devices:

```
"scripts": {
    "start": "cp App.standard.js App.js && react-native-scripts start",
    .
    .
    .
    "storybook": "cp App.storybook.js App.js && rnstl && storybook start -p
7007"
},
```

We'll also need to add some configuration for the loader in `package.json`. The following makes the loader look for `*.story.js` files in the `./src` directory, and generates a `storyLoader.js` file with the found stories:

```
"config": {
    "react-native-storybook-loader": {
        "searchDir": [
            "./src"
        ],
        "pattern": "**/*.story.js",
        "outputFile": "./storybook/storyLoader.js"
    }
},
```

Finally, we'll have to modify `storybook/index.js`, as follows:

```
import { getStorybookUI, configure } from "@storybook/react-native";

import { loadStories } from "./storyLoader";

configure(loadStories, module);
const StorybookUI = getStorybookUI({ port: 7007, onDeviceUI: true });

export default StorybookUI;
```

We are now set; let's write some stories!

 Check `https://github.com/storybooks/storybook/tree/master/app/react-native` for more documentation on `Storybook` for RN, and `https://github.com/elderfo/react-native-storybook-loader` for details on the loader we are using.

How to do it...

Let's write some stories. We can start with the `<RegionsTable>` component, which is quite simple: it doesn't include any actions, and just displays data. We can write two cases: when an empty list of regions is provided, and when a non-empty one is given. We don't have to think too much about the needed fake data, because we can reuse what we wrote for our unit tests! Consider the following code:

```
// Source file: src/regionsStyledApp/regionsTable.story.js

/* @flow */

import React from "react";
```

```
import { storiesOf } from "@storybook/react-native";

import { Centered } from "../../storybook/centered";
import { RegionsTable } from "./regionsTable.component";

const fakeDeviceData = {
    isTablet: false,
    isPortrait: true,
    height: 1000,
    width: 720,
    scale: 1,
    fontScale: 1
};

storiesOf("RegionsTable", module)
    .addDecorator(getStory => <Centered>{getStory()}</Centered>)
    .add("with no regions", () => (
        <RegionsTable deviceData={fakeDeviceData} list={[]} />
    ))
    .add("with some regions", () => (
        <RegionsTable
            deviceData={fakeDeviceData}
            list={[
                {
                    countryCode: "UY",
                    regionCode: "10",
                    regionName: "Montevideo"
                },
                {
                    countryCode: "UY",
                    regionCode: "9",
                    regionName: "Maldonado"
                },
                {
                    countryCode: "UY",
                    regionCode: "5",
                    regionName: "Cerro Largo"
                }
            ]}
        />
    ));
```

Adding a decorator to center the displayed component is just for clarity: the necessary <Centered> code is simple, and needs a little of the styling we saw in the previous chapter:

```
// Source file: storybook/centered.js
```

```
/* @flow */

import React from "react";
import { View, StyleSheet } from "react-native";
import PropTypes from "prop-types";

const centerColor = "white";
const styles = StyleSheet.create({
    centered: {
        flex: 1,
        backgroundColor: centerColor,
        alignItems: "center",
        justifyContent: "center"
    }
});

export class Centered extends React.Component<{ children: node }> {
    static propTypes = {
        children: PropTypes.node.isRequired
    };

    render() {
        return <View style={styles.centered}>{this.props.children}</View>;
    }
}
```

Now, setting up stories for <CountrySelect> is more interesting, because we have
actions. We'll provide two to the component: one when the user clicks on it to select a
country, and an other for the getCountries() callback that the component will use to get
the list of countries:

```
// Source file: src/regionsStyledApp/countrySelect.story.js

/* @flow */

import React from "react";
import { storiesOf } from "@storybook/react-native";
import { action } from "@storybook/addon-actions";

import { Centered } from "../../storybook/centered";
import { CountrySelect } from "./countrySelect.component";

const fakeDeviceData = {
    isTablet: false,
    isPortrait: true,
    height: 1000,
    width: 720,
    scale: 1,
```

```
        fontScale: 1
};

storiesOf("CountrySelect", module)
    .addDecorator(getStory => <Centered>{getStory()}</Centered>)
    .add("with no countries yet", () => (
        <CountrySelect
            deviceData={fakeDeviceData}
            loading={true}
            currentCountry={""}
            onSelect={action("click:country")}
            getCountries={action("call:getCountries")}
            list={[]}
        />
    ))
    .add("with three countries", () => (
        <CountrySelect
            deviceData={fakeDeviceData}
            currentCountry={""}
            loading={false}
            onSelect={action("click:country")}
            getCountries={action("call:getCountries")}
            list={[
                {
                    countryCode: "UY",
                    countryName: "Uruguay"
                },
                {
                    countryCode: "AR",
                    countryName: "Argentina"
                },
                {
                    countryCode: "BR",
                    countryName: "Brazil"
                }
            ]}
        />
    ));
```

We are all set now; let's see how this works.

How it works...

To view the `Storybook` app, we need to use the script we edited in the preceding section. Start by running the `storybook` script (it would be better to do this in a separate console) and then run the application itself, as follows:

```
// at one terminal
npm run storybook

// and at another terminal
npm start
```

The first command produces a bit of output, allowing us to confirm that our script works and that all our stories were found. The following code was slightly edited for clarity:

```
> npm run storybook

> chapter12b@0.1.0 storybook /home/fkereki/JS_BOOK/modernjs/chapter12
> cp App.storybook.js App.js && rnstl && storybook start -p 7007

Generating Dynamic Storybook File List

Output file:
/home/fkereki/JS_BOOK/modernjs/chapter12/storybook/storyLoader.js
Patterns: ["/home/fkereki/JS_BOOK/modernjs/chapter12/src/**/*.story.js"]
Located 2 files matching pattern
'/home/fkereki/JS_BOOK/modernjs/chapter12/src/**/*.story.js'
Compiled story loader for 2 files:
/home/fkereki/JS_BOOK/modernjs/chapter12/src/regionsStyledApp/countrySelect
.story.js
/home/fkereki/JS_BOOK/modernjs/chapter12/src/regionsStyledApp/regionsTable.
story.js
=> Loading custom .babelrc from project directory.
=> Loading custom addons config.
=> Using default webpack setup based on "Create React App".
Scanning 1424 folders for symlinks in
/home/fkereki/JS_BOOK/modernjs/chapter12/node_modules (18ms)

RN Storybook started on => http://localhost:7007/

Scanning folders for symlinks in
/home/fkereki/JS_BOOK/modernjs/chapter12/node_modules (27ms)


+--------------------------------------------------------------------+
|                                                                    |
| Running Metro Bundler on port 8081.                                |
|                                                                    |
```

```
| Keep Metro running while developing on any JS projects. Feel free to |
| close this tab and run your own Metro instance if you prefer.        |
|                                                                      |
| https://github.com/facebook/react-native                            |
|                                                                      |
+----------------------------------------------------------------------+

Looking for JS files in
   /home/fkereki/JS_BOOK/modernjs/chapter12/storybook
   /home/fkereki/JS_BOOK/modernjs/chapter12
   /home/fkereki/JS_BOOK/modernjs/chapter12

Metro Bundler ready.

webpack built bab22529b80fbd1ce576 in 2918ms
Loading dependency graph, done.
```

We can open the browser and get a view quite similar to the one we got for the web apps and React:

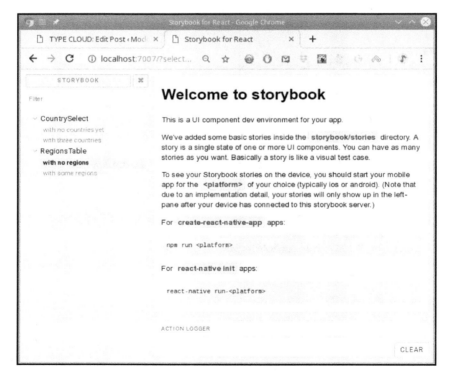

You can select stories in the sidebar, and the app will show them

If you select a story in the menu, the app will show it, as follows:

The app shows the story you picked in the browser

You can also select which story to show in the app itself by pressing the hamburger menu at the top left of the preceding screenshot. The resulting selection menu is shown as follows:

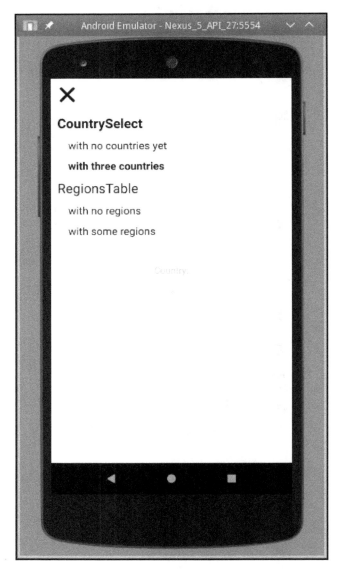

The app also lets you select what story to show

Finally, you can see the actions in the browser. Let's imagine you open the story for the country list with three countries:

The country selector lets you interact with actions

If you click on **Brazil**, the browser will show the fired actions. First, we can see **call:getCountries** when the `getCountries()` callback is called, and then **click:country** when you click on an option:

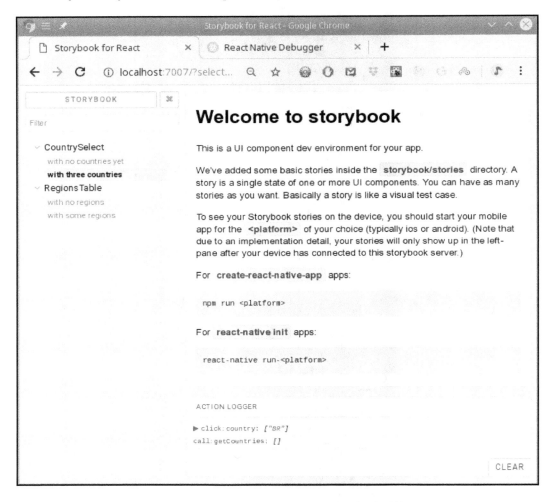

As with web apps, you can interact with stories and see what actions were called with which parameters

So, we've seen that adding stories is practically the same as for the web, and you get an extra tool to help in development—you should take this into account.

Debugging your app with react-native-debugger

Debugging a RN app is harder than working with a web app, because everything you want to do is done remotely; you cannot just run a fully powered debugger in your mobile device. There are several tools that can help you out with this, and in this section, we'll consider a "catch-all" tool, `react-native-debugger`, that includes a powerful trio of utilities, with which most (if not all) of your requirements should be fulfilled.

The basic tools you'll require for thorough debugging (and we already met them earlier) would be the following:

- Chrome Developer Tools, at `https://developers.google.com/web/tools/chrome-devtools/`, for access to the console and more
- React devtools (in its standalone version) at `https://github.com/facebook/react-devtools`, for dealing with components
- The `Redux DevTools` extension, at `https://github.com/zalmoxisus/redux-devtools-extension`, for inspecting actions and state

You could, of course, install each of them separately, and work with the trio, but having all of them together is undoubtedly simpler, so we'll follow that track. So, let's get on with debugging our code in this recipe!

 You can read about the basics of RN debugging at `http://facebook.github.io/react-native/docs/debugging`, and study `react-native-debugger` at `https://github.com/jhen0409/react-native-debugger`.

Getting started

We'll have to install several packages in order to get everything to work. First, just get the `react-native-debugger` executable from its releases page at `https://github.com/jhen0409/react-native-debugger/releases`. Installation is just a matter of unzipping the file you downloaded; execution simply requires running the executable within the unzipped directory.

We'll require a couple of packages in order to connect our app, which be get by running either on a simulator or on an actual device, with `react-native-debugger`. Let's install these with the following command:

```
npm install react-devtools remote-redux-devtools --save-dev
```

We now have everything we need. Let's look at a few details on integrating the tools (mostly, the Redux debugger) with our app, and we'll be ready to start debugging.

How to do it...

Let's look at how to set up our app so that we can use our debugging tools. To start with, we'll require a simple change in the store creation code, adding a couple of lines, as shown here:

```
// Source file: src/regionsStyledApp/store.js

/* @flow */

import { createStore, applyMiddleware } from "redux";
import thunk from "redux-thunk";
import { composeWithDevTools } from "redux-devtools-extension";

import { reducer } from "./world.reducer";

export const store = createStore(
    reducer,
    composeWithDevTools(applyMiddleware(thunk))
);
```

Just for the sake of it—so that we can actually get some debugging messages – I added sundry `console.log()` and `console.error()` calls throughout the code. For consistency, I wanted to use debug (from `https://www.npmjs.com/package/debug`), as we did earlier in the book, but it won't work, because it requires `LocalStorage`, and in RN you get `AsyncStorage` instead, with a different API. Just as an example, we'll look at some log output from `world.actions.js`. I didn't bother logging the output from successful API calls, because we'll be getting that through `react-native-debugger`, as we'll see:

```
// Source file: src/regionsStyledApp/world.actions.js

.
.
.
```

```
export const getCountries = () => async dispatch => {
    console.log("getCountries: called");
    try {
        dispatch(countriesRequest());
        const result = await getCountriesAPI();
        dispatch(countriesSuccess(result.data));
    } catch (e) {
        console.error("getCountries: failure!");
        dispatch(countriesFailure());
    }
};

export const getRegions = (country: string) => async dispatch => {
    console.log("getRegions: called with ", country);
    if (country) {
        try {
            dispatch(regionsRequest(country));
            const result = await getRegionsAPI(country);
            dispatch(regionsSuccess(result.data));
        } catch (e) {
            console.error("getRegions: failure with API!");
            dispatch(regionsFailure());
        }
    } else {
        console.error("getRegions: failure, no country!"):
        dispatch(regionsFailure());
    }
};
```

We have everything in place; let's try it out.

How it works...

First, run your app with the following command:

```
npm start
```

On your device (whether real or emulated), access the developer menu by shaking (on an actual device) or using command + *m* for macOS or *Ctrl* + *M* for Windows or Linux. At the very least, you want to enable remote JS debugging:

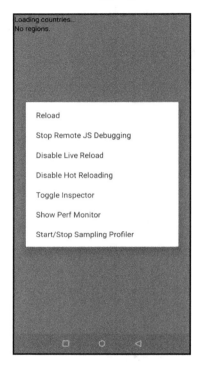

Using the device's developer menu to enable remote JS debugging

Now, open the `react-native-debugger` app by clicking on the executable you downloaded. If nothing happens, even after reloading the app, then the problem is surely due to a different port being set: in the menu, select **Debugger**, then **New Window**, and pick port **19001**, and everything should be fine. When you start the app, it should look like the following screenshot. Notice all our logs on the right of the screen, the first `Redux` actions in the top left, and the React tools in the bottom left (and if you don't care for some of these tools, right-click on the screen to hide any of the three):

Upon successful connection, you'll see the three tools in react-native-debugger running at once

If you check the **Network** tab, you'll see that the API calls from the app don't appear by default. There's a simple workaround for this: right-click on `react-native-debugger`, choose **Enable network inspection**, then right-click on the Chrome Developer tools and select **Log XMLHttpRequests**, and all calls will appear:

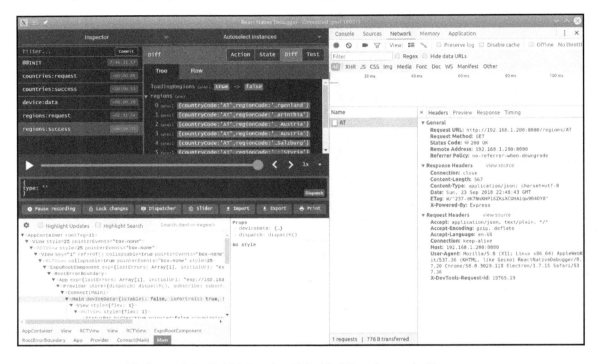

API calls are not displayed by default, but can be enabled by right-clicking on the react-native-debugger screen

You can also inspect `AsyncStorage`—see the following screenshot. I opted to hide `React` and `Redux DevTools`, as I mentioned previously, just for clarity. Since our app doesn't actually use `AsyncStorage`, I fudged it a bit: note that you can use a `require()` function on any module, and then use it directly:

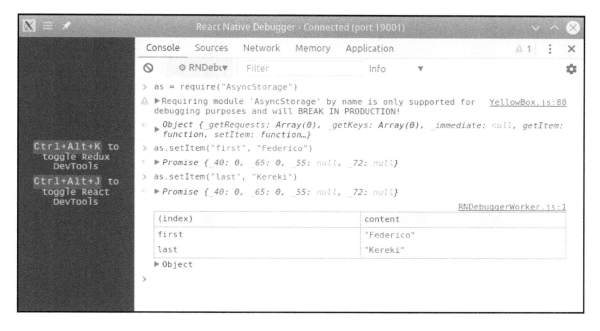

Examining AsyncStorage with the RN debugger

What else can we say? Not much, actually, since these tools are basically the same that we saw when using `React` for the web. The interesting detail here is that you get all of them together, instead of having to deal with many separate windows. Let's finish this chapter by considering an alternate tool, which you might just happen to prefer.

Debugging in an alternate way with Reactotron

While it's possible that `react-native-debugger` will work for most of your needs, there's another package that, while coinciding with many features, also adds some new ones, or at least give a twist to old ones: Reactotron. This tool can also work with plain `React`, but I opted to show it here with RN, because it's more likely you'll require it. After all, `React` tools for the web are easy to use without any undue complications, while RN debugging is, as we've seen, a bit more of a challenge. Reactotron is said to be more efficient than `react-native-debugger`, but I won't attest to that: check it out, and be aware that **Your mileage may vary (YMMV)**. Let's finish this chapter with a recipe to demonstrate this alternative way of debugging.

Getting ready

We'll need a pair of packages: the basic Reactotron one, along with `reactotron-redux` to help with Redux. Install them with the following command:

```
npm install reactotron-react-native reactotron-redux --save-dev
```

 Reactotron can work with `redux-sagas` instead of `redux-thunk`, and even with MobX, instead of Redux. Read more about this at `https://github.com/infinitered/reactotron`.

You'll also require the native executable tool that connects to your app. Go to the releases page at `https://github.com/infinitered/reactotron/releases` and get the package that matches your environment: in my particular case, I just downloaded and unzipped the `Reactotron-linux-x64.zip` file. For macOS users, there is another possibility: check out `https://github.com/infinitered/reactotron/blob/master/docs/installing.md`.

After installing all of this, we are ready to prepare our app; let's do so now!

How to do it...

It's a fact that you can use both Reactotron and `react-native-debugger` at the same time, but in order to avoid mixing things up, let's have a separate `App.reactotron.js` file and a few other changes. We have to follow a few simple steps. First, let's begin by adding a new script to `package.json` in order to enable running our app with Reactotron:

```
"scripts": {
    "start": "cp App.standard.js App.js && react-native-scripts start",
    "start-reactotron": "cp App.reactotron.js App.js && react-native-
scripts start",
    .
    .
    .
```

Second, let's configure the connection and plugins. We'll create a `reactotronConfig.js` file to establish the connection with `Reactotron`:

```
// Source file: reactotronConfig.js

/* @flow */

import Reactotron from "reactotron-react-native";
import { reactotronRedux } from "reactotron-redux";

const reactotron = Reactotron.configure({
    port: 9090,
    host: "192.168.1.200"
})
    .useReactNative({
        networking: {
            ignoreUrls: /\/logs$/
        }
    })
    .use(
        reactotronRedux({
            isActionImportant: action => action.type.includes("success")
        })
    )
    .connect();

Reactotron.log("A knick-knack is a thing that sits on top of a whatnot");
Reactotron.warn("If you must make a noise, make it quietly");
Reactotron.error("Another nice mess you've gotten me into.");

export default reactotron;
```

Here are a few details about some of the values and options in the previous code snippet:

- `192.168.1.200` is the IP for my machine, and `9090` is the suggested port to use.
- The `ignoreUrls` option for networking gets rid of some calls made by Expo, but not our own code, making for a clearer session.
- The `isActionImportant` function lets you highlight some actions so that they will be more noticeable. In our case, I opted to pick out the `countries:success` and `regions:success` actions, both of which include `"success"` in their types, but of course, you could select any others as well.

`Reactotron` also includes logging functions, so I added three (useless!) calls just to see how they appear in our debugging. I didn't want to show all the logging we added, but you would probably want to use the following commands so all your logging will go to `Reactotron` instead:

```
console.log = Reactotron.log;
console.warn = Reactotron.warn;
console.error = Reactotron.error;
```

Now, we have to adapt our store so that it will work with the `reactotron-redux` plugin. I opted to make a copy of `store.js`, called `store.reactotron.js`, with the following necessary changes:

```
// Source file: src/regionsStyledApp/store.reactotron.js

/* @flow */

import { AsyncStorage } from "react-native";
import { applyMiddleware } from "redux";
import thunk from "redux-thunk";
import reactotron from "../../reactotronConfig";

import { reducer } from "./world.reducer";

export const store = reactotron.createStore(
    reducer,
    applyMiddleware(thunk)
);

// continues...
```

Just for variety, and to be able to see how `Reactotron` handles `AsyncStorage`, I added a few (totally useless!) lines to set a few items:

```
// ...continued
```

```
(async () => {
    try {
        await AsyncStorage.setItem("First", "Federico");
        await AsyncStorage.setItem("Last", "Kereki");
        await AsyncStorage.setItem("Date", "Sept.22nd");
        await AsyncStorage.getItem("Last");
    } catch (e) {
    }
})();
```

Next, let's make some changes to our App.js file. These changes are minor: simply include the configuration file, and use the store I just adapted:

```
// Source file: App.reactotron.js

/* @flow */

import React from "react";
import { Provider } from "react-redux";

import "./reactotronConfig";

import { store } from "./src/regionsStyledApp/store.reactotron";
import { ConnectedMain } from "./src/regionsStyledApp/main.connected";

export default class App extends React.PureComponent<> {
    render() {
        return (
            <Provider store={store}>
                <ConnectedMain />
            </Provider>
        );
    }
}
```

Now, we're ready; let's see it work!

> For full documentation on Reactotron, check out the developers' web page at https://github.com/infinitered/reactotron. Reactotron includes more plugins that can help you when working with Redux or Storybook to do benchmarking of slow functions, or to log messages, so you may find many things of interest there.

How it works...

To use `Reactotron`, just start it (double-clicking should do the job) and you'll get the initial screen shown in the following screenshot. The tool will just wait for your app to connect; sometimes, it may take more than one attempt to get the initial connection started, but after that, things should move along swimmingly:

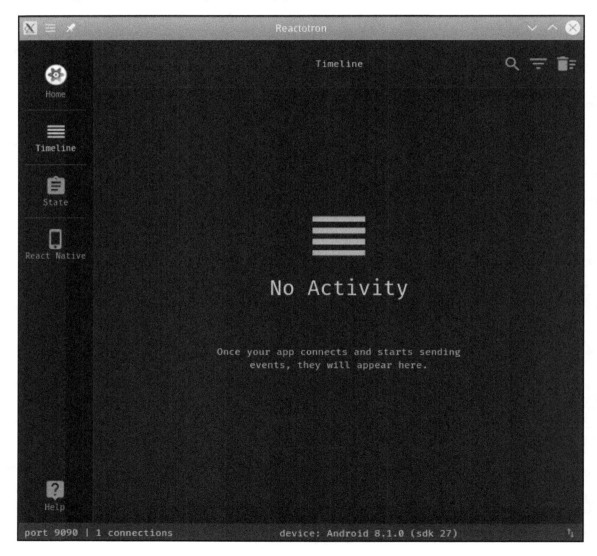

The initial screen for Reactotron shows it waiting for connections

After you start the application, you will see that it made a connection. `Reactctron` shows some details: for example, the device is on Android, running version 8.1.0, and we can also see the size and scale of the device. See the following screenshot:

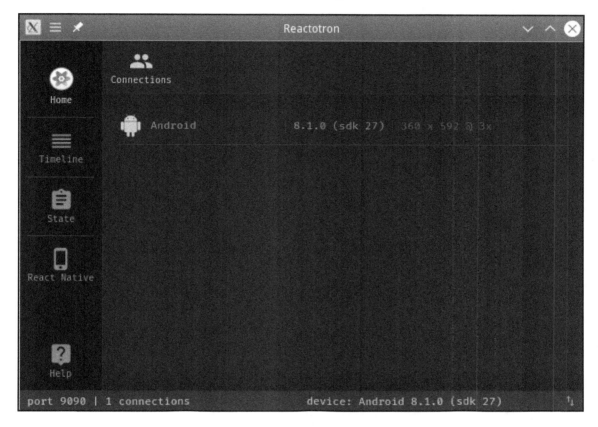

After a connection is made, you can see the details about the device

When the app starts, we get something like the following screenshot. Notice the highlighted action (`countries:success`), the **ASYNC STORAGE** logs, and the three lines from old movies that we added (trivia time, for movie buffs: who said those three lines?):

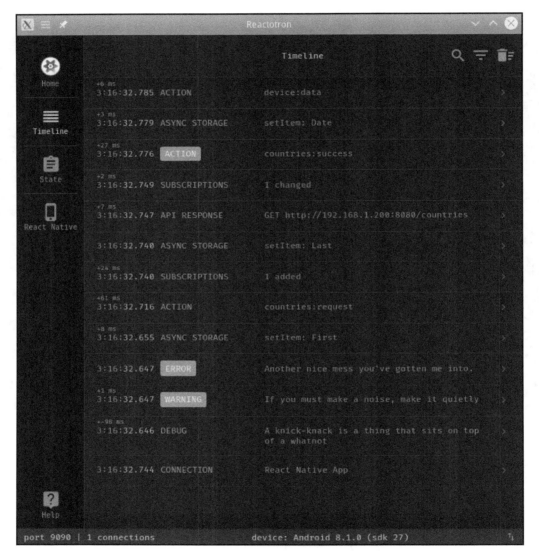

When our app starts to run, we get all these debugging texts in the Reactotron window

We can also see the state of the `Redux` store—see the following screenshot. I
inspected `deviceData` and one of the countries:

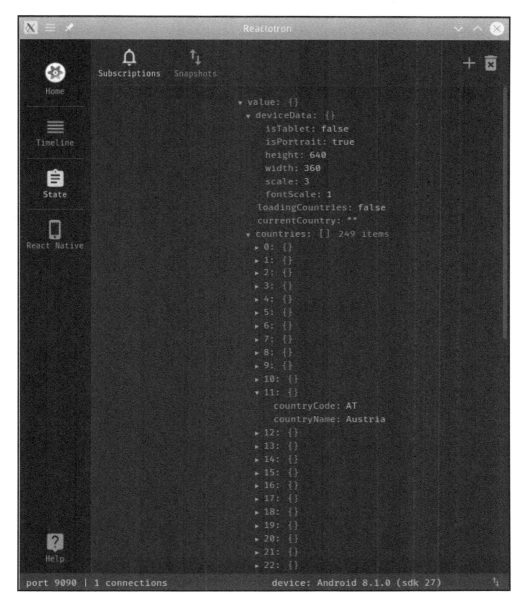

You can examine the Redux store to see what was put in it

Finally, I select **Austria** in the app. We can examine the API call that went out, and also the action that was dispatched afterwards; see the following screenshot:

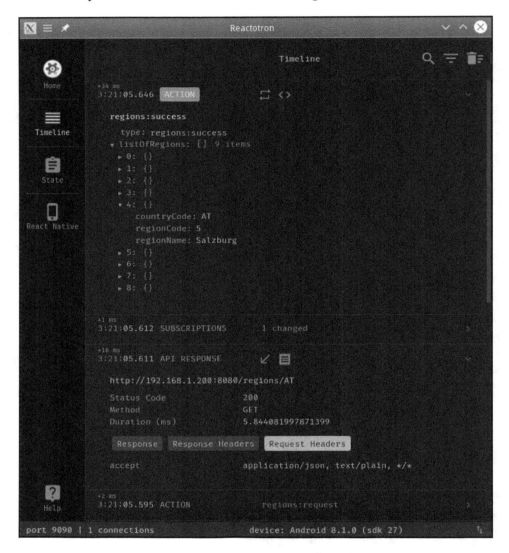

The results of selecting Austria in our app: we can examine the API call and the Redux actions as well. Here, we see the nine regions of Austria, and the details for the fifth one, Salzburg, of Mozart fame

`Reactotron` has, as we said, some different features, and for some purposes, it may suit you better than `react-native-debugger`, so it's a worthwhile inclusion in your arsenal of debugger tools.

Creating a Desktop Application with Electron

13

We will look at the following recipes:

- Setting up Electron with React
- Adding Node functionality to your app
- Building a more windowy experience
- Testing and debugging your app
- Making a distributable package

Introduction

In the previous chapters, we used Node to set up servers, and React to create web pages. In this chapter, we'll bring both together, adding another tool called Electron, and we'll see how we can use JS to write desktop apps that work exactly like any native executable app.

Setting up Electron with React

Electron is an open source framework, created by GitHub, that lets you develop desktop executables that bring together Node and Chrome to provide a full GUI experience. Electron has been used for several well-known projects, including developer tools such as Visual Studio Code, Atom, and Light Table. Basically, you can define the UI with HTML, CSS, and JS (or using React, as we'll be doing), but you can also use all of the packages and functions in Node, so you won't be limited to a sandboxed experience, being able to go beyond what you could do with just a browser.

You may also want to read about **Progressive Web Apps** (**PWA**) which are web apps that can be "installed" at your machine, very much like they were native apps. These apps are launched as any other app, and run in a common app window, without tabs or a URL bar as a browser would show. PWAs may not (yet?) have access to full desktop functionality, but for many cases they may be more than enough. Read more about PWAs at https://developers.google.com/web/progressive-web-apps/.

How to do it...

For now, in this recipe, let's first install Electron, and then in the later recipes, we'll see how we can turn one of our React apps into a desktop program.

I started out with a copy of the repository from Chapter 8, *Expanding Your Application*, to get the countries and regions app, the same we also used for an RN example. It just so happens that you can work perfectly well with Electron with a CRA-built app, without even needing to eject it, so that's what we'll do here. First, we need to install the basic Electron package, so in the same directory where we wrote our React app, we'll execute the following command:

```
npm install electron --save-dev
```

Then, we'll need a starter JS file. Taking some tips from the main.js file at https://github.com/electron/electron-quick-start, we'll create the following electron-start.js file:

```
// Source file: electron-start.js

/* @flow */

const { app, BrowserWindow } = require("electron");

let mainWindow;

const createWindow = () => {
    mainWindow = new BrowserWindow({
        height: 768,
        width: 1024
    });
    mainWindow.loadURL("http://localhost:3000");
    mainWindow.on("closed", () => {
        mainWindow = null;
    });
};
```

```
app.on("ready", createWindow);

app.on("activate", () => mainWindow === null && createWindow());

app.on(
    "window-all-closed",
    () => process.platform !== "darwin" && app.quit()
);
```

Here are some points to note regarding the preceding code snippet:

- This code runs in `Node`, so we are using `require()` instead of `import`
- The `mainWindow` variable will point to the browser instance where our code will run
- We'll start by running our React app, so Electron will be able to load the code from `http://localhost:3000`

In our code, we also have to process the following events:

- `"ready"` is called when `Electron` has finished its initialization, and can start creating windows.
- `"closed"` means your window was closed; your app might have several windows open, so at this point you should delete the closed one.
- `"window-all-closed"` implies your whole app was closed. In Windows and Linux, this means quitting, but for macOS, you don't usually quit applications, because of Apple' s usual rules.
- `"activate"` is called when your app is reactivated, so if the window had been deleted (as in Windows or Linux), you have to create it again.

> The complete list of events that `Electron` can emit is at `https://github.com/electron/electron/blob/master/docs/api/app.md`; check it out.

We already have our `React` app in place, so we just need a way to call `Electron`. Add the following script to `package.json`, and you'll be ready:

```
"scripts": {
    "electron": "electron .",
    .
    .
    .
```

We are set; let's see how it all comes together.

How it works...

To run the `Electron` app in development mode (we'll get on to creating an executable file later), we have to do the following:

1. Run our `restful_server_cors` server code from `Chapter 4`, *Implementing RESTful Services with Node*.
2. Start the `React` app, which requires the server to be running.
3. Wait until it's loaded, and then and only then, move on to the next step.
4. Start `Electron`.

So, basically, you'll have to run the two following commands, but you'll need to do so in separate terminals, and you'll also have to wait for the `React` app to show up in the browser before starting `Electron`:

```
// in the directory for our restful server:
node out/restful_server_cors.js

// in the React app directory:
npm start

// and after the React app is running, in other terminal:
npm run electron
```

After starting `Electron`, a screen quickly comes up, and we again find our countries and regions app, now running independently of a browser. See the following screenshot—note that I resized the window from its 1024 × 768 size:

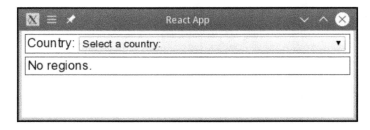

Our app, running as an independent executable

The app works as always; as an example, I selected a country, **Canada**, and correctly got its list of regions:

The app works as before; pick a country, and a call to our RESTful server will get its regions

We are done! You can see that everything is interconnected, as before, in the sense that if you make any changes to the React source code, they will be instantly reflected in the Electron app.

So far, we have seen that we can make an executable out of a web page; let's now see how to make it more powerful.

Adding Node functionality to your app

In the previous recipe, we saw that with just a few small configuration changes, we can turn our web page into an application. However, you're still restricted in terms of what you can do, because you are still using only those features available in a sandboxed browser window. You don't have to think this way, for you can add basically all Node functionality using functions that let you go beyond the limits of the web. Let's see how to do it in this recipe.

How to do it...

We want to add some functionality to our app of the kind that a typical desktop would have. Let's see how can we do that. The key to adding Node functions to your app is to use the remote module in Electron. With it, your browser code can invoke methods of the main process, and thus gain access to extra functionality.

 See https://github.com/electron/electron/blob/master/docs/api/remote.md for more on the remote module. There is also extra information that might come in handy at https://electronjs.org/docs/api/remote.

Let's say we wanted to add the possibility of saving the list of a country's regions to a file. We'd require access to the fs module to be able to write a file, and we'd also need to open a dialog box to select what file to write to. In our serviceApi.js file, we would add the following functions:

```
// Source file: src/regionsApp/serviceApi.js

/* @flow */

const electron = window.require("electron").remote;

    .
    .
    .

const fs = electron.require("fs");

export const writeFile = fs.writeFile.bind(fs);

export const showSaveDialog = electron.dialog.showSaveDialog;
```

Having added this, we can now write files and show dialog boxes from our main code. To use this functionality, we could add a new action to our world.actions.js file:

```
// Source file: src/regionsApp/world.actions.js

/* @flow */

import {
    getCountriesAPI,
    getRegionsAPI,
    showSaveDialog,
    writeFile
} from "./serviceApi";
```

.
.
.

```
export const saveRegionsToDisk = () => async (
    dispatch: ({}) => any,
    getState: () => { regions: [] }
) => {
    showSaveDialog((filename: string = "") => {
        if (filename) {
            writeFile(filename, JSON.stringify(getState().regions), e =>
                e && window.console.log(`ERROR SAVING ${filename}`, e);
            );
        }
    });
};
```

When the `saveRegionsToDisk()` action is dispatched, it will show a dialog to prompt the user to select what file is to be written, and will then write the current set of regions, taken from `getState().regions`, to the selected file in JSON format. We just have to add the appropriate button to our `<RegionsTable>` component to be able to dispatch the necessary action:

```
// Source file: src/regionsApp/regionsTableWithSave.component.js

/* @flow */

import React from "react";
import PropTypes from "prop-types";

import "../general.css";

export class RegionsTable extends React.PureComponent<{
    loading: boolean,
    list: Array<{
        countryCode: string,
        regionCode: string,
        regionName: string
    }>,
    saveRegions: () => void
}> {
    static propTypes = {
        loading: PropTypes.bool.isRequired,
        list: PropTypes.arrayOf(PropTypes.object).isRequired,
        saveRegions: PropTypes.func.isRequired
    };
```

```
static defaultProps = {
    list: []
};

render() {
    if (this.props.list.length === 0) {
        return <div className="bordered">No regions.</div>;
    } else {
        const ordered = [...this.props.list].sort(
            (a, b) => (a.regionName < b.regionName ? -1 : 1)
        );

        return (
            <div className="bordered">
                {ordered.map(x => (
                    <div key={x.countryCode + "-" + x.regionCode}>
                        {x.regionName}
                    </div>
                ))}
                <div>
                    <button onClick={() => this.props.saveRegions()}>
                        Save regions to disk
                    </button>
                </div>
            </div>
        );
    }
}
}
```

We are almost done! When we connect this component to the store, we'll simply add the new action, as follows:

```
// Source file: src/regionsApp/regionsTableWithSave.connected.js

/* @flow */

import { connect } from "react-redux";

import { RegionsTable } from "./regionsTableWithSave.component";

import { saveRegionsToDisk } from "./world.actions";

const getProps = state => ({
    list: state.regions,
    loading: state.loadingRegions
});
```

```
const getDispatch = (dispatch: any) => ({
    saveRegions: () => dispatch(saveRegionsToDisk())
});

export const ConnectedRegionsTable = connect(
    getProps,
    getDispatch
)(RegionsTable);
```

Now, everything's ready—let's see it working.

How it works...

The code we added showed how we could gain access to a Node package (*fs*, in our case) and some extra functions, such as showing a **Save to disk** dialog. (The latter function has more to do with the native look of your app, and we'll see more about it in the upcoming *Building a more windowy experience* section.) When we run our updated app and select a country, we'll see our newly added button, as in the following screenshot:

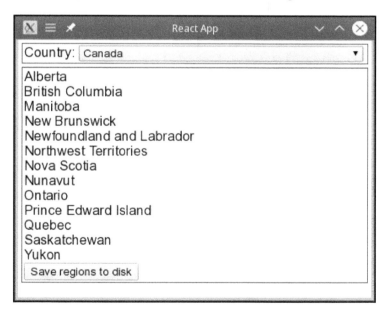

We now have a Save regions to disk button after the regions list

Clicking on the button will pop up a dialog, allowing you to select the destination for the data:

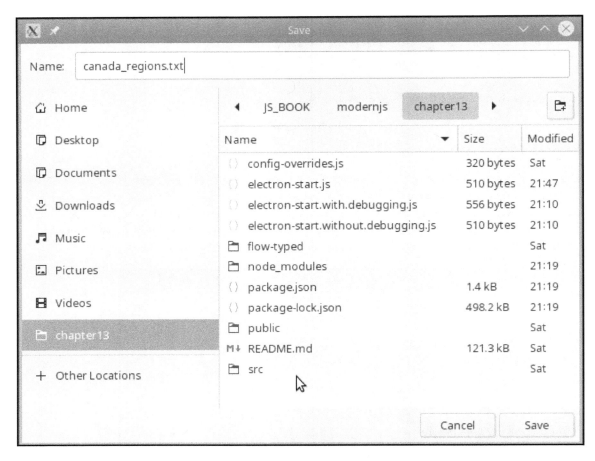

Clicking on the button brings up a Save screen, to specify to which file to save the results

If you click **Save**, the list of regions will be written in JSON format, as we specified earlier in our `writeRegionsToDisk()` function:

```
[{"countryCode":"CA","regionCode":"1","regionName":"Alberta"},
{"countryCode":"CA","regionCode":"10","regionName":"Quebec"},
{"countryCode":"CA","regionCode":"11","regionName":"Saskatchewan"},
{"countryCode":"CA","regionCode":"12","regionName":"Yukon"},
{"countryCode":"CA","regionCode":"13","regionName":"Northwest
Territories"},
{"countryCode":"CA","regionCode":"14","regionName":"Nunavut"},
```

```
{"countryCode":"CA","regionCode":"2","regionName":"British Columbia"},
{"countryCode":"CA","regionCode":"3","regionName":"Manitoba"},
{"countryCode":"CA","regionCode":"4","regionName":"New Brunswick"},
{"countryCode":"CA","regionCode":"5","regionName":"Newfoundland and
Labrador"},
{"countryCode":"CA","regionCode":"7","regionName":"Nova Scotia"},
{"countryCode":"CA","regionCode":"8","regionName":"Ontario"},
{"countryCode":"CA","regionCode":"9","regionName":"Prince Edward Island"}]
```

A final detail to note is that your app won't be able to run in a browser now, and you'll have to get used to seeing something as in the following screenshot, even though your code will run fine with `Electron`:

If you use Node's or Electron's functions, your code will no longer run in the browser, though it will perform perfectly well with Electron

That's it! Without much hassle, we were able to go beyond the limits of normal browser apps. You can see that there's practically no limit to what you can do in an `Electron` app.

Building a more windowy experience

In the previous recipe, we added the possibility of using any and all of the functions provided by `Node`. In this recipe, let's now focus on making our app more window-like, with icons, menus, and so on. We want the user to really believe that they're using a native app, with all the features that they would be accustomed to. The following list of interesting subjects from `https://electronjs.org/docs/api` is just a short list of highlights, but there are many more available options:

`clipboard`	To do copy and paste operations using the system's clipboard
`dialog`	To show native system dialogs for messages, alerts, opening and saving files, and so on
`globalShortcut`	To detect keyboard shortcuts
`Menu, MenuItem`	To create a menu bar with menus and submenus
`Notification`	To add desktop notifications
`powerMonitor, powerSaveBlocker`	To monitor power state changes, and to disable entering sleep mode
`screen`	To get information about the screen, displays, and so on
`Tray`	To add icons and context menus to the system's tray

Let's add a few of these functions so that we can get a better-looking app that is more integrated to the desktop.

How to do it...

Any decent app should probably have at least an icon and a menu, possibly with some keyboard shortcuts, so let's add those features now, and just for the sake of it, let's also add some notifications for when regions are written to disk. Together with the **Save** dialog we already used, this means that our app will include several native windowing features. Let's implement the following steps and understand how to add these extras.

To start with, let's add an icon. Showing an icon is the simplest thing, because it just requires an extra option when creating the `BrowserWindow()` object. I'm not very *graphics-visual-designer* oriented, so I just downloaded the **Alphabet, letter, r Icon Free** file from the Icon-Icons website, at `https://icon-icons.com/icon/alphabet-letter-r/62595`. Implement the icon as follows:

```
mainWindow = new BrowserWindow({
    height: 768,
    width: 1024,
    icon: "./src/regionsApp/r_icon.png"
```

```
});
```

You can also choose icons for the system tray, although there's no way of using our regions app in that context, but you may want to look into it nonetheless.

 There's another way of adding an icon to your app when you do the build, by adding an extra configuration item to the "build" entry in package.json.

To continue, the second feature we'll add is a menu, with some global shortcuts to boot. In our App.regions.js file, we'll need to add a few lines to access the Menu module, and to define our menu itself:

```
// Source file: src/App.regions.js

    .
    .
    .

import { getRegions } from "./regionsApp/world.actions";

    .
    .
    .

const electron = window.require("electron").remote;
const { Menu } = electron;

const template = [
    {
        label: "Countries",
        submenu: [
            {
                label: "Uruguay",
                accelerator: "Alt+CommandOrControl+U",
                click: () => store.dispatch(getRegions("UY"))
            },
            {
                label: "Hungary",
                accelerator: "Alt+CommandOrControl+H",
                click: () => store.dispatch(getRegions("HU"))
            }
        ]
    },
    {
        label: "Bye!",
```

```
        role: "quit"
    }
];
```

```
const mainMenu = Menu.buildFromTemplate(template);
Menu.setApplicationMenu(mainMenu);
```

Using a template is a simple way to create a menu, but you can also do it manually, adding item by item. I decided to have a **Countries** menu with two options to show the regions for Uruguay (where I was born) and Hungary (from where my father's father came). The click property dispatches the appropriate action. I also used the accelerator property to define global shortcuts. See https://github.com/electron/electron/blob/master/docs/api/accelerator.md for the list of possible key combinations to use, including the following:

- *Command keys,* such as Command (or Cmd), Control (or Ctrl), or both (CommandOrControl or CmdOrCtrl)
- *Alternate keys,* such as Alt, AltGr, or Option
- *Common keys,* such as Shift, Escape (or Esc), Tab, Backspace, Insert, or Delete
- *Function keys,* such as F1 to F24
- *Cursor keys,* including Up, Down, Left, Right, Home, End, PageUp, and PageDown
- *Media keys,* such as MediaPlayPause, MediaStop, MediaNextTrack, MediaPreviousTrack, VolumeUp, VolumeDown, and VolumeMute

I also want to be able to quit the application (never mind that the window created by Electron already has an × icon to close it!)—that's a predefined *role* for which you don't need to do anything special. A complete list of roles is available at https://electronjs.org/docs/api/menu-item#roles. With these roles, you can do a huge amount, including some specific macOS functions, along with the following:

- Work with the clipboard (cut, copy, paste, and pasteAndMatchStyle)
- Handle the window (minimize, close, quit, reload, and forceReload)
- Zoom (zoomIn, zoomOut, and resetZoom)

To finish, and really just for the sake of it, let's add a notification trigger for when a file is written. Electron has a Notification module, but I opted to use node-notifier from https://github.com/mikaelbr/node-notifier, which is quite simple to use. First, we'll add the package in the usual fashion:

```
npm install node-notifier --save
```

In `serviceApi.js`, we'll have to export the new function, so we'll able to import from elsewhere, as we'll see shortly:

```
const electron = window.require("electron").remote;

    .
    .
    .


export const notifier = electron.require("node-notifier");
```

Finally, let's use this in our `world.actions.js` file:

```
import {
    notifier,
    .
    .
    .
} from "./serviceApi";
```

With all our setup, actually sending a notification is quite simple, requiring very little code:

```
// Source file: src/regionsApp/world.actions.js

    .
    .
    .


export const saveRegionsToDisk = () => async (
    dispatch: ({}) => any,
    getState: () => { regions: [] }
) => {
    showSaveDialog((filename: string = "") => {
        if (filename) {
            writeFile(filename, JSON.stringify(getState().regions), e => {
                if (e) {
                    window.console.log(`ERROR SAVING ${filename}`, e);
                } else {
                    notifier.notify({
                        title: "Regions app",
                        message: `Regions saved to ${filename}`
                    });
                }
            });
        }
    });
};
```

We are set! Let's see what our more *windowy* app looks like now.

How it works...

First, we can easily check that the icon appears. See the following screenshot, and compare it with the very first screenshot in this chapter:

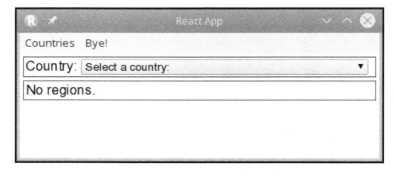

Our app now has its own icon, possibly not too exclusive or original, but better than nothing

Now, let's look at the menu. It has our options, including the shortcuts:

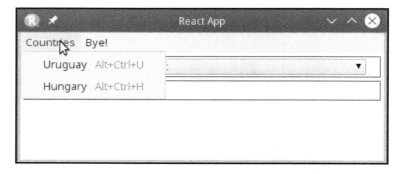

Our app now also has a menu, as any self-respecting app should

Then, if we select an option (let's say **Uruguay**) with either the mouse or the global shortcut, the screen correctly loads the expected regions:

The menu entries work as expected; we can use the Uruguay option to see my country's 19 departments

Finally, let's see if the notifications work as expected. If we click on the **Save regions to disk** button and select a file, we'll see a notification, as in the following screenshot:

Saving a file now shows a notification; in this case, for Linux with KDE

We've now seen how to expand our browser page to include Node features and windowing native functions. Now, let's go back to more basic requirements, and learn how to test and debug our code.

Testing and debugging your app

Now, we get to a common requirement: testing and debugging your app. The first thing I'll have to tell you is that there's no news in regards to testing! All the techniques we saw for testing browser and Node code still apply, since your Electron app is essentially just a browser app (albeit possibly with some extra functions) that you'll mock in the same way you did earlier, so there's nothing new to be learned here.

However, with regard to debugging, there will be some new requirements, since your code is not running in a browser. In a similar way as with React Native, we'll have to use some tools in order to be able to look into our code as it runs. Let's see, in this recipe, how to go about all of this.

How to do it...

We want to install and configure all the necessary tools for debugging. Let's do that in this section. The key tool for debugging will be electron-devtools-installer, which you can get from https://github.com/MarshallOfSound/electron-devtools-installer. We'll install it, as well as the Redux Devtools extension we used before, with a simple command:

```
npm install electron-devtools-installer redux-devtools-extension --save-dev
```

To use the Redux Devtools, we'll have to start by fixing the store, as we did earlier; nothing new here:

```
// Source file: src/regionsApp/store.with.redux.devtools.js

/* @flow */

import { createStore, applyMiddleware } from "redux";
import { composeWithDevTools } from "redux-devtools-extension";
import thunk from "redux-thunk";

import { reducer } from "./world.reducer";

export const store = createStore(
    reducer,
```

```
    composeWithDevTools(applyMiddleware(thunk))
);
```

For the tools themselves, we'll also have to tweak our starter code a bit:

```
// Source file: electron-start.with.debugging.js

/* @flow */

const { app, BrowserWindow } = require("electron");
const {
    default: installExtension,
    REACT_DEVELOPER_TOOLS,
    REDUX_DEVTOOLS
} = require("electron-devtools-installer");

let mainWindow;

const createWindow = () => {
    mainWindow = new BrowserWindow({
        height: 768,
        width: 1024
    });
    mainWindow.loadURL("http://localhost:3000");

    mainWindow.webContents.openDevTools();

    installExtension(REACT_DEVELOPER_TOOLS)
        .then(name => console.log(`Added Extension: ${name}`))
        .catch(err => console.log("An error occurred: ", err));

    installExtension(REDUX_DEVTOOLS)
        .then(name => console.log(`Added Extension: ${name}`))
        .catch(err => console.log("An error occurred: ", err));

    mainWindow.on("closed", () => {
        mainWindow = null;
    });
};

app.on("ready", createWindow);

app.on("activate", () => mainWindow === null && createWindow());

app.on(
    "window-all-closed",
    () => process.platform !== "darwin" && app.quit()
);
```

The good thing is that you can add all the tools from code, with no special installation or any other procedure. After these simple changes, you are done; now, let's see it work!

How it works...

If you start the modified code, you'll see that the Electron window now includes the classic Chrome tools, including React and Redux. See the following screenshot:

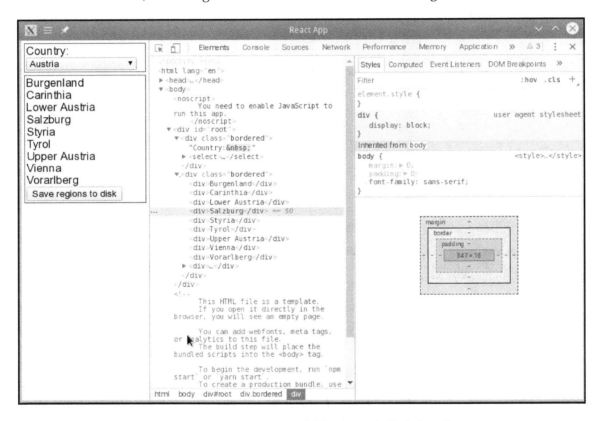

The electron-devtools-installer package lets you add all the tools you need, with a simple procedure

Apart from the console, you can use the `React Devtools` to inspect components:

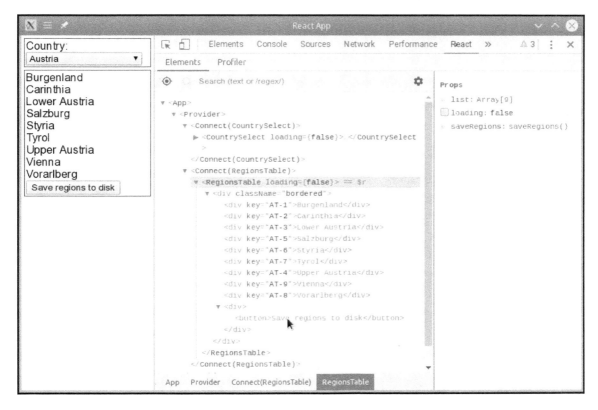

The React Devtools can be used to inspect components and their props

Similarly, the `Redux DevTools` let you inspect actions and the store. See the following screenshot:

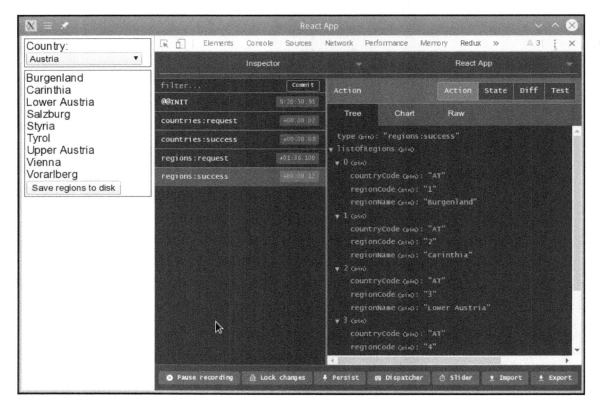

You also installed the Redux developer tools, which let you inspect everything Redux-related

As you can see, we've got all the tools we were accustomed to, with one exception—what about network calls? Let's see to that now.

There's more...

You may have noticed that the **Network** tab doesn't show the API calls done from the app. With RN, we solved that because the tools we used included the ability to inspect all network traffic, but that doesn't happen here. So, instead of an easy, automated solution, we'll have to do a bit of extra work. If you do all of your API calls with axios, you can simply modify its original methods to produce logging:

```
// Source file: src/regionsApp/serviceApi.js

    .
    .
    .

axios.originalGet = axios.get;
axios.get = (uri, options, ...args) =>
    axios.originalGet(uri, options, ...args).then(response => {
        console.log(`GET ${uri}`, {
            request: { uri, options, ...args },
            response
        });
        return response;
    });
```

The change shown will cause every successful GET to log everything you need, as in the following screenshot:

```
GET http://192.168.1.200:8080/countries ▶ {request: {…}, response: {…}}        serviceApi.js:29
GET http://192.168.1.200:8080/regions/CA                                       serviceApi.js:29
▼ {request: {…}, response: {…}} ▓
  ▶ request: {uri: "http://192.168.1.200:8080/regions/CA", options: undefined}
  ▼ response:
      config: (...)
    ▶ data: Array(13)
      headers: (...)
      request: (...)
      status: (...)
      statusText: (...)
```

Our changed axios.get() method produces a satisfying log

Of course, this is just the tip of the required changes. You'll have to add code for a failed call (so, add some logging in .catch(), too) and you'll also want to do this sort of change for the other methods (.post(), .delete(), and so on), but the necessary code is simple, so I'll leave it as an exercise for the reader!

Making a distributable package

Now that we have a full app, all that's left to do is package it up so that you can deliver it as an executable file for Windows, Linux, or macOS users. Let's finish the chapter by looking at how to do that in this recipe.

How to do it...

There are many ways of packaging an app, but we'll use a tool, electron-builder, that will make it even easier, if you can get its configuration right!

 You can read more about electron-builder, its capabilities, and its configuration at https://www.electron.build/.

Let's take a look at the necessary steps. First of all, we'll have to begin by defining the build configuration, and our initial step will be, as always, to install the tool:

```
npm install electron-builder --save-dev
```

To access the added tool, we'll require a new script, which we'll add in package.json:

```
"scripts": {
    "dist": "electron-builder",
    .
    .
    .
}
```

We'll also have to add a few more details to `package.json`, which are needed for the build process and the produced app. In particular, the `homepage` change is required, because the CRA-created `index.html` file uses absolute paths that won't work later with `Electron`:

```
"name": "chapter13",
"version": "0.1.0",
"description": "Regions app for chapter 13",
"homepage": "./",
"license": "free",
"author": "Federico Kereki",
```

Finally, some specific building configuration will be required. You cannot build for macOS with a Linux or Windows machine, so I'll leave that configuration out. We have to specify where the files will be found, what compression method to use, and so on:

```
"build": {
    "appId": "com.electron.chapter13",
    "compression": "normal",
    "asar": true,
    "extends": null,
    "files": [
        "electron-start.js",
        "build/**/*",
        "node_modules/**/*",
        "src/regionsApp/r_icon.png"
    ],
    "linux": {
        "target": "zip"
    },
    "win": {
        "target": "portable"
    }
}
```

 Read more about building for different platforms at `https://www.electron.build/multi-platform-build`. For more on all of the configuration options, see `https://www.electron.build/configuration/configuration#configuration`.

We have completed the required configuration, but there are also some changes to do in the code itself, and we'll have to adapt the code for building the package. When the packaged app runs, there won't be any webpack server running; the code will be taken from the built React package. Also, you won't want to include debugging tools. So, the starter code will require the following changes:

```
// Source file: electron-start.for.builder.js

/* @flow */

const { app, BrowserWindow } = require("electron");
const path = require("path");
const url = require("url");

let mainWindow;

const createWindow = () => {
    mainWindow = new BrowserWindow({
        height: 768,
        width: 1024,
        icon: path.join(__dirname, "./build/r_icon.png")
    });
    mainWindow.loadURL(
        url.format({
            pathname: path.join(__dirname, "./build/index.html"),
            protocol: "file",
            slashes: true
        })
    );
    mainWindow.on("closed", () => {
        mainWindow = null;
    });
};

app.on("ready", createWindow);

app.on("activate", () => mainWindow === null && createWindow());

app.on(
    "window-all-closed",
    () => process.platform !== "darwin" && app.quit()
);
```

Mainly, we are taking icons and code from the `build/` directory. An `npm run build` command will take care of generating that directory, so we can proceed with creating our executable app.

How it works...

After doing this setup, building the app is essentially trivial. Just do the following, and all the distributable files will be found in the `dist/` directory:

```
npm run electron-builder
```

You may want to add a new line to the `.gitignore` file so that the distribution directory won't be committed. I included a `**/dist` line to mine, paralleling the previous `**/node_modules` and `**/dist` existing lines.

Now that we have the Linux app, we can run it by unzipping the `.zip` file and clicking on the `chapter13` executable. (The name came from the `"name"` attribute in `package.json`, which we modified earlier.) The result should be like what's shown in the following screenshot:

The Linux executable runs as a native app, showing the same screen as we saw earlier

I also wanted to try out the Windows `EXE` file. Since I didn't have a Windows machine, I made do by downloading a free `VirtualBox` virtual machine from `https://developer.microsoft.com/en-us/microsoft-edge/tools/vms/`—they only work for 90 days, but I needed it for just a few minutes.

After downloading the virtual machine, setting it up in `VirtualBox`, and finally running it, the result that was produced was the same as for Linux, as shown in the following screenshot:

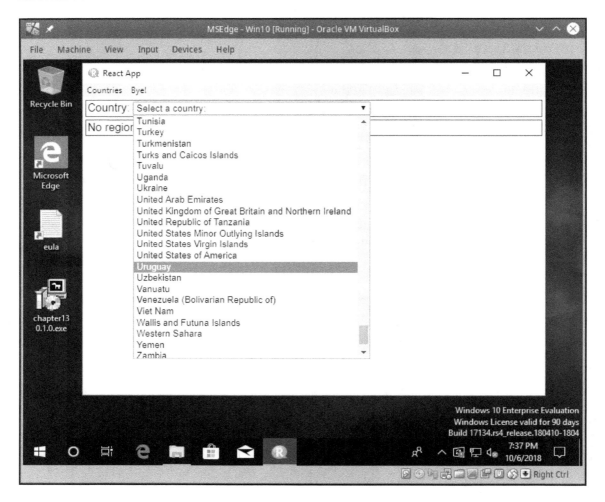

Our native Windows app runs equally in a Windows machine

So, we've managed to develop a `React` app, enhanced it with the `Node` and `Electron` features, and finally packaged it for different operating systems. With that, we are done!

Other Books You May Enjoy

If you enjoyed this book, you may be interested in these other books by Packt:

Building Enterprise JavaScript Applications
Daniel Li

ISBN: 9781788477321

- Practice Test-Driven Development (TDD) throughout the entire book
- Use Cucumber, Mocha and Selenium to write E2E, integration, unit and UI tests
- Build stateless APIs using Express and Elasticsearch
- Document your API using OpenAPI and Swagger
- Build and bundle front-end applications using React, Redux and Webpack
- Containerize services using Docker
- Deploying scalable microservices using Kubernetes

Learn Blockchain Programming with JavaScript
Eric Traub

ISBN: 9781789618822

- Gain an in-depth understanding of blockchain and the environment setup
- Create your very own decentralized blockchain network from scratch
- Build and test the various endpoints necessary to create a decentralized network
- Learn about proof-of-work and the hashing algorithm used to secure data
- Mine new blocks, create new transactions, and store the transactions in blocks
- Explore the consensus algorithm and use it to synchronize the blockchain network

Leave a review - let other readers know what you think

Please share your thoughts on this book with others by leaving a review on the site that you bought it from. If you purchased the book from Amazon, please leave us an honest review on this book's Amazon page. This is vital so that other potential readers can see and use your unbiased opinion to make purchasing decisions, we can understand what our customers think about our products, and our authors can see your feedback on the title that they have worked with Packt to create. It will only take a few minutes of your time, but is valuable to other potential customers, our authors, and Packt. Thank you!

Index

W

Web Accessibility Initiative (WAI) 353
web application
   adapting, with enhanced usability 338, 341
   elements, hiding 336
   elements, reordering 335
   elements, resizing 333
   elements, showing 336
   screen size, setting 330, 331, 332
Web Content Accessibility Guidelines (WCAG)
   353
Winston
   reference 212
   used, for adding logging 212, 214, 217

World Wide Web Consortium (W3C) 353
wrapper methods
   reference 542

Y

YAML Ain't Markup Language (YAML)
   about 264
   reference 264
yarn
   reference 30
yet another compiler compiler (yacc) 46

Z

zlib stream
   reference 145